Television
An International History

Television

An International History

Edited by ANTHONY SMITH

OXFORD UNIVERSITY PRESS

1995

Oxford University Press, Walton Street, Oxford OX2 6DP

Oxford New York
Athens Auckland Bangkok Bombay
Calcutta Cape Town Dar es Salaam Delhi
Florence Hong Kong Istanbul Karachi
Kuala Lumpur Madras Madrid Melbourne
Mexico City Nairobi Paris Singapore
Taipei Tokyo Toronto
and associated companies in
Berlin Ibadan

Oxford is a trade mark of Oxford University Press

Published in the United States
by Oxford University Press Inc., New York

British Library Cataloguing in Publication Data
Data available

Library of Congress Cataloging in Publication Data
Data available

ISBN 0–19–811999–2

1 3 5 7 9 10 8 6 4 2

Printed in Great Britain
on acid-free paper by
Bath Press, Avon

Contents

List of
Colour Plates

Notes on Contributors

Albert Abramson is a television historian/consultant, and previously worked as an engineer for CBS Television for thirty-five years. He is the author of *Electronic Motion Pictures, The History of Television, 1880–1941*, and *Zworykin: Pioneer of Television*.

Steven Barnett is a senior lecturer in communications at the University of Westminster and also teaches at Goldsmiths' College and the London School of Economics. He is a frequent contributor to the national and specialist press on media issues, and his books include *Games and Sets: The Changing Face of Sport on Television*, and (as co-author) *The Battle for the BBC*.

Dietrich Berwanger has worked as a television journalist in Germany and Kenya and is Head of the Television Training Centre in Berlin, an institute offering advanced training for television staff from Third World countries.

William Boddy is an associate professor at Baruch College and the Graduate Center, City University of New York, and has also taught at New York University, the University of Notre Dame, and the University of Wisconsin-Madison.

Susan Briggs is the author of *Keep Smiling Through* and *Those Radio Times* and co-author of *Cap and Bell: The First Twenty-five Years of Punch*. She has recently been carrying out research on the English family.

Les Brown is an US journalist and author who has covered television since 1953 for such publications as Variety, Channels, and Television Business International. He is the author of seven books, including *Les Brown's Encyclopedia of Television*.

Daniel Dayan is a fellow at the Centre National de la Recherche Scientifique in Paris, where he has co-ordinated research programmes on mass and intercultural communication. He is an editor of the French communication journal *Hermes*, and teaches media sociology at the Institut d'Etudes Politiques de Paris.

Elizabeth Jacka is a Senior Lecturer in Mass Communications at Macquarie University. She has published four books on aspects of the Australian film and television industry and has edited a book on the globalization of culture. She has worked at the Australian Film, Television, and Radio School and the Australian Broadcasting Tribunal.

Lesley Johnson is Professor of Communication at the University of Western Sydney, Nepean. She is the author of a number of major books including *The Unseen Voice: A Cultural Study of Early Australian Radio* and *The Modern Girl: Childhood and Growing Up.*

Hidetoshi Kato is Director-General of the National Institute of Multimedia Education in Japan, and also a member of the Board of Trustees of the International Institute of Communication and a Committee member of the Asian Mass Communication Information Research Center. His *Selected Writings* have been published in twelve volumes.

Elihu Katz is Trustee Professor at the Annenberg School for Communication at the University of Pennsylvania. He is also Scientific Director of the Louis Guttman Institute of Applied Social Research in Jerusalem, and Emeritus Professor of Sociology and Communication at the Hebrew University.

Charles Okigbo is the Executive Co-ordinator of the African Council for Communication Education. He has been Senior Lecturer in Mass Communication at the University of Nigeria, Nsukka, and Registrar of the Advertising Practitioners Council of Nigeria, and has published (as editor) *Advertising and Public Relations*, *New Perspectives in International News Flow*, and *Marketing Politics: Advertising Strategies and Tactics.*

Richard Paterson is Head of Media Education and Research at the British Film Institute.

Philip Schlesinger is Professor of Film and Media Studies at the University of Stirling. He has been a Nuffield Social Science Research Fellow, a Jean Monnet Fellow at the European University Institute of Florence, and is currently also a Professor in the Department of Media and Communication at the University of Oslo.

Colin Shaw CBE has been Chief Secretary to the BBC, Director of Television at the Independent Broadcasting Authority, and Director of Programme Planning at the Independent Television Association. He is now Director of the Broadcasting Standards Council.

Anthony Smith has been a BBC Television producer and the Director of the British Film Institute. He is now President of Magdalen College, Oxford.

Michael Tracey was head of the Broadcasting Research Unit, London and is now Professor and Director of the University of Colorado's Center for Mass Media Research, as well as holding the Chair of International Communication at the University of Salford.

Acknowledgements

I am extremely grateful to Andrew Lockett and Jason Freeman of the Oxford University Press for inaugurating this project and carrying it through the years of preparation so patiently. Liz Heasman has worked assiduously at tracking down the illustrations, bringing with her a wealth of experience from London's Museum of the Moving Image. I am grateful also to Mrs Judy Godley for taking care of the manuscript throughout its many stages; and finally, of course, to all the contributors to the volume.   A.S.

Introduction

Anthony Smith

n the opening programme of the world's first regular public service of television in 1936, an entertainer sang: 'The air has eyes that scan us from the skies | And ears that listen from the blue . . . So you needn't roam | From your own happy home, | The world will pass you in review.' Television had been one of the nineteenth century's confident predictions of the twentieth but it still took many decades of the new century to reach fruition and only in the second half of that century has it become a global phenomenon. But when it arrived it exercised an unanticipated and transforming influence: political life in democracies and non-democracies alike was thoroughly altered under the impact of television; a new 'consumer' economy came to depend upon it; in the sphere of culture it became the vehicle of the all-pervading Westernizing influences of the century. The world indeed 'passed in review', but television led to a kind of secondary environment of images in which we all now have to live.

As the twentieth century ends television is itself undergoing a technological and institutional transmutation, so thorough as to baffle or confound its own surviving pioneers and founders. Between the 1950s and the 1990s television was organized as a regulated and essentially national medium dependent on the scarce resource of electromagnetic frequencies. At the end of the era it is becoming a medium of abundance, with hundreds of satellite and cable channels becoming available (in some countries) in every home; these new sources of images, passing through new technologies and produced by a new generation of remarkably cheap miniaturized equipment, are emerging from jurisdictions outside the receiving countries. Television is becoming, at its roots, international, prolific, regulated lightly if at all. Television once provided the concen-

1

trated essence of a nationally authorized culture; now it is inextricably part of an international industry, increasingly beyond the daily control of the governments who have formal jurisdiction over it.

The inventors of television from the 1890s until the 1950s thought of it as an additional means for delivering information and entertainment, as an extension of telephone, radio, theatre, cinema; but it has now gathered to itself a range of functions beyond the entertaining and informing of audiences. What the inventors never quite realized was that television would become *normative*, that so much of what we see on the screen would contrive to suggest how things ought or ought not to be. We see a programme containing a depiction of family life and we learn to read it as a guide or as a barometer of a standard; we see a school and derive an impression of the expected behaviour of teachers and pupils. Television has come to delineate for us the boundaries of transgression; beneath the most routine or trivial entertainment the medium operates as a subtle instructor, with the complicity of the audience. It offers a continuous flowing river of experience from which we have come to draw much of the substance of our identities.

Many have tried but no one yet has succeeded in distilling the essence of the nature of its influence, but much passes between us and television that shapes and alters us. That is why television, almost since its inception, has been the location of so many vivid controversies. It may be difficult to trace the ideological influence of a single programme but no one denies that television amplifies the processes of change in fashion and ideas, sometimes sparking off political ructions while doing so.

This book is intended to offer the reader a broad account of the ways in which television has evolved. Television is an instrument which has come to play so vast a role in the world that it is impossible to treat it as a unitary phenomenon with a single line of history. Even the technical origins of television have to be traced to different parts of the world; its cultural impact can now be felt in every sector of our lives—non-viewers included.

Every means of public communication goes through a series of phases and is eventually superseded. In the last century and a half politicians have had to come to terms with the platform, the loudspeaker, the mass press, the poster, a local press, radio, cinema, and then television. No technology has eradicated any predecessor; rather they have all accumulated, each demanding fresh communicative skills and each somehow managing to impose its nature upon the process it was intended to assist. All have changed the organization of political life and all have altered the tone and poise of politicians. But the same range of changes has been visited upon entertainers and journalists, musicians and performers, artists, writers, teachers. Television has imposed its own ways upon everyone in society who needs to communicate something to an audience. By 1990 in the developed world 98 per cent of homes had come to possess a television receiver.

opposite Television and politics. Richard Nixon used presidential access to television to great effect: to deflect criticism, establish the national agenda, direct attention, and project his image as a world leader. But in the televising of congressional hearings in 1972–4, the power of the medium worked against him.

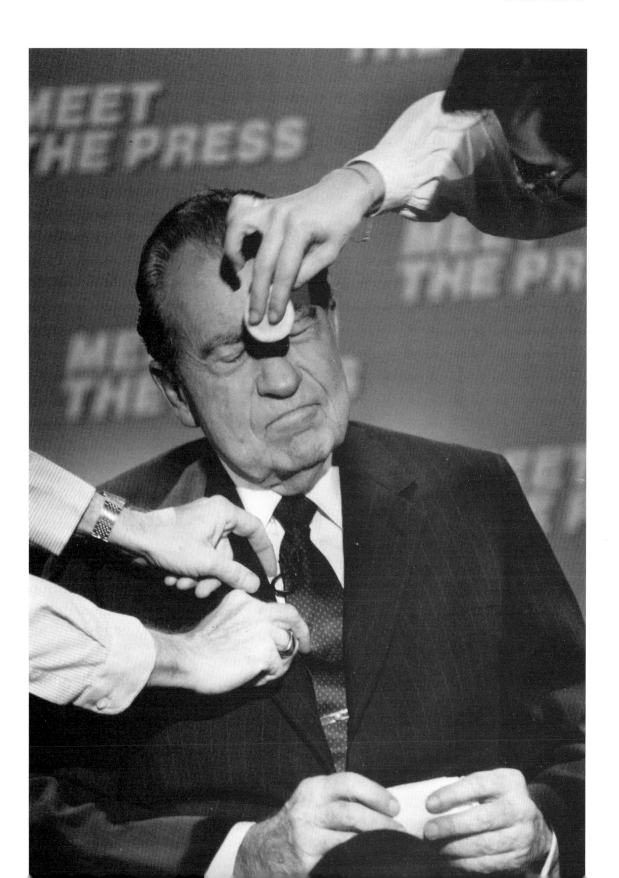

Our most influential images of authority today derive ultimately from television, usually from television fiction; from this we register at various levels of our minds the status of police, cabinet ministers, international organizations, heads of state; we learn to judge the relative measures of respect we offer to soldiers, priests, business leaders. Television images contain an implication of typicality and somehow suggest the point of justice, of balance, between the myriad of opinions latent in our minds.

The television image is held at a point of pressure between innumerable institutions—of regulation, of the market-place, of expressed and inchoate opinion—and it has thus come to govern the senses and the conscience, to offer an ordering of things, even to exaggerate the chaos and orderlessness of things. A child looks at the screen and discovers what it is or ought to be or might be to be a child; an old person sees how one reacts to the perils of age. In one society a violent social conflict can be set off by a pictured incident; in another the same conflict can be made to seem hopelessly beyond solution. If you look deeply into almost any television programme you can sense the second-order operations of the medium, even though at one level it proclaims its own superficiality, its openness to the laity in everything, its freedom to be taken or left. To use the phrase commonly employed by sociologists, television 'sets the agenda'. And so any study of television has to look at issues and institutions as well as at the history of the programmes themselves.

Such considerations have made it difficult to decide what to leave out of this book. I have included those countries where the history of television illustrates some of the major themes. The United States, of course, as the leading force in the medium is discussed in great detail, since it is necessary to understand how its commercial needs have led to the establishment of so many of the familiar genres, how its materials have come to fill the screens of many other countries. By contrast one can learn a great deal from an account of the evolution of television in the former Soviet Union, where for decades a totalitarian party used the medium to sustain itself in power but also undermined itself with the resulting combination of distaste and ennui. But little has been included concerning the position of television in the former satellite countries of the USSR; all of these are passing in the decade of the 1990s through a period of complete reorganization and privatization, the results of which are still far from clear.

For different reasons, little is said about China, where television is growing very rapidly but has as yet not exercised a significant influence outside the nations own vast borders. Were we producing this volume fifteen years from now, in 2010, we would no doubt be revealing the historical roots of important phenomena in countries which this volume has inadvertently played down. At any point in its history a backward glance would provide a different scene. The television of Brazil, for example, has proved to be a great world influence but in 1980 it was little known outside a few countries of South America and would have been ignored in a 'world' history. On the other hand, the BBC seems to us now to be still one of the great models for broadcasting institutions, but in the context of the multi-channel era now dawning it may decrease in salience and therefore also in historical significance. The whole public service model could turn out to have been heading into a historical cul-de-sac.

Even before television could have been said to have become a medium it was enmeshed in controversies. In Chapter 1 Albert Abramson charts the varied courses explored by the experimenters of the nineteenth century and after and William Boddy then takes on the story from the point at which the technical possibilities had become a fully-fledged 'medium'. Issues of how to organize the medium have continued without ceasing. Anthony Smith looks at the role of the state and of governments in shaping television institutions and at the different kinds of public service television which have been evolving from the earliest years.

Much of our book then concerns itself with the mainstream of genres and the geographical lines of influence and much of it is concerned with the history of television's specific forms of institutionalization. Richard Paterson writes about the history of the entertainment forms which have become the mainstay of the medium and Michael Tracey looks at news and public affairs and the ways in which the 'real' world of politics has become interwoven with the exigencies of television. Steven Barnett takes up the special place of sport on the television screen, while Elihu Katz and Daniel Dayan take up the vast issue of how the medium shapes our notions of history through the construction of the rituals of public life and the pageant of public events.

In Chapters 8, 9, and 10 we look at some of the ways in which television has invaded the mores of personal, family, and national life. Susan Briggs discusses the way in which the home and family have been reorganized around the phenomenon of television. Colin Shaw looks at the way in which the question of 'standards' has been handled—the core of the whole problem of what, once the institutional forms have been agreed, is allowed and disallowed on the screen, and the extent to which it is permitted to become part of the apparatus of social control. Philip Schlesinger concentrates on the special problems and paradoxes posed by terrorism, which has grown like a leech upon the medium.

Television is pre-eminently the medium of the prosperous. Les Brown examines the history of the powerful American networks which have operated as it were as the central thrust engines of the medium. Hidetoshi Kato takes up the story of Japanese television where it has similarly become a vast wealth-creating resource as well as an important cultural form.

It is in the non-prosperous area of the world, however, that television might have been thought to have most to offer, but in the context of the hardest developmental problems. Dietrich Berwanger examines the special problems and opportunities of television in the context of the Third World, which has been not nearly as culturally dependent on the 'First' World as appeared to be the case in the 1970s. Elizabeth Jacka and Lesley Johnson have looked at the way in which

Learning to manipulate the medium. The Kennedy–Nixon debates in the presidential campaign of 1960 were deemed to have helped Kennedy into office. He was clearly more confident under the pressure of studio lights. Eisenhower, shrewdly, had advised Nixon not to accept the challenge to live television debate.

Australia, at first poised in a sense between British and American models, has moulded television into an important resource of nationhood. Finally Charles Okigbo takes the continent of Africa (apart from the Republic of South Africa, which has special and exceptional problems), and examines the way in which television has carved out a special role in the most problem-ridden areas of the developing world.

Between, say, 1940 and 1970, television was a closed and somewhat mysterious medium. Programmes were created in awe-inspiring citadels by small groups of generally prosperous professionals and the general public enjoyed access to this growing medium only as passive viewers. But today children learn to use video as a new means of self-expression and in the minds of some the active use of television is thought to be a substitute for (or an extension of) literacy as we have traditionally known it. In some countries there are neighbourhood channels available for almost anyone to use. The great chasm between viewers and producers has in large measure been filled in and the sheer innocent mystique of television has evaporated. But is this not similar to what happened to writing and to printing in previous ages? Do we not see the equivalent of a new form of literacy in the classrooms where video is used? In the 'access' channels and in the advent of home video are we not witnessing processes parallel with the closing of the monastic scriptoria and the ending of the monopoly of the Stationers' Company?

These changes are occurring to television everywhere but at different paces in different societies. The gap between the provision of television in Africa, say, and North America is tremendous and in some places growing. The whole nature of the medium is altering in different places and situations; that is indeed why this seemed to be a good moment to pull together the various strands of television's multinational history. We start with its pre-natal existence in Victorian days and end with some discussion of the situation as it might become after the twenty-first century multi-channel transmutation.

Many of the fundamental certainties—some so fundamental as to be unargued—which are found in the pages which follow may well be challenged in future decades. For example, we show how American television came to dominate the international market for television programmes and thus enter deeply into the consciousness of scores of distant societies; so much so that we tend to think of American genres as central to the medium, as somehow the natural manifestations of the technology. It is American television which has shaped the context if not the content of popular culture throughout the world in the television era: but it is by no means a foregone conclusion that world television a generation hence will be so in thrall. In the vastness of Russia and its former satellite countries there is a cultural potential which could flow into the medium of television and into new programme industries. The visual skills in those societies are historically of a high order and their traditions date back to the early decades of cinema. The new myth-making of the mid-twenty-first century is as likely to emanate from Russia, from Japan, China, or South America as from the United States. There are industrial and investment issues to be resolved but as the medium becomes universal and abundant, other more historically rooted factors will come to influence the flows of the market-place of television material.

'Radio and more especially, television have . . . become the prime instruments for the management of consumer demand. . . . The industrial system is profoundly dependent on commercial television and could not exist in its present form without it.' So wrote J. K. Galbraith in *The New Industrial State* in 1967, at a moment when that view was more decidedly true of the United States than of other societies. But by the 1990s television was becoming ever more dependent, everywhere, on advertising revenue. Many of the new channels are being funded also by subscription, sometimes by advertising as well. The launching of mass consumer products has become ever more heavily dependent upon access to television and so in looking at the evolution of this medium one is looking at an unexpected prop for the whole economic system. That provides, of course, a further constraint on the culture of the medium and as the audience fragments—and as the larger *social* experience of television disappears—the pressures upon the programmes to perform the economic work are likely to grow more severe.

For the first half-century of television the biggest single institutional issue which remained unresolved was that of the relative legitimacy of public and private control of the medium. Indeed, radio and television together constituted a major battlefield in the fight between three distinct broadcasting 'ideologies': competitive commercial service, licence-fee funded public service, and a mixed policy. The argument has raged for decades as to which method of organization most encouraged native talent, most strengthened or weakened the medium in the face of government, and was most conducive to the creation of a diversity of interesting programmes. The argument has never finally been won by any party but the new technological opportunities seem now to suggest that nowhere can the traditional public broadcasting institutions continue to hold a monopoly. They are destined, all of them, to face commercial rivals, perhaps even a great array of these. But that will not mean that public service and state-run systems will die out; it does mean that they will have to define special and unassailable roles for themselves.

There are several other familiar certainties which are being swept away: we think of television as being of a certain size and shape, and with a slightly fuzzy image, inferior to the better kind of cinema screen. But by the year 2000 television sets will, even at the domestic level, tend to be much larger and many of them no longer in the familiar 4×3 format. We shall be moving slowly into a new era of higher-definition images, although it is too soon to predict whether a new 1,250-line system will replace the 525- and 625-line systems familiar around the world. What is certain is that many countries will have established a 16×9 format, rather similar to the modern 5×3 cinema screen and yielding a picture with a much harder edge (and with the sound commensurately improved). Our 'image' of the television image will thus begin to change.

Television has been a medium dependent upon a small squarish picture. It has been a medium of faces, close-ups, reactions, domestic interiors, with human emotions being explored through the facial muscles. The acting skills required by television, and the journalistic skills, too, have been shaped by the physical characteristics of the medium. One recalls the crown touching the head of Queen Elizabeth II, the gun pointed at the head of the Vietnamese prisoner, the face of Walter Cronkite, the kitchen scenes in *I Love Lucy*. The television of the next century will have to acquire a new aesthetic of the long shot, of the panoramic camera sweep, with deeper focus in crowd shots and with lateral space for more people in every shot. That will surely usher in a new set of narrative styles, in factual as well as fictional programmes.

What will be the judgement of the future on this medium of television, which many would say has more than played its part in late twentieth-century pessimism? Certainly the case made could be a negative one: the medium has short-changed human society while yet holding its attention, consuming much energy while ignoring the fundamentals of life. Television has, insistently, touched the audience at the most superficial levels but without seeming to accept responsibility for its own consequences.

Of course, there is a powerful rejoinder: television has merely reflected the society before it and should not be blamed for what it has merely observed. But has the medium held a mirror before the great object of its gaze or, rather, operated a gigantic reflecting device, with built-in tendencies to distort? It has made us see but has it made us look deeply? It has become our chief agency of history, in a novel and still half-understood manner, and in some hands has certainly tried to become also a means of peace. It may have aided the process of disrupting cultures, but it has helped much in the overthrow of tyrannies. It has wantonly manipulated our wants and distorted our true needs, but it has democratized and levelled, opening the eyes of millions to things of which they had been long deprived. It has reflected the ugliness of this century but taught hygiene and brought literacy to rural and urban poor.

The professionals of television have become a new kind of priesthood, mediating between events and audiences, making so many of the major cultural decisions. As with other priesthoods their power can be exaggerated and perhaps they have encouraged that exaggeration. But as the medium proliferates, cheapens, deregulates, and multiplies the numbers of those who control its messages during the coming decade there could well arrive a turning-point, a global reassessment, leading to major change in the shape of a reaction against the sheer ubiquity and overweening power of the medium. That would certainly be a moment to look forward to.

Part One

Origins and Institutions

1

The Invention of Television

Albert Abramson

elevision is the electrical transmission and reception of transient visual images, and is probably the first invention by committee, in the sense of resulting from the effort of hundreds of individuals widely separated in time and space, all prompted by the urge to produce a system of 'seeing over the horizon'.

Whether with tom-toms, smoke signals, or semaphore, human beings have always tried to communicate with neighbours beyond the horizon. The desire has been a matter of commerce, curiosity, or most importantly, warfare. Written messages were sent by ships, horses, birds, and shank's mare. But these were slow, cumbersome, and subject to the whims of weather, terrain, or the endurance of animals. The first steps towards *instant* communications were really taken by seventeenth- and eighteenth-century scientists such as Luigi Galvani, Allesandro Volta, Hans C. Oersted, André Ampère, George S. Ohm, Michael Faraday, and James Clerk Maxwell, who found that electrical currents could flow through certain materials as well as interact with magnetic forces. The first practical solution came in 1843 when Samuel F. B. Morse developed his 'telegraph' (distant-record) machine. This was a means of communication by which the letters of the alphabet were converted into electrical equivalents (the Morse code) that could be either recorded on paper tape or transcribed by trained operators. Since the code was transmitted over wires at almost the speed of light, it soon became the quickest means of point-to-point communication. Before long, electric wires were strung on poles connecting most of the major cities. These same wires were also run under the lakes and oceans of the world.

About the same time, other inventors were seeking means to transmit more

Le Théâtre chez soi par le Téléphonoscope, 1883.

than dots and dashes over these same wires. One of the earliest was Alexander Bain in 1843. In Bain's device, alphabetical letters were formed by a number of lines, each being connected by a separate wire. A comb-like probe containing insulated metal points scanned the type to be transmitted. At the receiver, a similar metallic comb reproduced the letters on chemically treated paper.

The Transmission of Symbols

A more advanced device was that of Frederick C. Bakewell in 1847 for transmitting handwriting, which used a metal foil inscribed with insulating ink wrapped around a cylinder. As the cylinder was rotated by clockwork, a metal stylus was used to glide over the foil. A similar device at the receiver provided means to shift the pens and to keep the devices in synchronism.

Another interesting device by Giovanni Caselli in 1855 used the actions of pendulums. At the transmitter a stylus connected by a lever to a pendulum would physically trace the object to be transmitted and would be electrically turned 'on' or 'off' as it scanned parts of the message. At the receiver, another stylus moved by a pendulum would be turned 'on' or 'off' in sequence and would create a replica (on some form of recording medium) of the image being transmitted.

The scanning of simple figures was quite important as it involved two of the foundations of the later system of instant visual transmission. The first was sequential scanning (dissecting) of the picture. The second was a means to synchronize (keep in step) the transmitter with the receiver. These primitive machines, while quite cumbersome, did work, and though of limited value at the time led to more important devices in the future. These systems were then called 'copy-telegraphs'. Today they are known as photo-telegraphy or facsimile (fax).

The next step was the transmission of audio over these same wires. In 1876 the telephone pioneer Alexander Graham Bell transmitted the sound of a voice by means of an electric wire and thus three means of instant communications came into existence, the telegraph, the copy-telegraph, and the telephone, and the time was ripe for the introduction of a visual transmission system.

In 1873, Willoughby Smith with Joseph May, an electrician working on the Atlantic Telegraph cable, reported that selenium rods used for continuity checks changed their resistance (conductivity) when exposed to varying light. This ability of certain metals to react to changes of light intensity was widely reported and manifested itself in plans for devices that would transmit pictures.

By the end of 1878, the combination of Bell's telephone and Edison's invention of the phonograph (1877) combined with progress being made in photography led the magazine *Punch* to print a cartoon of a new Edison invention the 'telephonoscope'. Here was depicted a two-way visual system on a wide screen depicting parents in London speaking with their daughter in Ceylon by means of an 'electric camera obscura' and telephone. Edison did not apply for a patent on

Edison's telephonoscope of 1878.

a motion picture system until 1889. It is ironic that *Punch* should have Edison invent an 'electric camera' before he invented the motion picture camera. But there were many schemes for visual communication gadgets at the time.

In 1880 Maurice LeBlanc detailed an ingenious method of transmitting moving images over an electrical wire. He described a scanning device (at both sender and receiver) consisting of two vibrating mirrors working together at two different rates of speed. The light from the image would be sent to a transducer (such as a selenium or Becquerel thermo-electric cell) to be converted into electricity. At the receiver, he proposed that two pieces of mica (as a shutter) would be moved according to the signal to control the light from a lamp. He suggested that because of persistence of vision, it would be possible to build up a likeness of the transmitted image. LeBlanc's 1880 fundamental paper contained in fact all the elements for a practical visual transmission system.

It was not long before the first practical solution appeared. In 1884, Paul Nipkow applied for a German patent for an *Elektrisches Teleskop*. The heart of Nipkow's patent was a revolving apertured disc. The disc had twenty-four holes in a spiral near the outer rim. Nipkow proposed that light from the subject would pass through the perforated disc on to a selenium cell. At the receiver, a similar perforated disc would be illuminated by a polarized light source. With both discs rotating at a constant speed, it was intended that an image would be built up and viewed through an eyepiece. This patent had all the elements (synchronization was presumed by a constant rotating speed) for a successful visual transmission system, and was soon followed by other ideas based on a rotating disc, including revolving mirror drums (Lazare Weiller), lensed discs (Louis Brillouin), and perforated bands and strips (Paul Ribbe).

Experiments with electrical discharges inside evacuated glass tubes started with the work of Heinrich Geissler and Julius Plücker in 1858. Plücker designed a

15

sealed glass tube filled with gas, with an electrode inserted at each end. When a certain voltage was applied to the electrodes, the gas in the tube ionized (incandesced), current flowed, and the tube glowed with a characteristic colour. This became known as a 'Geissler' tube.

Other scientists soon started to experiment with these tubes. Wilhelm Hittorf discovered in 1869 that a solid body would cast a shadow on the walls of the tube. In 1876 Eugen Goldstein concluded that the radiation came from the cathode and called them 'cathode rays'. William Crooks showed that the rays were projected at high velocities by electric forces near the surface of the cathode. Jean Perrin showed that the charge was negative in 1895. In 1897, J. J. Thompson proved that they could be deflected by an electrostatic field, and finally in 1897 Karl Ferdinand Braun developed the cold cathode ray tube that bears his name.

The Cathode Ray Tube

An International Electricity Congress was held in conjunction with the 1900 Paris Exhibition. On 25 August 1900 a paper was read by one Constantin Perskyi entitled 'Television', in which he described an apparatus based on the magnetic properties of selenium. This new term slowly supplanted the older names such as the 'telephot' or 'telectroscope' to describe the newly born art and science of 'seeing at a distance'.

The various theories of transmitting pictures by wire had created much controversy in the scientific community. A letter to *Nature* by Shelford Bidwell in June 1908, reviewing the various methods being proposed, concluded that, 'It was improbable for any system of television to view images hundreds of miles apart.'

This letter was answered by Alan Archibald Campbell Swinton who wrote that 'distant electric vision' was possible with tubes using cathode rays (at both the transmitter and receiver) properly synchronized and with the necessary means for converting light to electricity and back to light. This was the first mention in the literature of an all-electric television system.

Unknown to Campbell Swinton, both Professor Boris Rozing in Russia and Dr Max Dieckmann in Germany were also experimenting with cathode ray tubes as receivers. However, no one before had suggested the use of a cathode ray tube as an image transmitter.

Just one year later, in 1909, three different television systems were actually built and operated. The first (in order of publication) was that of Dr Max Dieckmann. His equipment consisted of a unique device at the transmitter with a cold cathode Braun tube for a receiver. The transmitter consisted of a rotating wheel that was fitted with twenty wire brushes. (It had no photo-cells or other light-transducing means.) The brushes actually touched the image to be transmitted, very much like the early devices of Bain and Caselli. At the receiver, the Braun tube with four deflecting magnets scanned a picture approximately 1.25 inches square. The electron beam was turned 'on' or 'off' as the rotating brushes touched the object, thus creating a picture on the screen. This was not a *true* television system as the transmitter was actually a form of telegraph sender rather than a transducer of light to electricity.

The second system was that of Ernst Ruhmer. It consisted of a mosaic of twenty-five selenium cells in rows of five each. Each cell when exposed to light was connected to a relay, which sent an alternating current over a line to a receiver. Here, there was a similar mosaic consisting of twenty-five incandescent lamps. At the receiver, there was one relay for each cell that would operate its own incandescent lamp. Only simple geometric figures could be shown. As it was a multi-wire (simultaneous) device, it was not a true television system.

The third was a quite different television device built and demonstrated by Georges Rignoux and Professor A. Fournier in 1909. The transmitting screen consisted of a bank of selenium cells, each connected to a separate relay. The relays were connected in sequence by a rotating commutator. As each relay was connected in turn to the commutator, it sent its signal through a single wire to a receiver. Here the signals were sent to a light valve (modulator) based on the Faraday effect of polarized light. (The light beam was aligned by a Nicol prism and then sent through a tube filled with bisulphate of carbon around which was wrapped a coil of wire.) As the current varied in the coil (due to scanning) the polarized light was 'rotated' in such a manner as to vary the amount of light passing through the tube. This modulated light was then sent through a set of rotating mirrors where the image was reconstituted on a screen. There were means provided to synchronize the receiver with the transmitter. This was a 'real' television system, the first on record as having been built and operated.

Rozing, Zworykin, and Swinton

Important work on a cathode ray system was also being conducted by Professor Boris Rozing of the Technological Institute of St Petersburg. In 1907, Rozing applied for a Russian patent proposing a television system using a cathode ray tube as a receiver. The transmitter used two mirror drums for scanning and dissecting the image. The mirror drums moved magnetic coils as they rotated, thus creating scanning currents for deflecting the electron beam at the receiving tube.

At the receiver, the currents were sent to a cold cathode ray (Braun) tube which had its beam deflected by either moving coils or plates. The beam itself was modulated (varied) in brightness by physically moving up or down between two small metal plates in the neck of the tube in accordance with the incoming signal. (At the time, there was no known method for modulating an electron beam, so this was quite ingenious.) The electron beam itself was deflected by coils using currents generated at the transmitter. This patent was second only in importance to that of Nipkow's of 1884.

Boris Rozing's laboratory.

It is claimed that Rozing had started working on such a device as early as 1904, and was actually building working apparatus. In 1908, he had carried out experiments with actual models and attempted to transmit simple images (slides, drawings, hands, etc.). In May 1911, he successfully demonstrated a distinct image consisting of four luminous bands to his colleagues at the Technological Institute of St Petersburg. For this he received a gold medal from the Russian Technological Society.

Professor Rozing built all of his apparatus (except for the cold cathode Braun tube that he purchased from a scientific laboratory in Berlin), including his own photoelectric cells. For this he had the assistance of a young engineering student by name of Vladimir Kosma Zworykin. Zworykin had been chosen by Rozing in 1911 to help him with his laboratory experiments as a result of his great interest in physics. Rozing introduced him to the new art of 'electrical telescopy', something Zworykin had never heard of before. Zworykin worked part time in Rozing's laboratory until his graduation in 1912. This was the beginning of young Zworykin's interest in cathode ray television.

In November 1911, A. A. Campbell Swinton became president of the Röntgen Society of London. He gave an inaugural speech entitled 'Distant Electric Vision'. He elaborated on his article of 1908 in *Nature* magazine and described a complete electric television system using cathode ray tubes for both transmitter and receiver. He admitted that his plan was an idea only, had never been constructed, and that it would take a great deal of experimentation and modification to be practical. However, the Röntgen Society was quite small and its journal's circulation quite limited, so his ideas were not widespread at the time.

With the start of the World War in Europe in 1914 interest in the new art of television diminished. But the war brought great advances in communications both by wire and radio. The end of the war found the (British) Marconi Wireless Telegraph Company in virtual control of long-distance communications between the United States and Europe. The Marconi Wireless Telegraph Company then tried to buy from the General Electric Company the Alexanderson radio alternator, which made these long-distance communications possible. This was brought to the attention of the US Navy Department, which objected strenuously. General Electric was told to reject the order. It was decided to buy out the American Marconi Company and replace it with a new American company to be formed by General Electric. This new company was to be called the Radio Corporation of America (RCA). A patent pool was formed and on 17 October 1919, RCA was incorporated. On 1 July 1920, an agreement was also reached with the American Telephone and Telegraph Company and its subsidiary the Western Electric Company, which were together known as the Telephone Group. This alliance did not last; two years later AT&T sold its RCA stock but remained in the patent pool.

Commercial radio broadcasting began in the United States in 1920 when Westinghouse Electric started operating radio station KDKA. This was so successful that on 30 June 1921, Westinghouse Electric was allowed to join the GE/RCA/AT&T consortium. KDKA was soon joined by hundreds of radio stations all over the United States.

Interest in television was also revived after the war. In August of 1921, the first patent for an electric camera tube was applied for by one Edvard Gustav-Schoultz of Paris. There is no record of this tube being built and no more was heard of the inventor.

In the United States, Charles Francis Jenkins had turned his attention from the motion picture (he had invented the first motion picture projector with Thomas Armat in 1895) to that of telephotography and television. In 1922 Jenkins applied for his first patent for transmitting pictures by wireless. It used a unique scanning device, 'prismatic rings'. These were glass prisms with varying surfaces that would bend the light from an object as they rotated. At the transmitter, the two prisms operating together would scan the scene (at two rates of speed) to analyse it and send the light to a photoelectric cell. At the receiver, two similar prisms reconstructed the image using a light valve of the Faraday type proposed by Rignoux. This light was projected on a type of fluorescent or phosphorescent screen.

Jenkins was assisted by both the General Electric Company and Westinghouse. He was the first experimenter to use the special neon light valve developed by D. McFarlan Moore of the General Electric Company in his receiver.

In December 1923, Jenkins demonstrated his television apparatus separately to Hugo Gernsback, editor of *Radio News*, and Watson Davis, editor of *Popular Radio*. They claimed that the apparatus was crude and cumbersome. Gone were the prismatic rings, prismed, mirrored discs being substituted. Jenkins was using

19

the sensitive Theodore Case Thalofide photoelectric cell at the transmitter and the General Electric Moore glow-lamp at the receiver. Both editors claimed that they could put small objects in the path of the transmitter and see them at the receiver. The signals were sent by a small radio transmitter across the laboratory. As far as can be determined, these were the first witnessed demonstrations of radio-television ever reported.

The Struggles of John Logie Baird

About this time in 1923, a young experimenter, John Logie Baird, started what was to be his life's work on television in London. With the financial assistance of Wilfred E. L. Day he was set up in a laboratory at 22 Frith Street, Soho. He filed for his first television patent in July 1923. It included a Nipkow disc at the transmitter with a bank of lights arranged to form an image on a screen at the receiver. This was the first of a multitude of patents taken out by Baird in his quest for a practical television system.

Another application for a camera tube was made on 29 December 1923, by Vladimir K. Zworykin of the Westinghouse Electric Company. It was part of a patent for an all-electric television system. The camera tube had an aluminum foil plate covered with a thin layer of potassium hydride. At the receiver, a Braun tube would reconstruct the image on a fluorescent screen. While this patent had many similarities to the original Campbell Swinton plan of 1911, it differed in one major aspect. Campbell Swinton's camera tube disclosed a mosaic of rubidium cubes, Zworykin's showed a plate covered with a layer of photoelectric material. This was to cause Zworykin much grief during the patent process and it took fifteen years before it was granted by the US Patent Office.

In April 1924, Campbell Swinton again described his all-electric television scheme in *Wireless World* and *Radio Review*. He had updated his ideas with the use of a hot cathode to create an electron beam resulting in better focus at the viewing screen. He lamented the hopelessness of his task unless one of the big electric companies with money and resources decided to get involved. This paper stimulated many researchers to start work on television projects, including the General Electric Company in Schenectady, the American Telephone & Telegraph Company, as well as many independent researchers, among them Dr August Karolus and Manfred von Ardenne in Germany and Kenjiro Takayanagi in Japan.

In January 1925 the Bell Telephone Laboratories (the research arm of the American Telephone & Telegraph Co.) started a research programme dealing with the problem of television, under the guidance of Dr Herbert E. Ives. He had been working on photoelectric cells for photo-telegraphy and invited Dr Frank Gray and John Hofele to head the programme. With the enormous technical resources of the new Bell Telephone Laboratories in New York City, the group

made excellent progress and by July 1925 were sending half-tone pictures from slides across the laboratory.

John Logie Baird and one of his early television machines.

Their mechanical system was based on the Nipkow disc for both transmission and reception. Their success came from the invention by Dr Frank Gray of the 'flying spot' scanner, developed around May–June 1925. In this device, the subject was bathed in a flying spot of light from an arc lamp behind the Nipkow disc. The reflected light went to four huge photo-cells that picked up the picture signal. This made half-tone television possible.

In April 1925, John L. Baird set up his apparatus in Selfridge's Department Store in London for three weeks and gave the English public their first crude demonstration of mechanical television. Then on 2 October 1925 Baird also independently discovered the principle of the flying spot scanner. He applied for a patent on this idea on 20 January 1926, and gave a demonstration of his new system to some forty members of the Royal Institution at his laboratory in Frith Street on 26 January 1926. This was the first public demonstration of television with half-tones ever given.

21

While it was reported that the pictures were 'faint and often blurred', the demonstration was considered a success. Baird and his associates were careful not to reveal how it had been done at the time. (The flying spot principle had been patented by G. Rignoux in France in 1908, by A. Ekstrom in Sweden in 1912, and filed for in August 1923 by John H. Hammond Jr. in the USA; issued in 1929).

In June 1925, Charles F. Jenkins made headlines in newspapers all across the United States. He again demonstrated his television system by transmitting the image of a revolving windmill five miles by radio from the US Navy radio station NOF in Anacostia, Maryland, to his laboratories in Washington, DC, an event witnessed by many United States officials.

Meanwhile in the autumn of 1925 (the exact date is unknown) Vladimir K. Zworykin assembled a complete, working electric television system for a demonstration to management at the Westinghouse Electric Company. With the help of his tube blower he built the first electric camera tube in the world and used a converted Western Electric oscilloscope tube for a receiver. He also constructed the rest of the system, which operated quite erratically.

Unfortunately the demonstration, which consisted only of an X painted on the face of the camera tube, was not considered a success by management. They recommended that he be put to work on something more useful. Zworykin was then forbidden by Westinghouse to do any more actual work on television (filing patents was permitted) and he concentrated on photoelectric cells and other devices that had immediate commercial value. However, this demonstration was the first of an electric camera tube to be displayed on a cathode ray tube.

Charles Francis Jenkins and his 1928 Radiovisor.

On 26 July 1926 Édouard Belin gave a demonstration in Paris of his new cathode ray television system to three important French officials. He revealed that he had been joined by Dr Fernand Holweck, Chief of Staff of the Madame Curie Radium Institute. The system was now called the 'Belin and Holweck' system after its inventors. It had been built and operated by Belin's chief engineer Gregory N. Ogloblinsky. The images were picked up by two small vibrating mirrors that were synchronized together. The receiver featured a metal cathode ray tube that had been designed by Holweck. The face of the tube could only show outlines of faces or figures. These pictures were 33 lines at about 10 frames per second. They gave the first demonstration of moving images on a cathode ray tube.

About two weeks later (2 August 1926) the cathode ray television system of Dr Alexandre Dauvillier of the Physical Research Laboratory of the Louis de Broglie Laboratories in Paris was revealed. He also used two small vibrating mirrors to dissect his image. However, his cathode ray receiving tube was quite modern. It was made of Pyrex glass, had a high vacuum, and used magnetic focus. His screen was made of willemite. He claimed to be producing 40-line pictures at 10 frames per second.

In October 1926, Kenjiro Takayanagi in Japan started his first actual experiments with cathode ray television. He claimed that he was able to transmit the Japanese character katakana (i) inscribed on a mica plate on 25 December 1926.

On 7 April 1927, the American Telephone & Telegraph Company gave their first public demonstration of television. This was a joint effort of the Bell Telephone Laboratories and Western Electric that was part of the Telephone Group. It consisted of a television programme transmitted by land-line (wire) from Washington, DC, to New York City. There was also a wireless (radio) transmission from Whippany, New Jersey, to New York City. It was claimed that there was no difference in the quality of the images transmitted.

Using a 50-hole Nipkow disc running at 18 frames per second, the pictures were of excellent quality. It was in fact the finest demonstration of television ever made up to that time. The Bell Laboratories admitted that they had been working on the project since 1925 and the demonstration required the services of almost 1,000 men.

This successful demonstration by the Telephone Group dismayed David Sarnoff, now Vice-President of RCA. Relations between the two giants of communications, the Radio Group (GE/Westinghouse/RCA) and the Telephone Group, were strained. Earlier (July 1926) Sarnoff had successfully removed the American Telephone & Telegraph Company from radio broadcasting and he certainly did not want them to have the lead in television research. Sarnoff immediately ordered both General Electric and Westinghouse Electric to double their research efforts to match those of the Telephone Group.

In San Francisco, California, a newcomer to the field of television, Philo T. Farnsworth, applied for a patent (7 January 1927) on a completely different elec-

Philo Taylor Farnsworth.

tric television system. His camera tube was an 'image dissector' that had a photo-electric plate upon which the light from the scene was converted into electricity. This created an *electron image* that was passed *en masse* by scanning coils sequentially to an electrode where it became the television signal.

Farnsworth had started work on his system in May 1926. He had obtained financing and was constructing all of his equipment in a small laboratory in Los Angeles. He soon moved to San Francisco, where he continued his experiments. It was claimed that by 7 September 1927, he was able to transmit lines of various widths in one direction, on a cathode ray tube, so that any movement at right angles was easily recognizable.

Farnsworth continued to improve his system. In January 1929, he hired a young engineer, Harry Lubcke, to work in his laboratory and by July 1929, Lubcke and Farnsworth had devised and built an all-electric scanning and synchronizing pulse generator. With it installed, Philo Farnsworth was now operating the first all-electric television system in the world. It consisted of his camera tube (the 'image dissector') and his magnetically focused picture tube (the 'oscillite'). There were absolutely no mechanical parts in the entire system.

On 13 January 1928, General Electric gave a television demonstration from its labs in Schenectady, New York. This was under the direction of Dr Ernst F. W. Alexanderson. It was a demonstration of a 48-line picture at 16 frames per second of 'live' images using the flying spot system of Dr Frank Gray. The images were received on three receivers located in the Schenectady area.

In April 1928, RCA applied for a permit for a television station to be constructed in New York City. It was to be operated by the Research and Test Dept of RCA at Van Cortland Park under the direction of Dr Alfred N. Goldsmith. This station W2XBS was part of a plan by David Sarnoff to have a television station operating by the end of the year.

On 8 August 1928, Westinghouse Electric gave a television demonstration of 'radio-movies' from their radio station KDKA in East Pittsburgh. It was a transmission of 35 mm motion picture film of 60-line pictures at 16 frames per second. The pictures were transmitted by land-line (wire) to the transmitter and back by radio (wireless) to special receivers at the laboratory. Westinghouse gave radio engineer Frank Conrad credit for this demonstration.

Conspicuously missing from this demonstration was Dr V. K. Zworykin. True to its word, Westinghouse had not allowed him to participate in it. Sometime late in November 1928, on David Sarnoff's orders, he was sent to Europe to inspect the various laboratories that had commercial agreements with the Radio Group (GE/Westinghouse/RCA), taking in Germany, Hungary, and France. In Paris he visited the laboratories of Établissements Belin and was shown all of their work in progress. Here he met Édouard Belin, founder; Fernand Holweck, chief scientist; Gregory N. Ogloblinsky, chief engineer; and one Pierre E. L. Chevallier, consulting engineer.

He was shown an advanced version of the 'Belin and Holweck' television system. It had a new picture tube that featured 'electrostatic focus'. This was accomplished by carefully controlling the voltages in two diaphragms that were in the path of the beam. The two-piece tube was metallic, continuously pumped (a Holweck speciality) with a glowing cathode that displayed 33-line pictures at 10 frames per second. It was rather crude, and, while quite sharp, could not display pictures with any more brightness than the usual Braun tubes using either magnetic or gas focus.

A Practical Television System

Dr Zworykin was elated by this disclosure. He knew that by making several important changes to this tube he had the answer to the problem of a practical television system. He made arrangements with Belin to purchase a Holweck cathode ray tube and a Holweck vacuum pump and bring them back with him. He also made plans to hire Ogloblinsky at an early date.

Zworykin arrived back in Westinghouse late in December 1928 and related his finding to Samuel Kintner, his superior at Westinghouse. Kintner showed very little interest in it and suggested that Zworykin go to New York and see David Sarnoff personally as he had gone to Europe on RCA's (not Westinghouse's) behalf.

This resulted in the famous meeting between Dr Zworkyin and David Sarnoff and their oft-quoted conversation. Zworykin convinced Sarnoff that he had the solution to a practical television receiver—to wit, one that needed no maintenance, had no moving parts, could be viewed in a semi-dark room, and operated by the average man in his home. He told him that he had the basic device working in his laboratory. This was true: he had converted the Holweck cathode ray tube to conform to his new ideas. When asked how much it would cost, Zworykin stated, 'some $100,000', a considerable understatement. But Sarnoff, who was quite eager to give RCA the lead in television research, gladly gave his consent and Zworykin was set up in his own laboratory at East Pittsburgh and provided financing and manpower to build a practical television system based on his revolutionary picture tube.

In February 1929, Zworykin ordered thirteen glass bulbs from the Corning Glass Company and began work on his new system. The first usable tube was assembled in April. A modified 35 mm film projector (Zworykin had no camera tube at the time) was to be used as a source of picture signals. Several top engineers from Westinghouse were assigned to the project. They included Harley Iams, John Batchelor, Arthur Vance, Randall Ballard, and W. D. Wright, an optical engineer.

The project went very well. On 9 May 1929, a demonstration was given of motion picture film using three sets of electrical circuits. Finally, on 17 August 1929, a demonstration was given by radio to a group of RCA and General Electric engineers.

The receivers were all-electric, with no moving parts. The seven-inch picture tubes, now called 'kinescopes' ('kineo' to move, 'scope' to see) could easily be viewed in a dimly lit room. Seven receivers were installed at various locations in East Pittsburgh (including one in Zworykin's home). Zworykin was allowed to use the KDKA Conrad short-wave radio transmitter late at night for his experiments.

Zworykin filed for a patent on the kinescope on 16 November 1929, and revealed it in a speech before the Institute of Radio Engineers on 19 November 1929. His paper was an oral presentation only, no demonstration was given. The speech was featured in papers, magazines, and journals all over the world. His development of the kinescope was the single most important event in the history of television. It made television as we know it today possible.

At Westinghouse, Zworykin was not content to rest on his laurels with the kinescope. With the arrival of Ogloblinsky from Paris in July 1929, he went to work to perfect a television camera tube. They used the same demountable Holweck cathode ray tube as the basis of their experiments. While only producing 12-line pictures, it proved that a camera tube with 'charge storage' was possible.

'Charge storage' was a long-sought-after goal. It meant that a camera tube would accumulate an electrical charge on each element that would continue to build up until scanned by the electron beam. As such the tube would have more sensitivity than a tube without it, such as Farnsworth's 'image dissector'.

In January 1930 all RCA television research was taken over by Zworykin, who moved his laboratory to the huge Victor Plant in Camden, New Jersey. Here he and Ogloblinsky produced many two-sided camera tubes. But they were hard to build (they were full of electrical and mechanical defects) and the resulting pictures left much to be desired.

Finally by July 1931, Zworykin and Ogloblinsky, who had been joined by Harley Iams, Arthur Vance, Sanford Essig, and Les Flory, had decided to take a new approach. They proposed to build a camera tube with a single-sided target, that is, one in which the electron beam and the light from the subject impinged on the same surface. Many variations of the single-sided design were built and tested. On 9 November 1931, the first tube displaying 'good' pictures was tested. Zworykin now named this tube the 'iconoscope' ('icon' for image and 'scope' to see). A patent covering this new design was filed on 13 November 1931. At last Zworykin and David Sarnoff had a camera tube that had the same potential as the kinescope. But the iconoscope was not revealed for two more years to the public.

In fact, the kinescope was now so bright that it was causing considerable flicker at the 24 frames per second rate in use. This was based on 35 mm sound film speed. On 19 July 1932, Randall C. Ballard of the RCA Zworykin laboratories applied for a patent for 'interlaced' scanning. This solved the problems of both flicker and limited bandwidth. While not a new idea (it had been

Vladimir K. Zworykin and a display of his television tubes.

done with Nipkow discs) this was the first time it had been applied to a cathode ray tube.

Each frame was divided into two fields (48 fields per second) and then inter-meshed so that it provided a continuous 24 frames per second picture. An odd number of lines (81 at the time) was necessary to make this system work. This important patent was soon incorporated into the RCA (and later the EMI) patent structure. At first it was done with a mechanical scanning disc, but by 1935 an all-electric interlaced scanning generator was finally designed and oper-ated.

In April 1931, it was announced in England that a new holding company, Elec-tric and Musical Industries Ltd. (EMI), had been formed by merging the HMV Gramophone Company with the Columbia Graphaphone Company Ltd. As the business depression was now world-wide, it was decided that by combining facil-ities, they could bring about certain economies of operations. A silent partner was RCA, which owned 27 per cent of the new company. David Sarnoff sat on the EMI Board of Directors.

EMI's first television project was to perfect a television system for the trans-mission of film based on the RCA/Zworykin kinescope. EMI's engineers from HMV included William F. Tedham (who was in charge of the project), C. O. Browne, R. B. Morgan, J. Hardwick, and W. D. Wright, formerly of Westing-house. From Columbia Graphaphone came Isaac Shoenberg, Allan Blumlein, P. W. Willans, and others. Sarnoff sent the EMI laboratories at Hayes, Middlesex,

27

several kinescopes for experimental purposes. RCA now had a powerful ally in its race for domination of the new television industry.

The EMI laboratories were also privy to the Zworykin experiments with an electric camera tube at Camden. Sometime in the summer of 1932, William Tedham and Dr Joseph D. McGee (who had come to work for EMI in January 1932) took it upon themselves to build an electric camera tube. According to McGee, it worked quite well for a short period of time. Dr McGee claimed that as it was not an 'official' (sanctioned) project it was not reported to the Director of Research, who was now Isaac Shoenberg. At any rate, it was the first working camera tube built in England. A patent for it was filed on 25 August 1932.

Early in 1933, EMI proposed to the General Post Office that it be allowed to go ahead with a television service. They suggested that with a few minor changes in the BBC's ultra-short-wave radio transmitter in London it could go ahead and produce receiving sets by the autumn of 1933.

Baird Television Ltd., which had been running an experimental low-definition (30 lines at 12.5 frames per second) television service for the BBC in London since September 1929, was quite upset by this and demanded that there be a competition for such a service. A demonstration to the General Post Office in April 1933 proved that EMI's system was far superior to that of Baird's. In May 1933, Capt. A. G. D. West became technical director of Baird Television Ltd. and immediately started a crash programme into cathode ray tube reception.

On Monday, 26 June 1933, at the Eighth Annual Convention of the Institute of Radio Engineers in Chicago, Illinois, Dr V. K. Zworykin presented a paper, 'The Iconoscope: A New Version of the Electric Eye'. In this paper he revealed the existence of the new RCA camera tube, the iconoscope. He made much of the fact that it used 'charge storage', which made it quite sensitive. However, just as with the kinescope in 1929, it was neither publicly exhibited nor demonstrated. Zworykin then went to Europe in the summer of 1933 and revealed the plans for the iconoscope to Isaac Shoenberg of EMI in England and Fritz Shröter of Telefunken in Germany. A camera tube laboratory was set up at EMI at Hayes with Dr J. D. McGee in charge. By 24 January 1934, the first EMI camera tubes were producing fair pictures. EMI raised its television standard to 240 lines at 25 frames. On 12 May 1934, Hans G. Lubszynski and Sydney Rodda of EMI applied for the first patent on a new, improved iconoscope camera tube. This new tube was called the Super-Emitron.

The rivalry between Baird Television Ltd. and EMI led the BBC and General Post Office to set up a committee to settle their differences. This was under the chairmanship of Lord Selsdon. It sent delegations abroad to study the state of the art in the United States and Germany.

On 24 May 1934, the Marconi Wireless Telegraph Company and EMI Ltd. merged to form Marconi-EMI Ltd. This powerful cartel left the Baird Television Company with Fernseh AG and the (English) General Electric Company as its only allies. GE was developing picture tubes. Fernseh was developing both an intermediate film system (using film that was speedily developed and projected) and the Farnsworth 'electron camera'.

In the summer of 1934, Philo Farnsworth gave the first public demonstration of all-electric television by a demonstration unit at the Franklin Institute in Philadelphia. His system consisted of his image dissector tube, an all-electronic scanning and sync generator, and his magnetically focused picture tube. The entertainment consisted of vaudeville talent, athletic events, and appearances of various politicians. Each programme was of fifteen minutes' duration.

The First Television Services

On 14 January 1935, the Selsdon Committee made its recommendations to Sir Kingsley Wood. It stated that a high-definition television service should be started in London with two companies, Baird Television Ltd. and Marconi-EMI Ltd. furnishing the technical apparatus. The transmission standard was to be at least 240 lines at 25 frames per second.

On 22 March 1935, the German Post Office (DRP) opened what was called a 'regular' medium-definition (180 lines at 25 frames per second) service from Berlin. It consisted primarily of the projection of motion picture film; no live coverage. It was not a success. The picture quality was quite poor. No television receivers were ever sold, programming was sporadic, and as a result of a disastrous fire it went off the air on 19 August 1935.

The competition between Baird Television Ltd. and Marconi-EMI was fraught with difficulties. The two companies would not exchange any information and would not co-operate in any way. At the Alexandra Palace, EMI planned to use a 'live' studio equipped with four Emitron cameras along with a 35 mm film projection unit. Baird Television Ltd. relied on a studio equipped with a flying spot scanner, an 'intermediate film' (a high-speed film developing process) system, a 240-line telecine Nipkow disc film transmitter, and the Farnsworth 'electron camera'. While Baird Television relied on the 240-line sequential scanning standard, Marconi-EMI proposed to use a new high-definition 405 lines at 25 frames per second interlaced (the Ballard method) television system.

The Eleventh Olympic Games were held in July–August 1936, in Berlin, Germany and were shown by television. The coverage was by the German Post Office (DRP), which was using iconoscope cameras furnished by Telefunken, intermediate film vans for outdoor events, and the Fernseh (Farnsworth) electron camera. Most viewing was done in the Olympic Village and in selected theatres throughout the city. Sadly, the transmitted pictures were quite unsatisfactory. They were unstable, having low image detail, and suffered from severe flicker.

By contrast, the opening of the London Television Service in London in November 1936 was a tremendous success. Both the Baird and Marconi-EMI systems were demonstrated and it was obvious from the start that the Marconi-

29

EMI high-definition 405-line interlaced picture was far superior to that of Baird's 240 lines, a tribute to Isaac Shoenberg and his staff.

The programming, under Cecil Madden, included game shows, musical numbers, drama, and a variety of 'outside broadcasts' that covered everything from the Coronation to cricket matches, boxing, and exhibitions. A steady stream of visitors from the United States (and elsewhere) were amazed at the uniformly high quality of the pictures, the regularly scheduled programmes, and the coverage of remotes (outside broadcasts).

The Marconi-EMI 405-line interlaced 25-frame standard was chosen in February 1937. This marked the beginning of modern television broadcasting as we know it today. The only problem was the high cost of the receivers. These were manufactured by Baird, Cosser, Ferranti, GEC, HMV, Marconi, Ecko, and several others. Costing from 37 to 170 guineas, less than 3,000 sets found their way into homes in London. Baird Television turned to large-screen cinema television.

On 30 September 1938, the London Television Service telecast the arrival of British Prime Minister Neville Chamberlain from Munich ('Peace in our Time') at Heston Aerodrome by means of its 'outside broadcast' unit. This was covered by three Emitron cameras and relayed 'live' to the Alexandra Palace were it was rebroadcast while actually happening. This was the first actual broadcast by television of a major news event as it occurred.

With the success of the London Television Service, David Sarnoff decided, in October 1938, to start a television service in the United States. This was to begin with the opening of the New York World's Fair in April 1939. Six American set manufacturers promised to have receivers ready for sale.

Television made its semi-formal debut in the United States on 30 April 1939. There was a speech by President Franklin Delano Roosevelt and shots of the Fair's activities. However, David Sarnoff had 'jumped the gun' and a week earlier (20 April 1939) had made a telecast dedicating the RCA Exhibit Building. While there was much enthusiasm for the new American system, few television receivers were sold to the American public. The National Broadcasting Company/RCA system was not able to provide a high-quality service similar to that of the London Television Service.

On 7 June 1939, Harley Iams and Dr Albert Rose of the RCA Laboratories announced details of a new camera tube called the 'orthicon' ('orth' for linear and 'icon' from iconoscope) which used a low-velocity electron scanning beam. It was considered a great improvement over the Zworykin iconoscope, which used a high-velocity scanning beam. Picture resolution was between 400 and 700 lines and it was supposed to be 10–20 times more sensitive than the iconoscope. Work on this new tube had begun in 1937, when Dr Albert Rose had joined Harley Iams at RCA.

The London Television Service was now a great success. Over 500 sets a week were being sold. By September 1939 over 20,000 sets were in use in the London area. However, with the invasion of Poland by Nazi Germany and the start of

World War II, the station was shut down with no advance notice on 1 September 1939. This was as if actual war conditions were being observed. The transmitter was turned off and all of the cameras and other equipment were carefully packed and stored away for the duration.

Television progress was lagging in the United States. NBC's experimental programming was sporadic and of very poor quality. Very few sets were being sold due to their high prices and there was very little public interest. In order to overcome this apathy, the Federal Communications Commission (FCC) stated that a commercial service could begin on or after 1 September 1940. RCA immediately announced a great sale of receivers at reduced prices. This upset the rest of the radio industry (Philco, Zenith, and the DuMont Laboratories). They feared, as in radio, that the NBC/RCA television transmission standards would become the official USA standard giving RCA another monopoly.

As a result, a National Television Systems Committee (NTSC) was formed in July 1940, to produce one set of universal standards agreeable to the entire industry. It would not do for the United States to have more than one set of transmission standards. A single 'lock and key' situation was needed in order that all receivers could receive the same pictures.

The NTSC submitted a report to the FCC in January 1941. It proposed a new set of technical standards for American television. Among them was a new 525-line standard and the use of FM for the audio portion. In May 1941, the FCC agreed to these standards and announced that commercial (sale of programmes) television could start in the USA on or after 1 July 1941. The issue of colour was to be taken up later.

On 1 July 1941, commercial television programming began in the USA. However, it was a lukewarm affair. Only NBC/RCA had paid, sponsored programming. CBS and DuMont, beset by technical problems, offered only limited fare. For the rest of the year, there was only minor television programming. Out of twenty-two licensees, only seven were actually broadcasting.

The bombing of Pearl Harbor by the Japanese on 7 December 1941 quickly put a halt to most programming in the United States for the rest of the war. Television returned to the laboratory, where it was to become a tool for guided missiles and long-range reconnaissance.

At first this war work depended on the newly developed RCA orthicon camera. But it had many defects and was not as successful as promised. Its war use in guided missiles and for reconnaissance was limited. The RCA Laboratories decided to improve its performance. The result was the development of the new highly sensitive tube called the image orthicon in 1944.

This tube was developed by Dr Albert Rose, Paul K. Weimer, and Harold B. Law of the RCA Laboratories. As a result, RCA came out of the war with a tube so sensitive that it could be used in normal room light. It was first demonstrated on 25 October 1945, at the Waldorf-Astoria Hotel. The original image orthicon camera was equipped with a single lens, but soon it was furnished with a four lens turret and an electronic viewfinder. This tube assured RCA supremacy in the development of post-war television all over the world.

With the war over, the BBC readied the Alexandra Palace for the resumption of telecasting. On 7 June 1946 it returned to the air. Although they had a chance to change their standards they decided to go along with the original 405-line standard.

In the United States some fifteen television stations went back on the air. They were still using their old iconoscope and orthicon cameras, which were slowly replaced with the new RCA image orthicon. With the rapid growth of television in the USA in the early 1950s, the need for programme material to fill expanding schedules was tremendous. As in radio, the big production centres were in New York, Chicago, and Los Angeles. Since the United States was divided into three different time zones, a major problem was broadcasting the same programme at the same hour across the country. In radio, this was done by means of magnetic recording of the audio programmes.

Recorders and Cameras

In television, this problem was temporarily solved by ABC, NBC, and DuMont with the co-operation of Eastman Kodak by the introduction of a system of television film recording called 'kinescope recording'. This was accomplished with a special motion picture film camera that photographed the television image on the face of a special picture tube. This film record could either be quickly processed and shown within a few hours, or more likely was processed and shown at a later, more convenient time. This was mainly done on 16 mm film. The accompanying sound was either recorded directly on the film or for better quality in some instances was recorded separately on a magnetic track. (Similar recording techniques were also started in Great Britain for basically the same reasons.) By 1953, it was reported that 100 million feet of film would be required each year for television recording in the USA.

However, this was an expensive, wasteful method. It was evident that a more efficient, less costly system of television recording was needed. The obvious alternative was to record the picture on magnetic tape, as was done with audio. But because of the wider bandwidth used by a television picture this presented some formidable problems. The first effort to solve this problem was by John T. Mullin, who was associated with Bing Crosby Enterprises in Los Angeles. He altered a standard audio recorder from the Ampex Electric Corporation of San Carlos, California, and gave the first demonstration of video signals recorded on magnetic tape on 11 November 1951. In order to get this wide-band signal on to magnetic tape, he ran the recorder at high velocity past stationary heads. He later used a multitrack high-speed approach that consumed an enormous amount of tape. Similar high-speed projects were being undertaken by RCA, the BBC Research Laboratories, and others.

The Ampex Corporation, now in Redwood City, decided to solve the video recording problem using a rotating head approach. This would allow them to run the magnetic tape at a normal speed of 15 inches per second. In December 1951, Charles Ginsburg was hired to build such a device. He was joined by a student engineer, Ray Dolby, and by June 1953 they were able to demonstrate very crude pictures. The project continued in September 1954, with the addition of Charles F. Anderson, Alex Maxey, Fred Pfost, and Shelby Henderson.

This ingenious team produced a revolutionary transverse recorder that was demonstrated at the National Association of Radio and Television Broadcasters Convention in Chicago in April 1956. It was a machine with a rotating four-head drum that used two-inch magnetic tape running at 15 inches per second. In addition to the picture, it included both a cue and audio track. The picture quality was quite good (better than any kinescope recording) and the resolution was over 320 lines. Playback of picture and audio was instantaneous, no processing was necessary.

This new recorder completely changed all television programming. No longer was a local station forced to show a programme as it came off the network feed. It could be played at any convenient time. The first videotaped network broadcast was made by CBS TV with *Doug Edwards and the News* from Television City in Hollywood on 30 November 1956. 'Time shifting' of television material had begun. The Ampex revolution was underway.

In September 1959, a different kind of video recorder was introduced by Norikazu Sawasaki of the Toshiba Corporation of Japan. It also used a rotating head system. However, the magnetic tape was scanned by a single head in a 'helical-scan' (slant-track) machine. This had many advantages as it could be run forward or backward, at various speeds and be still-framed for stop motion. (The Ampex Corporation also had a helical machine in their laboratories in 1959, but had decided not to reveal it in order to protect its original transverse machines.) This new helical format (but with two heads) slowly superseded the original Ampex machines and later became the industry standard.

By 1961, Ampex added a host of features to the basic machine. This included 'Intersync', 'Amtec', 'Color-Tec', and a rudimentary Electronic Editor. Finally, in April 1963, Ampex introduced EDITEC, the first electronic videotape assembly device. Not only did the videotape recorder enable 'time shifting', it made editing of programme material as easy as pushing a button.

In the USA, the battle for a compatible colour system continued. CBS had perfected its 'mechanical' colour system and it was adopted by the FCC in September 1950. However, this required a different set of transmission standards. But David Sarnoff and RCA were determined that only a colour system that could be fitted (electrically compatible) into the regular 6 MHz monochrome FCC USA channel should be adopted. As a result a second National Television Systems Committee was formed in 1950. Through the efforts of the major radio manufacturers, including Hazeltine, General Electric, Zenith, and Philco, a new set of transmission standards was agreed upon and was adopted on 17 December 1953. This meshed a colour system into the existing standards and was the basis for every new colour system later adopted throughout the world.

There was much effort made to improve the performance of and reduce the size and weight of new video recorders and cameras. In June 1962, Kurt Machein of Mach-Tronics Inc. of Mountain View, California, introduced the MVR-10, the first one-inch helical recorder. In 1964, for the BBC, the Ampex Corporation introduced the VR2000, the first 'high-band' (higher recording standard) video recorder with excellent colour quality. In July 1965, the MVR Corporation of Palo Alto, California, demonstrated the first single-frame video disc recorder. It could be used for 'instant playback', including still frames. In April 1966, the Westel Company of San Mateo, California introduced the Westel WRC-150, the first self-contained one-inch portable television camera with a video recorder. In April 1967 the Ampex Corporation introduced the first battery-operated portable colour video recorder, the VR3000.

In 1964 the N. V. Philips Company of the Netherlands introduced the 'plumbicon' (lead oxide) camera tube for colour television. It produced such excellent picture quality that it quickly made obsolete both of the RCA work-horses, the image orthicon and vidicon tubes. Less than three years later, some of the first tubeless cameras with solid state sensors were announced by Fairchild and RCA (1967), Westinghouse (1968), and the Bell Telephone Laboratories with their CCDs (charge coupled devices) in 1970.

The combination of lightweight cameras and portable video recorders soon made an impact on newsreel coverage. The new art of electronic news gathering (ENG) began and all film was rendered obsolete. News and special events could be covered by these cameras with portable microwave installations and by means of satellite communications could be seen instantaneously all over the world.

The introduction in 1978 of a 1,125-line, high-definition television by NHK in Japan was just one more step in the relentless pace for video perfection. Not only was television providing the fastest means of communication all over the world, but it was doing it with superb picture quality.

The desire to see over the horizon has manifested itself in a revolution that has encompassed not only television, but motion picture film and computer graphics as well, while the detail pictures from satellites exploring the planets and outer space is a harbinger of things to come.

2

The Beginnings of American Television

William Boddy

The first decade of commercial television in the United States set in place the major economic actors, programme forms, and regulatory structures of the vast American TV industry of the next thirty years. Moreover, the flood of exported American TV shows that began in the 1950s provided models of programme styles and popular taste for producers around the world.

The early regulatory decisions which established US standards for such matters as broadcast spectrum allocation, image quality, and colour versus monochrome service substantially govern American television today. The impact of these decisions on the competing private interests inside and outside the broadcast industry was to create a small group of extremely profitable station and network operators who quickly became powerful figures on the political and regulatory scene. Both federal regulators and industry interests were well aware from the 1930s that approval for commercial television operation under a given set of standards might influence investment in a way that would preclude a later shift to higher technical standards. Another legacy of these early regulatory decisions is the fact that US television operates under an inferior standard of image resolution and colour quality, part of a pattern of incoherence and duplicity in federal broadcast regulation. This regulatory background, and other ideological and economic constraints during television's early growth had influenced the commercial structures and programme forms of the medium in America, as well as the relation of US television to the rest of the world.

Broadcast regulation in the United States has been founded upon two opposing principles: that the federal licence confers a privilege, not a right, to the broadcaster to operate in 'the public interest' using public airwaves, and that the

NBC TV cameras in New York. Early network programmers used outside broadcast facilities to help fill their schedules, taking advantage of public events for live broadcasts such as this parade in Times Square in 1945.

licence establishes and protects the broad *de facto* property rights of private operators of television and radio stations under restricted oversight of network operations and programme content. Economic concentration within the burgeoning US television industry was early and pronounced. In 1954, the two major television networks and their twelve owned-and-operated stations took in over half of the total profits of a TV industry which included two other network operators and hundreds of local stations.

The chief cause of this concentration (which had its effects in the industry's internal practices, programme forms, and export policies) was the decision of the Federal Communications Commission (FCC) to locate television service in the VHF (very high frequency) portion of the electromagnetic spectrum which could support only twelve channels nation-wide and only three stations in most large cities. This quickly created a relatively small group of extremely profitable large-market station operators served by two dominant network firms, NBC and CBS, with the American Broadcasting Company (ABC) and DuMont television networks as also-rans in a two-and-a-half network economy. The DuMont network went out of business in 1955 while the ABC network struggled through TV's first decade to achieve a weaker, though competitive position by 1960.

The Manufacturing Industry

The direction of the American television industry in its first decade was largely charted by leaders of the radio broadcasting and set manufacture businesses, in particular TV's dominant firm, NBC-RCA. Emerging from the late 1930s and World War II, radio broadcasting found itself in a curiously ambivalent position of strength and defensiveness. Network economic strength derived from a decade of rising profits from network radio, reflected in advertising billings, stock prices, and ambitious plans for post-war spending in multi-million dollar broadcast talent contracts, facsimile broadcasting, international commercial radio networks, and in television itself. Simultaneously with the first round of the Justice Department's efforts to divest the Hollywood studios of their theatre chains and outlaw established distribution practices in 1938, the two broadcast networks faced a period of unsettling antitrust and regulatory scrutiny. An NBC executive in 1940 worried that 'the New Deal at last has come to the world of radio communications', and warned that the network was vulnerable to the same antitrust charges and legal remedies of dismemberment that the beleaguered Hollywood studios were currently undergoing. A new reform-minded FCC in Roosevelt's second term did challenge network radio practices, forcing NBC to divest itself of its smaller network (thereby creating ABC) and producing the infamous 'Blue Book' outlining the public service responsibilities of broadcast licensees.

The Defence of Commercial Television

Faced with possible New Deal-inspired antitrust and regulatory reforms aimed at the broadcast industry, the networks emerged from the war with a broad public relations strategy, emphasizing both their patriotic role in developing wartime military electronics and the philosophical defence of commercial broadcasting. While the television industry prospered tremendously from World War II defence contracts, an April 1942 NBC memorandum indicates the company's efforts to keep key technical personnel out of the war effort, 'to resist attacks made upon television engineers by other NDRC Labs as it is anticipated that we will need all the men we now have to carry forward the television development projects which are contemplated'. Despite such behind-the-scenes efforts, the electronics and broadcast industries emerged from the war in high public esteem and unquestionable wealth.

The second post-war network public relations strategy involved a new militant defence of the principles of commercial broadcasting, including a widely reported speech by CBS head William S. Paley to an industry group in 1946, which identified the recent public criticism of commercially supported radio programming as 'the most urgent single problem of our industry'. In terms which anticipate countless network defences of their television programme policies of the next decade, Paley explained:

First we have an obligation to give most of the people what they want most of the time. Second, our clients, as advertisers, need to reach most of the people most of the time. This is not perverted or inverted cause and effect, as our attackers claim. It is one of the great strengths of our kind of broadcasting that the advertiser's desire to sell his product to the largest cross section of the public coincides with our obligation to serve the largest cross section of our audience.

In response to those worried about the deadening hand of the broadcast sponsor, Paley told broadcast critics that 'the advertiser buys freedom for the listener at the same time he buys time and talent. For it is an historic fact that the only other kind of radio is government radio.' It was on precisely such polarized terms that the networks successfully defended their commercial television practices and privileges over the next decade.

Despite its wealth and political confidence, US commercial television did not immediately take off at the end of the war. There existed a bitter dispute between groups aligned with NBC-RCA who favoured immediate development on the VHF spectrum and those aligned with CBS, which wanted a delay in order to establish colour TV service on the wider ultra-high frequency (UHF) band. All the major actors, including the FCC, recognized the anti-competitive nature of the VHF allocations of the early 1940s, but the FCC was under considerable pressure to relaunch a commercial television service. RCA had not only a cumulative investment of 10 million dollars in television by the end of the war, but its formidable patent position in television was strongest in the VHF band. Political fears of being seen as holding up television and the need to stimulate new employment in post-war electronics persuaded the FCC to ratify the restricted VHF frequencies in 1945, while at the same time admitting that 'the development of the upper portion of the spectrum is necessary for the establishment of a truly nationwide and competitive television system'.

The qualified decision discouraged investment by potential VHF set owners and station operators, and their caution was fuelled by a series of regulatory petitions from CBS on behalf of UHF colour television. Some within and outside CBS at the time saw the network motivated less by concern for colour UHF television than by a desire to protect its network radio interests by delaying television altogether; unlike NBC-RCA, CBS had no patent or manufacturing stakes in television equipment, and both CBS and NBC were predicting a decade-long wait before the business of network television became profitable. CBS was therefore torn between a defensive involvement with VHF broadcasting as the only commercial TV system approved by the FCC and a desire to thwart or delay its rival NBC-RCA's interests in VHF television. CBS's ambivalence led to the unlikely spectacle of a broadcast disclaimer at thirty-minute intervals during all CBS telecasts: 'We hope that you will enjoy our programs. The Columbia Broadcasting System, however, is not engaged in the manufacture of television receiving sets and does not want you to consider these broadcasts as inducements to purchase television sets at this time. Because of a number of conditions which are

not within our control, we cannot foresee how long this television broadcasting schedule will continue.'

Furthermore, in support of its position before the FCC that VHF television standards were inadequate, CBS closed its New York City TV studios, refrained from applying for additional VHF broadcast licences, and warned other prospective VHF station owners that 'the sensible broadcaster who has not yet entered television might logically conserve his capital—might prefer to stay out of the field—until the new standards arrive and better pictures are at hand'. The regulatory uncertainty and anti-VHF campaign by CBS, what its annual report for 1945 called the 'militant CBS sponsorship of color television in the ultra-high frequencies', led to precisely the television industry stagnation that RCA had warned would be ruinous to the American economy.

As CBS pursued a revised UHF colour television petition at the FCC into the spring of 1947, it began to look as if post-war television would be a major industrial failure. By August 1946, eighty applications for TV station licences had been withdrawn at the FCC as Americans showed little interest in set ownership under

A salesman takes an order for the latest piece of television technology. With three million sets sold in the first half of 1950— 60 per cent on credit to middle- and low-income households—television was becoming something the average American family could not do without.

39

the unsettled industry conditions and only 8,000 sets were sold by the end of 1946. But the April 1947 FCC denial of the CBS UHF petition, ratifying the existing VHF standards, marked the real starting-point of US commercial television; within two months, sixty new station applicants had petitioned the FCC, and TV set sales finally moved upward. As a writer in the *Nation's Business* noted in July 1947, 'Television . . . is something the average American family has just about decided it can't do without.' By March 1948 *Newsweek* reported that TV was 'catching on like a case of high-toned scarlet fever'. Despite its first real growth in the second half of 1947, the early television industry faced a number of hurdles.

Training the Television Audience

Many commentators on early television suggested that the near-total attention the medium was expected to demand from viewers would preclude viewing periods of more than an hour or two a day, relegating the new medium to a decidedly secondary service to established radio. Television, one 1940 book argued, 'requires concentrated attention and cannot serve as a background for such activities as bridge playing or conversation. It is on this difference that many broadcasters base their belief that television will never replace sound broadcasting, but will supplement the present art with a more specialized service.' Other commentators pointed to the financial and personnel costs of supplying the vast programming hours of the television schedule. A 1940 *New Yorker* magazine writer offered a fantastical look back at 'The Age of Television' from the projected vantage-point of 1960, recalling that following commercial TV's launch in 1945, the huge advertising revenues demanded by TV's enormous station operating and networking costs caused the prices of advertised goods to soar, provoking bread riots in 1947. On the other hand, the author suggested, the prodigious personnel demands of the medium had abolished adult unemployment and guaranteed that any child passing a simple literacy test could become a TV writer and discontinue further education. Such satiric projections were based on the widespread industry admission that the costs of a full television programme schedule in the model of network radio might well be beyond the means of broadcast sponsors.

There were also early fears about the disruptive effects of television on the American home and family; a 1947 trade press observer worried that since television would demand complete attention, 'the housewife who is accustomed to listen to soap operas while she washes, irons, and does the housework, cannot watch a visual program while she does her chores'. The *New York Times* TV critic complained in 1948 that 'the American household is on the threshold of a revolution. The wife scarcely knows where the kitchen is, let alone her place in it. Junior scorns the late-afternoon sunlight for the glamour of the darkened living room. Father's briefcase lies unopened in the foyer. The reason is television.' A writer in *Parent's Magazine* in 1948 described her family's successful adjustment of daily routines to accommodate television, though she complained of adult neighbours 'who insist on conversing' during the evening's television entertainment. Many early commentators worried about eye-strain produced by prolonged TV viewing, and as late as 1951 *Parent's Magazine* found it necessary to alert readers that 'it is not advisable to wear sun glasses to view television'. Such complaints and anxieties point to the complex adjustments that early commercial television provoked in US domestic life.

The Search for a National Signal

There were also early doubts about the possibility of bringing television signals to virtually every American home as network radio had done in the mid-1930s. Because of TV's limitation to line-of-sight transmission and uncertainty over the economic viability of coaxial cable and microwave relay networks of scattered stations, the 1940s saw a number of exotic proposals to compensate for the expected limitations in TV networking, including the construction of a 300-mile-high transmitter in Kansas to cover the entire nation; 'Stratovision', a system of thirty-three airplanes flying in constant 20-mile circles 20,000–25,000 feet above the earth to cover the entire USA, and the revival of road companies of travelling actors to service disparate stations. Other critics of commercial broadcasting forecast that the geographical limitations of a commercially backed television system and the inability of sponsors to support anything like a full programme schedule would persist for five or ten years, arguing that the inevitable chicken-and-egg problem of small audiences and meagre programme budgets revealed the advantages of a BBC-style licence fee system for television support, and that the public interest would not be served by the expected decade-or-two wait before increased audiences could support full nation-wide service. Thus, an important dissenting argument against the model of commercial network television was quickly silenced by the speed with which the commercial medium reached undisputed viability and economic power.

By the autumn of 1947 there were still only 60,000 TV sets in the entire country, two-thirds of them in New York City, the result of set manufacturers' sales allocations to retailers in the nation's media and advertising capital, and TV programme-makers faced an unusual, if transient, audience demographic problem. In September 1947, 3,000 of 47,000 sets in NYC were operating in bars; the rest were located in homes of high-income families; however, because the TV sets in bars attracted many more viewers per set than those in private homes, the overall audiences were roughly equal. *Business Week* worried that 'satisfying them both means a big problem for televisors'; the television audience in bars preferred sports and news, industry observers believed, and programming intended for the higher-income home audience left them cold; moreover, there was insufficient sports and news material to fill the programme schedule. An observer in the summer of 1947 noted the programming slant: 'So far it's a man's

In the first years of US commercial television, the mostly male tavern audience represented a significant proportion of viewers, like this group at McCarthy's Steak House in New York City in 1951.

world in the program department, with sports and news events hogging the average station's 20 hour-a-week showbill.' The programme emphasis highlights earlier predictions of post-war television programming along lines thought to appeal particularly to men. An FCC commissioner wrote in 1941 that TV would offer remote coverage of sports 'and current disasters such as fires, disasters and floods, as well as many other interesting events'. Similarly, a 1943 *Newsweek* article, 'What Will Postwar Television Be Like?', predicted TV programming of two types: 'those which transport the viewer from his home to a place or an event, and those which bring someone or something into his living room'; the former would include 'fires, train wrecks, and political meetings' as well as sporting events. The problem of programming to the gender- and class-distinct audiences in and out of the home in early television was quickly 'solved' by the explosion in set sales by 1950.

The American Family Takes to Television

The change in TV audiences from high-income to middle- and low-income households has been offered by some industry historians as the motivation for a number of programming shifts of the mid-1950s, including the rise of the filmed situation comedy, the decline of live anthology drama, and the move from urban-based to suburban-based sitcoms. However, while this demographic shift in TV set buyers and viewers did occur, it happened much earlier than its commonly supposed programming effects. In fact, the speed with which families with low and moderate incomes took up television surprised many contemporary industry observers. While *Business Week* in January 1948 cited an audience survey describing the typical New York City television family headed by an executive, professional, or small business owner, a journalist writing in 1949 argued that predictions of the previous year that TV set sales would remain restricted to upper-income groups were no longer valid: 'TV is becoming the poor man's theater', he noted. By January 1950 one observer pointed to 'the almost reckless abandon with which money has been invested in television by the public even where ready cash was not available . . . Television is the poor man's latest and most prized luxury.' More than 3 million television sets were sold in the first six months of 1950, 60 per cent of them on credit, 'with the poor crowding the rich away from the counters', according to *Business Week*. An economist's study of 1950 TV set owners showed ownership declined with incomes and educational levels beyond moderate levels, while suburban and smaller-city households were much more likely to buy sets than big-city households, even though such viewers had more TV channels available. *Fortune* magazine saw a tribute to 'the resilience of the U.S. economy' in the continued boom in set sales in the face of tightening consumer credit, the imposition of a 10 per cent excise tax, and continued regulatory uncertainty over colour television.

As early as 1948, many trade observers saw a lucrative future for VHF television operators; in January *Business Week* proclaimed 1948 'Television Year', and proclaimed that 'to the tele-caster, the possibilities are immediate and unlimited'. Later that year, the magazine reported that 'television people are gambling that once the black ink starts to flow it will write big profit figures. They are rushing into television as fast as they can.' The continuing substantial post-war radio revenues subsidized early television development, as CBS and NBC slashed cultural and educational programming; moreover, an estimated 75 per cent of freeze-era local TV stations were owned by radio broadcasters who likewise pared costs and shifted revenues from the older medium. Also significant for NBC were the enormous profits generated for RCA from sales and royalty revenues from TV sets; in 1948 there were already sixty-six manufacturers of sets, with 75 per cent of the set market controlled by RCA, DuMont, and Philco. The high profits in early TV set manufacturing are reflected in the wild run-up in stock prices of TV manufacturing firms in 1949, with RCA's stock up 134 per cent that year; for one week in the spring of 1950, trading in the seven largest set manufacturers amounted to 10 per cent of total Wall Street trading.

There were undoubtedly some lean years for television programming despite the medium's steady growth in the late 1940s. In July 1947 the business press noted that television networks were 'no more than a gleam in a broadcaster's eye', and complained that 'the programs coming out of television's studios at present are reminiscent of "The Great Train Robbery" stage of movie progress'. The *New York Times* TV columnist wrote that 'thoughtful retailers note that

Although the second-set and portable television receiver markets did not emerge fully until the early 1960s, electronic hobbyists like this one in the 1950s (with a set powered from his automobile's cigarette lighter) anticipated the subsequent transistorized TV set's liberation from the domestic living-room.

there are not enough programs telecast even to demonstrate sets properly in a store'. With CBS caught flat-footed by its deliberate go-slow policy in VHF television production and networking facilities, *Life* magazine at the end of 1947 could point out that 'there is still only one network of consequence', complaining that television 'has disinterred some of the hoariest acts in vaudeville . . . [and] worst aspects of radio. . . . Only occasionally . . . does the entertainment seem almost mediocre.' Another journalist in 1948 complained that much TV programming 'is reminiscent of a junior high school graduation play', and *Fortune* in mid-1950 complained of 'program drivel that makes the worst movies and soap operas seem highbrow'. As early as 1949, critic Gilbert Seldes, who had served as director of CBS television between 1939 and 1945, was already lamenting what he saw as a decline in the programme quality since the earlier days when minuscule audiences freed programme-makers from the relentless need to address the widest public tastes: 'We seem to be watching, for the hundredth time, the traditional development of an American art-enterprise: an incredible ingenuity in the mechanism, great skill in the production techniques—and stale, unrewarding, contrived, and imitative banality for the total result.' Observers frequently expressed puzzlement at Americans' appetite for TV in the face of poor-quality programming in the late 1940s.

One factor behind this appetite was the enormous demographic changes brought on by suburbanization and the baby boom. Writing on the 'Possible Social Effects of Television' in 1941, RCA Chairman David Sarnoff predicted that

America's large cities would lose population to the new automobile suburbs between 1945 and 1960, arguing that television would provide a good fit with the new suburban households, linking them much like new high-speed roadways. As *Business Week* explained in 1956: 'Video dropped into the middle of a new social revolution: the mass exodus to the suburbs, new realms of leisure, rising incomes, and a tremendous demand both for things and for entertainment that had been pent up by war and depression.' The speed with which post-war commercial television gained economic ascendancy provided critics and policy-makers with a formidable *fait accompli* and discouraged commercial challengers and reformers.

The Social Impact

The new suburban home as imagined arena for television programmes had profound implications for freedom of expression in the medium, as a 1945 NBC executive suggested:

Television comes directly into the home. All the precautions that have been thrown around sound broadcasting to render it domestically acceptable may be automatically assumed to be essential for television. Furthermore, because the visual impression is apt to be more vivid and detailed and because to be understood it requires less imaginative response on the part of the observer than does an auditory impression, television must be much more carefully supervised if it is to avoid giving offense. This means that vulgarity, profanity, the sacrilegious in every form, and immorality of every kind will have no place in television. All programs must be in good taste, unprejudiced, and impartial.

Following complaints about New York-originated network programmes containing comic routines, actress necklines, and suspense and horror material thought unsuitable to domestic audiences in the nation's hinterlands, the TV industry quickly moved to establish industry-wide programme censorship. With prodding by Catholic pressure groups, FCC commissioners, and Congressional investigators, the networks in 1951 enacted a Television Code closely modelled in the Hollywood Production Code.

Political Pressures in the Television Industry

Also echoing contemporary events in Hollywood were the successful efforts of the anti-communist Right to shape the personnel and programme content of 1950s television. The 1950 publication *Red Channels: The Report on the Communist Influence in Radio and Television*, consisting largely of a list of over 150 actors and other television personnel with purported left-wing ties, quickly led to a decade-long pervasive political blacklist in network television. That year Jean Muir was removed from General Food's situation comedy *The Aldrich Family*; 1951 saw the resignation of playwright Elmer Rice in protest against the blacklist, and 1952 saw

45

the firing of Philip Loeb from the popular sitcom *The Goldbergs*, despite the efforts of the show's powerful star Molly Goldberg. In 1951 *Life* magazine wrote approvingly that the openly operating blacklist 'has served the good purpose of making "gulliberals" think twice before lending their names and talents to causes which are often Communist-inspired,' although the magazine lamented the fact that the anti-communist crusade had smeared innocents and 'cast a mantle of fear over a normally sunny profession'. Lauding the admittedly extra-legal vigil-antism of networks and sponsors, *Life* argued: 'In refusing to outlaw Commu-nism . . . Congress really passed the buck of fighting Communists to the American people. It is a tough and tricky task, in which each individual with any power in the matter—and sponsors have a great deal—must be his own general.' The anti-communist Right kept up the alarm in the early 1950s; Martin Berkeley, in a 1953 article, 'Reds in Your Living Room', warned that after being crushed in Hollywood by the House UnAmerican Activities Committee, the 'communist movement . . . then made calculated plans to seize the air waves of America'. Berkeley warned his readers that if such plans succeeded 'the Communist

The ubiquitous prime-time comedy-variety series of the 1950s brought veteran show business personalities to the new television audience. Jimmy Durante hosted the 1953–4 season of the **Colgate Comedy Hour** on NBC.

Party—through its secret members, its fellow-travelers, its dupes and sympath-izers—will have control of *every word* that goes out over the air waves'. In the spring of 1954 another conservative writer warned that TV's powers for persua-sion had attracted 'change-the-worlders' and 'uplifters', but noted with satisfac-tion both the plethora of right-wing commentators and personalities on the air and a TV sponsor's recent dropping of a commentator who had challenged Sen-ator Joseph McCarthy. Independent TV production companies and New York advertising agencies followed the networks' lead in full co-operation with the self-appointed anti-communist leaders, with pervasive and long-lasting effects on television programme content.

Thus, under these conditions of rising prosperity and ideological conser-vatism many of the persistent aesthetic features of American television program-ming were established and defended by the powerful economic interests in the early television industry. For example, one insight into what some contemporary critics see as US TV programming's dependence upon the soundtrack in a purported visual medium is the rationale offered by one 1948 advertising agency executive: 'I want those words to follow the set-owner in case he takes a notion to get up and go out to the bathroom while the commercial is running on the screen.' Similarly self-serving, if more fanciful, was CBS head Frank Stanton's 1951 argument on behalf of colour TV that 'color television wholly eliminates the interval in which your mind must take a black and white image into the dark-room of your brain and print it, on the intellect, as the true colored picture which the eye actually sees in nature. Thus, color television adds speed and clarity—greater impact and more information to each image and every sequence.' As we shall see, powerful private interests in commercial television were eager to seize upon and echo aesthetic claims if they served their strategic purposes in early television.

Many early TV critics in the USA attempted to deduce the aesthetic peculiar-ities of the dramatic medium from its technical limitations and its conditions of reception. Observers often lamented the tendency of TV to recycle talent and material from radio, movies, and the stage; they particularly cited TV's revival of vaudeville in the form of comedy-variety programmes, among television's most popular in the 1948–53 period. Early attempts to capture conventional theatre productions mid-proscenium were, the *New York Times* critic complained, 'not unlike seeing a series of picture postcards, with rather serious consequences to the play's fluidity and continuity'. Privileged by most critics were attempts to stage original drama for the medium; early television drama-makers faced constraints both financial (writers were offered only $25–200 for original TV scripts) and production-related, and such constraints often were translated by critics into the essential conditions of the art of television. One production exec-utive advised would-be writers in 1947 to consider the limitations of cramped studios, low budgets, and small TV screens and to 'write around living rooms, kitchens, offices, schoolrooms, etc.', for no more than three or four characters,

47

and urged TV directors to limit themselves to close-ups to convey the circum-scribed action.

Many TV critics deduced an essentialist mission for the medium, based on its reception in the domestic living-room; Gilbert Seldes wrote in 1950: 'The style of acting in television is determined by the conditions of reception; there is simply no place for the florid gesture, the overprojection of emotion, the exaggeration of voice or grimace or movement, inside the average American living room.' Seldes also argued that television possessed 'the capacity to transmit and deliver a rounded human character more completely than either radio or the movies. This is the source of its special power; this is what it must exploit to become totally successful.' He saw 'the sense of existing in the present' to be TV's essen-tial trademark, upon which 'a good director in television will base his entire style, the rhythm of movement, the frequency of close-up shots, the intensity of facial expression, the level of projection for the voice; on it the sponsor will build his advertising'.

Commercial television was growing despite the restrictive conditions of the VHF spectrum which caused competitive distortions in the television industry. The FCC froze station construction permits between the autumn of 1948 and the spring of 1952, (see Chapter 11) but by the end of the freeze the number of TV stations on the air had risen to 108, many of them quite profitable. By the mid-1950s the commercial structures of network television which would endure for decades were firmly in place. The networks used their profits and negotiating power arising from the scarcity of VHF licences simultaneously to effect a network seller's market in national TV advertising and a network buyer's market in the prime-time programming market. Faced with rising time and production costs, television advertisers moved away from single sponsorship of programmes to various forms of joint sponsorship, ceding programme licensing to the networks while retaining a censorship control over programme content in the form of informal or codified lists of proscribed subjects, characters, incidents, and language. At the same time, network licensing of prime-time programming reduced the market for independent programme producers to three network firms and allowed networks to demand ownership and syndication rights to their shows in exchange for a network time slot.

This financial model for the filmed programmes that would come to domi-nate network prime time and international programme markets was established as early as 1950 through network deals with a number of independent production companies, with Columbia Pictures' telefilm subsidiary Screen Gems making an early major Hollywood studio deal in 1952. The model typically involved network rights for two broadcasts of a typical thirty-nine episode annual season; the network licence fee would pay less than the full production costs of the programme, and to recoup the deficit, the production company would hope to resell the episodes to the domestic and foreign syndication markets. The 1952 ratings success of the thirty-minute filmed series *I Love Lucy* and *Dragnet* encouraged other production firms to enter the telefilm market, and the growing syndication revenues for network reruns in the USA and abroad in the mid-1950s led to the near extinction of live drama in network prime time by 1957. Furthermore, the rising programme licence fees by the mid-1950s attracted the major Hollywood studios into telefilm production, forming the industry relationships between programme producers and TV networks which largely endure today in American television.

In the midst of these programming shifts, the networks seized on the assertion by many early TV critics that the medium's capacity for the live transmission of dramatic or unstaged events defined its unique nature and mission as a rationale for network control of prime-time programming. Since only the networks could, by definition, provide interconnected live service to disparate stations, the networks defended their guardianship of the ontological essence of TV against those who 'would destroy the very lifeblood and magic of television', as CBS President Frank Stanton told a meeting of CBS affiliates in 1956. Ironically, the network privileging of live TV came at the very moment when the three networks moved irrevocably into filmed programming in prime time in pursuit of booming syndication revenues which live programmes could not attain.

Such stirring network defences of television's aesthetic mission and dire warnings against tampering with network power, often mobilized around Cold War or nationalistic themes, became commonplaces by the mid-1950s. In 1956 CBS President Frank Stanton told one group that the age of intercontinental nuclear missiles ('perhaps the most perilous time in our history') demanded an instantaneous civilian mobilization in the form of a divinely inspired network television system, arguing that 'it seems to be providential that we are thus able—at this pivotal point in world history—to reach into nearly every home in America simultaneously and at a moment's notice'. Stanton told a Congressional committee that year that nothing less than America's national unity was at stake: 'To curtail or destroy the networks' unique quality of instantaneous national interconnection would be a colossal backward step. It would make the United States much more like Europe than America. In fact, it would be a step in the direction of the *Balkanization*, the fragmentation, of the United States.' Arguing the political legitimation of the commercial use of the television airwaves, Stanton told another Congressional committee in 1956 that 'a network draws its validity in precisely the same fashion as an elected official of government—from election by and of the people'. As contemporary media economists have noted, the peculiar combination of concentrated private economic power and ostensible public interest standard in American network television led to sometimes tortuous justifications of oligopolistic privilege.

There were two major challenges to network sovereignty in the early television industry in the United States, the first from broadcasting's economic rivals in Hollywood and the second from philosophical nay-sayers and would-be reformers in the public realm. Contrary to some subsequent historical accounts, the Hollywood studios did not ignore television or limit their responses to Cine-maScope, 3-D movies, and other theatrical gimmicks. For example, a single major studio, Paramount, had interests in four of the nation's first nine TV stations in 1947, as well as stakes in significant television patents and in the DuMont television network. However, Paramount and the other major studios were also involved in a decade-long losing battle with the US Department of Justice over their distribution practices and ownership of movie theatres, and also faced a steep drop in the post-war theatrical box office unrelated to television, disruptions in post-war foreign markets, and an internecine political blacklist. The efforts of the studios to build a major presence in TV station ownership and network operation were consistently thwarted by the hostile actions of the FCC, and their efforts to develop an alternative to broadcast television in the form of large-screen TV in movie theatres were frustrated by FCC refusals of broadcast frequency allocations and coaxial cable rate regulation reform, as well as by public indifference and the costs of theatre renovation. Despite many ambitious Hollywood announcements of prospective theatre-TV plans between 1948 and 1951, fewer than 100 theatres across the country were ever equipped for its use, and theatre television dwindled into a series of infrequent and *ad hoc* offerings of prize fights and business conferences.

The 'Pay-TV' Controversy

The chief economic threat to the network-dominated commercial broadcasting model for television came from Hollywood proposals for pay television in the form of scrambled broadcast signals or cable into the home. As early as 1946 the electronics manufacturer Zenith began public tests of its Phonevision system, and in the period before 1952, when the economic viability of nation-wide advert-ising-supported network television was doubted by many, pay TV was seen not only as a boon to the Hollywood studios but as a solution to the economic prob-lem of supporting a nation-wide television service. Hollywood veteran John Houseman estimated in 1950 that pay TV could bring in for the studios four times the revenue of the theatrical box office, and despite difficulties in obtaining features from studios wary of exhibitor boycott threats, *Business Week* reported in 1952 that 'indications are that only FCC can stop pay-as-you-see TV in some form or another . . . If the FCC does go along, Hollywood may be more fabulously profitable than it ever has been.' Financial speculators pursued Hollywood feature film libraries in expectation of pay TV, and several surveys reported strong public interest in pay television in the early 1950s; one 1956 book reported the greatest interest in pay TV among those viewers most critical of conventional TV programming and among the wealthiest portion of the TV audience. Other surveys indicated that potential pay-TV viewers of sports and high-culture programming were quite insensitive to pay-TV pricing policies; in case of ballet, the same percentage of hypothetical viewers said they would pay for a ballet

programme whether it cost $0.25 or $1.00. Such affluent potential customers for pay TV were very attractive to the Hollywood studios and the networks were very fearful of their loss to broadcast sponsors.

The cast of **High Noon** watches baseball's World Series on set in 1951; within five years, Hollywood's large studios would become the major suppliers of prime-time programming for network television.

After a series of limited tests and regulatory delays, pay television seemed to be ready for a general launch by the mid-1950s, and the television networks launched a vigorous public relations and political campaign against it. CBS leaders William Paley and Frank Stanton described pay TV to CBS shareholders as 'a complex system which would force people to pay for looking at their own screens, . . . a betrayal of the 34 million families that have already spent $13½ billion for their sets in the anticipation that they would be able to watch them as much as they wanted without paying for the prerogative'. In a 1955 CBS pamphlet, Frank Stanton said pay TV 'would highjack the American public into paying for

51

the privilege of looking at its own television sets . . . . this is a booby trap, a scheme to render the television owner blind, and then rent him a seeing eye dog at so much per mile—to restore to him, only very partially, what he had previously enjoyed as a natural right.' Both CBS's Frank Stanton and NBC network head Robert Sarnoff paraphrased President Abraham Lincoln's anti-slavery rhetoric a century earlier to warn that 'television could not long remain half free and half fee'. The rhetoric of rights and righteousness in the networks' anti-pay television campaigns reached a peak when ABC head Leonard Goldenson complained to a Congressional committee in 1958: 'The FCC was created by Congress to develop and foster our American system of free radio and free television—not to authorize or encourage another system which could lead to its destruction, without first ascertaining the will of Congress.' As Goldenson's remark suggests, the networks lobbied Congress vigorously against pay TV, with considerable success; Frank Stanton reassured a 1957 gathering of CBS affiliates about the threat of pay television: 'I believe there has been some progress—at least as far as the Congress is concerned, where any prospects of legislative action in favor of pay television has been indefinitely postponed.'

Despite the networks' logical difficulty in arguing simultaneously that the public was uninterested in pay-TV programming and that its regulatory approval would destroy network broadcasting and with it endanger the American economy, their efforts to thwart pay television through regulatory delay were quite successful. Furthermore, by the second half of the 1950s broadcast television gained access to the most attractive product promised by pay-TV promoters, the enormous studio feature film libraries. Beginning with Howard Hughes's 1955 sale of the RKO film library, the bulk of Hollywood's pre-1948 features were released to television in a flood of 2,700 titles in 1956 alone. By the end of the decade, a series of multi-million-dollar deals between the studios and individual stations and syndicators resulted in the release to broadcast television of much of the feature product most attractive to potential pay-TV operators. It was not until the 1970s that Hollywood studio interest would turn again to pay television, following cable television's slow penetration into the homes of significant numbers of American TV viewers in the face of sustained FCC resistance.

Social Pressures on the Commercial System

The other major threat to the emerging network structure of early television in the USA was a more general challenge to the premises of unbridled commercial broadcasting itself, arising largely from progressive religious organizations, liberal reformers, and educators unhappy with their marginal role in American radio. Some of the reformers' energy was fuelled by a general unhappiness with TV advertising and with the implications of an advertising-driven mass culture. Observing the noisy internal battles among leaders of the would-be television industry in 1944, for example, *Christian Century* noted that 'so far we have heard no one asking the question about television that seems most important to us. When television comes into the postwar living room, will the ads come with it? . . . Advertising has been bad enough on the radio, but advertising on television could well prove an unmitigated horror.' Despite the claim by an NBC executive in a 1948 radio speech that 'advertising on television will be a potent educational force, and consequently will be of almost as much value to our American way of life as the entertainment itself', the same year *Time* magazine noted a general complaint that 'television grew—and behaved as outlandishly as an adolescent boy . . . and the first advertising binge had left the youngster with a bad commercial breath'.

The Educational Criticism

The most organized and sustained opposition to the hegemony of commercial television in the USA, however, came from educators. Since the debates around the 1934 Communications Act, the position of educators in broadcasting has been the touchstone for the more general criticism of American broadcasting. Postwar educators were still smarting over lost opportunities in educational radio in the 1930s, when federal authorities refused to reserve broadcast channels for

Strike it Rich, which featured contestants competing for audience sympathy with their hard-luck stories, was broadcast on CBS's prime-time schedule from 1951–1955. The press reported that its producers received 3,000–5,000 requests from would-be contestants each week; one public official denounced the programme as 'a disgusting spectacle and a national disgrace'.

exclusive educational use; they favoured encouraging donated time for educational programming from the commercial broadcasters but watched while commercial radio networks and stations dropped almost all educational programming in the rush to commercial television. Educators were now determined to represent themselves more effectively. The extended delay in station licensing brought about in the 1948–52 FCC freeze allowed educators to become better organized. Their arguments on behalf of educational television channel reservations, sometimes tinged with élitist rhetoric, offered some of the most profound criticism of the structures and programmes of American television, and educators offered genuine alternatives for television funding in the form of licence fees, private philanthropy, and government grants. A writer in the *American Scholar* in 1950 warned that 'television as merely another engine of power in the competitive struggles of our glorious "free enterprise system" will lead to cultural disaster', and critic Gilbert Seldes in his 1951 book *The Great Audience* argued: '*So long as mass media are considered as private entertainments*, with negligible effects on those who enjoy them, and with none whatsoever on those who pass them by . . . the mass media will consistently try to increase the numbers of their patrons and at the same time will steadily undermine the capacity to question, to criticize, and to protest.' Responding to fears of 'Big Brother' government control of non-commercial broadcasting, a writer in the *Yale Review* in 1950 wrote: 'The question is: do we dare leave radio to the Big Brother of the advertising agencies?'

The Ford Foundation Initiative

Funded by a series of grants by the Ford Foundation and spurred by a public concern over a post-war teacher shortage, 800 educational institutions petitioned the FCC on behalf of educational TV allocations between 1950 and 1952. The educators hired Telford Taylor, former FCC General Counsel and Nuremberg war crimes prosecutor, as counsel for a lobbying organization. Educators attacked both commercial TV's programming and economic structure; Taylor asked in the *New York Times* in 1950: 'What is to prevent television from degenerating into an interminable and unrelieved variety show?', and decried the programme decision-making of network television. 'There is no more reason for leaving this decision exclusively to the purveyors of candy, toiletries, sporting goods and Western outfits than there would be for letting them determine the school curriculum or the contents of children's books,' he wrote. Citing the need for commercial broadcasters to seek maximum profits, Taylor argued that 'given this basic situation, it is absurd to expect commercial broadcasting either to meet the needs of schools and colleges or to stress culture rather than popular entertainment'; he maintained that there is 'nothing "Un-American" about providing a new economic base for part of our radio-television structure', and concluded that 'it has become increasingly apparent that the most promising way to raise

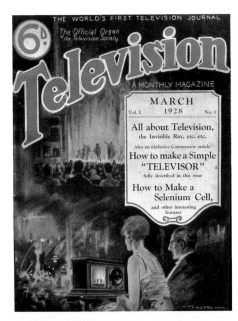

the standards of, and inject a real measure of variety into, television programming is to find the ways and means of supporting television from sources other than commercial advertising'. The Ford Foundation also funded the first major content analysis of TV programming in three US cities between 1949 and 1951 in support of educational channel reservations; the study found that advertising constituted 20 per cent of TV time, while educational programmes amounted to less than 1 per cent.

While the FCC's 1952 *Sixth Report and Order's* reservation of 242 channels for educational broadcasters seemed to offer educators their second chance, two-thirds of the reserved channels were in the UHF band. The FCC was unwilling to disturb prevailing VHF assignments in those markets where all VHF channels were already licensed to commercial operators, including the USA's largest markets of New York and Los Angeles. Lacking meaningful operating funds, the educational station owners' fortunes frequently sank along with those of commercial UHF broadcasters. Indeed, while the commercial TV networks and broadcasters opposed educational reservations on the VHF band, they did not lobby against UHF reservations for educators, suggesting that the dominant economic actors in commercial television correctly foresaw the limited utility of the UHF assignments.

While the first non-commercial educational TV station went on the air in 1953, four years later there were still only twenty educational stations in the entire country, many on the air only a few hours a day; as one mid-1950s observer noted, 'the financial position of most of the stations is precarious. A good stiff breeze would blow some of them away.' Until 1955, most of the Ford Foundation money, which provided the majority of educational TV funding for its first fifteen years, went into lobbying for non-commercial licence applications, not into sustaining programming or operating funds. A 1956 observer described educational TV stations as heavily dependent on donated vintage corporate public-relations films 'of dubious educational value', as lacking remote production facilities and programme links to their communities, and as operating in isolation and ignorance of the efforts of other educational broadcasters with no consensus, or even debate, about effective approaches to educational programming. Fearing that educational channel assignments left unused would be forfeited, many early educational stations went on the air with little planning for programming or operating support; in addition, many educational broadcasters and their institutional boards of directors, which drew heavily from conservative local business establishments, had an exceedingly narrow view of the mission of educational television, often limiting it to the narrow task of classroom instruction and as a way for financially strained educational institutions to defer hiring additional teachers in the face of booming post-war student enrolments. In 1956, the FCC began a series of reassignments of unused educational TV channels to commercial applicants, further demoralizing educational TV proponents. Disillusioned supporters saw educational broadcasting's 'second defeat' in the meagre accom-

Left: the Russian quiz show **What, Where, When?** (1984). Subsequent events in the Soviet Union were to dramatically alter the nature and structure of Russian television; by 1995 it was envisaged that a partly privatized Russian Public Television would be set up to compete with the commercial channels NTV and RTV.

Below: **Maski-Show**. The post-Gorbachev era brought out long-thwarted strands of programming, including political satire, but the new public television station Ostankino endured an appalling series of vicissitudes in the 1990s, not least when its General Director was assassinated by mafiosi within days of his appointment in 1995.

55

plishments of educational TV; by the end of the 1950s, there were still only forty-four educational TV stations, many broadcasting only a few hours a day, no meaningful national exchange of educational programmes, and no VHF outlet in New York City; 188 of the reserved educational channels still stood vacant due to lack of applicants. Educational television was still largely confined to the UHF band in 1960, at a time when only 7 per cent of the TV sets in the nation were equipped for its reception and the overall number of UHF stations fell to a low of 75.

Real growth in educational TV would wait until the early 1960s, when élite opinion, mobilized by the revelations of widespread fraud in television quiz programmes, FCC corruption, and an unleavened diet of escapist entertainment programming from the hugely successful network television industry, supported a new round of foundation and governmental interventions on behalf of educational broadcasting. In 1963 Congress provided matching funds for the construction of educational stations and also passed legislation requiring television sets sold in the USA after 1964 to be capable of receiving UHF broadcasts. Between 1961 and 1966, the number of educational stations on the air grew from 56 to 177. In 1967 Congress finally set up a funding scheme for the newly christened public television system, though the direct legislative appropriation scheme devised combined the defects of low funding levels with political interference in programme content, a situation which still obtains in American non-commercial television. The story of educational television's first decade, then, is one of brave hopes, hollow victories, and continued marginalization in the shadow of the prosperous and powerful commercial television industry. Like the economic challenge to network television from the Hollywood studios in the form of pay TV, the philosophical and public policy threats from sceptics of commercial television were easily turned aside by the TV industry.

The final theme explored here, the relationship between the American television industry and the rest of the world, forms a complex and uneven presence in the industry's first decade, though by 1955 US television's domestic fortunes were inextricably linked to foreign programme markets. RCA constantly reminded politicians and the public of the activities of European rivals during the run-up to commercial television authorization in the 1940s in hopes of sparking nationalistic fire behind its pressure for immediate VHF television, but during the post-war period up to 1955 the American TV industry was preoccupied with domestic television audiences, economic rivals, and regulatory threats: the Cold War issues coloured the industry's attitudes toward other TV nations.

The Overseas Strategy of American Television

Ideologically, the domestic battles for the 'American system of broadcasting', defined as network-distributed, advertising-supported programming to a large consumer audience in the home, had been waged and won by the US radio industry in earlier decades, but television provided new foreign territories for US suppliers of TV equipment and programming. In television's Cold War context, interests pursuing American markets abroad frequently invoked both the super-power rivalry with the Soviet Union and economic competition with other West-ern nations. Advocates of the export of US television technology worried about the Soviet Union 'getting the jump on us' in supplying equipment abroad, and argued that US-installed TV relays could also be used for military purposes in time of war. A post-war group of right-wing politicians, former Voice of Amer-ica employees, and private entrepreneurs successfully lobbied the Japanese Diet to adopt American television's technical standards and helped set up US-style TV systems in Thailand, Turkey, and the Caribbean. By the early 1950s the US government sponsored television exhibits at international trade shows, produced and distributed persuasive films for foreign TV stations, and set up Armed Forces television stations to serve its far-flung military outposts.

American television's rapid growth between 1947 and 1953 created a disparity between the number of sets sold in the USA and in other parts of the globe, and the US industry's efforts in this period were aimed largely at boosting the number of foreign TV stations and set owners. While NBC officials as early as 1947 foresaw the economic value of film recordings of network programmes for international distribution, the only significant potential market for some time remained the BBC. Only the UK, France, and the USSR had initiated regularly scheduled television services by 1950, and the new TV markets in Western Europe, Japan, and Latin America faced the common impediment of high set prices relative to national incomes.

In what was to become a major US export market, 1950 saw the beginnings of TV service in Brazil, Mexico, and Cuba following promotional tours of US equip-ment manufacturers; the American trade press expressed satisfaction in the US lobbying victory on behalf of the wide adoption of US technical standards and the advertising model in Latin American television. The typical Latin American TV system was initiated by politically well-connected national media moguls including Francisco de Assis Chateaubriand in Rio de Janeiro (who owned twenty-eight daily newspapers, sixteen radio stations, two national magazines, and a news agency) and Goar Mestre in Havana (owner of Cuba's largest radio network); in Mexico City, Emilio Azcarraga, owner of a chain of Mexican movie theatres, newspapers, and radio stations, joined forces with Romulo O'Farrill, 'publisher of one of Mexico's biggest dailies and a political crony of then-presi-dent Miguel Aleman,' as *Business Week* described him in 1953; together, the two men controlled 75 per cent of radio advertising revenues in Mexico. While the new Latin American TV stations were firmly planted in the US broadcasting model of unrestricted advertising support, the problem for the new Latin Amer-ican television moguls was gaining advertising revenues for broadcasts to popu-lations who could scarcely afford sets. For example, Azcarraga and O'Farrill opened a 3-million-dollar TV production centre in Mexico City at a time when there were only 30,000 sets in the entire country; the entrepreneurs supplemented their advertising revenues by charging public admission to the complex's twenty auditoria for televised sporting events and brought in additional revenues from a border TV station aimed at the US market. Likewise, despite the 1951 report that 'Cubans swallowed video with a thoroughly American hunger', and radio mogul Goar Mestre 'has copied the American model and used American equipment', by 1954 Cuba's private telecasters faced economic problems with rising programme costs and insufficient advertising revenues.

TV markets elsewhere around the globe were likewise anaemic in the early 1950s, at a time when the US television set and programme markets were booming. In the beginning of 1950, *Time* magazine cited the US industry's view of the European television market as ranging 'from the prenatal to the spoon stage'. By the autumn of 1951 the magazine reported that television abroad 'was popping out like the measles', but, outside the UK, most countries had very small numbers of set owners; the new newspaper-owned private TV network starting up in Japan, for example, had donated 1,000 US-made sets to opinion-leaders in an effort to spur sales and advertising revenues in 1951. That year there were 10 million sets in the USA, compared with less than 1 million abroad.

By the mid-1950s, however, just when set ownership levels in the USA were reaching what the industry feared were saturation levels, television use was taking off in many other parts of the world. In February 1955 there were 36 million sets in the USA and only 4.8 million in all of Europe, with 4.5 million of those in the UK; in February 1956 the number of TV sets outside the USA had more than doubled over the previous two years, to 10.5 million. In 1954, swelled by rising affiliate rosters, top programme ratings and unprecedented commercial revenues for its filmed prime-time sitcoms, CBS Inc. celebrated its best year ever and proclaimed itself the world's largest single advertising medium, boasting international affiliates in Mexico City, Havana, Puerto Rico, and twenty Canadian cities. Of even more lasting significance for international television, in the same year CBS initiated a subsidiary, CBS International, for foreign distribution of its network programming. The network's move into international programme distribution was quickly followed by NBC and ABC, and by the end of the 1950s the three networks were the dominant sellers of TV programming in the world.

The Networks and Independent Production

opposite Canine star Lassie, brought to TV after earlier incarnations in a popular children's novel, a feature film, and radio series, began a seventeen-year run on CBS in 1954 and has continued to earn huge revenues in international syndication.

The networks' strength in international TV programme sales flowed from their powerful position in the domestic US market, where their control over access to prime-time audiences allowed them to extract lucrative syndication rights over the programmes they licensed from independent producers. The networks' sway in the international markets for the TV programming did not derive from the sale of programmes they produced themselves, but rather syndication

control over programmes made by independent production companies which the networks gained as part of licensing agreements for original network release. In fact, CBS's telefilm arm withdrew from production of original programming for distribution in 1961 in favour of syndicating network-licensed independently produced programmes, 'eliminating the need for highly speculative investment in television pilot films and series', as its annual report explained. That year CBS Films Inc. sold 1,500 half-hours in fifty-five foreign countries; two years later CBS Films Inc. became the world's largest exporter of telefilm.

By the second half of the 1950s, the world market for American filmed TV programming was growing quickly; Japan was described as 'rapidly becoming as TV-obsessed as the U.S.' by *Time* magazine in 1958, and five of the top ten shows in Japan that year were US imports or Japanese-made clones of American programmes. Eighteen US telefilm distributors did a total of 20 million dollars of foreign business (exclusive of Canada) in 1958 and 30 million dollars in 1959; *The Lone Ranger* was seen in twenty-four countries and a single programme, *Lassie*, generated an estimated 4 million dollars in world-wide revenues by 1958. *Gunsmoke*, *Rin Tin Tin*, and *The Lone Ranger* were all in Mexico's top ten. The three American TV networks not only dominated the burgeoning international telefilm market at the end of the 1950s, they also made substantial direct investments in overseas production companies and television stations; as the head of ABC boasted in 1961: 'Television has a great future. . . . Half the people in the world are illiterate. Television can penetrate that barrier. . . . Television is a worldwide medium. You have to think globally. If you own a show, you own it worldwide.'

If American television's first post-war decade set up the industry structures and programme forms for its domestic TV audience, the subsequent decade saw the wide dissemination of its products around the world. By 1960, with US TV set penetration levels at 86 per cent and domestic sets sales growing at a mild 5 per cent annual rate, American telefilm distributors, led by the three networks, saw the TV's greatest potential in international markets. *Business Week* noted that year that 'The industry agrees that foreign TV is now just about where U.S. television was in 1947. It is just coming into its period of growth, and U.S. producers want to be in on the ground floor,' and the magazine noted with satisfaction that 'the bigger TV gets, the more it resembles the American product'. By the early 1960s the possible reciprocal effects upon American TV audiences of the huge international programme market caused a new self-consciousness about the US role in global television; as veteran TV critic Robert Lewis Shayon worried in 1961: 'There is hardly a foot of commercial TV film that is not destined, after appropriate dubbing, for the foreign rerun market. . . . The effect of this foreign market on the intellectual content of American TV film is significant. Such programs must not only be aimed at the lowest common denominator in this country; they must also be geared to the potential audiences of nations whose emergent cultures are largely at a primitive level.' This ambivalence of nationalistic pride at export prowess and defensive concern about tail-wagging foreign markets has been perennial in American trade and popular discussions of the global role of US media since the 1960s.

The changes in market structure which came belatedly to US television in the 1960s and 1970s—the UHF receiver act of 1963, federal support of public television in 1967, restrictions on network syndication and ownership of programming in 1971, the growth of cable television networks in the 1970s—all had their roots in long-running discontent with network commercial and programming policies of the medium's first decade. It is a testament to the political and economic clout of the US networks that they were able to preserve their oligopoly for decades in the face of eager and powerful potential competitors as well as numerous disaffected members of the American public. The tightly organized world of US network television elaborated in the late 1940s and early 1950s has had enormous and lasting effects on the international landscape of television to this day.

3

Television as a Public Service Medium

Anthony Smith

n the inter-war years governments everywhere were scrutinizing the new media of communication and wondering how best to organize them—to regulate them, tax them, censor them, govern them, repress or encourage them, and of course enable industry to make money from them. Radio was spreading rapidly from country to country and television was still passing through its experimental phase. But there were other new technologies in the process of establishment and these, too, had emerged from the scientific research of the late nineteenth and early twentieth centuries. These were also now subject to improvisation and experiment in the sphere of organization and public regulation. Airlines, telephony, cinema, and motoring were among them. Regulatory machinery was itself an area of experiment; models and examples were passing from country to country.

In the case of broadcasting it was evident from the beginning that a new tool of politics, as well as of entertainment, was being born and the form of broadcast organization or institution chosen in each country revealed something of the prevailing national political system—whether communist, fascist, or capitalist. Such issues as the choice between private capital and state supervision, the extent to which listeners and (later) viewers could become involved in the medium, and the limits placed upon the freedom of the broadcasters, were much influenced by the comparative experience of different countries and even more by the political ideology of the country concerned. Radio had been born into a world of radio hams, knowledgeable amateurs sending messages to one another through the ether, but television depended from the start upon research grants from governments and large companies: television was developed by professional technologists and they tended to be both competitive and national.

By the time television was viable (before World War II) the institutions of radio had already been given their basic structure and thus television automatically fell into the same forms of regulation; by the time television was fully developed (in the 1950s) governments realized something of the political potential of the medium and commercial operators were fairly certain that in time it would offer a tremendous bonanza.

There were of course other factors which influenced the regulatory decisions of governments: geography, economic status, and linguistic, regional, and cultural traditions would come to influence the early broadcasting institution. Of course, only governments can belong to the International Telecommunications Union (ITU) which apportions the spectrum and prevents radio interference, and so only governments, whether libertarian or authoritarian, could license the use of the spectrum and thus dictate crucial matters such as broadcasting hours, transmitter power, and the direction of signals. But the extent to which governments became more deeply involved depended upon the state of mind of the politicians in each country. Institutions often survive the political conditions which shape them, but in many countries the state of the broadcasting institution has acted as a barometer of changing politics.

None the less there were some improbable choices made by governments in the 1920s. In the newly constituted Soviet Union, then passing through the era known as New Economic Policy (NEP), Lenin thought that the medium of radio was destined to become a 'newspaper without paper and without boundaries' and, although he willingly invested in its technical development, he left it to amateur enthusiasts, as well as farms and trades unions, to set up their own stations; in 1924 a station in Moscow even took the form of a joint stock company. And at the same moment in the Netherlands, a group of religious and political associations initiated a system unique to the Netherlands, by which air time was leased from the Netherlands Transmitter Industry (the single company that had sought official rights to broadcast) and all of the programme hours were divided up among companies which existed primarily to advocate the views of the principal Christian denominations or of the main political parties. In Britain a new commercial entity, the British Broadcasting Company, was given a monopoly of public transmission of radio and the BBC in this its embryonic form was thus inaugurated by a consortium of equipment manufacturers.

Behind the diversity of forms there lay the great ideological rifts of the inter-war years, and as fascist and communist regimes took over country after country in Europe it became clear how important radio—as well as the infant medium of television—would become to the European dictatorships.

But there were other crucial shaping forces which crossed the ideological divisions. First of all a country had to decide whether to encourage broadcasting as a local medium, around each separate transmitter, or to try to start with a

The opening of Berlin's television studios, 1935. All receivers were in public places and transmissions continued until 1944. On 14 March 1934 Joseph Goebbels was sworn in as Minister of Propaganda, all broadcasting was taken over, and all programmes used to further the aims of the Third Reich.

complete and comprehensive national system, reaching all citizens simultaneously. Only slowly did broadcasting cease to be considered a kind of technical toy, the prerogative of the do-it-yourself pioneers.

For decades the most decisive factor was whether the country was large or small. Most of the geographically large countries (China, Canada, United States, Australia, Brazil) avoided national systems for a very long time, because of the impossibility of reaching their whole population or of doing so on a geographically equitable basis. On the other hand small countries tend to be close to other small countries and in these it is impossible to confine signals within frontiers. Austria, for example, had no technical means of reaching the entirety of its own territory without the signals spilling over into eight other countries. Luxembourg, from the start, took it for granted that its programmes would inevitably reach large numbers of listeners in surrounding lands and made it its policy to broadcast far afield; it evolved an unusual quasi-governmental system which derived large commercial benefit from advertising to neighbouring countries and offering them rather undemanding popular programmes.

Television and Land Mass

Another important factor—still active in broadcast planning—is the great variation in the cost of transmitting signals to countries with different kinds of terrain. The compact community of a metropolis or a small circular country such as Singapore or the Netherlands can be reached at a very low per capita cost.

On the other hand, Britain, with its Scottish and Welsh wildernesses and its population heavily concentrated in its great cities, has always faced considerable difficulty in achieving total national coverage for any single channel: but its broadcasting policy has always been to provide each national channel with as near total UK coverage as possible, and so rural Scots and Welsh (and the northern Irish) have always had their broadcasting transmission very heavily subsidized by metropolitan audiences.

A vast terrain such as that of the USA, with its population unevenly spread, is extremely difficult to cover efficiently with signals, and this fact came to influence broadcasting policy in the USA more than any other, for it made it necessary for broadcasting to be locally owned and controlled and only lightly regulated by central government: no single channel of either radio or television has ever been licensed to cover the whole territory of the union. The many time zones of the United States made it impossible for live programmes to reach the whole population. In the great cities broadcasting grew plentifully, with audiences able to choose from dozens and nowadays hundreds of signals; but in many rural communities, until recent times, radio and television signals have been very sparse indeed. The USA would have found it almost impossible to impose a European-style receiver licence fee upon viewers even if it had wanted to, simply because of the difficulty (before the era of the satellite) in providing the many states with reception of the same programme. It was left to the privately owned networking companies to link the hundreds of stations through commercial agreement across the great American land mass.

Canada's broadcasting structure is as heavily influenced by questions of terrain as any other, but it also exemplifies most of the other political, technical, and social issues: the major part of its population lived (and lives) within the shadow of a transmitter serving a major US city. At the same time the Canadian authorities are under pressure to make suitable provision for the vast and thinly populated areas, which include many tiny Inuit communities, with different languages and cultures; moreover the country is formally bilingual and there is strong political pressure to make French-language services available everywhere. Canada has long been aware of the potential of broadcasting to create a sense of nationhood in a society divided within itself and heavily influenced by its more powerful neighbour. Canada thus has been pushed, from decade to decade, sometimes towards free market 'deregulated' solutions (which end up leaving its audience in thrall to foreign stations) and at other times towards governmental, BBC-type solutions, which seem to be the way to solve its more geopolitical problems. It evolved the CBC, a politically beleaguered but nation-wide public broadcaster together with a host of commercial stations—also beleaguered by reason of their relationship with neighbouring American stations. The regulatory and cultural issues of broadcasting have come to be more intensely debated in Canada than in any other country.

As broadcasting became more important in politics, governments from tiny islands to superpowers found in it a prism through which they viewed the concentrated essence of all of their social and cultural tensions. For Canada national broadcasting was a chance to resolve a troubled national unity; but for Lebanon to attempt a single national system in radio would have put paid to any chance of unity. For Nigeria a national system could only exist in the English language, while all its indigenous peoples have to be reached through a multitude of stations using scores of tribal languages.

In both the Soviet Union and in India regionalism of broadcasting was the ideal method, for they could tailor the signals to fit the geographic contours of their internal national and language groups, under supervision of central government. But to reach the Lappish people as a group a broadcast signal has to cross the boundaries of three Scandinavian countries. In Britain the Welsh-speaking community for decades fruitlessly demanded its own television station, until the threat of a fast until death by a prominent Welsh nationalist persuaded the government in London to give in and grant a Welsh-language Channel Four (S4C) in 1980. So the structures which sustain broadcasting can act as the symbolic cultural cement which holds together the fragile links between communities, but they can also act as an explosive substance which sunders them.

Public service television is not necessarily *state* television although its existence can only be guaranteed by the state; it may attempt to function according to the traditional canons of disinterested journalism, offering entertainment and information intended to sustain public understanding or maintain a cultural tradition. It may also sustain a totalitarian political system. We shall look more closely at five countries—France, Germany, USSR/Russia, the UK, and the USA—which all illustrate public service television in one or more of its forms.

France

France was a country which saw from the start the latent possibilities of broadcasting as a consolidating force within a nation. French broadcasting shifted from privately owned status to being the system most closely controlled by government in Western Europe, only to shift back in recent years partly into private hands. France provides a case history of the way in which governments, when dealing with broadcasting, can imperil their own goals while learning slowly from their mistakes.

The first real radio station in France—Radio Paris—had been set up by a radio manufacturer with some finance from the Havas news agency, partly at the behest of the many amateurs who were experimenting with radio (as was happening all over the world) in the period after World War I. The Postal and Telegraph Administration charged Radio Paris a fee and established some ground rules. The French government had been broadcasting experimentally from the Eiffel Tower since before the war and so France had started up the

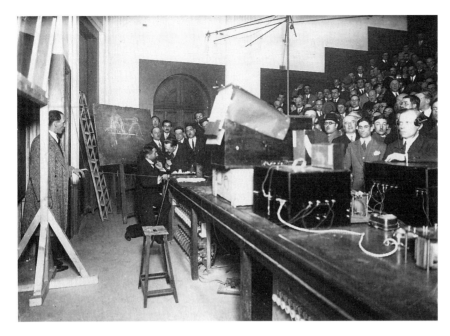

The first public demonstration of television in France, 1931. But full weekday television started up in France only in 1947 and the millionth TV receiver was not sold until 1958.

broadcasting age with a dual public/private system. For a decade after 1923 France enjoyed a spread of local commercial stations, all flourishing on advertising and often overlapping and competing. There were some public stations also, funded by small grants from government. At the end of the decade the PTT took over Radio Paris, placed a fresh series of controls on the private stations, and established a licence fee for all receivers, the proceeds of which were kept by the PTT and used to expand the public network.

Some of the dozen or so commercial stations which survived into the 1930s were owned by politicians who made direct use of them during the various lively elections of that decade. The PTT was of course under the direct management of a cabinet minister who controlled the content of news by direct telephone link to the publicly (PTT) owned stations. By 1939 the Prime Minister had placed the whole public network in his own direct management. For several years all news programmes outside Paris had been banned by official decree. When the German army marched into Paris in 1940 they seized all functioning stations as well as the infant television service and used them for domestic and overseas broadcasting. The Vichy regime in its zone in the south took over private as well as public stations, subsidizing and using all of them for its own propaganda.

Then in 1943 the Vichy government took a crucial step. It bought up the shares of SOFIRAD (Société Financière de Radiodiffusion) which in turn controlled the shares in Radio Monte Carlo, which broadcast from outside the territory of France. In the years to come the French government was to rely heavily on its indirect control of a series of 'radios périphériques', commercially owned stations located outside its frontiers.

67

Between 1945 and 1970 French broadcasting remained under a form of political tutelage which frustrated its own development and provided little scope for those who were not close government supporters. Soon after the Liberation all private stations on French soil were snuffed out and a decree of November 1945 established Radiodiffusion-Télévision Française (RTF), a civil service department, as the sole broadcasting entity. Its director reported to the Information Minister and was chosen by the cabinet. The Ministry of Finance ran its internal operations under civil service rules. Parliament voted its budgets. Constant consultations took place between RTF officials and senior politicians. Dozens of strikes took place, sometimes about pay and conditions but very often in protest against acts of official interference.

Television had been under development in France since the mid-1930s and under the new RTF system in 1947 it started up again, but its spread was extremely slow. French viewers close to Germany could receive foreign television but the rest of France saw no television other than its own. After seven years there were still fewer than 70,000 receivers and only a million had been distributed by 1958 when Charles de Gaulle returned to power. During the Fourth Republic (1945–58) there were so many successive governments that broadcasting policy did not fully develop.

President de Gaulle being interviewed in April 1969. De Gaulle 'guided' French broadcasting with a strong presidential hand. He saw it as a powerful instrument of French culture at home and abroad. De Gaulle became a skilled and effective television performer, despite his stiff bearing and wooden style.

De Gaulle, however, thought television very important. He had learned the value of radio during the Occupation, when he lived in London and participated in the overseas broadcasting of the BBC. Faced by a hostile newspaper press he now thought of broadcasting as a continuing source of political help. He appeared on television frequently, seated and speaking directly into the camera. Television was for de Gaulle the supreme means for diffusing the knowledge of French culture and of his own policies. Since the 1920s radio stations had been obliged to use correct French grammar and pronunciation and avoid all slang and local demotic usage. Now television became a positive tool of French national and international cultural policy. Management of programmes was conducted by means of an official liaison system, linking government and RTF, and the RTF was now transformed into an 'autonomous public institution', with its own director but no board, but with daily control from government. The Minister of Information could summon the heads of the various RTF departments from a row of buttons on his desk.

The arrangements made for the coverage of 1962 elections so egregiously favoured the Gaullist candidates that the resulting protest inaugurated a long-awaited process of change. A group of magistrates was briefly appointed to ensure fairness of access to the air by French politicians of left and right, but it was evident that the necessary reform would have to be more thorough. After two years of debate a new statute established the ORTF (l'Office de Radiodiffu-sion-Télévision Française—known popularly as l'Office) which provided the institution with some degree of institutional autonomy, with its own governing Council and the consequent ability to choose its own PDG (President Director-General).

But to the viewer there seemed to have been no change at all. True, there was a new Administrative Council, consisting partly of viewers' representatives, but the Council was dominated by Gaullists. There was to be fair and impartial coverage of the 1967 legislative elections, but that did not appear in practice to apply to de Gaulle himself, nor to his ministers, while his opponents were filmed from awkward angles and kept invisible in talk shows and documentaries. The National Assembly retained responsibility for the budget, and the interministerial 'liaison' system continued as before. A second television channel was started, with new programmes which dealt with some of the more delicate political issues of the moment, but within a year the government ordered these to be toned down.

In May 1968 there occurred a quasi-revolutionary eruption among the students of Paris. Barricades were thrown up and the staff of the ORTF covered the events fully and attempted to broadcast documentary material which set the background to the student dispute. The Information Minister ordered cuts and a one-day strike broke out, followed by a general ORTF strike, and then on 25 May a strike of 100 journalists began which was to last for months. The management promised changes and a few reforms took place, but quarrels broke out among

The television workers' strike which followed the May 'events' of 1968 jolted French governments into a long process of reform, liberalization, and privatization of broadcasting.

the strikers and by August they were all dismissed or moved to other jobs. The reforms amounted to an enlargement of the Administrative Council from sixteen to twenty-four, but sixteen of them were to be chosen by government. It was evident that nothing would change until de Gaulle retired, which he suddenly did in 1969, and was duly succeeded by Georges Pompidou.

Pompidou regarded reform of the ORTF as urgent and important. L'Office was now placed directly under the management of the Prime Minister while further major reforms were prepared. Several official reports were produced. The decision had already been made to introduce advertising, perhaps with the thought of putting a little pressure on the more politically recalcitrant newspaper press. But a scandal broke out over allegations of corrupt advertising, and political interference seemed to spread from the overtly political programmes even to the entertainment programmes which sustained the advertising, in fact to those strands of programmes in which, despite all the problems and the malaise, French producers had long enjoyed international recognition. The first wave of Pompidou reforms merely tinkered further with the ORTF, with government officials still regularly making direct suggestions to producers and management, despite the more liberal structure and the new commitment to balance in political programmes.

In France as elsewhere in the 1970s and 1980s politicians continued to complain that producers were communist or leftist and their programmes full of insidious propaganda, despite the great influence exerted by government over the ORTF. There were hopes that a more genuine independence would evolve when a former Socialist, Arthur Conte, was appointed PDG, but one of his early actions led to the resignation of Pierre Desgraupes, a widely respected and liberal-minded head of Television News. Then he proceeded to unleash a major controversy when he withdrew a programme which touched upon the rawest nerves in French political life: Marcel Ophuls had made a long documentary, *The Sorrow and the Pity* (1970), which explicitly referred to acts of collaboration by French people during the Occupation; Conte banned the programme and Philippe Malaud, the Information Minister, publicly agreed with the decision. In later years Conte was to publish a book of memoirs, in which he laid the blame for the public controversies and other problems of his time in office on ministerial interference (but the government stopped his appearing on television to discuss his book).

When Pompidou died, Giscard d'Estaing won the resulting presidential election and decided to rush through a complex and far-reaching set of reforms of French television. L'Office would no longer exist and in its place were to be seven autonomous organizations: two to run television channels, with a third to run regional television, and a fourth to be a new independent production company from which all the major programmes of the others were to be commissioned; the fifth to run radio, the sixth to take over all of the technical work of transmission, and the seventh to deal with research and archives. A new High Audio-visual Council would oversee the development of new technology and supervise a new public right of reply. The reform was presented to the French public and to the world as a true and sincere 'new deal'.

No one denied that these changes did finally provide France with a system which admitted it to the ranks of the world's mature and impartial television systems. There were many new opportunities for open political discussion. There was competition between channels. There was manifestly independent decision-taking. But ministers continued to order changes in programmes and every television departmental head was approved by a government minister. Every one of the seven companies contained a government politician on its council. A new stream of allegations began, this time of waste and financial incompetence, and indeed of corruption.

French television remained overall a state monopoly, although within a somewhat frenziedly competitive system, and the arrival of Mitterrand as President of the Republic in 1981 was quite clearly going to lead to an era of tremendous further change throughout French society. This began with the commissioning of the Moinot Report of September 1981, which made proposals for bringing about a greater separation between government and the broadcasting bodies: an Haute Autorité, composed of nine members chosen by different organs of state, would oversee budgets and regulate all broadcasting licensees. Political interference did not seem to diminish under the Socialist President—in fact, even more government supporters seemed to be being pressed into service in senior broadcasting positions. But there was in the 1980s a clear economic need for France to benefit from the new burgeoning technologies and remain ahead in the techni-cal race against Japan.

First the government licensed private radio, and hundreds of stations came legally into being to replace the hundreds of pirate stations which had been spreading across the map of France. A new pay-TV service, Canal Plus, was announced which would use terrestrial transmission and for which viewers would require a special decoder. Direct satellite broadcasting was to be started and cable television via optic fibres was to receive high government priority. Finally Mitterrand announced that there would be private commercial televi-sion—pirate television stations having begun to sprout already in Paris and else-where.

Just before the election of 1986 the government fulfilled this last promise by opening a new private network, La Cinq, of which 40 per cent would be owned by the Italian commercial television entrepreneur Silvio Berlusconi. The election resulted in the arrival of a Conservative coalition, with Mitterrand still the Pres-ident, which declared that it would soon revoke La Cinq's licence; in the event it found it possible only to redistribute the shares so as to admit the Conservative newspaper publisher Robert Hersant. It also kept a pre-election promise to abol-ish the still new Haute Autorité and replaced it with a very similar body, the Commission National de Communications et Libertés (CNCL); another promise had been to privatize the first channel (TF-1), which now passed into the hands of Monsieur Bouygues, with, for a time, Britain's Robert Maxwell as junior partner.

During both halves of Mitterrand's reign there was a steady growth in the political independence of television despite continued political jockeying. For one thing there were more people of differing political outlooks working in the medium. Many more acquired stakes in radio or television. In the profuse outpouring of new stations there was a net growth of political independence.

But there remained a vigorous official insistence on a privileged position being accorded to the language and culture of France, at a time when among both intellectuals and politicians *le défi américain* had become a talking point. All parties feared the effects of a foreign flow of programme material, through the new technologies in particular. France could not resist that flow, any more than any other nation in Europe. Within the European Community there was a grow-ing attempt to implement the Community directive which stipulated that, after the initial period of establishment, all cable and satellite companies should ensure that 65 per cent of all their programmes were European in origin. In the 1993 elections Mitterrand's position was shaken in a Conservative landslide, and a further drastic wave of policy changes in the French television system was confidently expected.

French television during the Fourth and the early years of the Fifth Republics was frequently derided for its lack of political independence; it was held up as an example of what can happen when politicians get their hands on the medium.

But French television in those years was by no means a failure technically or creatively. It certainly provided a great deal of good entertainment and high-quality cultural material. It fulfilled the national goal of preserving the French character of the principal modern medium of entertainment.

The USSR

The same can be said, perhaps surprisingly, of the more authoritarian society of the Soviet Union, where the idea that entertainment was a new kind of social right had failed to take root at all. In official terms, broadcasting existed in the Soviet Union to improve society, to explain and celebrate the triumph of communism, to make certain that the audience understood the great sacrifices which had made their Soviet system possible. Where television (or radio) dealt with social problems—drink, drugs, crime—it was only to show the solutions which were now being administered. But even in this highly purposeful context material which amused, uplifted, and relaxed viewers did creep into the programming schedules.

Television has never in fact reached the whole of that vast territory. Soviet technicians had developed the Molniya (lightning) satellite in the mid-1960s, which sent signals out close to the ground across union territory, but it was only to link the twenty major transmission centres, so ground connections were necessary everywhere. While Moscow could boast four channels (and much of their material was sent out to the various (now independent) republics, most cities had only two channels and they originated material only for a few hours a day. In the late 1970s a new geo-stationary TV satellite brought about a massive increase in coverage.

The founders of the communist movement had selected cinema rather than radio as their supreme medium of social and political agitation and after the Revolution radio was allowed to develop without a great deal of party or official involvement. When Lenin died in 1924 the manufacture of individual receivers had not gone far. There were experiments with loudspeakers in public places and a great deal of wired radio to places of work. But during the 1920s the Communist Party gradually took over the existing stations, and by 1933 the Council of People's Commissars took over full control of the medium from the post office, and a junior cabinet minister ran it from day to day. There were still little over a million receivers in the entire union and although this number quintupled by the start of World War II, only a fifth of the total were individual, i.e. non-wired, sets: when war started these were nearly all confiscated. Only in the late 1940s was it possible for Soviet listeners to receive short-wave broadcasts from the BBC, Voice of America, and other stations which provided credible news and a wide range of contemporary music.

Television had started in a similar manner to radio in the 1930s, with amateurs constructing receivers and stations in half a dozen cities. Prime Minister

73

Khrushchev realized in the 1960s that television would have to be a key item in the new consumer society which he was intent upon building, and by the time he fell from power 14 million receivers had been distributed and some even sold by the innovative method of hire purchase. Until the collapse of the Soviet Union and the communist system in the 1990s, the same Khrushchev-reformed governing structure existed for both media: a State Committee for Radio and Television ran broadcasting within a special department of the Council of Ministers or cabinet. An excise tax was imposed on all receivers at the time of purchase; the licence fee which was used to help finance radio and early television was dropped, but in more recent years paid television advertising was introduced, although it must have contributed only a tiny proportion of the programme costs.

By the mid-1970s 50–60 million receivers had been sold around the USSR, but they were notorious for poor manufacture and the programmes were heartily and in fact openly disliked by many viewers. The drabness and propagandistic tone of the programmes helped to bring home to the mass of the people, perhaps more than anything else, the unsatisfactory nature of their political system. Even Brezhnev urged the brightening up of the news programmes and the introduction of rather more up-to-the-minute information about the state of major world stories. Gorbachev, from the moment he came to power in 1985, travelled the country urging improvement in the content of the media. Gradually change

Making television receivers in Minsk, Belarus. The expansion to mass distribution of television was delayed in the USSR until the 1970s, when the Molniya (lightning) series of satellites—in an elliptical orbit—became fully operational at twenty locations. Radnga (rainbow), a geo-stationary satellite, followed in 1975. Fifty million sets (often not working) were quickly sold.

Russian news programming before and after perestroika: *left* **Vremya** 1977 and *above* **Vesti** (presented by Svetlana Sorokina) 1993.

occurred and better use began to be made of the extensive and high-quality technical facilities which had been built to serve the channels at their Moscow headquarters. Even video recorders and cassettes now began to be manufactured, although more reached the USSR from abroad, spreading a taste for Western entertainment.

The attempted coup against Gorbachev in 1991, which was followed by the Yeltsin regime, the dismemberment of the union, and the destruction of the communist system, transformed the practices of Russian television. The three channels remained but the broadcasting personnel now embraced a new freedom in reporting. Their reporters, in renamed daily news programmes, had to cope with the chain reaction of social, political, and economic change. Their task for the first time entailed investigation as well as narration. Even under Gorbachev the Chernobyl disaster had forced Soviet journalism to confront the tensions between accurate reporting and social responsibility. Now they had to absorb the implications of their new role as one of the forces governing an open society, albeit one that appeared to be slowly disintegrating. Russian television reporters, with an extraordinary story to tell their viewers, began to discover the problems and issues entailed in investigative reporting; a vast avalanche was set in motion, of suppressed information about their national history and about urgent problems of the present (nuclear leakages, the rise of metropolitan mafia gangsterdom, widespread unemployment, hyper-inflation, political corruption). The events grew in drama, the more viewers were able to learn.

Within a month of the attempted coup, President Yeltsin issued his Order No. 500 which established a provisional system for the licensing of commercial television under the Ministry of Mass Media and Information, and the Ministry of Communication. Soon, a new sixty-two-article Law on the Mass Media was enacted which abolished censorship but spelled out in great detail the rights and responsibilities of journalists—it also laid the foundations for an organization similar to the American Federal Communications Commission, which would in future regulate frequency use and also establish the framework of new mass media institutions. Russia's new Federal Broadcasting Commission has ten members: three appointed by the President of the Republic, three by the constitutional court, and six by the two chambers of Parliament.

However astonishing the contrast between the era of Stalin in the Soviet Union and that of Yeltsin in Russia, there can be no country which has undergone changes in its broadcasting institutions and in attitudes towards broadcasting so profound as those of Germany.

Germany: Federal Republic and Democratic Republic

Germany was one of the pioneering countries in both media. The German Post Office transmitted concerts as early as 1920 for the benefit of wireless amateurs. It was a terrible time for German culture and the economy. The country had been cut down in size at the end of World War I; its monarchy had been abolished, and much of its population hived off into other countries; while paying reparations to the victorious powers, its currency collapsed, a mark sinking in value to billionths of a pound or dollar. The administrative system of early German radio is fascinating for what it foreshadowed: although the Nazi era brought about the complete destruction of what was built in the 1920s, some of the early ideas about the involvement of parties and citizen groups in the running of the mass media returned in the era of television. After the reunification of Germany in the 1990s it was as if a sixty-year task was being finally completed.

A Radio Society was set up in 1925 at the instance of the German Ministry of the Interior; its task was to organize all of the small private stations which were springing up. The rules of the Society stipulated that the German Post Office was the regulatory authority, and indeed the Post Office had already imposed an expensive licence or tax on all receivers which was partly used to finance the programmes sent out by the Society to its member stations. Every province or *Land* government set up a radio committee to judge the social value of the output of the stations, and a management committee watched over each station, appointed by national and *Land* governments. The news was sent out by wire from an official news service and disseminated by the stations. The purpose of this draconian system was to guarantee fairness between the political parties as Germany rapidly descended into chaos, and also to frustrate the designs of the growing Nazi Party. Until the Nazis actually seized power the cultural quality of German radio was extremely high, with a wide range of music, drama, documentaries, and discussions. Under the growing influence of central government the news and political information were neutral and innocuous to the point of nullity.

The Nazis' seizure took place in 1933 and they were determined, like other European dictators of the time, to use radio to transform the consciousness of the public through propaganda. It was the perfect medium for spreading Nazi philosophy. The many local clubs and societies of listeners were absorbed into the Nazi machine and used for identifying deviant individuals. Cheap 'People's Radio' receivers were efficiently manufactured, and these could receive only the two permitted channels. Transmitter strength was increased.

The network of committees disappeared and local programming too. Jazz music disappeared, as did other material of non-German origin. Each station was given a single manager selected for party fidelity and racial purity. The Nazi Party Office of Broadcasting reported, like the Propaganda Ministry, to Joseph Goebbels himself. Meanwhile the Berlin-dominated system provided the world with a number of demonstrations of the vast newly revealed power of broadcasting: first came the Saarland plebiscite, then the Anschluss or seizure of Austria, and then the seizure of the Sudetenland and Czechoslovakia: before

Listening to radio in Germany, 1932. In that year a new Radio Commissioner within the Ministry of the Interior was appointed to supervise all news and political programmes. Within twelve months Hitler's first head of radio had been appointed to run the instrument by which 'the entire nation will be drenched through and through with our philosophy'.

each coup the population concerned was deluged with propaganda, saturated to the point of somnabulism. Listener protest led to some modification.

German radio under the Nazis perfected the art of propaganda to a degree never achieved in any other medium. News of victories would be delayed and then heralded with excited anticipatory announcements intended to raise the emotions of listeners to a high key. Bombed stations would be got on the air again in minutes. Even after the collapse of Berlin Nazi propaganda by radio continued from the last Nazi redoubts. And when the Red Army finally seized Berlin it took over the national radio system, denying the Allies access to it and providing Germany with another unitary propaganda radio.

In the mid-1930s the Nazi leadership turned its attention to television and set up, even before the BBC did, the world's first regular television service, but it was transmitted to public places rather than private or domestic receivers. The service was to continue in Berlin (and another also in occupied Paris) until 1944; even before the war this service had adopted a clear-definition 441-line standard. But the shape taken by post-war television in Germany was largely dictated by the actions of the Allies as they attempted to inaugurate a Nazi-free broadcasting system in the years between 1945 and the establishment of the Federal Republic in 1949. The allied occupying powers went about the task in different ways.

In the zone of Germany occupied by American troops every major city was given its own station, while the British and French zones established single centres of broadcasting, all drawing upon the experience of their own national systems. But the three western sections of Germany were gradually knitted together and the different practices harmonized; under the new West German constitution the governance of broadcasting, as an element of the cultural sphere, was to reside with *Land* governments and not with the central Federal government. In the Soviet zone, in Berlin, a centralized system was created and the *Land* system eventually abolished altogether. The intention behind eastern and western approaches was in one way the same—to prevent the return of a Nazi demagogue to the centres of power.

In fact, in their search for ways to anchor the new German television to the democratic system, the Allies rediscovered and built upon techniques of the 1920s. In every *Land* the broadcasting station was provided with a Radio Council, containing representatives not only of the new political parties, but also of churches, unions, cultural organizations, business, and industry. The councils were all different and have all evolved differently, mostly becoming far more politicized than was originally envisaged. But these councils are unique among the broadcasting institutions of Europe in that they possess real power, notably over the appointment of each *Intendant* or General Manager and in their role as supervisors of the budget. The advisory boards of other European systems have no real budgetary or managerial power at all. In some cases the *Land* legislature decides who should be appointed to the Councils and from the start several of the Radio Councils leaned towards one or other political party. In 1954 the largest station, NWDR, which broadcast throughout the large and populous British zone, was divided into two, with signals now emanating from separate stations in Hamburg (NDR) and Cologne (WDR).

There then began (to the consternation of the allied occupation authorities) the *Proporz* system by which the parties shared out among themselves, in proportion to their power in the *Land* parliament, the senior posts within the stations. If the *Intendant* was from party A, the Chief of Programmes would turn out to be a known supporter of party B, and the next appointment lower down the tree, perhaps the Head of News, would be from party A, and so forth. But there was no such representation of citizens or viewers in the new German Democratic Republic; there the State Committee for Broadcasting, under a party official of cabinet rank, ruled the broadcasting system (television arrived in 1952) and imposed an 'improving' tone upon the medium, every programme attempting to justify the regime in the eastern half of the country. The most famous programme of the Democratic Republic was called *The Black Channel*, and almost symbolized the Cold War in its incessant, hectoring, joyless, word-twisting blather; it consisted of excerpts taken from FRG television, which was widely viewable in the East, reinterpreted by the reporter Karl Edouard von Schnitzler to demonstrate the evils and weaknesses of the West. (In the event it was the GDR which imploded and the Federal Republic which absorbed it: the western television system simply took over the eastern and remoulded it to the pattern of the former, *Proporz* system included.)

The constitution of the Federal Republic prevented central government from licensing or regulating any domestic broadcasting system. But there were extreme imbalances and inequalities among the many stations which survived from the occupation years: for one thing, the population of FRG was unevenly spread and yet the licence fee was the same everywhere, leaving some stations perilously poor and others extremely rich. The stations therefore linked themselves into a 'Working Group', the ARD (Working Group of Public Service Broadcasting Administrations) which formed a kind of national network across the federation both through the exchange of programmes and the redistribution of revenues.

The Federal Republic gradually emerged as a world economic power and the question of further German television channels became pressing in the early 1960s. There were many in German industry who wanted the federal government to start licensing commercial stations, but in 1961 the Supreme Court reconfirmed the exclusive rights of the states to regulate radio and television. The ARD stations thought it too expensive to duplicate its existing arrangements and gradually in discussions between the *Länder* representatives a scheme emerged: all the states (but not the federal government) would jointly establish a second German channel (ZDF), this time with a nationally selected Broadcasting Council consisting of no fewer than sixty-six people; it would have a central set of studios in the twin cities of Mainz and Wiesbaden and would be granted,

Karl Edouard von Schnitzler, whose political commentaries from East Berlin became part of the fabric of the Cold War.

by all of the states, a share in the total and now increased licence fee revenue (which had not been raised since the 1920s). Like the ARD stations, ZDF would sell advertising in one or two time-blocks each evening, but not within programmes. Later in the 1960s the ARD stations did decide to add extra programmes of their own, transmitted from each regional centre as a 'Third Programme', but consisting in the main of rather more intellectually demanding material.

During the 1980s television began to change throughout Europe. The fear of the culturally lowering effects of commercial television began to subside. New technologies made it easier and cheaper to start new networks. New media empires (including German ones) sprang up around the world, hungry for new challenges and objects of investment. Video, satellite, and cable started up and threatened to compete with any national television system which failed to satisfy its home audiences. In Germany some of the *Länder* agreed to permit commercial stations (Bavaria and the Rhineland-Palatinate the first among them). The smaller *Länder* of Lower Saxony and Schleswig-Holstein (which formed an element of the large Hamburg-based NDR) announced the intention of breaking away and starting their own stations. The Supreme Court accepted that the *Länder* had the right to license commercial stations, so long as they maintained the same 'Radio Council' system of governance. But then there was the problem of cable which had long existed in Germany as a means for relaying ARD and ZDF signals; now it was decided that new cable systems should be constructed by the *Länder* (rather than by the federal Post Office) and cable began to spread very rapidly across the channel-starved map of Germany. The great multi-media concerns of Bertelsmann and Springer began to interest themselves in satellite and a number of consortia were formed to link Germany with new European satellite channels. The vast wealth of the new Germany, despite the problems of recession, is thus obliging the new electronic media to serve its needs, even though Germany, East and West, for decades resisted anything but public services in its broadcasting.

Great Britain

The United Kingdom is one of the few countries in Europe which has not passed through an era of authoritarian rule since the birth of broadcasting in the 1920s. It was the first country to establish a regular daily television service direct to the home and to start the evolution of the special professions of television, both technical and creative. The BBC, still the cornerstone of British television, has existed without interruption since the start of broadcasting, but there have been major changes of public policy and major internal changes behind its institutional continuity. Of all the broadcasting organizations in the world the BBC has been the most widely admired but has none the less proved difficult for others to copy successfully.

John Charles Walsham Reith was six-foot-six and thirty-three when he became General Manager of the BBC in 1922 and he remained in charge for sixteen years. Few individuals have so influenced the lives of a nation. Deeply God-fearing, he was obsessed with a sense of his own failure and after leaving the BBC never was given a post which, in his own phrase, 'stretched him to more than a fraction of his capacity'.

Towering over the history of the early BBC is the figure of its founder Lord Reith, who entered the world of radio after running a munitions factory in America during the latter part of World War I. The new BBC and the medium of radio seemed to offer him the opportunities for national leadership and quasi-religious prophecy for which he yearned. (In the longer run the medium of broadcasting was to disappoint him.) Reith's shadow still looms over the organization which he founded, even though most of its revenue is now consumed by television (a medium which he regarded with a certain apprehension) rather than by radio and even though it is now one of a number of television institutions competing for the UK audience—over which Reith's BBC held an unassailed monopoly.

81

Reith believed that the education and moral improvement of the public was the real purpose of radio, but carefully selected entertainment was an acceptable means for carrying out the task. The BBC seized every opportunity to establish standards of every kind in the minds of the listeners: in guiding, for example, the grammar and pronunciation of the English language and in attempting to create a more enlightened electorate; Reith fought against the secularization of Sunday; he made broadcasting 'a servant of culture'—by which he meant the high culture of classical music. 'As we conceive it,' he once wrote, 'our responsibility is to carry into the greatest possible number of homes everything that is best in every department of human knowledge, endeavour or achievement.' This intention was stressed even in the permitted standards of dress, speech, and behaviour of the BBC's staff, which grew under Reith from just four in number, including himself, to many hundreds. It was under Reith that the government established the system by which a Board of Governors (appointed by the cabinet minister responsible for broadcasting, normally the Home Secretary or Interior Minister) held supreme power over the Corporation and appointed the Director-General and the most senior staff. The BBC was presented by Parliament with a Royal Charter, signed not by the Prime Minister of the day but by the sovereign; this is highly permissive in character, providing the Corporation with a wide range of powers but inserting a 'reserve' or emergency power for government to prohibit any material or class of material—a power which has only very seldom been

Helen McKay singing 'Here's Looking At You' at Alexandra Palace on 29 August 1936 as part of the Radiolympia demonstration television transmissions.

The sheet music and lyrics of 'Television', sung at the opening of the BBC service on November 1936 by Adele Dixon. The service operated for two hours a day, including revues, variety, ballet, illustrated talks and demonstrations. Filmed extracts from London West End shows were broadcast, as well as a varied range of sports from outside the new studios.

invoked. Between the BBC and Parliament there exists a 'Licence and Agreement' which stipulates the remit of the BBC in greater detail and establishes the funding system based upon the licence fee. In regulatory terms, it is the simplest of systems but has depended for its efficient functioning upon a great deal of human understanding between government and broadcasters and upon a measure of institutional self-discipline.

Reith established the idea in the mind of government that a broadcasting institution had to be free of all political interference, although he never permitted his broadcasters to step far from the general orthodoxies expressed in Parliament. During the great testing time of the General Strike of 1926 his radio services suddenly became crucial, but he found it hard to identify, during the convulsion, a *national* interest as distinct from the view pressed on the BBC by the government. He insisted on keeping the licence fee, collected by the Post Office, as the sole source of revenue and on preventing any form of advertising, apart from that in the programme journals. He opposed, successfully, any measure which might

83

lead to the breach of the BBC's monopoly—and this remained unbroken until the arrival of commercial television in the 1950s. But during the 1930s a large part of the British audience did in fact turn to the commercial stations transmitted from continental Europe.

The BBC began a television service in 1936 and continued it until the day the war began. On its return to the air in 1946 some of the same programmes and personalities were still available and the receivers still worked. The BBC seemed to many to embark on the development of the medium without enthusiasm and it was only when the Conservative Party came to power six years after the war and decided (after acrimonious debate) to set up a commercial channel to rival the BBC's, that the BBC responded and worked to build a mass audience. The coronation of Queen Elizabeth II was shown on television in 1953 and this provoked a sudden growth in the number of viewers.

The commercial television companies which commenced transmission in 1955 did not at first make money, but after a false start they became suddenly extremely profitable and remained so until the 1990s, when their collective national monopoly of television advertising revenue was in turn broken. By that time several of the commercial companies had become the nuclei of vast new multi-media corporations. For forty years this group of companies were franchised by a public body (the Independent Television Authority, later renamed the Independent Broadcasting Authority) which was not dissimilar in approach and style from the BBC's own Board of Governors. The liveliness of the programmes on the commercial channel provoked a revolution in the BBC's approach: Reithianism was by no means abandoned but there was an attempt to create programmes which reflected the actual living culture of the British people, in music, comedy, and commentary. The *Tonight* programme introduced the demotic and the amusing into daily information and built up a team of personalities with whom great numbers of the public identified. From that team the satirical programme *That Was the Week that Was* emerged, chaired by David Frost. Week by week it broke television taboos and social taboos. It was television which in Britain acted as the barometer of the great attitudinal shifts of the 1960s.

The 1960s were a time of great prosperity for both rival systems and each, with its respective monopoly of licence fee and advertising, passed through an era of plenty. Colour television arrived and the licence fee was raised for every set which was able to receive it; as colour spread across an audience of nearly 17 million homes, the income of the BBC rose rapidly, even faster than necessary to satisfy its needs. In the 1970s, the era of high inflation, a reverse process was to set in and the BBC began to become the poorer relative to its commercial rival. But the BBC by then had two channels with which to compete.

Before each fresh stage in the development of broadcasting in Britain the government has set up a special official committee or commission of inquiry to work out a nationally agreed policy. In its first years the BBC had been a company owned by the radio manufacturers, but became a corporation when it received its first Royal Charter. The Charter was renewed and revised approximately once a decade, usually as the result of a new technological development or a decision to expand the national scope of the medium.

The official inquiry of 1935 proposed that the BBC's remit be altered to include television, and another of 1962 recommended that it be given a second channel. In the late 1970s a further inquiry proposed that a fourth television channel be set up along novel lines and this was finally established in 1980 as a commercial company, owned by the regulatory authority, the IBA, but with independent directors, and financed by a special grant derived from the total revenue of the fifteen commercial companies which were permitted to sell advertising on the new fourth channel, although they neither owned nor controlled it. Thus a third 'monopoly' was instituted in Britain for a third, rival, institution—Channel Four. Only Channel Four was eligible to draw upon the special levy imposed upon the commercial companies of the ITV channel, but they could extend their monopoly of advertising to include its highly regulated commercial air time. It was a somewhat complicated formula but it meant that one of the founding principles of Britain's approach to television was retained—that enterprises fighting for the same audience should not find themselves competing for the same sources of revenue, for that way, it was believed, lay an inevitable lowering of standards and a pandering to the lowest common denominators of audience taste. That principle was abandoned in the reformed structure of British television which was inaugurated in January 1993, after many years of debate within the government of Mrs Thatcher.

One can see within the relatively long continuities of British television a number of separate eras. In the Reith era, before television, programming was originated almost entirely within the Corporation. That seemed to be the way to control standards—from the top—and thus to fulfil the monopolistic vision of the BBC. The BBC acquired its own orchestras, both for serious and 'light' music; it operated its own repertory company of actors and employed its own news reporters. The system was carried over into television, although the new medium also took over some practices and traditions from the film industry. But until the great break of the 1960s the BBC, like other public service television companies in Europe, attempted to provide and control all that it needed by way of input.

The world of the late 1960s presented the BBC with a number of problems of culture, as well as of commercial competition. The dominant generation seemed to be the new post-war youth, especially that sector of them who were passing through further education. There was a clear gulf between the generations and a powerfully expressed desire on the part of the young to slough off, in broadcasting as elsewhere, the lingering inhibitions and constraints of the Victorian world, in particular all those concerned with the representation and discussion of sexuality. This was expressed in the new music of the time, as well as in drama and art, in attitudes towards education, and, most of all, in the political protest movements against the H-bomb and the war in Vietnam. The Reithian BBC could not possibly survive these pressures, and in the prosperous conditions of the time it was possible to meet new demands through diversification, accretion, and experiment; also, of course, by recruiting a new generation of programme-makers to fill the programmes of the BBC's new Channel Two.

The events of the year 1968—in Vietnam, Paris, Czechoslovakia, Amsterdam, Chicago, Washington, Berlin, and the universities everywhere—had a tremendous impact upon the conduct and culture of television. New technologies of news gathering arrived in time to reflect and amplify the effects of the demonstrations and battles, invasions, and 'happenings' of all kinds. New writers expressed the mood of the time in television drama and soap opera, in a new era of frank comedy and explicit talk programmes. An accommodation was made between the old and the new, but a new opposition to the liberalization of the BBC was established which was to harry it for the next quarter-century. The yearning for the certainties of the Reith era never abated in some parts of the community, and the counter-claims for total freedom of expression, public accountability, and open access to the medium remained equally clearly expressed. But there was, in the era of Sir Hugh Greene's tenure of Reith's old office, a kind of settlement and this survived more or less intact until the arrival of Mrs Thatcher.

The Establishment of Channel Four

There were many who had long been unhappy with the social changes of the 1960s, which appeared to stem from the medium of television. Around the figure of Mrs Mary Whitehouse and the Festival of Light an increasingly powerful social force emerged, protesting in effect at what appeared to be both the ultimate manifestation of materialism and the final secularization of culture. It was at times fused with the political right and seemed to yearn for a world of extinguished values. For its part, it thought the loss of that world was the result of a conspiracy, led in part by the BBC.

The new Channel Four, the plan for which Mrs Thatcher inherited from a committee of inquiry set up by her Labour predecessor Harold Wilson, gave expression to a newly identified set of cultural needs, while adding to the commercial armoury of the independent television companies. Some part of the new channel's Parliament-given remit was to afford opportunities to a fresh generation of would-be independent television producers and film-makers. After the virtual collapse of British cinema there came about a kind of fusion between a new world of television programme-makers and a new generation of potential film-makers. The new channel made itself responsible for encouraging and commissioning work from this burgeoning world of small companies. Hundreds of independents had sprung into being. Channel Four took some highly innova-

tive material from them, and some from independents in other parts of the world, including the Third World. Many programmes were commissioned by the commercial ITV companies.

Channel Four gave expression to some of the cultural freedoms desired by the 1968 generation and something of the entrepreneurial culture of the Thatcher era. It established a new cultural 'settlement' in Britain in the conditions of the 1980s, a combination of commercial opportunity and political radicalism, traditional values and those of the new ethnic communities of Britain. Through the somewhat ingenious institutional improvisation of Channel Four, Britain was provided with a container, as it were, of a new pluralism, the resolution of a series of fresh cultural tensions.

Several problems confronted the world of public television, including the BBC and the two IBA-regulated channels, at the dawn of the new decade of the 1990s. Declining public sector finance meant new pressures for television to earn more of its own finance and to cut costs. The new world of non-institutional programme-making brought pressures on the Corporation and the companies to provide them with more opportunities. Industry was vexed by the monopoly of television advertising in Britain. Competition would reduce advertising costs but thus reduce the revenues available on the commercial channels for programme-making. A reorganization of the commercial sector of Britain's television took place at the end of 1992 after a new report, the Peacock Report, and a very hard-fought debate, one of the last of the Thatcher era.

The British System after 1993

First, the regulation of television was separated from the regulation of radio and a new Independent Television Commission was created to replace the IBA and to offer new contracts to television companies on the basis of a kind of auction— not a completely open auction, but one restricted at first to largely British capital, and to companies which could prove their ability to meet the exacting standards of a 'quality threshold' before they were permitted to bid. Channel Four was to be separated from the ITC, selling its own advertising time, in competition with the commercial channel, which was to be constituted by the linking of the new, post-auction, companies, under the supervision of the ITC. After two years it would be legal for other companies, including foreign ones, to purchase the shares of the commercial companies, but not of Channel Four, which is a kind of non-profit trust. These changes meant that competition for revenue had finally arrived in British television and that the commercial companies were no longer the money-printing machines of the past. The entire atmosphere of the medium changed almost overnight; a new generation of entrepreneurs arrived, some from quite different worlds, and quite unused to the protected, regulated ambience of the ITV system as it had existed since the 1950s.

The BBC also was at the brink of an era of great change, for it was now under

Facing, above: **Faustus, Faustus, Faustus**, Miklós Jancsó's 1984 nine-part drama series tracing Hungary's stormy history in the twentieth century, was adapted from *The Blessed Descent to Hell of Dr Faustus* by László Gyurkó.

Facing, below: a whole new category of programmes, 'reality television' has sprung up in the United States in recent years. The American Cable Channel, Court TV, has pioneered the live televising of trials— notably the O.J. Simpson case in 1995.

THE ELEVENTH HOUR:
WHO WILL CAST THE
FIRST STONE

The logo of Channel Four's **Eleventh Hour**, one of the many new and radical experiments produced by independent companies 'saying new things in new ways' with which the Channel opened up in 1982.

public scrutiny, as government prepared to present a new Charter when the old one expired in 1996. The BBC had to find a way to maintain (through direct production and through commissioning of independents) two channels of programmes of high quality. A new Director-General, John Birt, arrived in 1993, and his task was to create a new national rationale for the BBC in the era of multi-channel competition and then to make the whole machinery of the Corporation work more efficiently and cost-effectively. The BBC would have to prove that it could function in the new climate, without either succumbing to simple hour-by-hour competition or abandoning its historic mission. But its staff (at one time 27,000 in number) would have to be greatly reduced and many more of its activities hived off to outside, commercially competitive, supplying companies. Large numbers of BBC staff departed, to sell their skills back to the BBC and to other channels. The BBC itself started the process of creating an internal market of producers, using their budgets to purchase all of the special services required in their programmes. Sections of the BBC which failed to pass muster in this system of 'producer choice' would close and their function go to an outside company.

In virtually all of Europe both forms of broadcasting had begun as public services; commercial channels arrived much later, in order to compete, to complement, to exploit newer technologies, to assist in the growth of consumer economies. Some countries (Norway, for example) eschewed all forms of commerce in television, until the 1980s. But by 1992 almost every country of the Continent either had commercial satellite or cable, or had launched a terrestrial commercial channel, or had, at least, allowed advertising on one or more of its indigenous channels.

Public Service Television in the United States

In the United States, on the other hand, public service television had had to struggle for a place against diverse, increasingly profuse, and entirely commercial channels. But America has always possessed a public sector dimension to its broadcasting. The Radio Act of 1927 established 'public interest, convenience and necessity' (a phrase borrowed from public utility legislation) as the discretionary yardstick for the licensing of stations. In 1934 President Roosevelt, then in the midst of a mass of 'New Deal' schemes and legislation, brought about a new Communications Act which set up the Federal Communications Commission (FCC) as the agency by which federal jurisdiction would be established over all telecommunications in the United States. There was much discussion at the time of the importance and value of non-profit broadcasting, educational stations in particular, but no special provision was made while frequencies were being distributed, for radio in the late 1930s and for television a decade later.

By 1948 it became evident that there was insufficient space available for the vast numbers of licence applications for TV stations which were building up, and the FCC imposed a freeze on all new stations—a freeze which lasted for four years. In 1952 the UHF band was opened up and at the insistence of one of the Commissioners, Freda Hennock, an allocation of frequency space for 242 non-profit educational television stations was made by the FCC, but no arrangements were made for federal cash to be supplied to help them (see Chapter 11).

It was a full decade before a further Educational Television Facilities Act provided for money to be given to the rather patchy growth of educational television which had taken place in the interim. The new Act stipulated that no agency of federal government would have the right to control or interfere in the content or curriculum of the educational programmes transmitted. The Ford Foundation had poured large sums into educational television and had nurtured it to a point of professional maturity, but the commercial networks were always nervous of the possible consequences of the growth of public sector competition. Yet to many Americans it seemed wrong that the USA should be denied access to the kind of programmes which public services were providing all over Europe, in Britain especially by the middle of the 1960s. The Carnegie Commission report of 1967, encouraged by President Lyndon Johnson, proposed a massive set of

changes to the entire system of American educational television and new legislation followed within a few months.

The Public Broadcasting Act of 1967 established the Corporation for Public
Broadcasting, which was provided with greatly increased federal funds to
disburse among the many educational stations. That all of America's non-profit
stations had to be 'educational' in a formal sense was now abandoned, and the
most powerful of the stations were now resourced to pursue the more open and
discretionary 'public service' remit as that is understood in the UK and elsewhere. A unified, though highly diverse, entity emerged, linked through a new
Public Broadcasting System (PBS), which thought of itself, somewhat optimist-
ically, as a fourth network (after the three commercial ones). National Public
Radio was also established and like its television counterpart started to spread
nation-wide.

Throughout the Nixon and Reagan years public television had a very difficult
time. As Les Brown explains in Chapter 11, there was tension between CPB,
which hands out federal subsidy, and PBS, which organizes the distribution of
programmes through the system. There was tension between the stations and
between these and CPB and PBS. There was a greater tension between the White
House and the whole world of non-profit television, which both Nixon and
Reagan believed was irreversibly subject to the influence of east-coast liberalism.
(Vice-President Agnew delivered a number of notorious and 'chilling' broadsides
against the alleged biased liberalism of the commercial networks, but he was
swept away in the course of a corruption scandal.)

Public television stations in America remained starved of funds and—somewhat to the puzzlement of visiting European broadcasters—found it necessary
to raise their funds in part through public appeals, often on television and often
through the holding of week-long auctions of goods and memorabilia. The non-
profit stations have often been accused of spending as much air time raising funds
as the commercial stations do with their advertisements. None the less, the
record over thirty years of American public broadcasting presents a picture of
effective public service, albeit reaching minority audiences, and valuable experimentation. Perhaps the most internationally far-reaching contribution has been
in the field of Children's programmes (most notably *Sesame Street* and *The Electric
Company*); but in the field of news programmes the *MacNeil–Lehrer Report* entered
public consciousness as a successful and sometimes searching alternative to the
powerful news coverage of the commercial networks. Public television also
helped to re-establish a tradition of classic and social drama (or single plays)
which had been successful in the early years of commercial television but which
had died when the main networks found it impossible to remain competitive
unless their programmes ran in long continuous seasons. But American public
television also performed the task of importing the best of British (BBC and
commercial) documentaries and fiction material.

A great deal of programming has originated through co-production between the larger US public stations and European (mainly British) producers; this system of co-production, made possible by sponsorship money from large US corporations, had brought production finance into European television which would otherwise not have been available because of the prohibition of sponsorship in much of Europe. Public television in America has been the great unifier of European and American television culture, where the commercial networks have been the source of a profitable one-way traffic eastwards across the Atlantic.

The continued existence of public service television is not inevitable. The political culture is changing everywhere as technology and public attitudes change. Nor will the crucially enabling licence fee exist for ever. It is sometimes argued that competition, consumer choice, and a diversity of technologies will between them give rise to as full a range of material as the viewing public desires. The question is whether there ought always to be television channels available, or at least programmes, of a kind which could not exist simply in an open market. Other means of entertainment do not demand permanent public subsidy and do not need state oversight or compulsion. But it has generally been believed that the sheer universality of television makes it necessary for every audience to have guaranteed access to programmes which no commercial system can be relied upon to supply. Television is now so deeply inscribed in the practices of democracy that the latter has come to be dependent on it.

Public service in television is simply television produced for motives of service rather than motives of profit. Today as the technologies for projecting moving images multiply it is increasingly likely that much of the material produced by public service systems will also find a home in cable or cassette or satellite—certainly if we begin to see 500-channel cables in our homes. The non-terrestrial channels appear to take up to about 40 per cent of the available audience, sharing them among an increasing number of outlets. Terrestrial television appears to have a long-term future, after all, including the established public service channels. These have a sporting chance of surviving for a further generation at least and from them we may expect to continue to receive the imagery of national pageant, the kind of entertainment that touches the nerves, discussion of the kind to which audiences turn at great moments of decision, and much of our socially shared cultural experience in an era when 'narrow-casting' is becoming ever more narrow. Where there are many twigs and branches there is need of a sturdy trunk.

Part Two

Forms and Genres

4

Drama and Entertainment

Richard Paterson

elevision drama and entertainment programming are at the heart of every broadcasting schedule. They offer a mirror and a window to the culture of the audience they seek to serve. They inspire and entertain, criticize, challenge, and amuse. They play a part in defining the make-up of citizenship in a modern society. That they also recruit audiences to the television screen to sell to advertisers greatly influences what is produced.

From its very start in the 1930s television used and developed existing forms—radio, film, music hall, theatre, literature—to create its own unique range of programme fare. Television also invented its own genres, with radio still a rich source of new ideas, to this day. It has been subject to a process of continual change, with constant innovations, whether aesthetic and formal, or merely commercial in search of new audiences, bringing about phases of experiment which alternate with phases of exploitation or mere duplication of successful formats. Every novelty found to be successful is almost inevitably adopted elsewhere, by competitors at home and abroad. But entertainment and drama have evolved alongside the rest of television's programming output, affected by television's place in the home and in the wider culture.

What is possible within programme production has always been affected too by technological change—studio drama was transformed when video recording arrived; the studio-bound nature of production became outmoded with the advent of portable video cameras; special effects technology brought new creative opportunities; wide-screen technology will soon alter the parameters yet again. Changing regulatory frameworks, especially the intensification of

95

Beat the Clock, one of television's original game show formats, in its original US version (1952).

competition, have had an impact both on innovation and on the tendency to replicate.

The most important influence has been and remains the economics of the industry. Drama is traditionally the most expensive genre, while entertainment can be produced more cheaply, its main costs arising from the need to secure star performers. For some time, indeed, the cost of drama has been one factor in the developing globalization of TV production: in recent years, there has been a growing reaction in many countries against the flow of American programming throughout the world. But even US programming, which once could amortize its entire costs in its domestic market, now needs revenue from the global market to cover costs of production and make a profit.

The question of whether television is adequately serving the cultural needs of audiences is a live one in every society. Imported series are used to fill out the schedule, and the consequence is that viewers see the world interpreted in terms of American images. But regional television trade patterns suggest that the notion of American dominance is over-simplified, given that locally produced drama usually achieves bigger audiences than American programming.

The concerns with 'effects' of television on social attitudes have been a major issue at different times in different countries. Television drama has sometimes been deemed too violent, and believed to have a detrimental effect on the morality and values of the society. It has also been criticized for failing to represent the diversity of its audience or for stereotyping. In television entertainment there appears to be a systematic distortion of reality favouring life-styles and aspirations of higher status groups who tend to live in more exciting and glamorous surroundings. In recent years women's cultural expression has increasingly been reflected in programme output. Whereas previously programmes were made for women (the daytime soap operas being possibly the obvious example), the feminist critique of soap opera has now exerted an influence over what is made, and how women are represented.

Much criticism has been levelled at television for being an essentially escapist medium. Programming is often accused of lacking intrinsic merit or purpose, as being undemanding and formulaic. Television is felt not to achieve its educative potential and to offer a cheapened experience. In this account escapism is seen as wholly negative: *being* entertained, *living in* a fantasy, getting *away* from real-life problems. However, other research has found something more complex: television viewing is as much about coming to terms with problems of life, reality seeking, as escaping from them into fantasy. Television can alter perceptions and understandings of the world in which the individual lives.

These are very different views and indicate the paradoxes of television's role in late twentieth-century societies.

Golden Ages and Changes

For television drama the mid-1980s and early 1960s are regarded as a golden age—though this is usually clouded by a large degree of misremembering. Grand gestures were possible within the emerging markets in the USA and in the UK. Innovative scripts and *mises-en-scène* were allowed and even encouraged, within the restricted technology which confined production to the studio. The realism of single television plays fitted the politics of the Cold War, the culture of an emerging consumer society, and new welfarist ideologies.

A lead was taken in developing the art of television, particularly in television plays. Commentators have attributed this to the need to attract middle-class audiences to watch and purchase television receivers, and it is certainly the case that the TV play did not outlast the period of initial mass marketing.

In the USA the dramatic fare of the 1950s was offered in anthology series like Philco Television Playhouse or Kraft Television Theatre. Original plays were transmitted live from New York each week and were very popular. Little-known actors (like Paul Newman or Rod Steiger) played in dramas written by the likes of Paddy Chayevsky, Rod Serling, or Gore Vidal and directed by new talents such as John Frankenheimer or Sidney Lumet. Significant examples included

Chayevsky's *Marty* and Serling's *Requiem for a Heavyweight*. At that time the key influence on TV drama was Broadway theatre. The lack of videotape recording technology and the continued uncertainty of live performance contributed an edge to the productions. However, once pre-recording and editing arrived there was a fundamental shift in output which coincided with a move of production to Hollywood. Previously uncooperative film studios realized the profitable opportunities of supplying television with programmes. The networks gradually replaced New York-based anthology dramas with filmed series, while paradox-

Paddy Chayefsky's **Marty** (1953), written specially for television, showed the artistic potential of the new medium. Picture shows Rod Steiger and Nancy Marchant.

Gunsmoke, the television Western series which recounted the story of Marshal Matt Dillon (James Arness), ran for 20 years.

ically many of the most creative talents were under attack and being forced out of the industry through the infamous McCarthy witchhunts of the early 1950s.

There was a certain inevitability about the changes. Series were easier to schedule and allowed the networks to amortize fixed costs over a longer period. And as had been discovered before with radio, continuity of a programme contributed enormously to building its popularity over time.

From Hollywood the Disney studio led the way with *Disneyland*, a weekly series. Warner Bros. followed producing adventure dramas under the anthology title Warner Bros. Presents, which included examples of the emerging popular Western genre then a staple of Hollywood film production. Out of this stable came such long-running filmed series as *Cheyenne*, *Wagon Train*, *Rawhide*, *Gunsmoke*, and others. Indeed *Gunsmoke* ran for twenty years until 1975, while *Bonanza* ran for fourteen years to 1973. These series also had the advantage of filming and transmitting in colour.

The popularity and then waning of the Western can be viewed against a rapidly transforming American society—the period from the emergence of the Civil Rights movement in the late 1950s through the period of the Vietnam war: an age of increasing disillusionment in which the male bonding of the Western, unhindered by attachment to women or concern for minority cultures, became an anachronism. Alongside the Western series, adventure and action were

99

provided by an increasing number of crime series which eventually supplanted the Western.

In Britain and other European countries with a strong public service ethic the TV play retained its pre-eminence in drama output for a much longer time. In Japan, however, like the USA, the rapid rise of commercial television led to an early demise for the single play form after a brief flourishing in the late 1950s with famous examples including *I Want to be a Seashell* by Yoshiko Okamoto.

Early British examples of live television included *1984* and *The Quatermass Experiment*. With the advent of video recording, ever more adventurous TV plays emerged in Britain—under the rubric initially of commercial television's Armchair Theatre, from 1958 (with examples such as Alun Owen's *No Trams to Lime Street*) and then, from 1963, on BBC with the Wednesday Play. Notable examples included Jeremy Sandford's *Cathy Come Home* and Nell Dunn's *Up the Junction*, both directed by Ken Loach using a naturalist non-studio documentary style, and both having a considerable social impact. Armchair Theatre and the Wednesday Play gave young dramatists—from David Mercer (with *And Did Those Feet?*), John Hopkins (with *Talking to a Stranger*), and Dennis Potter (with the Nigel Barton plays)—an opportunity to develop strong themes and a television aesthetic which included the multi-part series. Subsequent critically acclaimed examples have included Dennis Potter's *Pennies from Heaven*, Jim Allen's *Days of Hope*, G. F. Newman's *Law and Order*, and later Alan Bleasdale's *Boys from the Blackstuff*, maintaining a political eye on the culture and politics of the nation through the 1970s, within a surprising aesthetic range.

TV drama in Britain could evolve in this very different way because it was defined by a non-commercial ethic that allowed and encouraged innovation. It did not exclude American-type action series and British producers imitated these through *The Saint* and *The Avengers*. At the same time in Britain television series aimed at middle-brow audiences were produced, to great success both domestically and abroad, including *The Forsyte Saga* and *Upstairs Downstairs*, as well as such reflections on national biographies as *The Six Wives of Henry VIII* and *Edward and Mrs Simpson* and later literary adaptations such as *Brideshead Revisited* or *Tinker, Tailor, Soldier, Spy*. This particular strand of short-form series has continued to have considerable importance in the schedules of broadcasters in Britain and other European countries, less enthralled to the commercial pursuit of audience untainted by notions of purpose.

The craft of the *television* writer emerged in the 1950s and 1960s. In those countries without a viable film industry indigenous screen writers, and directors too, have found an outlet for their work within television. Television has acted as a nursery slope for new talent as well as functioning as the most important screen window for a nation's culture. Many talented directors who later received worldwide acclaim began their careers in television. One apposite example is Emir Kusturica, the Bosnian film director, who first worked for TV Sarajevo in the early 1980s.

This particularly European tradition of encouraging and developing a diversity of cultural output has come under pressure in the drama field only with the commercial pressures of the 1980s and 1990s. Previously, taking Denmark, for instance, as an example of European public broadcasting, in broad terms the move had been from classical plays in the 1950s to modern experimental plays in the 1960s, TV movies in the 1970s, with a return to nostalgia in the 1980s. There was of course a much greater variety of forms than these generalizations imply and this tendency has increased as imitation across borders has become the rule.

Sometimes TV drama has achieved a major impact. The ability of television to draw attention to the drama 'event' as a marketing ploy has been utilized on many channels, both commercial and public service, across the world. It was used with huge success by the US networks in the 1970s. The mini-series, *Roots*, *Holocaust*, *The Day After*, or *Rich Man, Poor Man*, secured huge audiences and set a pattern of scheduling and formatting which lasted several years. *Roots* was a milestone in television history in the USA with the highest rating at that time

Alan Bleasdale's five-part drama **Boys from the Blackstuff** (1982) reflected the impact of unemployment on families in Liverpool and had a significant impact in Britain in the early 1980s.

The television adaptation of Alex Haley's **Roots** became a major cultural phenomenon in the USA in 1977 as huge audiences followed the story of Kunta Kinte, a young African warrior captured by American slave traders.

ever for an entertainment programme. In the UK this phenomenon blossomed in the early 1980s with Granada series such as *Brideshead Revisited* and *Jewel in the Crown*, to be followed later by *Prime Suspect*. In Germany *Das Boot*, *Heimat*, and *Die Zweite Heimat* have received similar treatment.

Equally, some television series have become the object of cult status. Whether *Doctor Who*, *Blake's Seven*, or *Star Trek*, they have led to bizarre imitation and fan behaviour, including not infrequently congresses to discuss the finer points of narrative development.

In recent drama output, in Europe in particular, television companies have worked increasingly with the film industry because of economic factors. There have been varied outcomes and for some the dominance of a TV aesthetic has undermined the essentially cinematic. The relationship to cinema began to emerge as a significant one in the 1970s in Germany through ZDF, and in France, first with the public service broadcasters, and then in the 1980s with Canal Plus. In the 1980s in Britain a similar pattern was followed with the emergence of Channel Four as a major financier of British film output, some premiered through theatrical release. Important films from this source have included Stephen Frears's and Hanif Kureishi's *My Beautiful Laundrette* and more recently Neil Jordan's *The Crying Game*.

Other national systems which arrived later on the television landscape too have had brave successes—Tagore's *Rakta Karobi* (1980), a 165-minute studio drama set in a surrealistic cavernous gold mine in Bangladesh, for instance. These are the exceptions alongside the run of the mill output. In Brazil, for example, TV Globo has had a policy of producing major mini-series, such as adaptations of Jorge Amado's *Tent of Miracles* or Joao Guimarães Rosa's *The Devil to Play in the Backlands*, alongside its dominantly serialized output. Often such programmes have been influential within a national cultural formation seeking to challenge alongside the normative certainty, assurance, and identity offered by the greater part of the output.

Drama Forms

One-off dramas have had an ever more precarious situation within the schedule in recent years. In the USA they were replaced from the late 1950s by the filmed drama series as the Hollywood studios came to terms with television. The series had a number of advantages—all of which have gradually influenced all TV production: regular characters and situations with a returning audience, schedule anchorage, efficient production, easy sale of advertising. It should never be forgotten that commercial television programming is there to attract audiences which can be sold to advertisers.

The filmed drama series dominated ratings in the USA from the early 1960s, and were sold on cheaply across the world to equal success with international audiences: *Cheyenne, Bonanza, Dragnet, the Untouchables, Star Trek*—derivative often from film action genres.

These popular programmes have had a huge impact on audiences—they are a common currency for discussion world-wide—although they are not highly regarded by critics. Their essential appeal to audiences is similar to the appeal of the action film, itself a symbol of American dominance in audio-visual trade. These programmes of the 1960s and after remain in syndication even today, serving the secondary and tertiary market in the USA and the many overseas markets. Programming is a commodity which is ripe for further exploitation and the dominance of American distribution companies has allowed them to achieve and maintain a significant market share.

In Europe with the domination, indeed in most cases until recently monopoly, of public service broadcasters the evolution of television drama forms followed a slightly different path. Action series took longer to establish (other than in the UK where successful imitations such as *The Avengers* were sold to the USA), and the one-off, critical social or cultural drama, in anthology form remained a schedule staple. Short-form serials often based on literary classics remained popular.

Serialization, a form first adopted in radio drama, particularly with daytime soap operas in the USA, later spread to become an essential element in television schedules around the world. It evolved in many ways serving daytime, children's, and prime-time audiences in different ways in different countries.

Serials

The factory production of television has its longest history in US daytime soap operas and in game shows. The earliest serials were published in weekly maga-

103

zines. Radio in the USA in the 1930s developed the format for selling soap powder to female audiences during the day. Television inherited the form and used it in the struggle for daytime viewers in the USA. Essentially television soap operas are open-ended stories usually within a domestic setting. Their story-lines in the USA have reflected the daily hopes and despairs of average middle-class families in suburban or small town settings. Numerous story-lines interweave to create a complex narrative web which centres on human interest stories and the lives of the soap's leading characters.

Over the years there have been distinct shifts in character, style, and setting. Medical soap operas such as *General Hospital* in the USA or *Emergency Ward 10* in Britain became a subgenre while more recently the youth audience has been served by serials such as *Neighbours*, *Home and Away*, or *Grange Hill*. The impact of the soap phenomenon has been studied in terms of how they provide potential role models for viewers and their use as the currency of everyday conversation. The key factor, of course, is their popularity with audiences in virtually every country of the world, and their relatively low production costs for drama output.

The serial form has undergone different mutations in different territories: in the UK *Coronation Street* or *EastEnders* are prime-time soaps, now imitated across Europe with programmes like *Lindenstrasse* in Germany. The top-rated fiction in Japan in the early 1990s has been *Kimino Nawa*, a fifteen-minute narrative based on a popular radio series which started in the 1950s. It is broadcast each morning at 8.15 by NHK. For many years another serial, *Oshin*, was a morning event in Japan.

Other examples have ranged from *Glenroe* in Ireland to *Country GP* in New Zealand, *The Awakening* in Singapore to *House of Christianshavn* in Denmark, *Kampos* in Cyprus to *Pobol y Cwm* in Wales. In India the initial attempt to use the drama serial as a vehicle for the pro-social message with *Hum Log* in 1985 was based on earlier Mexican success with this use of popular drama. *Hum Log* became popular only when these elements were dropped and the more usual domestic drama dominated. After this success other serials were produced and the serialization of the religious epic, *Mahabarat*, became something of a national event in securing huge audiences. Nigeria, too, with *Cock Crow at Dawn*, attempted the pro-social in the mid-1980s (encouraging a return to the countryside and agricultural self-sufficiency).

In Brazil, Mexico, and the other countries of Latin America, the telenovela emerged as the generic mutation, with a range of target audiences, stripped across a week so that every day a new episode is shown at the same time. The novela as a form grew out of the radio novela—pioneered in Cuba with *El Derecho de Nacer* (1946) in pre-Castro days and developed in Brazil (from 1964) and Mexico. The most distinctive difference of the Latin American telenovela from Anglo-American serials is the range of styles and settings. And of course they are complete narratives in around 100 episodes, unlike the never-ending soap operas.

Novela story-lines tend towards the romantic and melodramatic with an emphasis on upward social mobility usually through romantic attachment, and they are expected to have a happy ending.

At their most powerful they make political statements with potentially huge impact. *Roque Santeiro* broached the questions of myth, power struggle, and the role of the church in Brazilian society at the time of fundamental political change as the military government relinquished power. In Mexico there is even a tradition of the historical telenovela which will deal with a fundamental aspect of national history. Examples include *La Tranchera* (1986) about the creation of modern Mexico between 1917 and 1938 and *The Carriage* (1971–2), based on the struggles of President Benito Juárez to maintain an authentic Mexican government between 1864 and 1867. In Chile in the mid-1980s during the Pinochet dictatorship an attempt to show friction within family relationships and the presence of a Nazi refugee in Chile was censored as it was deemed to give a distorted view of Chilean reality (*La Dama del Balcón—The Lady on the Balcony*).

The phenomenal success of telenovelas in attracting audiences has accrued considerable economic power to TV Globo of Brazil and Televisa in Mexico, and

Domestically produced serials and series are often popular with national audiences, **Kampos** from the Cyprus Broadcasting Corporation offered a mirror to life on the island in the early 1980s.

105

The Carriage used the telenovela format to tell the story of Benito Juárez on Mexico's Televisa.

led to original novela production in Colombia, Venezuela, and Puerto Rico. In Brazil they have remained an essential part of the schedule for TV Globo—which runs three per night, six days of the week. The imbalance in trade flows has led to a number of new entrants: in Chile after 1976 there was a concerted move to achieve a national fiction through novelas. Success in overseas markets, particularly for TV Globo, which has sold to over 100 countries, has included a strange reverse colonization pattern *vis-à-vis* Portugal from the Globo output.

Interestingly some of these novelas have become quasi-event television in emerging societies to which they have been exported: *La Escrava Isaura* in China, Czechoslovakia, or Cuba, *Gabriela* in Angola, *The Rich Also Cry* in Russia. As a sociologist suggested, in Czechoslovakia *Isaura's* success could be explained because it was shown 'in a situation of social disappointment, the public seek consolation in fairy tales, as was the case in Czechoslovakia after 1968'.

Indeed the export of serials has become more widespread in recent years. The

Australian soap operas *Neighbours* and *Home and Away* have brought huge audiences in the UK while American daytime soaps have been successful in Italy and France.

Purposes of Drama

Drama output from any television station offers viewers national images and myths alongside imported culture. It is a right of citizenship in the modern world to have access to different views in both current affairs and drama on television. The important debate about the purpose of drama has to be constantly renewed in every nation. The BBC has in recent years proclaimed its mission to act as the national theatre of the airwaves.

Societies in flux have increasingly turned to television for a sense of direction and purpose. For this same reason control of the media has so often been a priority for new regimes. In the 1960s and 1970s in the then Communist bloc television drama served a number of roles: propagandist, pro-social, and national. Much of the output was dull and unchallenging. In Ceauşescu's Romania in 1971 a World War II drama series *The Search* showed the preparations for the anti-fascist uprising in August 1945; in 1976–7 *Independence War* 'celebrated' the centenary for Romania of independence from the Ottoman empire. In Hungary in 1983 as the control of Soviet communism eased, Miklos Jancso's *Faustus, Faustus, Faustus* told the sombre chronicle of post-war Hungary from Liberation to 1973 through one man's story.

The popular sitcom **Claffy** from the Jamaica Broadcasting Corporation.

Similar national pretensions informed Iranian television in the mid-1980s with *Sarbedaran*, for example, based on the revolt against the Mongolians in 1357. In the wake of the overthrow of the Shah and the coming to power of a fundamentalist Islamic regime TV drama was used to serve a particular need and purpose. In Turkey in the early 1990s the public station TRT attempted to seize the mantle of quality in response to commercial pressures and produced the mini-series *Ataturk's Children* on the struggle for Turkish independence. In Singapore the serial *The Awakening* in the 1980s told the story of the struggle against British colonial rule.

At root television drama plays a major role in all television systems because it aspires, even without self-conscious reflection, to address the cultural identity of its audience. The fear of all-pervading American imported entertainment as the dominant order of TV is true only to the extent that it was widely sold and provided audiences world-wide with high-cost productions which they could interpret (even subvert in their reading) and comprehend—but the insidious side-effects can be overstated. It has been repeatedly proven that whenever local drama fare is available it always secures the largest audience—whether *The Mukadota Family* in Zimbabwe, *Mirror in the Sun* in Nigeria, or *Claffy* in Jamaica.

One example of cultural specificity which perhaps unsurprisingly eschews the American style format is the samurai drama series in Japan, with its violent but stylized sword fighting. Although the popularity of this genre has waned in recent years with an ageing demographic profile amongst its audience there has been a minor revival and 1990s examples include *Nobunaga* (set in the sixteenth century), and *Ooka Echizen* and *Mito Komon* (set in the nineteenth century). However, as in other countries romantic melodrama and detective stories are ever popular in Japan.

Genre

Within TV drama there are enduring thematics and genre—crime, action, melodrama, the familial are invariably present. Their roots can usually be traced to a popular fiction form in other media. It is in these culturally specific frames that the representations and myths of a society are reproduced and reformulated.

At worst replication of generic successes leads to format TV. However, genre conventions are only a starting-point. Producers working within the confines of a given genre with specific audience targets can and have created highly innovative work. Examples such as *Hill Street Blues* or *Miami Vice* had considerable impact with reverberations for the aesthetics of TV crime shows world-wide.

Crime

The crime genre is a universal fiction form which on television encompasses *Inspector Derrick* and *Tatort* in Germany, *The Sweeney* in Britain, *Highway Patrol* or *Kojak* in the USA. The appeal and importance of such programmes can be judged from their longevity and presence in all national programme schedules. They are derivative, often directly, of crime literature and cinema.

They are a variant of popular tales which can be understood as a means by which we renew the commitment of people to their society. Crime fiction can be seen to carry some of a society's responses to sources of danger or anxiety. But it is also responsive as a genre to contemporary neuroses. The moral fable re-establishes an equilibrium whenever disorder seems to threaten. The detective story is a fiction of alienation addressed to an experience of anxiety.

The nineteenth-century detective story evolved by the 1930s to become the *roman noir*, with film equivalents, as the genre came to terms with organized crime and official corruption. The integrity and individualism of the Sherlock Holmes-like figure was replaced by the detective working against the ambiguities of the corrupt city. The urban crime story after a period of parallel production eventually replaced the Western in film and television—the colonization of the frontier is replaced by the hero in the underworld of the city, maintaining his integrity in the face of corruption and anomie. The law enforcer is both a protective hero and a scourge on dishonest government. In contemporary USA, in particular, the crime melodrama speaks to contemporary anxieties and concerns. It is preoccupied with vulnerability and threat, but provides ways in which the threat can be, and indeed, is, overcome or countered.

Television crime stories play out fundamental social moralities before a national audience. But their place on the schedules has been constrained by the increasing concern with the effects of violence in programmes which have at times affected programme content.

Action-packed crime series are popular in many countries. Germany's **Tatort** has been a ratings winner for a number of years.

Dramatic licence and the romanticization and paradoxical status of the modern hero had increased with time, with a parallel shift in treatment. Any history of the crime genre has to reflect on the decline of the realist imperative, the increasing violent action scenarios and the later impact of a postmodern aesthetic. This can be gauged by the changes between *Dixon of Dock Green* or *Z Cars* and *The Sweeney* and *The Professionals* in Britain, or between *Dragnet*, *Perry Mason*, and *Highway Patrol* and *Starsky and Hutch* or *Cagney and Lacey* in the USA. More recently the use of more schematic narratives, in *Hill Street Blues* and *Miami Vice*, adapting innovations from documentary and music video in a *mélange* of styles, still retained the underlying message of reassurance. That more recently there has been a return to the familiar and the domestic milieu, and a return to the realist aesthetic, with series like *The Bill* in the UK, can be attributed in part to the increasing concerns about the genre's influences in the wider society.

Melodrama

The generic formatting of television drama led to much imitation of the 'melo-dramatic' successes of the late 1970s. The hugely successful prime-time melodrama series *Dallas* and *Dynasty*, which had grown out of the American daytime soaps, were cloned world-wide.

The US networks had wanted to attract a greater share of male viewers to examples of the genre in prime time. They altered the form to give more emphasis to prominent male characters than had been the case for daytime soaps. With higher production budgets available for prime-time programming the visual realization owed much to filmic melodrama, while settings were transferred from the suburban middle-class milieu to glamorous bourgeois settings. Their huge success in international markets followed the earlier pattern of American dominance of the trade in TV programming and led to the coining of the phrase 'wall-to-wall *Dallas*'.

Chateauvallon, a much talked about Euro-soap, was a deliberate response in France: a challenge to US dominance; while in Germany *Schwarzwaldklinik* played a similar role. *Schwarzwaldklinik* took elements from German cinema and from the prime-time melodramatic format to offer national myths to a national audience—it borrowed the glorification of landscapes and folk life from the 'Heimatfilm', together with the trustworthy doctors and hospital stories long successful in medical dramas. In India *Khandaan* adopted the same high-cost family drama formula, while in the Philippines *Mansyon* was a local derivative of *Dynasty* and *Victoria Hills* from *Falcon Crest*. Turkey's public television produced *The Eagles Fly High*, a *Dallas* clone.

Television drama serves a range of purposes. It can act as a national theatre devoted to representing nations to themselves. For TV executives it is part of a quest for audiences: habituated viewing underpinned by the aspiration of entertaining as many people as possible for a variety of ends. Its centrality to the purposes of broadcasting cannot be understressed.

The global success of **Dynasty** and **Dallas** led to many imitations including the Turkish **The Eagles Fly High** (TRT).

Entertainment Formats

Entertainment on television is not a distinct genre but a continuum of programming which extends from drama at one end to coverage of the real world at the other. It includes comedy, game shows, quizzes, and variety shows. It is television's space for expressions of abundance, but also in part, like drama, for coping with society's neuroses.

There are two traditions in the understanding of entertainment. One view sees it as easy, pleasurable, hedonistic, and democratic, as opposed to the serious, refined, and cognitively difficult areas of high culture. Entertainment offers available pleasures in the face of the problems of life. This can be seen either as reconciling audiences to the status quo; or, as a way to lead people to question and criticize the status quo by reference to the ideal world in the entertainment utopia. Abundance, energy, and community are seen then in distinction to the dreariness of everyday life.

Game shows are hugely attractive because they are cheap to produce and when successful they generate large audiences. Formatting is central to many of the most successful game shows. Many of the factory-line-produced American game shows have been adapted to local conditions and delivered huge audiences in Europe and elsewhere. It was a trend which started with programmes like *The $64,000 Question*, the very first big money quiz show in the USA, which premiered in 1955 and transferred to Britain's fledgling commercial television service in the 1950s.

Other successful formats adapted elsewhere include *Fort Boyard* from France which became *Crystal Maze* in the UK, and *Wetten Dass* from Germany which became *You Bet!* in Britain. Programmes such as *The Price is Right* or *The Dating Game*, owned by Goodson Todman, have been formatted for markets throughout the world (*El Precio Justo* in Spain, *Kac Para?* in Turkey, *Der Preis ist Heiss* in Germany). Also adapted across the world is *Wheel of Fortune*, which became *La Roue de la Fortune* in France, *Glucksrad* in Germany, and *Rad van Fortuin* in the Netherlands. These programmes have considerable ratings pulling power, and are produced and retained for this reason.

The legalistic framework within which game show formats are encompassed indicates the lucrative nature of this business in triviality. This is not to decry the impact and importance of game shows. They are flexible. They can be scheduled at any time. Audiences find them relaxing and challenging. There is an in-built tension between chance and rules in a games structure—between the predictable and unpredictable, the controllable and the uncontrollable, which creates enjoyment. Quiz shows can be categorized by their relation to knowledge, and one of the pleasures which comes from watching is that the viewers can measure their own performance against that of contestants. They offer puzzles for viewers to solve, both literally in answering questions and metaphorically in terms of supporting different contestants, and in so doing they actively participate in the creation of their own pleasures. Indeed in Japan the game show form gains the largest audiences. In 1993 *Show by Shobai*, a quiz show about world business, topped the ratings, while variety or quiz shows made up much of the most popular programme fare.

In Slovenia game shows were inflected for political ends during the struggle to separate from the former Yugoslavia. National moments and vernacular inflections intruded into the construction of *She and He* through the orchestration of the game show host Milo Trefalt, showing that even such forms evolve in relation to wider cultural influences—in this case the invention of a new nation-state.

Perfect Match (Grundy, Australia), which was reformatted as *Blind Date* in the UK and as *Herzblatt* in Germany, hooks into a different social phenomenon.

These programmes offer the romantic casino on air and like melodramatic fiction open a space for identification or sympathy for the 'characters'. They tap into an interest in reality similar to that of infotainment programmes ranging from *Rescue 911* in the USA or *999* in Britain, which reconstruct the exploits of the emergency services, or *America's Funniest Home Videos*. In all these formats real people's lives are opened up to the public gaze. This genre of programming became extremely popular in the late 1980s. As they are much cheaper to make than drama and audiences have shown that they like them, they seem likely to remain on the schedules for some time.

The fading popularity of certain genres has been a marked feature in the changing schedules of television across the world, particularly in competitive situations. In the early days of both American and British television the variety show format was popular. Both *The Ed Sullivan Show* in the USA and *Sunday Night at the London Palladium* in Britain featured a range of singing, dancing, and comedy acts and were presented by a strong compère. Such shows virtually disappeared from the schedules in the 1970s in the USA and UK. However, the variety show has for many years remained a staple in the television schedule of many other societies: *Sábados Gigantes* (*Giant Saturdays*) in Chile, *Bei Bio* in Germany, *Sacrée Soirée* in France, *Hola Raffaela* in Spain, *Amigos Siempre Amigos* (*Friends Always Friends*) in Chile, *Superstar* and *Student Canteen* in the Philippines. The continued popularity of the form in Italy has led to a number of hybrid outcomes such as the now infamous *Culpo Grosso*, which sits alongside many traditional variety shows on both RAI and the Berlusconi-owned channels. In Brazil and across the rest of Latin America the long-form variety show continues to be extremely popular with programmes like *Fantástico* and *The Silvio Santos Show*.

Comedy

Many believe that it is within television's comedic output that many of the neuroses of societies first appear on television. Whether it be the position of women, the demystification of divorce, old age, different sexualities, or ethnicity, we find in the situation comedy the first expressions of the changes in the domain of the private.

Comedy is institutionalized humour which contrasts social norms and values in a public forum. Comedy's attack is restricted by the consensus (about values and norms) on which it depends for recognition. In this sense all comedy is extremely national-cultural specific, even though some common themes have travelled, so that something like *Till Death Us Do Part* based on a British working-class bigot could be reformatted for the USA as *All in the Family*, or Thames's *Man about the House* with a story-line based on a bachelor sharing a flat with two bachelor women as *Three's Company*. Equally some American situation comedies attain universality in their address—*M*A*S*H* offered a moral address on the

opposite Formatted game and quiz shows have proliferated. They are cheap and easily adapted to national mores. **The Price is Right** has been an international success.

travails and humanity in war during and after the Vietnam conflict; *The Cosby Show* offered a positive image of family life, able to amuse across different cultures.

Formatting of sitcoms has been attempted quite frequently. That it does not often work confirms the distinctive national characteristics of humour. Situation comedy is not a form which works in Latin America, for instance. There sketch shows dominate such as *Las Mil y Una de Sapag* (*Sapag's Thousand and One*) in Argentina.

Comedy offers a safe space within a society from which to witness social transgression. Jokes destroy hierarchy and order and denigrate dominant systems of value. The humorous context means that views can be expressed which allow the assimilation of more liberal attitudes to social problems. The form allows the temporary challenge to hierarchies of ordered social relationships and effects a relief, albeit not sustained, from the constraints of social dominance and subordination. Many sitcoms have dealt with entrapment—characters unable to escape the constraints of their class, gender, marital status, or work position. Those watching and identifying have been offered ways of coping, or even ways of escaping, literally. They may also create a shared community in which at its most banal viewers can share catchphrases or points of conviviality and laughter.

Less inhibited by social mores and conventions—though still ultimately recuperative and conventional—the unseen political impact of situation comedy may have been considerable. As well as the unsettling images of bigotry in *Till Death Us Do Part* or *All in the Family*, situation comedy has asserted the feminist cause through humour (*Roseanne*) and undermined many of the prejudices against retired people (*Golden Girls*).

The basis of most situation comedy is that all characters will revert to their original position at the end of every episode. Problems are invariably resolved. Characters are stereotypical, or recognizable as social types. Situation comedy on television in the UK and USA first developed using known comic personalities who had shows constructed around them. *Hancock* or *Lucy* used the 'realistic' almost intimate mode of delivery with self-contained narratives. Lucille Ball remains the most memorable of the zany actresses in domestic situation comedy in TV's formative era.

There is a remarkable parallel between the themes of successful situation comedies and the social history of modern society. In the 1960s the key British sitcoms dealt with class and social mobility (or lack of it): *Hancock*, *Steptoe and Son*, *The Likely Lads*, and *The Liver Birds*. In the 1970s there was a heightened debate about gender roles and the undermining of traditional familial roles and structures: sitcoms which focused on these issues included *Butterflies* and *Agony*. In the middle of this period the race issue had first emerged in *Till Death Us Do Part* and in *Love Thy Neighbour* in the late 1960s and early 1970s, at a time when the British culture began to come to terms with its new multicultural realities. The most popular hits of the 1970s and 1980s—*Dad's Army*, *'Allo, 'Allo*, *Hi-de-Hi*, *Last of the Summer Wine*—had a clear relationship to a popular memory based on nostalgia, with particular emphasis on the Second World War.

Representations in comedy have been particularly sensitive indicators to changes in attitudes in society. The USA's *Three's Company* and *Charlie's Angels* were, in the late 1970s, part of the era when women's sexuality became represented in a more unabashed, though often sexist way. Frank discussion of personal issues became possible in *All in the Family* or *Maude*. *Happy Days* in the mid-1970s was successful in showing a teenage loner coping.

In the 1980s the multicultural diversity of society was used as a context for programmes like *No Problem!* or *Desmond's* in the UK, while in the USA *The Fresh Prince of Bel Air* bore the same messages. The late 1980s saw the onset in the UK of a new type of humour exemplified by *The Young Ones*, *The Comic Strip*, and similar comedies which set out to undermine the realistic narratives of most comedy with absurdist disruptions. For the 1990s lower-middle-class aspiration in *Only Fools and Horses* and the role of the old in *One Foot in the Grave* provided comic relief.

Various situation comedies have sought to amend the traditional format of returning characters to their original situation by introducing a serial narrative structure. *The Fall and Rise of Reginald Perrin* and *Butterflies* in Britain, and *Soap* and *Mary Hartman, Mary Hartman* in the USA were early examples of the narrativization trend. There has also been a transfer of sitcom elements to other genres. So, for example, in Britain *Minder* has mixed generic features from crime series and situation comedy, as did *Moonlighting* in the USA. The enrichment and diversification of the genre has not precluded star vehicles, with Lenny Henry in Britain and Bill Cosby in the USA two important examples.

Situation comedy has remained a staple of American and British television because of its popularity. Many early American sitcoms remain in syndication— from *Lucy* to *The Beverly Hillbillies*, *The Mary Tyler Moore Show*, and *Sergeant Bilko* to Jackie Gleason's *The Honeymooners*, while British sitcoms are repeated regularly.

The other comedic form which emerged on television during the important formative 1960s was satire. This development has never been particularly strong and has tended to wax and wane according to the political climate in different countries. In Britain *That Was the Week that Was* with political satire, songs, and sketches and *Monty Python's Flying Circus* with its grotesque humour emerged in the 1960s and were complemented by *Rowan and Martin's Laugh in* in the USA. NBC later introduced *Saturday Night Live*, which launched the careers of many American comedians including John Belushi, Dan Akroyd, and Chevy Chase. By the 1980s the emergence of *Spitting Image* in Britain, and *La Bebete Show* in France, was seen as bravely maintaining the tradition of political satire. *La Bebete* and *Spitting Image* rely on latex models of politicians and others who are lampooned. That the tradition is alive is confirmed by the emergence of *Saluti e Baci* in Italy, which deals with corruption in that society, while in Germany in the early 1990s

The enduring popularity of television satire: France's **Les Guignols de l'Info**.

a satirical comedy *Motzki* was produced about Germany's unification problems, causing widespread offence in the best traditions of the form. Russian television in its post-Soviet days has adapted Russian comedic traditions in entertaining satirical variety shows such as the *Masks* series.

Politics and TV Forms

The key questions about television drama and entertainment concern its impact and influence. We need to understand the relationship between the different aesthetics and forms and how they change or affect peoples' view of the world. It is not a simple relationship by any means and needs to be considered in the light of varying political contexts, changing audience demand and understanding, and the aspirations and intentions of producers.

Representation questions have been high on the agenda for many activist groups in the 1980s and early 1990s, replacing an earlier concern with the avoidance of challenge through the use of realism. There has been a belief that the melodramatic form can be subversive of dominant values. The popular as a resource for oppositional views is no more provable than the effect of violent representations on the young. However, as noted above, it is a more likely effect than the simple escapist thesis so prevalent in the 1960s, and research has shown diverse and surprising range to the interpretations of what would be considered mainstream programming.

The impact of 'political correctness' in the 1990s has been considerable in affecting how television has handled representations of women, ethnic minorities, and the disabled. Indeed the creativity of screen writers has encompassed these changing modes of thinking.

Censorship is a matter which is seldom far from the surface in considering television's role in society. Its operation, both directly and indirectly through the self-censorship mode, tests the limits of tolerance in any society. Cases of attempted censorship such as the row in Britain over *Death of a Princess* about a member of the Saudi royal family are probably outnumbered by those films or programmes never transmitted or even made. These are usually examples where the political culture could not face up to its own internal contradictions. Examples abound in Latin America in the 1970s, while in Britain programmes covering Ireland or the peace movement have encountered difficulties. (*Shoot to Kill* and *The War Game* are but two examples.)

Technological change in recent years has boosted the availability of channels for all kinds of 'niche' programming. In Europe entertainment channels, often playing out imported US material, have tended to act as pathbreakers. The 'aesthetic' heart of TV has changed and is changing in this development. The co-production fix and the centrality of formatting have begun to dominate. The longer-term cultural and political consequences are unknown. The worst excesses which many fear as permanent changes may quickly change—in Italy the dominance of US imports on the Berlusconi channels in the 1970s was transformed to support for domestic production through the late 1980s.

Whether different types of programming are needed in the new environment is an open question. The Game Show Channel or Ha! (The Comedy Channel) or Telenovelas are just three of an ever-increasing range of genre channels to have emerged in recent years. Film and television have been on the path of convergence since the decision by the US studios to work with rather than against television. Now each is intertwined inextricably with the other—organizationally and in terms of programme exploitation.

The global cost equations are posing real questions about the sufficiency of supply and quality. Changing patterns of ownership of TV broadcasters are raising serious questions about domination and political influence, and relatedly about whether we will much longer have images of our own culture on our screens.

Whether it be stereotyping or cult status, political impact or violent effect, television cannot evade its responsibilities to its audiences as the main modern medium of communication. Change is taking place fast and programming is becoming available in an ever-increasing range of delivery modes, but the case for adequate representation of the diversity of cultures in future output must continue to be made in every society.

5

Non-Fiction Television

Michael Tracey

Television and the Real World

There are few people today who do not have a sense of the rest of the world. They may not be massively knowledgeable, they may have little more than flickering images in front of the mind's eye. But chances are that their sense of what is going on elsewhere on the planet is derived from television. In particular their sense of key moments in history has been defined by television programmes, which in effect constitute the punctuation points of television history and thus provide its grammar. The Coronation of Queen Elizabeth II in 1953. Images of Soviet tanks crushing the Hungarian revolution of 1950. June 1963, Buddhist monk Quang Duc immolates himself in a protest against the South Vietnamese government. The cameras are there. August 1963, Martin Luther King stands on the steps of the Capitol building in Washington and tells 200,000 demonstrators and millions more through television 'I have a dream'.

In 1963, a global audience saw the painful coverage of JFK's assassination and funeral and the agonizing moment as the funeral cortège passed, the cameras watched, and JFK's son, John Jr., saluted his father's passing coffin. In August 1965 came a searing report from Morley Safer of CBS from the village of Cam Ne in Vietnam, which was being torched by GIs bearing not just weapons but cigarette lighters, a cruelly banal image that in many people's eyes was a turning-point in the attitude of the American public towards the war. In the early 1960s the TV public of the USA watched, largely in horror, as civil rights campaigners were brutalized in the southern states. In 1968 TV film was smuggled out of Czechoslovakia of the invasion by Soviet forces, crushing the Prague Spring of Alexander Dubček. In that same year came reports of the Tet offensive, which put to death for ever the official line that the USA was winning the Vietnam war and offered one of the most searing images of the war as police chief Nguyen Ngoc Loan shot in the head at point blank range a Vietcong suspect, blood shooting forth like a scarlet geyser from the wretched youth's temple. July 1969, hundreds of millions of people watched Neil Armstrong make his one small step for man, one giant leap for mankind, as he set foot on the surface of the moon. 1974, Richard Nixon, brought down by the scandal of Watergate, moving up the steps of the helicopter that was to take him into ignominious early retirement, turning on his heels, defiantly facing the cameras and through them America and the world, holding his arms aloft and offering one final victory salute. 1975, Saigon is about to fall, and television viewers throughout the world, but particularly in the USA, are horrified by pictures of a young girl, naked, running along a road, her face creased by pain and fear, her skin peeling away from her body, the effect of napalm, our napalm.

In the summer of 1981 countless millions spent hours in front of their television screens watching a young woman, Diana, marry the 'world's most eligible bachelor', Prince Charles in St Paul's Cathedral. In 1984 Michael Buerk's searing journalism from Ethiopia finally alerted the world to the fact that in that war-ravaged country was a famine of biblical proportions, with images of tiny corpses wrapped in off-white cloth, a totally lifeless landscape. 1985 there was Live Aid, the Bob Geldof-organized charity concert from Wembley Stadium which sought to raise money for the starving and which Geldof, perhaps with a certain hyperbole, claimed at the time was being watched by 1,000 million people. 28 January 1986 the world watched in horror as the space shuttle *Challenger* exploded shortly after take-off, its fiery end captured by the cameras of CNN alone, the videotape of its final moments played time and time again. 1989, during the Romanian revolution as the people of the country were overthrowing the repressive government of Nicolae Ceaușescu, protesters took over the television station, broadcasting their demands for change. The signal was carried by a Soviet satellite, cherry-picked by CNN, and broadcast around the world.

February 1991, the first night of the Gulf War, and millions of viewers sat in front of their TV screens, as the voices of CNN reporters Bernard Shaw, John Hollinworth, and Peter Arnett reported from underneath a table in their hotel room in Baghdad on the US air assault on the Iraqi capital. Then President Bush was watched in 75 million American homes and many more elsewhere as he announced the war, and the first pictures started to come through of the air assault, images like those from a video game as high-tech aircraft avoided the blue fire-fly trails of Iraqi anti-aircraft fire. August 1991, an attempted *coup d'état* against Mikhail Gorbachev, away at his holiday dacha on the Black Sea coast; but the cameras kept rolling, the commentators kept talking to the television audiences of the world, positioned across from the Russian White House as Boris Yeltsin and his supporters said defiantly, 'No, there will be no coup'. May 1991, the cameras gave us the images of Chinese students calling for democracy in Tiananmen Square, Beijing, until the moment when the authorities decided that television going around the world was far too potent a force and pulled the plug, literally. 1992, and videotape is shown, repeatedly, of several Los Angeles police officers beating the helpless Rodney King.

All these moments, to which the key was the television camera, suggested that the planet had become not so much a global village, more a colossal television lounge, with huge audiences watching multiple versions of their own lives. And yet the very nature of the examples, which so readily present themselves to the eye, speaks to slowly evolving trends within non-fiction television: the move from the searching and the analytical to the dramatic, the immediate, the wrought, the superficial. If television as it developed after 1945 became the poetry of the age, the stanzas got progressively shorter, less taxing, and more devoid of meaning.

At 3 p.m. on 2 November 1936 the BBC inaugurated the first television service in the world. There were speeches, jugglers, and comedy dancers. At 9 p.m. Leslie Mitchell introduced the first edition of *Picture Page*, 'a magazine of topical and general interest'. Thus at the very beginning of television non-fiction was prominent, but already nudging up against more obviously entertainment-oriented programming. Sales of TV sets were stimulated by the television coverage of such notable events as the Coronation of George VI and the return to Heston airport in 1938 of Neville Chamberlain who, following his meeting with Hitler, was shown on the tarmac declaring 'peace in our time'.

In the USA NBC's television service was inaugurated when Franklin Delano Roosevelt opened the New York World's Fair on 30 April 1939, and the station produced a three-and-a-half-hour broadcast of the event. CBS went on the air on 1 July 1941, and its evening schedule, which was to say the least threadbare, included fifteen minutes of news.

From its earliest days then, television was viewed as a means of showing the viewer 'reality' as well as entertainment. However, the early use of television for the coverage of political and other current events was somewhat laggard. For example, in Britain in the early 1950s, during the period of the BBC's monopoly, the only political discussion which took place on television was on a programme called *In the News*. Opposition to this nevertheless came from both the major parties, and the programme slowly disappeared, only to be reincarnated on ITV's *Free Speech*. BBC TV news, which began on 2 January 1950, was remarkably conservative. It was not until 4 September 1955 that the BBC showed the faces of its newscasters, though even then they were still not named. The BBC, particularly in the guise of its Head of News, Tahu Hole, was by turns neurotic and obsequious. No story, for example, could be carried unless it had been confirmed by several sources. And if the Royal Family did *anything* the account would inevitably lead the bulletin.

ITN started in September 1955, and its first editor-in-chief, Aidan Crawley,

BBC cameras capture the arrival of Harold Wilson back in London from his Huyton constituency shortly before his 1964 General Election victory.

decided to call the presenters *newscasters* rather than *newsreaders*, and thought of ITN as television's 'first popular newspaper', which not only showed the newscasters but named them. ITN established its lead over the BBC journalistically when it brought back film in 1956 of the Hungarian uprising, and of British and French troops landing at Suez. In 1957 ITN's Robin Day landed a world exclusive in an interview with Egyptian leader Nasser that was noted for its journalistic sharpness. The BBC, ever hidebound by propriety, strictly followed the 'fourteen-day' rule, which prohibited discussion of any subject to be raised in Parliament within the prior two weeks. The rule persisted until 1956.

The Corporation also put distance between itself and elections. The Rochdale by-election in 1958 was in fact the first British election to be televised. The assumption up until that time had been that to cover any election on television would be in breach of the Representation of the People Act. A commercial company, Granada Television, within whose franchise area Rochdale lay, decided to challenge this belief. The following year saw the first British General Election covered by television. That of 1964 is regarded as the first real 'TV' election in Britain, with a clever manipulator of the medium, Harold Wilson, as leader of the Labour Party, up against the hapless Conservative Prime Minister, Alec Douglas Home, who came over as someone from a politically bankrupt, other age. Wilson led the Labour Party from 1964 until his surprise resignation in March 1976. His time in 10 Downing Street was pockmarked by tussles between himself and the BBC. At the time of the General Election of 1966 when Wilson won a major victory, relations were so strained between him and the BBC that he refused to be interviewed in the special studio which the Corporation had set up on his train as he returned in victory to London. In 1971, there was a huge row over a programme called *Yesterday's Men*, a documentary about what life was like for Wilson and his colleagues after they lost power in the election of 1970.

By 1974 Wilson's image was being carefully manicured by the English film director David Wickes: new suits, clean shirts, a valet, and a make-up man, to make sure that the candidate did not have the Nixon problem of appearing 'shiny and sweaty'. Wickes had been schooled in American political campaigns, and the model of John F. Kennedy was at the front of his and Wilson's minds.

In the United States NBC's first regular news programme, begun in 1947, was *Camel News Caravan*, presented by John Cameron Swayze. NBC had a deal with Fox Movietone which supplied newsreels on 35 mm film. CBS's Television News with Douglas Edwards received newsreels from Hearst-MGM's Telenews. The television news which was emerging emphasized short treatments of stories on the grounds that the stations did not want to bore the audience. It was in response to this trivialization that current or public affairs programmes developed, in which the news could be given an in-depth treatment.

The United States had developed a tradition of covering elections much earlier than Britain. The Republican National Convention of 1940 was the first of its kind to be televised, and the election returns were televised from an NBC auditorium improvised into a newsroom. Viewers saw the newstickers tapping out reports, reporters rushing around, and commentators explaining the results as they came in. Not much has changed. Shortly after the attack on Pearl Harbor, 7 December 1941, CBS presented a 90-minute TV documentary on the Japanese attack, the first of its kind. In 1942 NBC ran a training programme for air raid wardens, the first organized attempt at educational television. On 23 June 1948 a telecast of the Republican National Convention in Philadelphia was picked up by a plane flying at 25,000 ft over Pittsburgh and rebroadcast to a nine-state area of 525 miles. The end of the war was marked by television coverage of the opening session of the United Nations Security Council at Hunter College in New York. Truman's State of the Union address in 1947 was the first covered by television, and in that year the first surgical operation was televised, at a meeting of the American College of Surgeons at a New York hotel.

In 1951 Estes Kefauver, chair of a committee which was investigating crime, permitted the Senate hearings to be broadcast live. Huge audiences were drawn to the spectacle of gangsters and their girlfriends being interrogated by Committee Counsel Rudolph Halley. It was these hearings, which had taken the American public to the heart of the political process, that catapulted Kefauver to national fame and to a run for the presidential nomination in 1952—funded by the monies he made by selling the story of the hearings to the *Saturday Evening Post*.

In 1952 there was a clear sign of the way in which television was evolving when the actor Robert Montgomery coached Eisenhower in relaxing in front of the cameras. The 1952 campaign also saw slick one-minute commercials for Eisen-hower. Adlai Stevenson refused to play along with the manicured rise of Ike, much preferring long speeches and discussions. He lost the election. Senators and Congressmen began to take courses in how to speak in front of the camera. Delegates at conventions were warned not to pick their noses lest the camera catch them in the act. The 'actor's smile' emerged as a necessary prop for any successful politician, and conventions were 'redesigned' to suit the needs of TV and its audience. The Eisenhower administration had led the Presidency into using television in the way in which Roosevelt had used radio.

It was in the 1952 campaign that Nixon delivered his legendary Checkers speech. Accused of financial impropriety, Nixon asked for, and received, air time to defend himself. The defence speech he offered was 'I'm not a quitter, and we're keeping the dog'—a reference to a gift of a dog from a supporter to his daughters. The speech was brilliantly successful and saved Nixon's career, and the Eisenhower–Nixon ticket won a major victory at the polls.

On 26 September 1960 Nixon debated with Kennedy on television, in what proved to be a disaster for him. He looked ill, almost seedy, especially in contrast to the sun-tanned Kennedy. The director of the transmission, Don Hewitt, was persuaded by JFK's people that the candidates should stand at lecterns rather than sit. Nixon had been in hospital for surgery on his leg and thus was in consid-erable discomfort, and kept shifting his weight from leg to leg. There were all kinds of accusations that CBS deliberately misled Nixon, for example on the colour of the studio walls, which he was told would be dark, thus suggesting a light suit. The walls were light. JFK turned up in a dark suit. The reaction shots also showed Nixon sweating, biting his lip, wiping his forehead—not surprising given that he was running a temperature. The effect, however, was to portray someone who looked dishevelled and shifty. Seventy-five million Americans watched the debate, and others listened on radio. Polls seemed to indicate that those who watched thought Kennedy had won, those who listened, Nixon. More than 115 million Americans watched at least one of the debates, and the percent-age of the electorate that voted rose from 60.4 per cent in 1956 to 64.5 per cent in 1960. We see here the moments in which television matured into the national debating chamber, as news and documentary moved to the heart of the televi-sion schedule.

Kennedy's press conferences as President were the first to be televised live. At the time of the Bay of Pigs affair in 1961 and the Cuban missile crisis in 1962, he effectively used the medium to speak directly and comfortingly to the American people. Indeed it was during this time that using television as the place to find out things was becoming *the* national and international habit. If there is one moment, however, at which one can say the medium finally matured into some-thing of enormous significance, it was the coverage of JFK's assassination and funeral: days on end of uninterrupted coverage, soothing the national and international mind by informing, telling the people what was happening, reflect-

Cuban refugees in the USA watch anxiously as President Kennedy broadcasts during the 1962 Cuban missile crisis.

ing, and consoling. The veteran producer Fred Friendly commented: 'It was broadcasting's finest hour. And I think it may have saved this country; at least it got us through that period until we had a succession to the next president. . . . Television was for those four days the sinew, the stabilizing force, the gyroscope that held the country together.'

In 1962, after he had lost the California gubernatorial election, Nixon had observed to reporters that 'you won't have Richard Nixon to kick around anymore'. However, Nixon did return to power in 1968 and demonstrated a serious distrust for journalists in general, and particularly of certain newscasters he deemed unfriendly. Indeed, he was so suspicious of 'unfriendly' newscasters that during the 1968 election, he appeared on a series of programmes which in effect were commercials paid for by his supporters. Nixon was seen chatting to sympathetic housewives, blacks, farmers, in short to a middle America which was his natural constituency. As President, Nixon used direct addresses to the American public, but became more and more frustrated and angry as he found his comments critically analysed by network pundits. In response, Vice-President Spiro Agnew was encouraged to attack television, most famously in a speech on 13 November 1969, in which he described the networks as those 'nattering nabobs of negativism' and not so subtly reminded them that they broadcast with licences issued by government. The consensus seemed to be that following Agnew's assault the networks bent the knee a little. They certainly helped Nixon with their coverage of his visit to China in 1972. Eventually, however, with their portrayal of Nixon's manifestly disingenuous commentary on the Watergate scandal (when men hired by the Republicans broke into the headquarters of the

Democratic Party and the Nixon White House proceeded to cover up its involvement) and of the Senate hearings, TV finally helped bring Nixon down.

If the 1950s saw the rise to power of Nixon, the Iago of American politics, so these years also saw the rise of someone who came to personify the vast journalistic potential of the new medium, Edward R. Murrow. Murrow's *See It Now* began in 1951, and rapidly became successful and powerful. In 1953 Murrow took on Senator Joe McCarthy. He did so in the episode of *See It Now* called *The Case against Milo Radulovich, A0589839*. Radulovich had been forced out of the Air Force by the McCarthyite forces which so dominated US politics at the time, because of the alleged political sympathies of his parents. The programme led to his reinstatement. In March 1954 *See It Now* did a further programme in which Murrow, in a more direct confrontation, dissected McCarthy's accusations against alleged communists in public office. In a famous remark in the commentary he said: 'This is no time for men who oppose Senator Joseph R. McCarthy's methods to keep silent.' The programme was the beginning of the end of McCarthyism, brought down by the brilliance of the production and the massive credibility of his accuser, Murrow. There is one small but telling and important footnote to this famous programme. Everyone understood that there might be enormous repercussions for the network by taking on McCarthy. It was even suggested that CBS could be forced out of business. Murrow asked William Paley, the Chairman of CBS, if he wanted to see the programme before it went out. Paley declined, trusting Murrow's judgement. Just before the broadcast Paley phoned Murrow and

The man who brought down McCarthy: Ed Murrow on the set of **See It Now**.

McCarthy rehearses his speech before going on CBS in November 1953 to reply to the increasing attacks on 'McCarthyism'.

said, 'I'll be with you tonight, and I'll be with you tomorrow.' When CBS gave McCarthy air time to rebut the Murrow attack he only served to damage further his own case and reputation, coming over as a ranting bully and bigot. The *See It Now* programmes acted as a backbone transplant to others and later in 1954 a Senate committee called McCarthy to account for his accusations of communist infiltration of the armed forces. In one historic moment, with the television cameras showing the crumbling character of McCarthy, the Army's defence counsel Joseph N. Welch asked, with venom in his voice, 'Have you no sense of decency, sir? At long last have you no sense of decency?'

See It Now ended in 1958, a victim of the commercial pressures which even then were beginning to build. Just before Murrow's departure he and Friendly, working with producer David Lowe, collaborated on another documentary that as with so much of Murrow's work was to enter legend. The programme was called *Harvest of Shame* and portrayed the plight of the nation's migrant workers. The ending to this is a classic example of what made Murrow the greatest television journalist we have ever seen, and probably will ever see, his words a product of extraordinary professional expertise reflected through a deep humanity: 'Those are the people out there who make us the best fed people in the history of the world. They don't earn a living. They have no constituency. They can't do anything to help themselves. Maybe we can. Good night and good luck.'

The turbulence of the 1950s demonstrated for the first but far from last time the potential of reality to make for gripping television: the Suez crisis in 1956 and the Israeli invasion of the Sinai; Khrushchev's denunciation of Stalin and then crushing of the Hungarian revolution; the launch of *Sputnik* in October 1957; the sending of troops in 1957 to Little Rock, Arkansas, to enforce desegregation of public schools; Castro's seizure of power in 1959; Khrushchev's visit to the USA in 1959 and his bombastic defence of Marxism to the TV interviewer David Susskind. All these events were feeding the growth of television.

The 1950s in the USA also saw the rise to fame of a number of extremely talented television journalists, such as Murrow, John Daly, Walter Cronkite, Chet Huntley, David Brinkley, Howard Smith, and Edward Morgan. Programmes

Drinkers at a pub in Wandsworth, London listen intently as Prime Minister Eden warns that Britain can never accept the seizure of the Suez Canal by Egyptian President Nasser.

such as *Meet the Press*, begun in 1947, *Face the Nation*, Mike Wallace Interviews, *CBS Reports* with Walter Cronkite, *The Huntley–Brinkley Report*, and Murrow's *Person to Person* presented political celebrities open to scrutiny by highly skilled interviewers. In fact such was the impact of these programmes in the 1950s that Sunday afternoon became known as 'politics time' and politicians sought out these occasions to make major announcements, ensuring front-page coverage on Monday mornings. From a production standpoint their programmes remained, well into the 1960s, somewhat wooden and studio bound. This was the age before jet travel and satellites, light camera equipment and recording gear, which, beginning in the 1960s, were radically to transform news and current affairs programmes.

The reputations of both television's coverage of political affairs and of certain key personalities were greatly boosted by the increasing involvement with elections. The first programme with which Walter Cronkite was involved was CBS's *Pick the Winner*, broadcast during the election of 1952. The programme provided a forum for candidates to air their views. Huntley and Brinkley came together at the 1956 Republican convention.

The 1950s were proving to be very much the beginning of a golden age of public affairs documentary. In 1952 NBC produced the 26-part series *Victory at Sea*. Within a few weeks of *Harvest of Shame*, NBC produced a major programme, *The U2 Affair*, and NBC produced *Yahni No*. In Britain in the 1950s there was an equally powerful development of the documentary tradition: 'The aim is to forge a new style of television journalism' was how the BBC's *Radio Times* put it in September 1952. The film-maker John Grierson had defined documentary as 'the creative treatment of actuality'. The tradition on television was best represented by Norman Swallow's series *Special Enquiry* and the documentaries of Denis Mitchell. Swallow described the origins of his series: 'We were inspired by Picture Post and, in television terms, by the Ed Murrow and Fred Friendly series See It Now . . . . together with the old British documentary tradition . . . up to that point (television's) treatment of what we call current affairs subjects had been a little pompous. It was mostly so-called experts . . . and the thought was that we would do something in which our presenter would in fact be one of us, so the presentation would be from the point of view of the audience, of the public, not from the point of view of someone who knew everything about it or thought he did.' This documentary tradition thus focused on stories about housing, education, youth, old-age, race, food poisoning, disability. Here was being articulated the belief that a proper, even necessary, function of TV is to examine the condition of society.

This was clear evidence of the *See It Now* technique being adopted around the world; the moving of the focus from the powerful to the ordinary, from political élites to the man in the street, from the centre stage of formal politics to the anterooms of human life, always tied to a tough crusading journalism. In Britain the programme that most obviously followed down this path, all the while evolving

into a magazine format, was *Tonight*, which started in 1957, the brainchild magazine of the brilliant, quixotic, but sometimes difficult Donald Baverstock. Baverstock recruited from the recently defunct *Picture Post* such names as Fyfe
Robertson, Trevor Philpot, Slim Hewitt, and Kenneth Allsop. He also employed
directors like John Schlesinger, Jack Gold, and Kevin Billington, all of whom went
on to establish major directorial reputations. It was a brilliant success, a blend of
the important and the quirky. Perhaps even truer to the tradition of *See It Now*
was the Granada programme, *World in Action*, produced initially by an
Australian, Tim Hewatt. Hewatt believed in slaying dragons, drawing hard
conclusions always on 'our' behalf against 'them'. He was less than sympathetic
to any crude interpretation of objective journalism, seeing in it a sort of professional castration. A consequence was an inevitable and not infrequent clash with
authority, for example in the 1970s over the always contentious issue of Northern
Ireland.

In the 1960s the documentary tradition, which had developed in the 1950s,
continued to flourish. In 1960 CBS presented an unprecedented total of 765 hours
of news and public affairs, including *CBS Reports*, *Eye-witness to History*, *Face the
Nation*, and *Twentieth Century*. By the 1960s it became a regular event for the
networks to interrupt their schedules for breaking news stories and to pre-empt
regular programmes to keep the audience abreast of developments. At the height
of the Cuban missile crisis, ABC pre-empted six hours for news reports. CBS did
ten hours of uninterrupted coverage of John Glenn's flight into space. There

Walter Cronkite pictured in 1952.

were also numerous and successful specials dealing with public affairs: e.g. CBS's *Eisenhower on the Presidency*; ABC's *Meet Comrade Student*; NBC's *Circus*.

In the 1960s the networks also turned their attention to documenting what was happening in the rest of the world. NBC produced *Profile of Communism* and *The Kremlin*, and its multiple-award-winning *The Tunnel*, which documented the actual escape of refugees from East Germany. ABC produced *Saga of Western Man*, a four-part series on significant periods in history, and a documentary version of Theodore White's *The Making of the President*. CBS produced such programmes as *The Roots of Freedom*, *The Law and Lee Harvey Oswald*, *Dialogues of Allan Nevins and Henry Steel Commager*, *Ten Years after Stalin*. In 1963 NBC cleared an entire evening's schedule for *The Negro Revolution*. On 10 September 1967 ABC devoted 4 hours of prime time to a documentary *Africa*, narrated by Gregory Peck, which won the George Polk award. ABC also won an Emmy for its documentary on Westminster Abbey, and much praise for *Ivan Ivanovich*, a detailed examination of the life of a Soviet family. A CBS news special in 1967 presented a conversation between Eric Severeid and longshoreman-philosopher Eric Hoffer. The public reaction was enormous and 'showed that stimulating ideas when presented in a natural, nonstagy way could capture an audience as thoroughly as more elaborate productions'. NBC produced such memorable documentaries as *Khrushchev in Exile* and *Bravo Picasso*.

In Britain in the early 1960s the BBC produced the massively successful *The Great War*. It established a tradition which was to be brilliantly reflected in Thames Television's *The World at War*, in 1978 the series *Palestine*, in Kenneth Clarke's *Civilization* and Alastair Cooke's *America*, and in the 1981 production *The Troubles*.

The coverage of war and domestic 'civil war' always provides some of the most intractable problems facing news and public affairs programming. American television had enormous troubles in dealing with Vietnam, and for much of the war was uncritical of US policy. Morley Safer's *Vietnam* (1967) was traditionally objective but managed to show something of the dark side to the war's execution. Felix Greene's *Inside Vietnam* (1968) was a rare portrayal of the war from the standpoint of the North Vietnamese. CBS's *The Selling of the Pentagon* (1971) revealed the relationship between the Pentagon and arms dealers, causing major controversy. Walter Cronkite was the first TV anchor, and 'the most trusted man in America'. In 1968 he travelled to Vietnam. On his return he broadcast his view that the United States should withdraw, on the grounds that the price for winning was too great. A few weeks later, in March, President Lyndon Johnson withdrew from the candidacy for the next election. On the following day he told a meeting in Chicago: 'Historians must only guess at the effect that TV would have had during earlier conflicts on the future of this nation, during the Korean War for example, at the time our forces were pushed back to Pusan, or World War II, the Battle of the Bulge . . .'. TV animated the anti-war campaign, something well understood by such student radicals as Abbie

Hoffman, and the protests at the 1968 Democratic Convention also showed that 'the whole world is watching us'.

One of the arguments—in military eyes, lessons—of the coverage of the Vietnam war was that television could undermine public morale. It was a lesson well learnt by the emerging officer class of the USA and Britain, who in such later wars as the invasion of Grenada and Panama, the Falklands conflict, and the Gulf War made sure that the constraints on all television journalists were considerable.

In similar vein there is always a problem of how television covers internal wars. There was for example a huge argument in 1972 over the BBC's decision to screen a televised inquiry into the problems of Northern Ireland, *The Question of Ulster*. There was a moment in fact when it appeared as if the Home Secretary, the cabinet minister then responsible for broadcasting, would use his emergency powers and, for the first time in British television history, veto the broadcast. His cabinet colleagues dissuaded him from such a draconian measure. There were, however, to be repeated confrontations between British television and the government over coverage of Northern Ireland: an interview in 1979 with the Irish National Liberation Army, the group which murdered the MP Airey Neave; filming in 1979 in the village of Carrickmore which the IRA 'occupied' for the benefit of the cameras; and most recently a Thames TV programme, *Death on the Rock*, which in effect suggested that the Special Air Service had assassinated in broad daylight three unarmed suspects. All of these programmes caused enormous tension between the broadcasting authorities and the government.

Perhaps some of the most stunning television—certainly in journalistic terms—has come with the coverage of assassinations and assassination attempts: the stabbing of Japanese politician Inejiro Asanuma in October 1960; JFK and Oswald in 1963; Robert Kennedy and Martin Luther King in 1968; George Wallace in 1972; Reagan in 1981; the attempt on the whole Thatcher cabinet in 1984. Or there are the dramatic sieges and confrontations, hijackings, picket line violence, urban insurrection. Hostage taking has also brought drama and audiences to the coverage of current affairs. In 1979, when Iranian students seized the American embassy in Tehran, ABC News president Roone Arledge decided to have a nightly programme on the crisis, produced by Robert Siegenthaler. The series, called *America Held Hostage*, became the successful nightly current affairs programme *Nightline*.

Sometime around 1970 there was in the United States the beginning of a move away from the traditions which had been pioneered in the 1950s and a discovery of the potential importance of local news. Local stations had come to realize that news was cheap, reliable, popular, and therefore good for revenues, while also lending a spurious respectability. The reality was that local news was singularly untouched by substance or journalistic merit. What was happening in fact was a significant erosion in serious television journalism. In the 1980s as the networks became part of larger conglomerates, considerable pressures were brought to

131

Barbara Walters, who became in 1976 the first woman to anchor a major network news programme in the USA—and also at the time the highest paid on-camera newsperson in American television.

bear on news divisions to increase profits and reduce costs, demands which tend not to be in the best interests of good journalism.

The coverage by television of the real world in a real way was by the 1970s beginnning to change, from an ethos of journalism to one of entertainment. The pleasure principle, based on assumptions about what the audience wanted, was becoming dominant. The process would gather pace in almost every major television society throughout the 1970s and 1980s. As ever, though, the exemplar of this change was in the United States. Documentaries and prime-time public affairs began to all but disappear. An assumption was made that the long-form documentary could never be as popular as any entertainment programme, and therefore would always make less money. This is in itself a highly questionable argument, since there were many examples of documentaries which were journalistically powerful but which also attracted good audiences. The most significant aspect of the assumption, however, was that it reflected a changing attitude inside the networks, an attitude, moreover, which was to spread to many parts of the globe. Former CBS News president Richard Salant put it well when he told a conference in 1990 that twenty years ago the network bottom liners did not expect the network news division to turn a profit, and that he took pride in being known at CBS as 'the executive in charge of losing money'. The entertainment programmes like sitcoms made the money and documentaries and other public affairs programmes were regarded as prestigious loss leaders. This is no longer true, in almost any country. And it is certainly not true in the USA, where the idea of *infotainment* moved to centre stage in the treatment of public affairs, and the personality of 'the anchor' seemed to become more important than the content of the information being communicated.

The long-form public affairs programme was, however, also a victim of the success of new magazine programmes, the most famous of which is *60 Minutes*, first broadcast on 24 September 1968. It is the most consistent top ten programme of the past twenty-five years, has been number one in the ratings on sixteen occasions and has never been lower than tenth. It is the only programme in American television history to be the top season programme in three different decades, 1979–80, 1982–3, 1991–2. In other words *60 Minutes*, a public affairs programme, can lay claim to being the most successful programme in the history of American television.

Its success has depended on a number of factors. The three or four stories per episode format allows it to range from the serious to the amusing, to the almost flippant. It reflects large issues through human experiences; it has a certain fearless, prosecutorial style, the good guy against the bad, us against them; it is populist without being trivial; and fronted and produced by the very highest calibre professionals. It is not long-form but in some ways while it is less grainy, not so earthy, it continues the traditions of Murrow and Swallow. And it makes huge amounts of money. Its success has been copied in such programmes as *20/20*, *48 Hours*, *Prime Time Live*, *Street Stories*, and *Day One*.

These are all reasonably agreeable efforts, journalism which remains accessible. In some sense, though, they had and have within them the seeds of what may be the next age of public affairs television, in which all such programming is soaked with the values of commerce, entertainment, the bottom line rather than those of the good journalist. The most obvious examples of this are the debased use of television in election campaigns, and what has become known as 'reality television'.

One important, though somewhat controversial form of non-fiction television is the 'fly on the wall' documentary. One of the best-known examples of this technique of documentary programme-making was Paul Watson and Franc Roddam's *The Family* in 1974 which, some argued, nudged the genre from observation to manipulative entertainment. The success of this programme, however, guaranteed the continued place of the documentary serial with the British television schedule. *Sailor* in 1976 was another prominent and successful example. Philip Donnellan had been making observational documentaries for the BBC since 1958 with his *Joe the Chainsmith*. In 1980 he produced the controversial *Gone for a Soldier*, an examination of the life of British soldiers from 1815 to 1979. Mike Grigsby produced *A Life Apart* (1973) about deep-sea fishermen, and *A Life Underground* (1974) about coal-miners for Granada. The Hungarian documentarist Robert Vas made *Refuge England* (1958), *Nine Days in '26* (1974) about the British General Strike, and *My Homeland* (1976) about Hungary.

Sir Kenneth Clarke
presenting an episode from
the immensely successful
Civilization.

Analysis and Manipulation

By the early 1970s the excitement of early current affairs television was evaporating. Analytical pragmatism became more the order of the day, with the start for example of *Channel Four News* in 1982. Beautiful spectaculars also became popular, prompted by the huge international success of Kenneth Clarke's *Civilization* (1969).

In many instances politicians have gone to considerable lengths to seek to control what people see and hear, and in some democracies there have nevertheless been severe and official restraints on television. In France, for example, where broadcasting was traditionally under very tight political control, between 1956 and 1959 there was not a single programme broadcast dealing with the conflict in Algeria. Every major moment in French politics after 1958 was marked by de Gaulle's television appearances in which he sought to use the medium to galvanize popular support. The most dramatic such moment occurred one night in April 1961 when a French army coup in Algeria challenged his authority. His television appearance calling for national unity and condemning the coup attempt was seen as a crucial factor in rallying public opinion. Television covered his every move, his every appearance, while systematically ignoring those of his opponents. In 1962 the Gaullists used television in their campaign to change the constitution in order to strengthen the Presidency. For months they appeared on numerous news and current affairs programmes explaining why in the national referendum the public should vote for change. The opposition candidates were given only ten minutes each to explain their views. In 1964 when Gaston Defferre announced his candidacy for the Presidency the news report lasted all of thirty seconds and managed not to show his face. When de Gaulle decided to pursue closer relations with China in 1963 a spate of pro-Chinese documentaries began to appear on French television. In similar vein in 1968 both radio and television tried systematically to ignore the May events that almost toppled the government.

Similar control of television can be seen elsewhere. In Mexico in 1988 the government-dominated Televisa was prevented from giving opposition candidate Cuahtemoc Cardenas air time. In Cuba, Fidel Castro, after he seized power in 1959, used television to fashion a new political reality, and the studios of Station CMAB-TV in Havana became the real location of power. Every night Castro would speak for hours on television. Television was nationalized soon after he seized power and became Castro's personal instrument of power. Major decisions would be announced during these performances—agrarian reform, the imposition of the death penalty for terrorists and saboteurs, the declaration of a socialist state, and so on. Castro defined these performances as an advanced form of democracy, by-passing normal electoral processes. Television was used for show trials of opponents of the new regime or of captured infiltrators from the USA. In fact television in Cuba established as its main task the creation of a new socialist consciousness. It was almost as if under Castro television became the seat of government.

In the Soviet Union television remained relatively undeveloped until after Stalin's death in 1953. Gostelradio—the USSR State Committee for TV and Radio Broadcasting—had its duties defined by the 23rd Party Congress, to 'mould a Marxist-Leninist outlook and promote the political and cultural development of all the Soviet people'. Therefore broadcast programmes had such titles as *The Leninist University of Millions*, *Your Leninist Library*, and *I Serve the Soviet Union*. Something similar prevailed throughout the Warsaw Pact, and in many developing countries. This clearly affected the character of non-fiction television, in the sense that news and public affairs programmes would be heavily influenced by the prevailing state ideology. These examples point to an assumption which has been evident throughout the whole history of television, the belief by most politicians in the power of the medium to influence and control events. For example, Ian Smith, after he had made the unilateral declaration of the independence of Rhodesia from the British Commonwealth in 1965, said that control of television was necessary to win 'the war for the minds of men'. Sometimes the political uses of television lead to cynicism. Writing about the Indian television service, Doordarshan—'the tedium is the message'—one Indian journalist, Arun Shourie, observed: 'The function of radio and TV is to lie on behalf of the government.'

There were no news programmes on Soviet television until 1957, and then just once a day. Its use by the late 1950s became central to the ideological campaigns of the party as defined by the Seven Year Plan of 1959–65. In 1960 the Central Committee argued that television was being 'inadequately used to propagandize the achievements of the Soviet people in political, economic and cultural life and to exhibit Soviet man, the builder of Communism'. Television news and public affairs programming inevitably became highly ideological. In the beginning television news in the Soviet Union essentially consisted of reading bulletins from Tass, though by the 1960s there was more use of film. Local stations would produce programming with such titles as *We shall fulfil the seven-year plan ahead of schedule*, *Lenin's ideas are becoming a reality*, and *Through heroic labour we shall carry out the grandiose communist assignment*. Other programmes would be interviews with workers who had fulfilled their production quota.

One success for Soviet television was in covering the country's achievements in space, including the first transmission from a manned spacecraft in August 1962. In the 1960s also the political class became more effective in using what were recognizably Western television techniques. For example, when Kosygin returned from an Asian tour in 1965 his report to the public was handled like that of any Western leader: advance text made available to journalists, background maps, a teleprompter. However, even as television was developing many party officials remained more trusting of the traditional propagandistic methods of leaflets and public meetings. Television was altogether too impersonal for the run of the mill Leninist. With a certain prophetic quality Dizard concludes that TV would be a threat to the ideological certainties of the regime because of 'its capability as a mirror of everyday reality . . . potentially threatening the very foundations of Soviet ideology'.

In every other East European society television was similarly used as an instrument of propaganda. There was, however, some indication of viewer hostility to, or at least distaste for, news and current affairs programmes which were overly ideological. In East German television in the late 1950s and 1960s there was much use of the tradition of 'political cabaret' with satirical comment on such things as fascism in West Germany, NATO, and imperialism. In China, where television did not begin until 1959, again inevitably news, commentary, and public affairs programming was overtly ideological.

It was China, however, which in 1989 provided some of the most powerful political television of modern times, when the students began to call for democracy in Tiananmen Square. They had chosen their timing well, since Mikhail Gorbachev was there for a summit and with him the usual hordes of the world's press. The students understood the potency of the moment and the need for the world's cameras to record not process but symbol. With a touch of genius they constructed their own papier mâché version of the Statue of Liberty and immediately captured the hearts and minds of the American public and those of other Western liberal-democratic societies. And as the cameras looked down from the windows of a Beijing hotel they captured an even more awesome sight that quickly went to every television home around the world. A lone student, wearing dark trousers and white shirt, standing in front of and for a time halting a line of tanks. It was an extraordinarily potent symbol of individual human rights confronting an oppressive state.

There was a strong tradition throughout Europe of rigorous control of the ways in which elections were covered. This included regulations on who could appear, and with what ratio of time; the curtailment of entertainment, dramatic discussion, and documentary programming which might be politically sensitive. All this was done to ensure strict impartiality. In the communist bloc countries at election time television was used to persuade people to vote rather than to offer different points of view. There were after all no different points of view. Without exception European countries, including those with commercial television stations, did not permit the sale of air time to politicians.

In the late 1950s and through the 1960s discussion and talk emerged throughout Europe as a staple of the television schedule. The techniques were similar to those used in such US programmes as *Meet the Press*, or where guests are questioned by members of a studio audience. Austria developed cross-border discussion programmes with its communist neighbours. Belgium developed one of the early phone-in programmes in which the public could question politicians. In Sweden there was a readiness to discuss issues on television which elsewhere would not be addressed until relatively recently, homosexuality for example or advocacy of the overthrow of the political system by Nazis or communists. The Swedes were also an early advocate of the belief that while there should be a commitment to balance in programming this could be achieved over the whole schedule rather than within one programme. A controversial opinion did not therefore have to be answered within the same programme. This approach also came to characterize West German current affairs programmes. Indeed in Germany certain programmes came to be seen as to the left and others to the right, the balance being achieved by having both in the schedule. So, for example, NDR's *Panorama* was left-leaning, while Bayerischer Rundfunk's *Report* leaned right. The bias within these programmes was more implicit than explicit. In another strand of German television, however, there were deliberate biases on display, for example the programme *Kommentar*, in which someone was invited to editorialize about a topic of the day, which might or might not be political.

The collapse of the Soviet Union, in which television played a vital role, inevitably changed the whole issue of how the medium should deal with political and social life. One commentator, Sergei Muratov, wrote: 'TV not only made visible the mechanism of the reconstruction of our society, but also itself more and more became a part of this mechanism, turning from a product of glasnost to a condition for it'. As the change was happening the 'nomenklatura' tried to control the content of programmes, only to find their efforts lambasted by the newly liberated press. At one huge demonstration in Moscow participants carried placards which read 'Goebbels prize—to the first programme of the Central TV'. What had persisted was what Muratov calls 'nomenklatura tv',

which was informed by a belief that if you are armed with a syringe then the person in front of you must be a patient. Hence the reason why the main news programme, *Vremya*, was broadcast on four channels simultaneously—to maximize the effect. Muratov adds, 'Nomenklatura broadcasting engendered a special kind of tv news information independent of facts.' What has sprung up, for example on the new Russian channel Vesti (News), is the offering of opinion and interpretation, highly polemical and subjective in nature: 'television turned into an institution of political missionaries . . . The figure most usually seen on the screen today is an agitator and propagandist . . . Our television combines in itself a heritage of authoritarianism with absolute freedom of journalistic self-display.'

As the issue of the future of Russia continued to become ever more contentious public affairs television became the site of the struggle between the competing forces. In March 1993 police prevented an extreme nationalist, Alexander Nevzorov, from entering the TV studios in St Petersburg on orders from local government officials who had sacked him. Nevzorov used his ten-minute programme *600 Seconds* to espouse what were seen by the Yeltsin forces as deeply reactionary, pro-Soviet positions. In January 1993 Yeltsin had appointed as head the main CIS television service Ostankino the leading liberal figure Valery Bragin.

It is nothing new for political parties to seek to manipulate the mass media for their own ends. 1988, however, seemed to offer evidence of the sheer extent to which this had now gone. As the US presidential campaign wound down an editorial in the *Nation* noted: 'The campaign now concluding may not be the dirtiest or dullest in recent history, but it is certainly the most mediated. Absolutely nothing of interest has happened since this summer's conventions that has not been plotted by the candidates' handlers for media presentation or staged by the media themselves, in fact, for dramatic effect—that is to say, commercial exploitation' (14 November 1988). The campaign was seen to be cynically negative, manipulative, driven by image over substance, sound-bitten (tiny little, meaningless clips of candidates' utterances), spinned (the candidates' people telling journalists what the real story/interpretation was), lying, unanalytical, obsessed with visuals which said little but looked good. That it was so was largely because television allowed it to be so. There were exceptions: public television's the *McNeil–Lehrer Report*, CNN's *Inside Politics '88*, ABC's *Nightline* all tried to offer in-depth coverage. They were, however, at the margins of the schedule, that is, either on little-watched channels or scheduled late in the evening. The sorry condition of the bulk of the coverage led to the conclusion, 'As this year's campaign draws to a close, many reporters and news executives find themselves in agreement. "Television news has been coopted by the image-makers and the media managers" says former network correspondent Marvin Kalb . . . "the manipulators learnt that by controlling the pictures you end up controlling the content".' (*Time*, 14 November 1988.) Politics had become a performing art for

opposite Manipulation of the media is all: Nancy Reagan turns to wave to her husband after her address to the 1984 Republican National Convention in Dallas. He was watching proceedings from his hotel suite.

television, and the conductors were no longer from the Murrow school of journalism, rather from the theatre of the absurd of the likes of Roger Ailes and Lee Atwater. Lloyd Morrisett wrote with a tone that bordered on fearful despair in the wake of the 1988 election:

Most political analysts contend that television has undermined rather than strengthened civic life. They point especially to the way the medium is now used in presidential campaigns . . . [which] offer slogans instead of substance, negative ads in place of statements of belief and purpose. Virtually no attempt is made to educate voters or to address their concerns. What the public receives are the products of managed news and photo opportunities: what it is left with is the idea that one candidate is as bad as the other. Candidates' irresponsibility, the complicity of the media, and the growing apathy of the voting public is causing our system of choice and popular representation to atrophy.

What had chastised Morrisett to utter such words of bleakness was research which showed that in the 1988 election 36 per cent of all the media coverage had been of the campaign as a horse race; 20 per cent had dealt with conflicts between the candidates; and only 9.7 per cent had been discussion of the issues.

In the 1992 presidential election and in the subsequent use of television by President Clinton in the first months of his administration there was a further turning away from traditional television journalism. This suggested not so much an attempt to manipulate news and public affairs programmes, rather they were simply ignored. This is no place to write an account of the apparent malaise of the political classes in almost every major society. What is clear, however, is that because of the continued pressure of economic decline and the intense though barely articulated sense of political instability among citizens of many different countries, there has emerged a deep disenchantment with and a turning away from the core institutions of democratic society, including mainstream journalism. A new home for the dispossessed and the disenchanted, especially in the United States, was the talk shows offered by the increasingly dominant cable television. When candidate Clinton was reeling from the allegation that he had had a long-time mistress, Gennifer Flowers, he turned not to the traditional journalistic outlets but to the New York radio talk show host Don Imus and the television talk show *Donahue*, hosted by Phil Donahue, whose usual fare would be 'mothers who have fallen in love with their daughter's boyfriend' and who once, during a programme on cross-dressing, conducted the whole programme wearing a woman's dress.

Into the 1990s: The New Trivial Pursuit

It is in this context that we can begin to see a major shift in the dominant character of television journalism. The perceived importance of non-fiction television, whether it was being produced within a Western liberal model or the more authoritarian models of the former and current communist world or the democratic dictatorship of the likes of President de Gaulle, lay in the perception that here was an important means of nurturing important public debates about issues that mattered. In effect non-fiction television rested on the Enlightenment belief in the importance of rational discourse about human affairs. This is not to suggest that everything that was being done, every documentary, every news programme, every public affairs programme was inevitably of the highest quality. What was to be applauded was the intent. That is why the little story of Paley's phone call to Murrow is so important. It is why all those moments with which this essay began were so 'obviously' important to so many people: they seemed to capture in their pristine singularity matters of enormous import to national and international populations. If one pans across the decades, however, the pattern that begins to emerge is one of a shift from those commitments to communications which to many eyes are ever more impoverished, such that citizens are less enlightened, more entertained.

Talk shows, for example, have become one of the major sources of political discourse within the United States, with perhaps the most famous being *Larry King Live* on CNN. During the course of the 1992 election, from January to November, Bill Clinton appeared forty-seven times on talk shows, including sixteen appearances on Larry King; Ross Perot appeared on thirty-three talk shows, including fifteen on King; and Bush appeared just sixteen times, three times on King. The Larry King show was deemed to have been crucial to the campaign of Ross Perot in particular, and indeed it was on that programme that he announced his candidacy. In an analysis of the names and phrases most mentioned by all the major media—print and television—the couplet of 'Larry King and Ross Perot' came in third. Perhaps the most memorable such appearance was when Clinton appeared on *The Arsenio Hall Show*, which is purely entertainment, wore a pair of sunglasses, and played a version of 'Heartbreak Hotel' on his saxophone. It is now seen as a turning-point in his fortunes, but, as the wits observed, Elvis was running for President. The point of contention is that such shows are relatively easy for a politician to handle, since the questioning tends not to be as probing as would be the case with a Sam Donaldson of ABC or Jeremy Paxman of the BBC. In other words the programme becomes an opportunity for a politician to get the message out without the intrusive mediations of the journalist. For the viewer they seem to capture that resentment at the political and journalistic class and to provide 'information' in a neatly agreeable, accessible, easy to digest manner. They can thus be remarkably useful politically. The programmes have in fact become the McDonalds of political discourse, and became known to political strategists as 'direct-contact TV'.

Another major development—made both possible and necessary by the niche programming of cable—is the rise of the live coverage of press conferences and speeches. CNN does much of this, as does C-Span, the cable satellite public affairs network. While these can be fascinating for the person who is obsessed by politics, they yet again represent the sidelining of television journalism and thus of the understanding that can flow from the offering of analysis. Yet another example of this is the electronic town meeting in which politicians buy or are given air time to take questions from a studio audience and from viewers over the phone.

Elsewhere the process seemed to be if not quite as bad as in the USA, certainly moving in that direction. Prior to the 1992 British election one commentator noted: 'The public relations spin-doctors from all the parties patrol the [parliamentary] lobby; stop off at the bar; and whisper secrets in the corridor. . . . the major television and radio news and discussion programmes are getting fed up with the bullying attempts by all the parties to control topics for debate and appearances by their spokespersons' (Sarah Baxter, *New Statesman*, 31 January 1992). The problems of covering the election, of having to play a game defined by the politicians, began to nurture scepticism and irony among at least some journalists. One such, Jeremy Paxman, needled by what was described as the 'sheer volume of absurdity and falsehood in this campaign' suggested as the election was called that there would be 'four weeks of humbug . . . torrents of half-truths . . . rattle-toothed zealots bickering' (27 March 1992). Paxman, who is one of the more important current affairs presenters on British television and frequent interviewer of senior politicians, once said that he was fond of Claud Cockburn's watchword, 'Why is this lying bastard lying to me?' At the heart of the campaign was a film by John Schlesinger about John Major called *The Journey*, which took Major back to his roots, and was described as having 'intriguing echoes of Billy Liar and Midnight Cowboy', rather in the way in which *The Boy from Hope* film about Clinton had echoes of *The Waltons*. Another commentator of the British television-election scene pointed out that one of the best-known political interviewers, Sir Robin Day, who had established a reputation in the late 1950s and through the 1960s for professional, effective interviewing to which politicians responded equally effectively, now believed that the political interview 'has somehow ceased to function as it ought to . . . [it is] virtually a dead duck'. Compared to political leaders of the past modern-day politicians 'are content to dole out their prepackaged texts . . . . It is public relations that determines today's campaigns, with television at the leading edge of PR strategy with both British parties employing a technique borrowed directly from the American campaign trail, media pulse analysis' (Stephen Barnett, *New Statesman*, 21 February 1992). Market research is used to pin-point 'effective' buzz words and sound bites from floating voters, to be passed on by the PR consultants to their political clients. The essence of any appearance on television thus becomes the making sure that the 'one-liners' appear. Private polls are commissioned to establish where on issues and image the party is strongest. Barnett concludes—and remember that he is speaking of British television: 'Image making, phrase testing and agenda setting has invaded almost every aspect of political television. Consequently television becomes little more than a passive promotional tool manipulated by political parties, rather than an opportunity to promote understanding and help citizens make informed electoral decisions.'

What we have been witnessing in panning across the history of 'non-fiction' television is a moving away from a commitment to the idea of rational discourse, at the centre of which must lie information and analysis, and the coronation of pleasure at the heart of all we do and think. Consider that at the heart of the 1992 presidential campaign was a debate about what became known as 'family values'. The debate, however, was anchored to a tussle between the Vice-President of the United States and Ms Murphy Brown, a sitcom character played by Candice Bergen. The most obvious and powerfully contentious debates about race and the police now occur in rap music videos.

The boundaries between the real and the unreal thus are becoming hopelessly blurred. There is of course nothing new in this. Drama-documentaries, for example, have long been part of public affairs output. The issue, however, is one of the integrity of the exercise and the manner in which it is undertaken. There is clearly a difference, though not one readily identified in the abstract, between, say, Ken Loach's *Days of Hope*, Peter Watkins's *The War Game*, and NBC's *Kill Me if You Can*, about Caryl Chessman, and CBS's six-hour mini-series, *Columbus*, which was historically disastrous but presented as a 'true account'. The trend in the United States towards the dramatic recreation of events, something of a craze in 1989, has also led to considerable errors of judgement. For example, ABC News showed videotape of an American foreign service officer giving a briefcase to a Soviet diplomat. The film looked very much like a surveillance tape, crosshairs, time and date at the bottom, and so on. What they forgot to tell their view-

The blurring of the boundaries between the real and the unreal: **The War Game**, Peter Watkins's 1965 drama-documentary vision of a nuclear attack on Britain was considered by BBC Director-General Sir Hugh Greene as too shocking to be broadcast. It was eventually shown in 1985.

above 'Reality television':
Real Stories of the Highway Patrol and **Emergency Call**.

opposite Perhaps the single most important development in the history of non-fiction television: CNN.

ers was that the whole thing was a dramatized version of an alleged event. In November 1992 NBC broadcast a report on one of their public affairs programmes, *Dateline NBC*, which showed a 'test' of a General Motors truck impacted by another car and bursting into flames. The film was to support the story-line that these trucks were unsafe. GM cried foul, but NBC said they stood by the story. GM asked to see the truck used in the test only to be told that it had been scrapped. GM found the truck, examined it, and announced to the world something which NBC had forgotten to mention, that in order to ensure that the truck did burst into flames on impact the producers of the item had rigged explosive devices. They had blown up the truck to dramatize what they said was happening in reality. As Daniel Schorr said, on another occasion, of docu-drama: 'At best they simplify reality, at worst they pervert it.'

Schorr's observation here takes as given that in news, public affairs, documentary, drama-documentary we are discussing something to do with 'reality'. One development in television which has begun in the United States and which appears to be spreading to other countries is 'reality television'. A whole category of programmes has emerged in the past few years presenting a curious combination of the documentary, the magazine, news, low-market tabloid journalism, the sensational, the prurient, the voyeuristic. These programmes are all about reality, they are all non-fiction, but they are the constituent parts of great TV journalism. The titles of the programmes tell something of the genre: *Rescue: 911*, *Top Cops*, *Unsolved Mysteries*, *Cops*, *Code 3*, *Real Stories of the Highway Patrol*, *Cop Files*, *Great Detective Stories*, *Beyond the Call*. All of these are made possible by the use of lightweight video cameras and obviously the large theme which seems to define them is watching the forces of law and order going about their business. Other new reality programmes, such as *Inside Edition*, *A Current Affair*, and *Hard Copy*, are a kind of tabloid journalism dealing with what can only be described as the sleazier side of life, almost inevitably with some kind of sexual component. A public opinion survey in March 1993 indicated that 50 per cent of the public

June 1, 1980, Turner Broadcasting Launches Cable News Network

For Over 13 Years, The World Has Been Turning To CNN

1981 Iran releases hostages after 444 days.

1982 Argentina invades Falkland Islands.

1983 Soviets hold press conference to explain the downing of KAL Flight 007.

1984 The world mourns the assassination of Indira Gandhi.

1985 Shiites hold 39 hostages in TWA hijacking.

1986 Challenger explodes 74 seconds after liftoff.

1987 Wall Street crash sends financial shock waves worldwide.

1988 Pan Am Fight 103 is bombed.

1989 Students demonstrate at Tiananmen Square.

1990 Nelson Mandela released from prison.

1991 Gulf Crisis escalates into war.

1992 Yeltsin supplants Gorbachev as communism falls.

1993 Christiane Amanpour reports from the besieged city of Sarajevo.

For over 13 years, viewers around the world have relied on one television network for coverage of history as it happens. 24 hours a day. No other news service compares.

CNN INTERNATIONAL
The World's News Leader

Contact: Edward Boateng
Turner International Network Sales Limited
CNN House, 19-22 Rathbone Place, London W1P 1DF, U.K.
Tel: + 44 71 637 6764 Fax: + 44 71 637 6713

believe that programmes such as *Hard Copy* and *Inside Edition*—which in British terms are really the equivalent of the *Sun* newspaper—provide viewers with a good way of obtaining information about what is going on in the world. That is perhaps the most disturbing trend of all.

One consequence of the success of 'reality television' has been to push the networks' entertainment divisions, for example in their movies of the week, to look for real-life sensational stories—movies about the World Trade Centre bombing and David Koresh and the Waco tragedy, for instance. All three networks produced 'fact-based' dramas about Amy Fisher, the Long Island teenager who shot her lover's wife.

Perhaps, however, the single most important development in the history of non-fiction television took place in 1980 when Ted Turner, an Atlanta business-man, station owner, and Americas Cup yachtsman, gave the world the Cable News Network, a mixture of news leavened with analysis and discussion. It is reasonable to argue, though not necessarily with applause, that we have not been the same since and never will be. By offering a twenty-four-hour news service, with often live and lengthy coverage of events from around the world, CNN has had a major impact on how we think about political and social events. CNN *World Report*, which offers unedited, three-minute pieces from about ninety different television organizations around the world, provides an inflection to political discourse, to our sense of news, which simply was not possible before. It was, in particular, the crisis which led to the Gulf War which elevated the importance of CNN, if only because in the first instance it was the one place that one could see and hear at length the competing positions. There was a memor-able photo on the front page of the *New York Times* which showed George Bush and his aides watching the progress of the war on TV. The set was tuned to CNN. And at another tense moment when the Defense Secretary Dick Cheney was being interrogated by reporters he said, 'We are getting our information from CNN just like you.' Turgut Ozal, the president of Turkey, told a CNN crew that he was watching a live interview with Bush on CNN when Bush told reporters that he was about to call the Turkish president. Ozal got up, walked next door to his office, and picked up the ringing phone. It was Bush.

Conclusion

One of the defining characteristics of television, spanning the past five decades, has been a pervasive belief in almost every country where it developed in its potential for enrichment. The notion of enrichment is one loaded with nuance, subtlety, ambivalence. Essentially, however, the notion invokes the belief that we can be better than we are, and in particular can better think about our condition as a social, political, and cultural species. To think one has to have the where-withal to absorb and mull over ideas, complex and simple. And in most cases someone has to provide the information and the ideas with which we can then work. Overwhelmingly that source of information in the post-war decades became television.

Perhaps the single most powerful evocation of the potentiality of the medium to do something other than entertain through fiction and comedy took place in the USA in 1958. Edward R. Murrow was an enormously well-known broadcast journalist, first on radio when he sent back elegantly crafted radio reports to the American listening public from a London being heavily bombed by the Luftwaffe. He became the most prominent television journalist of his age in the 1950s. In 1958 Murrow spoke to the annual meeting of the Radio and Television News Directors' Association. He told them: 'This instrument can teach, it can illuminate; yes and it can even inspire. But it can do so only to the extent that humans are determined to use it to those ends. Otherwise it is merely wires and lights in a box. There is a great and decisive battle to be fought against ignorance, intolerance and indifference. This weapon of television could be useful.' If there is a theme to this account, it is that as the social and economic organization of television shifted so did the commitments to, and character of, its non-fiction programming. As a business ethic prevails the ability to sustain a notion of journalistic responsibilities becomes, at the very least, challenged. The history of non-fiction television increasingly appears as if it is moving from the powerful professionalism and dignity of an Ed Murrow to a crass tabloidism which panders rather than serves.

6

Sport

Steven Barnett

From the original Olympic Games in Greece and the chariot races of ancient Rome to the jousting tournaments of medieval England, and to the arrival of modern soccer and athletics, those who did not attend an event or game did not share in the experience. The role of sport differed from society to society, but in one respect all sport was the same, in the sense that the only way to share the immediate drama of the experience was to play or to attend. Not even the most eloquent word-of-mouth description nor the most vivid reporting prose could substitute for the passion and involvement of live spectating.

Then came radio. For the first time in history, it was possible to convey to people outside the immediate arena the drama of an event as it unfolded. It required skill and imagination to paint vivid pictures with the spoken word while simultaneously following the action, but suddenly the old or poor or half-hearted could witness big sporting events without being physically present.

Then came television, and the watching of major sporting contests was no longer the exclusive preserve of those who were physically and financially able to come in person. Almost imperceptibly, two completely unrelated activities—the screening of television programmes and the participation in sporting events— have become inextricably intertwined. Around the world, there are sports which owe their popularity (or their demise) to television, and there are television channels which owe their success and sometimes their very existence to sport. The consequences have not been confined to individual sports within individual countries. Just as television's power to create a 'global village' has brought to most countries a knowledge of places and cultures which were previously unknown, so it has taken previously esoteric sports across national boundaries. Sports like soccer, rugby, ice hockey, and swimming are international languages which have been adopted in countries where previously they lay dormant. Television has allowed one country's passion—cycling in France, sumo in Japan, baseball in America—to excite the imagination and fuel new sporting fashions elsewhere. Truly international events like the Olympics and soccer's World Cup have introduced audiences across the world to new sports and new countries. The consequences have not just been sporting ones. Who knows how many youthful European ambitions to travel to Zambia, Tonga, or Brazil had their origins in a brilliant 400 metres athlete or an outstanding World Cup soccer match between two obscure teams?

But its transnational influence has not always been positive. Some countries are fearful of seeing their indigenous sporting traditions obliterated by images of more glamorous sports being beamed in by satellite. Recent visitors to some West Indian islands have been struck by the spontaneous games of basketball which are springing up and replacing the traditional make-shift games of cricket on spare patches of grass. It is the satellite pictures of American basketball games—featuring predominantly black sporting heroes—which are universally blamed. At one point in the UK, British commentators were concerned that American football might be supplanting soccer as the national game. Throughout the world, the evolution of sport's relationship with television has been full of these contradictions: a fascinating, emotional, often painful evolution. This chapter looks at that evolution in Britain, but many of the implications are

The notorious Berlin Olympics in 1936 were the first Games to be televised. But cinema newsreels were still the most dominant visual mass medium and provide most of the footage that survives today. It was not until thirty years later that television began to establish its international role.

universal. The troubled marriage of sport and television in Britain is a case history which shows up many of the technical, financial, and institutional issues which have cropped up in most societies.

In the UK it has been, as the sports pages jargon might have it, a game of three halves. The development of sport's relationship with television has mirrored exactly the tensions and pressures represented by three phases in the evolution of British television: the BBC monopoly phase from television's first appearance to the arrival of ITV in 1955; the duopoly phase, when two BBC channels faced one and then two heavily regulated commercial channels until 1989; and the new age of outright competition, with most obligations removed from terrestrial commercial channels and the arrival of new specialist channels beamed into people's homes via satellite. The structures and philosophies of British television in those three phases have dictated the nature and impact of televised sport.

The Monopoly Phase

It all started with a Wimbledon tennis match on Monday 21 June 1937. Ownership of TV sets was confined to around 2,000 well-heeled Londoners, and at 3 o'clock in the afternoon they became the first people in the country to watch a live sporting event from the comfort of their living-rooms. The pictures were blurred, the match (involving British champion Bunny Austin) unmemorable, and few at the time fully appreciated the wide-ranging significance of that particular tennis match.

At the beginning, the relationship with television was not one to which sports bodies willingly committed themselves. Over the next twenty years, a succession of BBC managers had to encourage, cajole, and inspire sports administrators to persuade them of the benefits which the new machine could bring. But having convinced the All England Tennis Club the BBC's first Director of Television, Gerald Cock, set his sights on the national game and suggested to the Football Association that both the international England v. Scotland match and the FA Cup Final would make good television material.

The FA Council's immediate reaction foreshadowed fears about television's impact on attendances which would feature for the next fifty years. What would be the effect of live transmission of a blue riband event on all the less significant matches being played in the London area at the same time? To date, highlights of big games had been provided by cinema newsreels in which films were transmitted days, if not weeks, later. This was a new, unpredictable, and potentially ruinous development which administrators did not trust.

Cock tried to reassure the FA, and wrote that permission would 'not be regarded as a precedent but as a trial'. He was well aware both of the potential contribution which television could make to sports spectating and of the collaboration which would be required from the sports themselves. He ended his letter: 'Television is on trial. Here is the beginning of a great new industry, the

Above: the media gathers in Tiananmen Square, 1989. The protesting students understood that it was necessary for the world's cameras to record not process but *symbol*: their papier mâché Statue of Liberty, and the lone student confronting a line of tanks, conveyed in potent fashion the struggle for human rights.

Below: President Gorbachev addresses a news conference in Moscow in 1991. The collapse of the Soviet Union, in which television played a vital role, had a profound effect on the issue of how the medium should deal with political affairs.

Right: sport meets new technology to end the era of the couch potato. Interactive cable will allow tomorrow's sports viewer to participate in the viewing process: choose your camera angle, your statistics, or your moment for a slow-motion replay.

Below: Sumo. Television has allowed one country's passion to excite the imagination and to fuel new sporting fashions across the world.

progress of which depends to a great extent on the co-operation of institutions such as the Football Association.'

In the event, Cock's arguments prevailed. On 9 April 1938, England v. Scotland provided the world's first television pictures of a soccer match, and three weeks later Huddersfield Town and Preston North End contested the first televised FA Cup Final. But as the number of sets gradually increased and more sports were approached, the reservations initially expressed by the FA began to gain currency. Even before war had been declared, and television had begun its seven-year banishment, the era of sympathetic experimentation was giving way to more hard-headed assessments of potential damage.

Immediately on its post-war resumption, television saw a great deal of sport in the schedule. There was Wightman Cup and Wimbledon tennis, the first Test Match against India at Lords, speedway from West Ham and Wimbledon stadiums, racing from Ascot, and the varsity Rugby Union match from Twickenham. Towards the end of 1946, Head of Television Maurice Gorham listed only two refusals to co-operate, of which the first—an ice show from Wembley Pool—would have provoked more amusement than concern. Arthur Elvin, managing director of Wembley Stadium, objected to the BBC's additional lighting 'not only because it tended to melt the ice surface but because he was afraid his patrons would expect similar lighting on evenings when we were not there to provide it'.

The second refusal was indicative of a more serious, though in the end temporary, problem. The British Boxing Board of Control, which had given permission to televise a middleweight championship fight, withdrew their offer. Like many other sporting bodies, they were becoming fearful that cinemas might 'rediffuse' television pictures and charge for admission. The BBC could offer no guarantee that this would not happen (it was not against the law) and all sporting bodies started to fret about the possibility of losing control over access to relayed pictures. The issue was taken up by the newly formed Association for the Protection of Copyright in Sports, a loose alliance of sporting bodies which shared a growing fear about how this new technology might threaten the control of administrators over their own events.

There were a few incidents of withdrawal but before disruption could grow any further, the matter was resolved—not for the last time—through government intervention: unauthorized cinema rediffusion became impossible without a special licence from the Postmaster-General. Although promoters' fears of pirating were not wholly allayed, they were superseded by a more serious problem: television's effect on attendances.

A few promoters had a positive outlook, and were convinced even at this early stage that television offered valuable free publicity which would encourage 'accidental' viewers to follow up their television experience with a paying visit. Twickenham reported in 1949 that, for the first time, tickets for the England v. France international had been oversubscribed and many applicants disappointed.

The magic eye. Members of an early Arsenal team gather in wonderment around the new technological wheeze. But soccer's administrators were more concerned about what television would do to gates and income.

There were attendance records for steeplechasing at Sandown Park and record crowds on the first Saturday of the 1948 Wimbledon championships. Nevertheless, with television households approaching a quarter of a million by the end of 1949, opposition voices were growing louder and fear was contagious. An APCS document in February 1950 stated explicitly that 'it is not the object to get more money for the promoters by selling the rights but to protect the whole sporting spectacle system'. Although the APCS represented too many disparate interests for total unanimity to prevail, it had a marked effect on sports output—so much so that questions were eventually asked in the House. On 17 May 1950, Ernest Marples MP asked the Postmaster-General Ness Edwards, 'Will the right honourable Gentleman bear in mind that undoubtedly sporting events are at the moment the most effective spectacle on television?'

No doubt recognizing the potential sport has to galvanize political hostility, the Postmaster-General established a Sports Television Advisory Committee (STAC). Sports associations agreed to allow the BBC to show 'sports events of the order of 100 events per annum' for an experimental period to allow the Committee to assess the direct and indirect effects of television. The Committee was to report 'from time to time as it may see fit'. Although the restricted geographic availability of television allowed for some unique controlled experiments, the Committee's findings were predictably inconclusive. After its first—and ultimately only—report was delivered in May 1951, the conclusions were summarized in three points by the then Director of Television G. R. Barnes:

1. Some time must elapse before it is possible accurately to estimate the effect of Television on gates.
2. It is the televising of important events like the Cup Final and Professional boxing which have a marked effect on attendance.
3. This effect is greatest on the smallest clubs.

Little was resolved, and some bans remained in place including the 1952 FA Cup Final. It was only in the face of intense resistance (particularly from the Football League, which was firmly against television) that the FA agreed to the televising of the classic 1953 'Stanley Matthews' final, whose pictures are regularly replayed today.

Although this issue continued to simmer, it was gradually overtaken by events: sports bodies and BBC managers geared themselves to the imminent arrival of competitive television. The prospect of a commercial competitor, desperately opposed by many influential people within and outside the BBC, had particular repercussions for sport because the BBC could no longer offer a price to sports bodies on a take-it-or-leave-it basis. Not only would they face the possibility of escalating costs for television rights, but there was a real risk of losing the right to cover major sporting occasions.

It is ironic, in the light of future events, that at no stage during this monopolistic period did money feature as the defining issue in the TV–sport relationship. As Gorham noted at the end of 1946, 'the question of permitting television will continue to be judged solely on its promotional value until much larger fees are paid'. This was partly due to the limited availability of television sets, but also to the non-commercial and overtly public service nature of the BBC. A corporation accountable to its licence payers, and with one channel on which to cater for all television tastes and preferences, was obliged to marshal its resources carefully. It could not make outrageous payments for single events beyond the 'facilities' fee, and there were strict prohibitions on any kind of commercialism. When boxing promoter Jack Solomons offered a championship fight to the BBC in 1947, he agreed to waive any fee in return for an opening announcement along the lines of 'by courtesy of Jack Solomons and Vernons Pools'. The response from Gorham was unequivocal: 'I am afraid I must turn down the suggestion of acknowledgement . . . Vernons Pools are not the organisers of the fight, and to acknowledge them as well as Solomons would be sponsorship without alloy.'

Public service obligations, and the absence of any commercial competition, therefore inhibited any tendency towards spiralling costs. By 1954, with the approaching threat of competition from a new independent sector, the BBC were forced to reconsider their philosophy of televising sport and their reaction to commercial competition. At a meeting between the BBC and eleven representatives of the APCS on 21 April 1954, Director-General Sir Ian Jacob outlined the BBC's approach. The BBC was not concerned with exclusive rights, but with obtaining facilities for broadcasting 'all events of interest to the public'. It wanted to work with promoters to ensure that sport could reap the benefits of television without undue damage: 'The question of the money payment involved was less important, in the Corporation's view, than that of preserving all forms of sport in a healthy condition.' Jacob warned—presciently—of competitive television's tendency to strive for exclusivity and 'to exploit sports to the utmost'.

It was an argument which conveniently combined an altruistic public service attitude to the health and welfare of sport with the more self-interested institutional motive of sustaining the BBC's dominant position. It was a philosophy which ensured that, contrary to the expectations of many senior BBC managers at the time, sport was one area where in the years to come commercial television rarely embarrassed its opposition.

From Monopoly to Duopoly

It was not long before sport became one of the first battlegrounds in a fledgling ITV's attempt to assert superiority. The first non-BBC transmission was broadcast to the London area by Associated Rediffusion Television on 22 September 1955. It was to be almost a year before commercial television covered more than half the country, but even in its embryonic stage ITV saw the value of a mould-breaking major attraction to announce its arrival. There was no better candidate than the country's most popular sport, and—just like the new satellite competition thirty-five years later—ITV went for live coverage of league football.

They faced two obstacles. First, league secretary Fred Howarth was still opposed to live soccer on Saturday afternoons because of the effect on smaller clubs. The notion of playing televised games at a different time was unthinkable. Secondly, like many other sports administrators, he was profoundly distrustful of the new arrivals. In August 1955 he told Head of Outside Broadcasts Peter Dimmock: 'The BBC have always been very straightforward with us and we don't even know who are behind these commercial people.'

The following year, however, both reservations were being severely tested by an offer of £50,000 from the Midlands franchise ATV in return for live coverage of matches postponed until 6.15 p.m. Dimmock reported that the Football League Management Committee were finding it difficult to refuse, but one month later the Committee finally rejected all proposals and deferred indefinitely the whole question of television coverage. The affair had concentrated the BBC's mind on its own competitive strategy and whether it should avoid a bidding war for live events. Dimmock acknowledged that this sort of competition probably represented 'the first of many similar situations that will arise as ITV gathers strength and increases its coverage', and wanted to press for film rights so that a 'telerecording'—recorded highlights—could be transmitted at a later time. It took another nine years before Dimmock's idea was translated into what was to become the hallmark of British football coverage and the centre-piece of Saturday night programming—recorded highlights on *Match of the Day*.

Deprived of the national sport for non-financial reasons, ITV could not even use financial muscle to gain exclusive rights to major events in other sports. When commercial competition in television was just a glint in the eye of a few Conservative MPs, the BBC was conscious of the importance of sport to its role not simply as public service broadcaster but as national broadcaster. As early as May 1950, it had announced a list of 'events from which the BBC would not wish

Television's forerunner: how the 1931 Derby was transmitted live from Epsom Downs to a Metropole cinema screen twenty-five miles away.

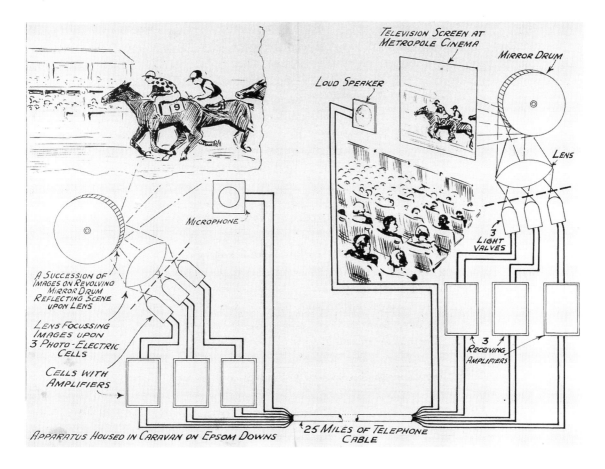

to be excluded'. This comprised boxing (world professional title fights); football (Cup Final plus internationals); cricket (Test Matches); horse racing (Derby, Grand National, St Leger, Royal Ascot); tennis (Wimbledon plus Wightman and Davis Cups); rugby union internationals; and the Boat Race.

As the glint turned to reality, there were apprehensions within the BBC and within Parliament that, as Bernard Sendall records, 'wealthy commercial interests might outbid the BBC and . . . deprive BBC viewers of events they expected to see on the "national" service'. The BBC therefore evolved the principle of non-exclusivity: any negotiation with the BBC would not preclude an agreement with other television stations and no one would be able to exclude the BBC by virtue of agreements with other stations. It was a philosophy which, according to Dimmock at the time, would cover the BBC both ways: 'This seems to me to offer a safeguard for BBC viewers without precipitating the political storm that might arise if we bought exclusive rights. It would also enable us to protest strongly if the ITA obtained exclusivity at a major event . . .'.

It was not easy to persuade Parliament of the need to preserve major events from exclusive purchase. On the one hand, Conservative MPs were aware of the electoral consequences of major sporting events being lost to a channel available to barely half the population. On the other hand, a free market philosophy dictated that the legitimate interests of sporting bodies should not be inhibited by statutory constraints on competition.

At least one government spokesman referred to the relevant section as 'the most difficult problem in the Bill', but an apparently insoluble dilemma was eventually resolved through a non-statutory compromise. The Postmaster-General was given power to draw up a statutory instrument 'with a view to preventing the making of exclusive arrangements for broadcasting of sporting or other events of national interest' which was never invoked because the broadcasters voluntarily agreed a list of ten events which would be non-exclusive. These were: the English and Scottish FA Cup Finals; the Grand National and Derby; Test Cricket involving England; the Boat Race; Wimbledon tennis; soccer's World Cup finals; the Olympics; and the Commonwealth Games when held in Britain. Thus, the BBC's presence at all major sporting occasions was assured in an arrangement which, while born of unique circumstances in 1955, was sustained until 1990.

This disqualification from exclusive access to major events made it difficult for ITV to establish itself as a serious contender in television sport. Unlike its satellite competitor thirty-five years later, it could not use sport as a weapon for enticing viewers away from established viewing patterns. This was particularly important for ITV's sports programming, because it suffered from a number of inherent disadvantages.

First, with ITV's structure based on a series of regional franchises, it was difficult to formulate a coherent sports policy. Different regions had different sporting priorities, which militated against a determined and co-ordinated stand against the BBC. Although there were sporadic attempts to launch a centrally funded sports network along the lines of Independent Television News, there was never enough will or momentum for the project to succeed. Secondly, established sports bodies remained wary of these upstart commercial characters. They would welcome additional revenue, of course, but there was still a lingering and very British distrust of commercial imperatives and the way in which financial gain rather than the public interest might dictate decisions. As Garry Whannel has pointed out, the Oxbridge and RAF influence within the BBC contrasted sharply with the backgrounds of those running the first four ITV franchises 'with their roots in film and show business'. Val Parnell, Lew Grade, and the Bernstein family were unlikely to be seen by the sporting establishment (themselves mostly Oxbridge) as reliable guardians of the nation's sporting heritage. Thirdly, there was the enormous power of the BBC's reputation as traditional purveyor of British sport. For nearly twenty years, with interruptions only for war and the occasional copyright problem, the BBC had brought to increasing numbers of British citizens the cream of Britain's sporting achievement. This twenty-year advantage had allowed the BBC to develop what Asa Briggs calls 'a remarkable team of commentators'. Looking back at some of those names, it was easy to see why some administrators were reluctant to surrender their respective sports to the obscurity of anonymous commentators.

Dan Maskell and Freddie Grisewood at Wimbledon, Kenneth Wolstenholme and Alan Weeks for soccer, Raymond Glendenning and Harry Carpenter for boxing, Harold Abrahams and David Coleman in athletics were all quickly hailed as the voices of their respective sports. Cricket provided a host of knowledgeable and entertaining contributors, including John Arlott, E. W. Swanton, Rex Alston, Peter West, and Brian Johnston. By the end of the 1950s, just as ITV was struggling to establish itself, these commentary teams had created a familiarity and authority which guaranteed for their employer a formidable reputation in British television sport.

By the end of the 1950s, the BBC had established two regular sports programmes as the platform for their dominance in the field: *Sportsview*, a fast-moving and authoritative Wednesday evening programme with Paul Fox as editor; and *Grandstand*, a three-hour Saturday afternoon programme which still forms the centre-point of BBC sport thirty-five years after its first transmission. Weighed down by all its disadvantages, ITV could not match the BBC's style and variety and, in Sendall's words, 'handled sport rather gingerly', with coverage which was 'sparse, random and sometimes amateurish'. Amidst calls from the ITA to improve its sports coverage, ITV launched *World of Sport* in the autumn of 1964 to challenge *Grandstand*, but struggled to overcome their lack of experience and inability to win over key sports.

The drive for improvement was given impetus by the new ITV franchisee London Weekend Television in 1967. Having brought in a successful football manager and negotiator, Jimmy Hill, to head their sports team, LWT sought to sharpen up and widen their sports coverage. In a major coup, they won rights to the final of the prestigious one-day cricket tournament, the Gillette Cup, in 1968. One of the most exciting finishes in the competition's history should have provided the crowning glory. Unfortunately, with the match hinging on the last over, ITV ran out of time and cut for commercials followed by the next programme.

It was a small incident which confirmed everyone's worst fears and prejudices about ITV: too inflexible to run over, too driven by money to withhold a commercial break, too insensitive to the integrity of a sporting occasion to sustain full coverage to the end. It did little to improve ITV's stature in the sporting industry, and illustrated how the BBC had established a standard of professionalism and a set of expectations which any commercial channel would now have to meet.

In fact, that is precisely what LWT aspired to do in its soccer coverage, investing in more technical resources and a new team of personalities in order to add a different dimension to televised soccer. Although widely acclaimed, LWT's efforts did not convert large numbers of viewers and ITV continued to be outrated two to one for major international events like soccer's World Cup and the Olympic Games. The interruption of commercials did not help, and the feeling grew within LWT that exclusivity was the only way to challenge the BBC's continued superiority. In November 1978, director of programmes Michael Grade launched a spectacular but ultimately unsustainable coup.

The target, once again, was soccer. In tandem with the routine negotiations which the BBC and ITV were jointly holding with the Football League, Grade and LWT sports chief John Bromley were concluding a highly secret unilateral deal. Its announcement created an uproar which ITV could not withstand. According to David Docherty, 'a ferocious battle ensued during which the BBC threatened court action and, with a fixation verging on paranoia, vilified Grade'. The upshot was an agreement that the BBC would surrender its Saturday night monopoly of soccer, and that the two channels would alternate the Saturday night/Sunday afternoon transmissions. With fifteen years of television football tradition finally fractured, Saturday evening soccer lost its appeal. Audiences dwindled and by the mid-1980s there were question marks over the entertainment value of recorded sport in general. The joint contract was maintained—at least for the moment—but, in an ironic historical twist, the emphasis turned full circle from recorded action back to live. September 1985 saw Britain's first live league soccer match.

It was not just the comparative dullness of recorded sport that bothered ITV, but ITV's continued second place in any coverage shared with the BBC. There emerged the basis for a sports policy which saw ITV into the satellite era—a 'live and exclusive' tag. It was a useful advertising slogan, and it was the only formula for clawing back the BBC's continued advantage. All it needed was some high-profile exclusive contracts.

By the end of the 1980s and the beginning of satellite competition, ITV had notched up three key victories. In 1984, it convinced the Amateur Athletics Association that its coverage could do justice to the burgeoning British talent in athletics. Athletics was an ideal target. First, the athletics audience was liked by advertisers who—despite the respectful distance traditionally maintained between programme-makers and air-time sales staff—were becoming increasingly influential. Second, emerging personalities like Sebastian Coe, Steve Ovett, and Daley Thompson were ideal promotional vehicles for announcing ITV's sporting arrival. Television's ability to elevate individual sporting characters had been recognized from its earliest days, and exploited to the full in the fiercely competitive environment of American television. Here were ready-made characters to suit ITV's ambitions.

At several moments during these complex negotiations, ITV executives looked with some envy across the Atlantic where outright competition ruled unchecked. ABC, in particular, had started life as a fledgling network, a minnow compared to the CBS and NBC giants. But its executives had realized early on that exclusive sport held the key to network supremacy. In particular, they latched on to the Olympic Games as the ideal promotional soap-box for the rest

Within a generation, watching televised sport was to become a private living-room experience. In 1948 those who were not at the opening game of the baseball World Series could share the communal live experience by watching television sets on Boston Common.

of their programming wares. Their cause was helped in gruesome style by their exclusive coverage of the 1972 Munich Olympics. There had only been limited competition for the rights because audiences were still moderate, but that all changed when the horrific drama of a terrorist kidnapping of Israeli hostages unfolded on screen. It sent ratings soaring, and ensured the permanent place of the Olympics as a priceless screen commodity. The crisis had barely been resolved before ABC's sports negotiator had snapped up the rights to the 1976 Montreal games.

Those games clinched ABC's sporting hegemony and the Olympics as a television spectacle without peer. With spectacular images in ice-skating and gymnastics, the games were widely acknowledged as a sporting and television triumph. More importantly, those two sporting weeks lifted the network from third place in the ratings to a clear first, which it maintained for the rest of the decade. Through its access to such a high-status event, the stature and image of the network was elevated.

But ABC's approach to sport was not solely based on exclusivity. It developed a philosophy about sports coverage which increasingly started to influence the thinking of sports programme-makers around the world: entertainment value. Arledge, for example, founded his approach to college football coverage squarely on the need to get the audience emotionally involved: 'If they didn't give a damn about the game, they still might enjoy the programme.' And the primary purpose of the commentary team was to ensure that an audience not entirely convinced of the unalloyed joys of American Football would find the programme irresistible. In the words of Howard Cosell, ABC's star commentator: 'There is no damn way you can go up against Liz Taylor and Doris Day in prime-time TV and present sports as just sports.'

As part of the entertainment attraction, it was increasingly necessary to focus on individual personalities rather than the sports themselves. In Britain, less accustomed to the dictates of the market-place, this provoked a hostile reaction from traditional sports followers. Amid accusations of over-commercialized coverage, ITV hyped up a 'celebrity' race between Zola Budd and Mary Decker-Slaney. Billed as a grudge match after Budd's accidental tripping of Slaney during the 1984 5,000 metres Olympic final, the race was given enormous publicity and stood accused of ignoring mainstream British athletes in the desperate search for a good story. Traditionalists hated it, but 11 million watched on television.

Meanwhile, the sudden influx of wealth to a traditionally amateur sport began to create new tensions, as criticisms grew about the increasing emphasis on material gain. Annual income for athletics, which stood at around £750,000 in 1984 mushroomed on the back of ITV's generosity to over £5 million by 1989. The professionalization of athletics, already under way in a small and discreet way via appearance fees in 1984, was given enormous impetus by the value of athletics to British commercial television. The result has been not only the elevation of status and income for a few select individuals but—in the eyes of some followers—a gradual corrosion of the amateur ideal. Television's need for drama has ensured greater emphasis on the track events at the expense of field, and on shorter races at the expense of longer ones.

Few such subtle considerations afflicted professional soccer, and in 1988 it became the first sport to benefit from satellite television. Just as ITV had done thirty years earlier, a new commercial broadcaster saw football as its route to success. The newly formed and ill-fated direct broadcasting operation, British Satellite Broadcasting, offered the Football League a staggering £200 million for a ten-year deal. This was trumped by an offer of £44 million from ITV over four years—which given the long-term effects of inflation was a substantially more lucrative price. Here was the first indication that a cash-strapped licence-funded public broadcaster would face an impossible squeeze against ferocious commercial competition. For all its reputation as the voice of Britain's sport, the BBC could not compete, and for the next four years it was unable to show a single minute of First Division soccer.

Inevitably, with such large sums at stake, the Football League had to learn to live with some of the dictates of a television schedule. The half-time break was extended from 10 to 15 minutes, immediate post-match interviews became commonplace, and several of the more appetizing big name clashes were rescheduled to suit ITV. Some uncomfortable lessons were being learnt which led one commentator to conclude: 'English football is now handcuffed to television and nobody can doubt which of the two is under arrest.'

In 1989, ITV achieved its final coup: exclusive rights to the Rugby World Cup finals, held in Britain for the first time in 1991. The attraction, once again, was an up-market audience profile so beloved of advertisers as well as another dent in the BBC's sporting image. This time coverage was meticulously arranged to avoid any accusations of insensitivity to the game through positioning of commercial breaks and undue emphasis on personalities. It was, by previous standards, an almost untarnished success.

While ITV spent the 1980s vainly trying to undermine the BBC's reputation and girding itself for the satellite challenge, Britain's newest terrestrial arrival brought a completely different perspective to television sport. Channel Four's ingenious structure enabled it to fulfil its statutory obligation to make programmes which were innovative and different. Under the tutelage of ex-Olympic medallist Adrian Metcalfe, Channel Four brought an approach to television sport which was dictated neither by tradition nor by a quest for ratings nor by the demands of advertisers. In sports programming, Channel Four has been the living embodiment of television's ability to create rather than exploit sporting passions. Its first achievement was to construct, out of virtually nothing, a following for American Football which still survives. The choice was based on a desire to find something different which was more than just a sporting event—something which represented part of the dynamic life and culture of another country. Coverage was designed to do two things: first, to take British viewers who were entirely unfamiliar with a game which to them resembled organized thuggery in fancy dress, and guide them through the rules, tactics, and intricacies; second, to place the sport itself within a cultural context which explained something of its history and its importance to the American way of life. Not only did it swiftly attract audiences of more than 3 million, but the gridiron pitches which started to appear on public parks bore testimony to its sudden popularity.

Much the same approach was followed with sumo wrestling, although the physical proportions required for participation disqualified most viewers from active involvement. Its television origin owed as much to the enormous complexity and fascination of its rules and rituals as to the excitement of the sport itself, and it introduced several million viewers to a piece of Japan which had previously been strange and incomprehensible.

There were other more mainstream successes on Channel Four, such as cycling and volleyball, and a series of programmes called *Challenge to Sport* which enabled more obscure sports like tug-of-war, karate, and archery to make their bid for more coverage. Uniquely amongst the four terrestrial channels, Channel Four was able to make experimental forays into dozens of less familiar sports which—if given a chance—audiences might find captivating. There has certainly

Twenty-four hours of sport. Unlike the wide-ranging terrestrial channels, dedicated satellite channels can cater around the clock for almost every sporting taste. But increasingly they are buying exclusive access to major events which were once universally available.

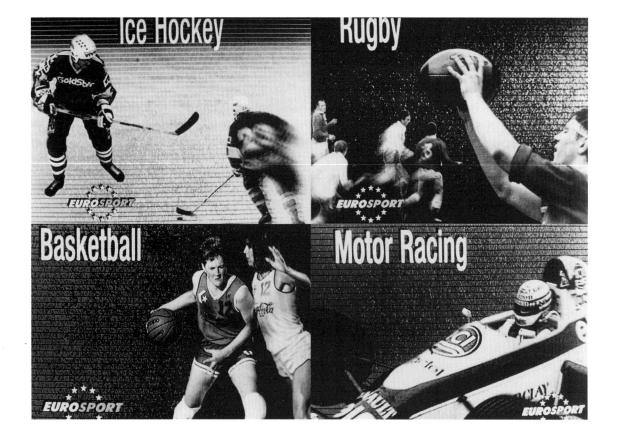

never been a shortage of sports clamouring for just a tiny slice of valuable air time, on the proven assumption that a little television can generate more spectators and more participants.

From Duopoly to Deregulation

In less than two years, the British broadcasting landscape was transformed, making an immediate and permanent impact on television sport. 5 February 1989 saw the launch of Rupert Murdoch's four Sky satellite television channels, one of which was dedicated entirely to sport. It took just three weeks for Sky to demonstrate the vital importance of sport to satellite and the implications for viewers: on 26 February only a few thousand viewers could watch a much-anticipated heavyweight championship fight between Mike Tyson and Frank Bruno, after Sky had prised the rights from ITV. By the end of 1990, Sky had swallowed its direct broadcast rival BSB. The newly emerged British Sky Broadcasting set about establishing itself in the minds and affections of British viewers who were not accustomed to paying for satellite dishes or subscription fees. Just like ITV thirty-five years earlier, it set its sights on exclusive live access to major sporting spectacles.

There followed, amid widespread dismay, exclusive rights to the cricket World Cup in March 1992. And two months later, it was a deal involving league soccer yet again which provoked a ferocious battle and furious recriminations. From under ITV's nose, BSkyB snatched exclusive rights to show live coverage of the new Premier League in a £306 million deal over four years which gave the BBC recorded highlights. It returned *Match of the Day* to the BBC's Saturday night schedule, but infuriated soccer fans, who were unwilling to pay the £6 per month subscription fee which Sky Sports were now charging. It also enraged ITV executives, who saw the BBC as co-conspirators in a deal which removed live league from terrestrial screens for the first time in eight years.

West Germany, three years earlier, had seen precisely the same phenomenon. In 1989, the German-based media conglomerate Bertelsmann made the All England Tennis Club an offer for Wimbledon television rights which the European Broadcasting Union could not match. These rights were sold on to television companies throughout Europe; in Germany itself they were passed to Bertelsmann's own subsidiary, the satellite-delivered and subscription-based private channel RTL Plus. While this represented a major coup for an as yet unprofitable satellite venture, it created a major problem for German viewers. Because RTL Plus was barely accessible to half of German homes, and because the public service channels refused to pay what they considered to be extortionate sums of money for peripheral rights, the majority of West German viewers were denied any pictures from Wimbledon. Unfortunately, this happened to be a year when both men's and women's singles titles were won by West Germans.

Thus there quickly emerged a new philosophy of television sport based

163

An example of the extraordinary power of new camera technology. The famous 'stump camera', pioneered in Australia, provides a unique view of the cricket ball's flight.

neither on satisfying public service principles nor on satisfying the demands of advertisers. The satellite approach was founded on buying up rights to popular sports and charging viewers who wanted to watch them a direct subscription fee. On the one hand, it introduced another stream of revenue for television; on the other, as the football deal demonstrated, it shattered a forty-year-old tradition of universal television access for nothing more than the cost of a licence. It has become fashionable in the new consumerist environment to talk of television 'product' rather than programmes, a reification process which precisely describes how competitive commercial channels have sought to exploit sport with the connivance of revenue-hungry sports bodies. Although new channels have vastly increased the volume of television air time devoted to sport, the result has not been noticeably beneficial to viewers. At the end of 1989, Matthew Engel wrote in the *Guardian*: 'Watching the best-presented sport in the world on national television has been a reason for living here. The advent of satellite TV is likely to change all that, as sports choose to sell their major events to smaller audiences for more money.'

The process was accelerated by two provisions within the UK's 1990 Broadcasting Act, which applied the prevalent free market political ethos to broadcasting. First, the listed events provision, which for thirty-five years had guaranteed universal access to the country's major sporting events, was abolished. It will not be long before one of those valuable events is sold to a satellite channel in return for a share of the enormous subscription revenues which such events could generate. Second, the protective funding structure for Channel Four was removed, requiring it to sell its own advertising air time in direct competition to ITV (see Chapter 3). While its remit to be different remains, the new reliance on advertisers will inevitably involve more populist programming. Channel Four's most recent sporting acquisition, Italian League Soccer, was an effective spoiling exercise for the BSkyB deal, but could hardly be interpreted as fostering minority interests and fresh sporting insights.

One of the great features of the first fifty years of televised sport therefore seems to be doomed: the ability of television not just to serve as a platform for launching unfamiliar sports, but to create a bandwagon of popular appeal. In the 1950s, it was showjumping which the cameras transformed from a pre-war preserve of élitist aristocrats to mass peak-time appeal. The reasons for its success owed as much to technical limitations as to the sport itself or the personalities involved. With heavy, stationary cameras which could cope most effectively with a fairly confined (and preferably open air) space, showjumping was the ideal foil. As Dorian Williams, the voice of BBC showjumping, subsequently explained, the screen could accommodate everything that was essential: the horse, the rider, the fence. A traditional British love affair with animals, of course, also helped.

For the same reason, the 1960s saw a great deal of televised swimming. And the 1970s launched the snooker phenomenon which survives (albeit with declining interest) today in the mid-1990s. Its origins lay in a programme launched on

BBC2 in 1969 designed to test the effectiveness of colour television. The combination of colour, easy and cheap coverage, and simple rules meant that technological pragmatism and audience tastes coincided to establish a new television fashion. Today's technologies are not inventing new television sports so much as enhancing old ones. The ubiquitous microchip is giving us cameras inside cricket stumps, cameras looking over the shoulders of racing drivers, cameras attached to the inside of goals, cameras underwater, in fact cameras which can go anywhere and follow anyone required by an inventive sports producer. The result has been some quite spectacular pictures, confined almost exclusively to the mainstream sports which make the investment worthwhile.

It is in these presentational issues—as well as in the number and types of sports being covered—that the most serious changes have occurred over the last fifty years. The way in which pictures have been conveyed is one element of the presentational mix. Another is the commentary which accompanies pictures. And a third is the way in which sports are promoted and packaged through trailers and other pre- and post-event coverage.

The last, in particular, has been transformed by the new demands on sport of a more competitive and commercial television environment. Both in promotional and on-screen presentational terms, the production ethos increasingly owes more to the retention of marginal or 'soft' viewers with a tendency to channel-hop and less to a faithful portrayal of the essence and integrity of a particular sporting event. Thus, it is not unusual for championship fights or tennis matches to be billed as 'grudge matches' with the emphasis on hostility and confrontation. Satellite coverage has imported two Australian devices which are completely divorced from any sporting context but aimed squarely at audience retention: an on-screen cartoon duck which accompanies cricketers dismissed for zero (in cricketing terminology, a 'duck') back to the pavilion; and the notorious 'honey shot' which involves a camera lingering on attractive female spectators in the hope that male viewers might then be dissuaded from switching channels. Women, for whom sport tends to be less appealing, are enticed through trailers featuring muscle-bound young men in various stages of training or combat which are of questionable relevance to the sport in question. And in the international arena there is a growing tendency to engage in a macho and aggressive nationalism that elevates the most humdrum contest to a battle of apocalyptic proportions. These are charades of tension building which contribute little to an appreciation of the skills, tactics, or subtleties of the contest: the warfare terminology initiated by television is echoed by newspapers, carried into the grounds, and eventually creates an atmosphere of hostility which panders to populist jingoism and vulgarizes the game.

Garry Whannel, in writing about professional ideologies which underlie the production process, has proposed a useful journalism/drama/light entertainment triangle to encapsulate programme practices in general. Although he places sport at the centre of these three disciplines, it seems that increasingly the

Sport or show business? An early example of some blurred boundaries as Mohammed Ali and Joe Frazier demonstrate their muscle power with chat-show host Dick Cavett.

new television environment is driving sport towards the entertainment/drama axis. As Whannel says, 'sport stars show up on chat shows, showbusiness stars appear on Cup Final Day and all meet up on the new breed of game show'. Sport has always created heroes and villains, while television has always magnified and elevated individuals. In an era when personalities win ratings, and ratings are the criterion of success, a potent combination of the two has created a new breed of superhero and supervillain. The Michael Jordans and Mike Tysons will never go hungry, and nor will the channels which buy exclusive rights to their contests.

Journalism in its investigative sense has never been an intrinsic part of the television sport culture: cricket coverage would pointedly avoid controversial discussion of South African rebel tours, soccer coverage would discreetly ignore racist chants directed at black players from the terraces. But the new philosophies have driven us even further away from a detached and critical view of the sporting world, which is now almost exclusively the preserve of the print media.

The BBC, despite its public funding, is not exempt from these competitive pressures: it retains a commitment to serve the generality of licence payers and therefore struggles to retain its hold on its sporting tradition. Against all the odds, it has succeeded in sustaining that reputation—albeit with tacit acceptance that the advertising and sponsorship logos 'inadvertently' featured on a strictly non-commercial channel is a valuable contribution to corporate PR. But it cannot be long before the enormous revenue potential of subscription television leaves the BBC, once again, to bring recorded highlights to those without money or inclination for new technology.

Conclusions

A critical and decisive factor in the development of the sport–television relationship in the UK was a national, non-commercial, and monopolistic broadcaster with an implicit responsibility for looking after the best interests of sport as well as the interests of viewers. The absence of purely financial criteria allowed broadcasters to take decisions which were, in their view, not detrimental to the sports they televised.

As competition to the BBC evolved, sport became a crucial weapon in the battle for channel supremacy and survival. In the era of specialist subscription-funded channels, the role of sport in attracting paying viewers to new channels will be even more important. In a sophisticated media world, when most formulas for drama or soap opera or light entertainment have been exhausted, sport offers an ideal combination of the dramatic and the unexpected. Increasingly, of course, the drama requires some enhancement and the less committed sports fan needs to be attracted. As the head of Sky Sports Dave Hill said at a conference in 1991 'sport as drama and sport as soap opera—that's what people want to watch on television'. The result is a television recipe which may not always be faithful to a sport's traditions or integrity.

These are not conclusions confined to the British experience. Across the world, satellite channels and new commercial channels are challenging traditional patterns of screen presentations of sport and placing a premium on major sporting events. Show business values are becoming more prominent, and are seeping via the major international events into the sports television culture of most countries. America's high-glitz Hollywood extravaganza which defined the 1984 Los Angeles Olympics spawned imitations as well as criticism, and channels world-wide are competing to introduce variations of the all-singing all-dancing routines to accompany major events.

Meanwhile, television's unique ability to unite a nation through free access to its big sporting occasions is being eroded by the sheer commercial value of sport in an increasingly competitive broadcasting environment. Sport remains an international language, enchanced in its cross-frontier significance by two generations of universal free access via television around the world. But increasingly, that access to sport as it happens will be restricted to those with the money and inclination to pay for it. We have reached the age of the electronic stadium and the electronic turnstile.

From sport's perspective, with the spotlight on big occasion money-spinners, the obvious loser is those minority activities for which the television soap-box can mean much-needed sponsorship money as well as much-appreciated exposure. The winner—at least financially—is the mainstream professional sport in which star participants demand material rewards commensurate with their status. Television can provide the sort of income which gate receipts and sponsorship alone never could. In the professional world, the two industries of sport and television are now mutually dependent and almost inseparable, with sport increasingly obliged to bend its collective knee to the dictates of television in return for those material rewards. To what extent this might be healthy for the integrity of the sports concerned is an issue which should be concentrating the minds of sports governing bodies around the world.

7

Political Ceremony and Instant History

Daniel Dayan and Elihu Katz

ecall the funerals of President Kennedy and Lord Mountbatten, the royal wedding of Charles and Diana, the journeys of Pope John Paul II and Anwar el-Sadat, the pre-election debates of John Kennedy and Richard Nixon, the Watergate hearings in the United States Congress, the confirmation hearings of Mr Justice Thomas, the revolutionary events of 1989 in Eastern Europe, the Olympic Games, and many more. These are the television programmes of special occasions. Every nation has them. Their hallmark is their rarity, their being different from everyday television. They depart from the conventions of non-stop transmission.

If everyday television is dominated by the imperative of a schedule and the aesthetics of flow, this chapter is about the television that is based on interruption, on the idea that something important needs to be said that will reconnect society to its centre. Different from the mundane television of series and scandals, these broadcasts have a festive character that is evident both in their construction and reception. On such occasions, there is ceremony to be seen on both sides of the screen; people gather in each other's homes to share the viewing experience. Like holidays this kind of television declares 'time out' from the routines of broadcasting and the routines of daily life. It demands that we stop all other activity to celebrate an event that embodies a shared value.

To characterize these events generically, it is not enough to say that they are broadcast live and pre-empt other programming. It is important to add that their organizers are not the broadcasting organizations, that they originate outside the studio, and are typically well rehearsed and well advertised, rather than spontaneous. They are not major news events such as the Kennedy assassination, but major ceremonial events—which are also news—such as the Kennedy funeral. The broadcasters transmit these events reverentially, and hail them as 'historic'. When successful, people tell each other that viewing is mandatory, that they must put all else aside. When successful, they electrify very large audiences—an entire nation, sometimes the whole world. They are rare realizations of the technological dream of the electronic media—to reach everybody, directly and simultaneously.

Indeed, the earliest policy debates over the nature of television broadcasting raised the possibility of a television dedicated to collective purposes. For example, during the late 1930s in Germany, two rival models were considered. The Ministry of Propaganda advocated the placing of television sets in public places, while the Ministry of Posts favoured a home-based model of collective viewing. Indeed, street viewing characterized the early days of television in many countries—Japan, for example (see Chapter 12), or rural India, and even in the West where TV was a featured attraction in bars and restaurants—before the sets became affordable to individual householders. While the latter ultimately prevailed, fascist regimes included, the former has not altogether disappeared. In fact, one can say that the two models blend into each other whenever homes open their doors to collective viewing, or when viewers everywhere converge on the same programme.

Television Events and National Identity

There is a pre-natal link between television and political ceremony. Nation after nation has inaugurated its television system by broadcasting events meant to celebrate continuity, community, and centre. The coronation of Elizabeth II is the paradigmatic example of how nations link the launching of television broadcasting to a major presentation of national identity. To take another example, Israel began its television broadcasting following the 1967 war with the live broadcast of a victory parade that displayed the reunification of its national capital.

Following the inauguration of television, the ceremonial broadcasts that call for this kind of collective viewing recede into the background while the routine of day-to-day broadcasting takes over. Yet, episodically, they reappear to mark other major turning-points. Ceremonial broadcasts are not primarily informative, nor are they meant to provide mere entertainment. These broadcasts are, first of all, integrative. This is why they are typically promoted (but not necessarily controlled) by establishments. When they are successful—and this is not always the case either—the events evoke the same exhilarating sense of community that characterized the inaugural event. Viewers feel that they are experiencing history. But ceremonial broadcasting is at odds with history as told by television news, an antagonism that is made all the more salient as the news, increasingly, is broadcast live, also deals with events, and often with the same

actors and the same situations. The news, however, heightens conflicts while television ceremonies function to mitigate them.

Such 'media events' recall the continuity of social identity. In most cases, the focus is on national identity, as in the Royal Wedding of Diana and Charles, for example. Some events offer straightforward affirmations of national continuity through the live broadcasting of commemorations such as Holocaust Day in Israel, the centennial of the Statue of Liberty, the bicentennial of the French Revolution. In some cases, however, the reference may be to a wider identity, even a primordial one; thus, the Pope's televised travels express the continued vitality of the Catholic Church, and the Olympics mark the progress from ancient Greece toward the dream of a world community. Continuity rests here on the existence of shared narratives.

A second type of continuity addressed by television concerns not narratives but institutions, not retellings but replacements that ensure the continuity of the social system. So that each generation may find its place, key symbolic roles have to be filled by successive actors. Whether in sports or in politics, one hero has to give way to another. This must be done (and be seen to be done) according to the

The collective memory of live media events is reinforced by their incorporation into the other genres of television and cinema—as in this celebration of the British Royal Wedding on the soap opera **Coronation Street**.

171

rules, whether of ascription or achievement. Thus, televised ceremonies such as pre-election debates spotlight the process through which representative individuals are chosen, generation after generation. The result itself is celebrated in investitures and inaugurations. Such rites apply not only to ascension but to the vacating of roles through death or deposition. Think of the funeral of Churchill or the farewell address of Richard Nixon. Like the rites of passage familiar to anthropologists, media events of this type are part of the cultural order that implements societal continuity by transcending the limitations of nature and biology.

A third type of event is mounted in response to discontinuity. Thus, some events are hastily improvised in the midst of trauma. The best examples are live broadcasts of the state funerals of assassinated leaders such as Mountbatten, Kennedy, Indira Gandhi, and Aldo Moro. Such events are designed to contain damage and to insure the stability of the prevailing order. In a sense, they are 'shock absorbers'.

By their anachronistic invocation of the vocabulary of the American frontier, the moon landings suggest a fourth type of event that serves, paradoxically, both to propose change and, at the same time, to alleviate the very discontinuity it is designed to introduce. Examples of this type include the live broadcasts of the ostensibly disruptive journey of Anwar Sadat to Jerusalem, or the Pope's disruptive first visit to communist Poland. Both events were subversive of the prevalent state of things. Both nevertheless stressed continuity through the invocation of

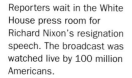

Reporters wait in the White House press room for Richard Nixon's resignation speech. The broadcast was watched live by 100 million Americans.

symbols—of biblical brothers, of Polish martyrs—that connected them with earlier traditions. This is also what happened during the extended live broadcasts of the Watergate Senate hearings. The call for interrupting the tenure of a President was justified in terms of the very norms that define the Presidency as an institution. Tradition was disrupted, but the disruption was blamed on the President himself. The Senate hearings introduced a dramatic change, but they did so in the name of continuity.

Ensuring continuity is always done from the point of view of the dominant order. Continuity is constructed in accordance with its interests. One should not look here for traces of what Walter Benjamin calls the 'history of the vanquished'. Still, this process is not always smooth or consensual. Dominant orders are far from stable, especially in democracies. In fact, they are in constant need of re-equilibration. Media events often give voice to alternatives and oppositional plans of action, including some that had previously been abandoned as hopeless. Certain rare events are ceremonial expressions of change itself—as were the live broadcasts of the confrontations in the central squares and parliaments of Prague, Bucharest, Moscow, and Berlin during the transformation of Eastern Europe at the turn of the present decade.

Broadcasts in this genre, then, are intimately connected with history. They invoke history to establish their meanings and importance, but in doing so, they sometimes leave a visible mark on history. In considering the relation between television and history, this chapter critically examines the claim of television to the title of historian and custodian of collective memory. It ponders how the audio-visual representation of events in progress may affect their outcome and consequences. It asks how pre-electronic societies engaged their far-flung members in ceremonies of collective identity and national deliberation.

Precursors of Television Events

Television ceremonies are obvious continuations of earlier ceremonial forms, and, like them, are concerned with the integration of societies in space as well as time. In the sociology of Émile Durkheim, all ceremonies serve to represent a society's structure and values to itself. Such symbolic representations hold societies together, by focusing attention on what Edward Shils calls the 'centre'.

The anthropology of ceremony provides us with many examples of occasions in which centre and periphery connect. Pilgrimages offer a first set of such examples. In Christian tradition the typical pilgrim journeys to the shrine alone, leaving his identity behind; in ancient Jewish tradition, pilgrimage to the Temple in Jerusalem was undertaken in families and small groups. But whether undertaken collectively or alone, the journey eventually confronts the pilgrim with a mass of other pilgrims ready to submit themselves to what Victor and Edith Turner call the 'pedagogy of the shrine'. The shrine serves here as a 'centre', both as a geographic point of convergence, and as a symbolic construct meant to ensure

173

the unity of the group. Walter Benjamin also evokes the notion of pilgrimage to describe the experience of an original work of art by someone who has made extensive preparations to visit the far-off museum in which it is housed. Benjamin suggests that 'the age of mechanical reproduction' has diminished the 'aura' of these works of art and with it, for better and for worse, the imperative of making the journey.

In contrast to pilgrimages which bring the periphery to the centre, other ceremonial forms bring the centre to the periphery. In the late Roman empire, for example, dignitaries representing the centre went successively from city to city, and were received at the gates in a repetitive ceremony called the *adventus*. Improving on the model of the *adventus*, and aiming to unify not an empire, but the Church, the Christian procedure of 'translation' distributed fragments of the remains of a holy figure. By enshrining these relics, each community, no matter how peripheral, gained access to the sacred centre, directly and permanently.

In an analysis of royal 'progresses', Clifford Geertz, the anthropologist, discusses the ways in which monarchs in different societies—Hassanian Morocco, nineteenth-century Bali, Elizabethan England—symbolically take the centre 'on tour' throughout their kingdoms. This formula—ritual display of the symbolic centre at different points in the periphery—was adopted at the time of Abraham Lincoln's funeral, where centre and periphery were again connected by means of transportation. The railway train carrying the embalmed and continually retouched corpse of the slain president plied its way from town to town. Unification was achieved through the successive re-enactment of a standardized ritual in different spatial segments of the community.

Yet another means of giving the periphery access to the sacred centre is evidenced in ceremonies such as the Passover Seder, the American Thanksgiving, and the Christmas Dinner. The iconic focus for these events is no longer physical. It is neither a visitor nor a holy relic, but an ideal centre that has been enshrined in memory. We call these 'diasporic ceremonies' because they are celebrated in widely scattered communities by small groups of families and friends, sharing the knowledge that all the others, however remote, are similarly and simultaneously focused.

Radio took advantage of this formula in its earliest days. The BBC's Lord Reith arranged for the King to deliver his Christmas message to a nation of expectant households, seated around the loudspeaker. Franklin Roosevelt's immensely consequential talks to the American people were introduced as 'fireside chats'. Thus was the geographic problem of connecting centre and periphery solved by means of communication rather than by means of transportation. As in 'translation', the centre was brought to the periphery. As in 'diasporic ceremony', the household, often augmented by extended family and invited guests, was the unit of reception.

In contrast to both 'translation' and 'diasporic ceremony', the ceremonies celebrated by radio, and later by television, required neither relics, nor memories. An *adventus* without transport and transposed into an intimate register, radio and television events no longer needed to be inscribed in a tradition; they could even be events in progress. The 'centre' could be ceremonially displayed in an event that had never before been celebrated. The new diasporic ceremonies were thus moved from past to present, from the commemorative 'there and then' to the live 'there and now'.

What radio initiated, and television spectacularly fulfilled, changed the very nature of the public sphere by canonizing events in the making. That which was only now happening was turned into a new type of ceremonial focus. Consider

The text of the Haggada focuses the attention of myriad small groups gathered at the Seder table to re-experience, simultaneously, the Jewish exodus from Egypt 3,000 years ago.

Enacting fantasy: the moon becomes real. The first live pictures of the moon's surface, 1965.

the moon landing. Television invited the world to assume a ceremonial attitude towards an ongoing event by framing a technological experiment as a symbolic occasion. But since the event had no past, and came without centuries of commentary that had fixed its meaning, television itself had to provide the instant gloss that would turn the event into an embodiment of central values.

In this case, as in others, television is invested with the right 'to declare a holiday'. This means that television provides a frame that signals the sacred character of an event in progress. The consequence is that audiences assemble by the hundreds of millions into holiday gatherings, confirming the legitimacy of the ceremonial framing and reinvesting the event with a new type of aura that derives from its centrality to a multitude. In other words, we are proposing an irony: that this most elaborate of the media of communication, when combined with the ceremonial character of diasporic reception, may be reinstituting some of the aura lost to works of art in 'the age of mechanical reproduction'.

The aura restored by television is not bestowed on the 'original', however, but on the reproduction. In the process of reproducing an expression of the centre, television so profoundly alters it as to raise the question of whether the reproduction is not more authentic than the original. Indeed, there may no longer be an original, in the sense that television montage can consist of the coexistence of so many pieces of space and time that their connection to any original is severed. Walter Benjamin anticipated this in his championing of film as the art without an original. What he did not anticipate was the way in which electronic events would be received simultaneously and collectively. Nor could he have anticipated how television, even more than radio, has become custodian of the centre. Entitled to pronounce what belongs in the centre, television has become part of the centre, if not the centre itself. Its very presence bestows aura.

Characteristics of the Genre

All genres may be considered 'contracts' in which producers and consumers voluntarily agree on the commodity to be exchanged and the terms of the transfer. This is also the case for 'media events'. Of course, totalitarian leaders may mount events that coerce the broadcasters to perform them, and the audience to go through the motions of celebration. Alternatively, the transmission may be sabotaged by parties unwilling to allow the event to reach its audience, as when an unidentified hand unplugged the live broadcast of Khomeini's return to Iran.

By the same token, the audience may be coerced, not to attend but to stay away, as was the case in the broadcasting of Sadat's funeral by Egyptian television, when a government that had lost faith in its assassinated leader denied public access to the funeral site. When events are derailed in this way, they lose their ceremoniality, and although they may maintain high interest, they are no longer different from great accidents and scandals. They have become major news events.

Ceremonial events, on the contrary, entail active and successful negotiation over each event among its organizers (the Royal Family, the International Olympic Committee, the National Aeronautic and Space Authority, etc.), its broadcast-producers, and its audiences. Thus, the first televised presidential

Who's the fairest of them all? Nixon and Kennedy in the first televised presidential debates, 1960.

177

debates in the United States in 1960 required suspension of the equal-time rule by the Congress so that free time could be offered only to the candidates of the two major parties without fear of being sued by the splinter parties. It involved agreement between the broadcasters and the candidates (Kennedy and Nixon) over the exact format for questions and answers, the time allotted to each candidate, the identity of questioners, the number and length of reaction-shots (of opponent, of audience). It required the television audience to come dressed as citizens, to sacrifice the evening's entertainment in favour of a political contest. If a ceremonial event is to succeed, the audience must agree to its elevated definition. Audiences must be willing to take a ceremonial role: that of citizens in presidential debates, that of mourners during the funerals of assassinated leaders, that of supporters cheering the home team in the Olympics.

If one of the partners to the contract refuses assent, the event collapses or fails. Thus, organizers of the Middle East peace talks at Camp David in 1979 refused journalists access to the deliberations; broadcasters sometimes refuse government proposals to mount commemorative events. Audiences, too, have refused events such as the live broadcast of the award of the Nobel Peace Prize to Prime Minister Begin, or the live broadcast of Richard Nixon's trip to China. Many such events are cancelled when consensus is not reached, and others, although mounted, fail to be remembered because they did not 'fire'.

Some failed events, however, are derailed from the inside, so to speak, not through coercion of any sort, but through progressive revelation of a divisive nature, which contradicts the consensual form of ceremony. Thus, the US Senate Committee hearings over the nomination of Clarence Thomas to the Supreme Court were transformed from a ceremony of ratification into a courtroom contest of mutual recrimination over issues of sexual harassment, women in the work-force, racial discrimination, and character assassination. The divisiveness associated with these controversial issues in the news stole the spotlight from the ceremony as planned. Yet from the point of view of democratic participation, this was far from a failure. There are moments in the life of a society when the public sphere opens or closes. There are moments of admission and moments of exclusion, moments when everyone feels competent to enter the fray and moments when very few do so. The reframing of this event focused attention on a situation about which most viewers felt they had something relevant to say. What had begun as a problematic ceremony ended as a true debate over fundamental issues.

In anticipation of a ceremonial broadcast, viewers are enjoined by each other to stop whatever they are doing, and turn on the television. There is graphic evidence that viewers treat such occasions as festive: they dress up, invite others, serve refreshments, applaud or otherwise respond, offer their own commentary, exchange telephone calls, and generally prove their awareness of the collective dimension of the event. Eric Rothenbuhler demonstrates this process in his report on 'the living-room celebrations' of the Olympic Games. 'Festive' is the best word to describe the effervescent nature of the occasion, even if it must be expanded to take account of those events that are not joyous. Thus, the televised events surrounding the funeral of John Kennedy offered a focus for the four-day vigil of grieving, soul-searching, and attempts to understand what had happened, interweaving different frames. What began as news—the assassination—was gradually transformed into ceremonies of mourning culminating in the funeral. But news events, the most prominent of which was the shooting of Lee Harvey Oswald by Jack Ruby, repeatedly challenged the ceremonial frame.

If we were to sum up the major characteristics of these events, we should say that they are (1) live, (2) pre-planned and publicized, (3) interruptions of the schedules of television and of daily life, (4) organized outside the broadcasting organization. They (5) evoke the enthralled response of a willing audience, and (6) invoke deeply rooted narrative forms that are associated with heroics. It is to these forms of story-telling that we now turn.

The Scripts of Television Events

Media events are not only collectively received, they are celebrations of the collective. Their scenarios—we call them Contests, Conquests, and Coronations—are so familiar that they permit the narration of events in progress almost as if we were certain as to how they will end.

What we call Coronations refer not only to monarchic events; they characterize inaugurations of all sorts, such as official funerals and commemorations. In short, they mark the rites of passage of the great. The Coronation script is used to illustrate the workings of collective norms in the action or life of an individual or institution. Coronations are constructed as homages; they signify a commitment to existing norms. They call on spectators to reiterate loyalty to norms and confidence in the men and institutions that embody them.

Contests are the ceremonies of sports and politics; they are designed to identify the best contender or the best team. While Coronations are mostly ascriptive in their choice of heroes, Contests are pure celebrations of achievement; their message is that the winner won *by the rules*. When they are framed as media events, sports contests become expressions of symbolic rivalry between contestants and symbolic unity around the rules. Similarly, political contests are mounted at decisive turning-points in democratic societies. Competitors are invited to face each other within an agreed set of rules at parliamentary hearings, party political conventions, and presidential debates. Contests highlight the desirability of political debate before a public that serves as judge; they confer equality on the representatives of different points of view. They celebrate pluralism. Ironically, even totalitarian societies mount political debates when they need to acquire democratic respectability.

Conquests are perhaps the most consequential of media events; they are also the rarest. They consist in dramatizing political or diplomatic initiatives aimed at the radical transformation of public opinion on a major issue. Conquests are made possible by the charisma of their protagonists and by the fact that they reactivate the repressed aspirations of a society. Thus, Sadat voyages to Jerusalem, while the two countries are nominally still at war; thus, John Paul II visits Poland, confronting the communist leaders of the most Catholic nation in Europe. In both cases, a great man contemplates the means for breaking a long-standing deadlock, announces a radical solution, and risks his life to enact it. In both, the main protagonist crosses unarmed into enemy territory, and talking over the heads of local leaders converts their people to a new vision, and to collective action.

Each of these scenarios has a dominant visual metaphor. The Coronation can be envisaged as a procession, with well-wishers lining the aisle. The Contest calls for an arena filled by supporters. Conquests need a frontier for the hero to cross to the cheers of his own side, and the anticipation of the other.

The three scenarios draw upon different types of legitimacy and different styles of authority (as Max Weber describes them). Coronations invoke the authority inherent in tradition. Contests are based on agreed procedures; they are legalistic by nature and end in a rational judgement. While Coronations and Contests are rule-bound events, Conquests consist in defying the rules, a defiance that both confers and presupposes charisma. Thus Sadat challenged the rules of diplomacy while the Pope challenged the ban on religion in a communist regime.

The differences among the three scripts hint that their distribution among societies will be far from even. All societies have Coronations, because there is no society without traditions. On the other hand, Contests—certainly political Contests—favour regimes that privilege pluralism and are open to the possibility of orderly change. Totalitarian societies abhor Contests, unless they are 'fixed', and delight in Coronations because they celebrate authority and their outcome is known in advance. As for Conquests, their charismatic dynamic is always subversive and they are rightly feared by establishments. Only regimes that are desperate, or those that can afford to take risks, can tolerate the live broadcast of charismatic events. Poland had no choice but to invite the first Polish Pope; this was meant as a concession to popular fervour in the wake of an explosive economic situation, and as an antidote to possible revolution. As it turned out, the agreed script was thrown aside, and Poland got both Pope and revolution. The Coronation of a native son was turned into a Conquest.

The case of the live broadcast of the Pope in Poland demonstrates that scripts are objects of prior negotiation, not only analytic constructions projected on events by commentators and academics. The case of the Pope also demonstrates that rescripting may take place during the event itself. Such rescripting may be highly conflictual, as evidenced by the turmoil caused by the visits of the Pope to many Latin American countries. Similarly, some members of the Senate Committee on the ratification of Justice Thomas protested vehemently against

the change of script that involved the surprise appearance of Professor Anita Hill after the hearings had been adjourned. A less conflictual example is the case of Sadat's visit to Jerusalem where the two main protagonists, Sadat and Begin, nevertheless attempted to pull the script in different directions (Begin towards recognition of the legitimacy of the state of Israel by an Arab leader, Sadat towards regaining the territory lost in the 1973 war).

In another case of script changing, there was no conflict at all, so spontaneous and acceptable was the change. This is the case of a commemoration by Korean Television of the suffering in the North–South war. The broadcast included a small interview segment: bereaved South Koreans described the conditions in which they became separated from their families. These presentations evoked such overwhelming response that a decision was made to extend the programme to allow relatives to seek each other over the air through the co-operation of local stations in the national network. The programme continued for eight days and is probably the longest single live broadcast anywhere. Parenthetically, during the broadcast, more families were successfully reunited than had been the case over the previous thirty years. Thus, a commemorative programme that had been scripted as a memorial was rescripted as a reunion, and yet again into a prelude to actual contact between the two Koreas.

Totalitarian regimes specialize in commemorative ceremonies such as this 1973 May Day parade in the former Soviet Union, but avoid live broadcasting of events that may go wrong.

While the Korean event fits the corpus of media events in almost every way—it interrupts the flow of daily life, interrupts the schedule of broadcasting, and preoccupies an entire population to the exclusion of all other concerns—its script differs from Contests, Conquests, and Coronations in that it does not focus on an individual hero. Rather, it features an anonymous succession of unknown people, each of whom emerges briefly from anonymity holding up a placard with his or her name, address, and telephone number. If these actors become symbolic at all, it is at the collective level.

Such is the case for other events that share this people-to-people character. Urban marathons are a good example. A crowd of amateur runners is seen 'progressing' through the city streets, cordoned off from everyday traffic and everyday violence in a display of togetherness that has become a tradition of live broadcasting. Not a race, these are events in which the public, at home and in person, search for such non-heroes as their dentists, priests, mothers-in-law, baby-sitters. Only the identifiable professional runners remind us that it is something of a race after all. In this type of event—which seems more recent than the others—the collective dimension is celebrated directly, not through representation by a symbolic figure. Here, participants and non-participants are interchangeable; the audience sees itself as hero.

Television Events and the Writing of History

Broadcasters invariably proclaim this type of event 'historic'. Even recurrent events that have great import—such as international sporting events, presidential debates, or summit meetings—are labelled this way. While such claims seem hardly more than advertisements, they point to the fact that television has entered into competition with the historian for the role of chronicler of the present and interpreter of the past. In this view, television pre-empts the right of historians (and newspaper journalists) to decide what should be labelled historic, how it should be told, and what it means.

Yet, offering the experience of participating in history as it happens does not mean that the role of historians has been taken over by television. Television narratives have distinct ambitions. True, they diverge from those of the historians, but they confront the latter with new problems and new questions. These are problems of accuracy, and questions that prompt historians to adopt a reflexive attitude towards their own discipline: what, for instance, is the relation between event and process? What is the influence of the observer on the matter observed?

Television history as 'tiger leaps'

The historiography of television hops from event to event, ignoring the progressions and evolutions that link them. Television ceremonies explore discrete events, not long-running processes. Television's stroboscopic narrative forsakes

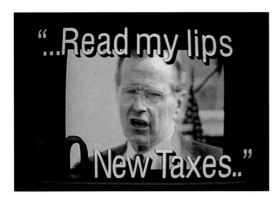

Above: televised politics. Recent US presidential campaigns have been seen to be cynically negative, unanalytical, manipulative, and driven by a preoccupation with image over substance. Many believe that through its complicity in this process, television has undermined rather than strengthened civic life.

Right: Bill Clinton lampooned in the French satire show **Les Guignols de l'info**.

Below: television and the family. The family, however deviant and extended, has remained at the heart of soap operas worldwide. Pictured here is Germany's **Lindenstrasse**.

Above: a pilgrim's progress. Pope John Paul II on a visit to Cameroon. The Pope's televised travels function as an important expression of the continued vitality of the Catholic Church, a public affirmation of the religious community.

Below: television and terrorism. Terry Waite at a Beirut press conference in 1985 before being kidnapped. He was later released in 1991 and was the focus of massive news attention; the media generally presented the story as a triumph of human endurance and heroism, downplaying the political background.

historical progression in favour of detailed close-ups. As for television ceremonies the fact that they are broadcast live makes it evident that they are narra-
tions of the 'now'.

Thus, unlike historical accounts in which events are inserted into carefully
reconstituted continuities, television broadcasts achieve their contextualization
through what Benjamin called 'tiger leaps' into the past. Rather than search for
immediate antecedents, the narrators and actors of televised ceremonies seek to
associate the events at hand with similarly significant events often disregarding
actual connections and observable continuities. These other events are
metaphors. They illuminate the meaning of the present event and offer the viewers a libretto of its development. Thus, the Kennedy assassination became the
Lincoln assassination; the visit of Sadat to Jerusalem was set against the background of Jewish–Arab relations in the Golden Age of Andalusia; the Polish
Catholics addressed by the Pope re-enacted the plight of the early Christians.

By invoking events that are paradigmatic but temporally distant and discon-
nected, broadcasters telescope time in favour of symbolic relevance, following
the lead of those who proclaimed the French Revolution 'Rome reincarnate'.
Thus, the live broadcasts of Coronations, royal weddings, and funerals offer a re-
enactment of the past, even if this past sometimes turns out to be a forgery.
Conquests often extend further into the past, suppressing the immediate context
in favour of an earlier era to which the present may be associated. Chronicles of
this type, we have already shown, attempt to achieve radical but orderly change
by portraying a dramatic act (Sadat in Jerusalem, for example) as the reinstatement of a forgotten continuity. In giving voice to the heroes of Conquest, television allows them to introduce conceptions of time, space, and collective memory
that link their proposals to prior (but not immediately preceding) conceptions of
these parameters.

These 'tiger leaps' are clearly at odds with history as a science. Television
history aims at grasping the 'constellation' that a given moment has formed with
some earlier time. It illustrates the alternative history evoked by Benjamin, a
history whose task would consist in redeeming from oblivion those aspects of the
past that have been erased because they represented defeated options. Yet, if
some of our events—especially those we call Conquests—represent a conscious
attempt to revive long-forgotten possibilities, they are no more than a tiny
minority. In most cases, ceremonial contextualization through 'tiger leaps into
the past' belongs to what Yerushalmi describes as a ritual route towards the
constitution of memory—as opposed to a historical route. Indeed, by focusing
on discrete events and linking them to paradigmatic models, television's
approach replicates the mnemonics of oral tradition rather than the record of the
written word.

By now, the politics of memory has turned into a fully-fledged field of historical investigation. Considerable attention is being devoted to the various modes
of recontextualizing events over time. Far from competing with the work of

Daniel Dayan and Elihu Katz

right The assassination of President Lincoln. Reaching only one city at a time, Abraham Lincoln's funeral cortège travelled for twenty-one days. *below* Reaching the whole world simultaneously, by contrast, the mourning for John F. Kennedy lasted four days, the funeral itself only some hours.
Live coverage of major news events—such as Kennedy's assassination—document disruptions of social order. Live coverage of ceremonial events—Kennedy's funeral, for example—are restorations of social order.

historians, television events invite historians' scrutiny; they offer a powerful illustration of the workings of collective memory. Historians will recognize that 'historic' on television means 'legendary' and that ceremonial television is preoccupied less with the factual than with the meaningful.

Hiding behind ceremony

Television ceremonies are consensual events, moments of agreement among masses and élites about what is important, and what the important means. But these events, and what lies behind them, are creatures of the moment, and may conceal more than they reveal. What did go on behind the scenes while Sadat's visit or Kennedy's funeral monopolized the screen? The need for journalists and historians to answer questions like these has become all the more important.

There is no alternative to historical scholarship when the facts themselves are in doubt, in cases such as the reporting of the Gulf War, for example, or the broadcast alleging a massacre in Timisoara, which fanned the flames of the Romanian revolution of 1989. What may be legitimate in the case of consensual ceremonies which make no secret of their integrative ambition seems much less acceptable in controversial, or potentially controversial, events where the ceremonial format serves to bridle the functioning of a free and critical press. The simultaneity of an event and its transmission often makes it impossible to meet the basic requirements of accuracy such as checking on the credibility of sources and the authenticity of images. The task becomes almost impossible when live, pre-planned broadcasting is no longer the privilege of ceremonial events, but also applied to news events.

Increasingly, news events are also broadcast live and, sometimes, even masquerade as ceremony. Thus live broadcasting of the Gulf War, or the Falklands expedition, or the intervention in Somalia was made possible because the timing of these events, and their logistics, had been made known in advance, as if their organizers were proposing a ceremonial frame for the actions to come. This advance scripting of major news events is what Daniel Boorstin would rightly condemn as 'pseudo-events'. When the coverage of a war is no longer distinguishable from its celebration, historians are urgently needed to tell us what actually happened.

Influence of narrators and narratives

But if television events do not usurp the writing of history, they may nevertheless refocus it on new objects. They may, as we have seen, constrain the historian (and the rest of us) to consider the differences between history as a discipline and the other channels of collective memory. They constrain the historian to take account of the social role imparted to narratives and narrators and to consider the influence of different forms of chronicling on the directions taken by society.

Apart from the story that unravels on screen, the sheer size of the witnessing audience may incite to collective action. Triggering a society-wide conversation,

Daniel Dayan and Elihu Katz

Gulf War, 1991: television was there, but did the tree really fall?

opposite: The Graphic, 1915: artists' sketches and photo-journalism are precursors of the televising of events.

the event may lead to drastic changes in public opinion and even to the rise of social movements. That the observer—whether broadcaster, journalist, or historian—may affect that which is being observed is even truer here than in the constantly cited examples from the physical sciences. Leaving aside the issue of manipulative intent, surveillance itself has an effect. Television's historiography invites historians to reflect on its impact—and their own.

Nor can historians afford to overrate television's revival of the art of the chronicle, which diverts attention from large-scale evolutions in order to refocus it on the intricate texture of events. Rather than being enveloped in a larger process, the event becomes a process in itself. Unravelling its intricacies calls for the adoption of a new, almost ethnographic, approach. Television may thus have affected the writing of history by reintroducing a specific interest in events after these had been banished in the name of deeper-seated and more abstract trends. While a history of long-range processes turned its back on the role of agency and the relevance of voluntaristic action, telling history as event reinstates both actor and subject. Historians may pronounce this new focus misplaced but they have no choice but to take the rehabilitation of the event into account.

A final point deserves the historians' attention: the integrative function of ceremonial television is all the more evident as we enter the era of electronic

fragmentation. The new media technologies are pulling television in two directions—towards individuation (in the sense that no two people will see the same programme at the same time) and towards globalization (the whole world will see the same programme at the same time). The nation-state as a political community is overlooked in this industrial tug-of-war, and ceremonial television, of the sort described here, may be the only shared experience that will hold nations together in the future. Historians, anthropologists, and other social scientists have all the more reason, therefore, to take note.

Part Three

Television and Society

8

Television in the Home and Family

Susan Briggs

ome life has never been the same since the advent of television, particularly since television began to be considered as *the* household medium in a very large part of the world. None the less, broadcasters, critics, academics, and viewers have never been in agreement about the domestic consequences of television, for many reasons.

Since television entered the home—and each home has had its own family and television chronology—much else has changed besides the mere size of the television audience. The family itself as a unit has been under pressure for reasons of which television has been only one. Changes in family structure and the rise in the number of single parent families have transformed the scene. 'Family values' have themselves been in question. But even before these changes there were many kinds of homes, and many kinds of families. Reactions were not the same. Joseph Klapper, research pioneer, rightly refused in 1960 to draw a sharp distinction between the habits of 'television families' and 'non-television families' without examining whether the differences which were thrown up in family surveys antedated the purchase of a television set.

Taking the world as a whole, it is even more difficult to generalize about the impact of television on the family because of the variety of political, economic, and communications systems. When television was geared to the market and derived its revenues from advertising it was used to tempt viewers to gaze at other consumer goods from automobiles (which took families out of their homes) to better and brighter kitchens (designed to keep them in them). It served as an invaluable instrument in an age of increasing 'consumerism'. When it was geared to the power of authority and was totally dependent on government for finance it was used for political propaganda, and in the process both inculcated values and contributed in the longer run to their subversion. In countries with public service broadcasting systems, organized with varying degrees of independence, television often encouraged critical discussion of the family as an institution. It also illuminated differences between opinion groups and pressure groups, many of the latter professedly committed to 'family values'.

When the first half-century of American television was celebrated at a Smithsonian exhibition in 1989, *Time* magazine asked just what the revellers should be celebrating, television as a technological device, as an entertainment medium, as 'a chronicler of our times', as a business enterprise, or as 'a social force'? In fact, the exhibition, which was called American Television from the Fair to the Family, concentrated, as many opinion and pressure groups have done, on the impact of television on the home. Early advertisements for television were shown with elegant models watching the screen in sophisticated surroundings. Television was a luxury then as well as a novelty. Very soon, however, advertisers began to promote television as a force making for family togetherness: 'There is great happiness in the home where the family is held together by its new common bond—television.' Later advertisements had a sharper focus after television became a mass medium. Predictions proliferated. One Los Angeles survey in 1949 even forecast that the divorce rate would fall in America, thanks to television.

The world-wide relevance of this particular American half-century, celebrated in 1989, can be challenged. It was a fact that RCA had introduced 'the modern system of television' at the New York World Fair fifty years before in 1939, but the American television audience, the first of such audiences in the world, did not grow fast until the late 1940s and 1950s. The Second World War had held back the progress of television in the United States and in Britain had brought it to an abrupt halt.

The number of viewers in Britain and Germany was, of course, extremely small. In Britain there were only 20,000 television licences in 1939 and television was serving the needs of only a small relatively well-off audience in the London area. It was Britain, however, with a very different broadcasting system, and Germany with a different political system, that had introduced television services in 1936 before television took hold in the United States.

The main impact of television in Britain before that date had not been on 'viewers', a new term, but on the press, which did much to publicize it among people who never saw it, while its main impact in Germany had been on Nazi leaders who were fascinated by broadcasting technology. None the less, even before 1939, there were occasional revealing comments on the likely impact of television on the home and family. Thus in the class-based society of pre-war Britain a working-class Cockney woman, interviewed after watching a television demonstration in 1937, could exclaim, 'Blimey! . . . if we ever get one of these things at home, we shan't have an excuse to go out to the pictures . . . and we shan't be able to get rid of the men on Saturday afternoons, either. They'll want to sit in front of the fire to watch the football match.'

The fact that the radio set (and in some cases the gramophone) had entered the home before the television set was of crucial importance both in Britain and the United States, as it was to be in other countries, and not surprisingly in the early years there were sceptics on both sides of the Atlantic who doubted whether television would ever supplant radio inside the house. For example, Raymond Postgate, writer on wine, food, and history, suggested in 1939 that working-class homes were not big enough to take television screens: there was not enough wall space. In his view television would become an amusement only in homes that had several rooms. 'Not more than ten per cent of the population will take it up permanently,' he predicted. 'But in cinema houses, as a rival feature to films, it may become very popular.'

As late as 1951 Derek Horton, author of a book called *Television's Story and Challenge*, believed that the future lay in big-screen television viewed in special theatres. Television was spectacle. He refused to believe that 'television will ever make families want to stay at home night after night peering at their little screens'.

By then, however, there were many people, at least in Britain, who were convinced that the television set would supplant the wireless set in the home, even in the working-class home. It was already becoming a familiar piece of furniture, often the most expensive piece of furniture that a lower-income-group family had ever bought or hired. As the *Daily Mail Ideal Home* book put it undra-

An early cartoon from the pages of **Punch**.

"I didn't realise you had Television, dear."

matically in 1950, 'Sound broadcasting is already essential to the life of the nation and the family unit . . . It will not be long before television occupies a somewhat similar position.' Two decades later, a more dramatic statement of the by then established power over people of television was that of the authority on pop culture Arthur Asa Berger in 1973. Drawing a comparison between (American) television and drugs he wrote: 'Once you are hooked on them it is difficult to get off them . . . both depend upon "turning on" and passively waiting for something beautiful to happen.'

In the early years of television in a number of other countries, Italy in particular, television was not a home-centred medium. It was associated with public places. The same is still true of television in some developing countries, where the cost of a television set is too high for most families to afford.

II

Even before television became a mass medium, considerable interest was shown in the habits that it would be likely to induce, foster, restrain, or suppress. How, for example, would it affect other activities both inside and outside the home? Would it make viewers more open to outside influences and therefore better informed or would it simply make them more passive?

Most of the early research concentrated on quantitative assessments of hours spent on viewing. Time-use surveys were collected in different countries, and from them deductions were drawn as to the extent to which television displaced, for example, radio listening in the home and cinema attendance outside it. Japanese time-studies of what happened during each twenty-four hours in a seven-day week, developed during the 1970s, were perhaps the most sophisticated examples of such research. Meanwhile, a long-term American study compared a sample of 2,021 respondents in 1965 with another sample of 2,475 respondents in 1975. During the decade it was found that time spent on work, housework, and leisure showed considerable constancy both across time and across social groups. The largest change in the use of time was within 'leisure': television not only usurped time previously devoted to the mass media that it replaced, i.e. radio and the movies, but also cut into time previously not spent on the media at all.

In Britain in 1993 *Social Trends* could report that 'watching television and visiting or entertaining friends or relatives' had remained the most popular home-based leisure activities over the previous fifteen years. The average number of hours of television viewed per week rose from 16.2 in February 1967, to 19.9 in February 1977 to a peak figure of over 26 hours a week in 1986 (after which the figure declined very slightly). Significantly, the media periodicals *Radio Times* and *TV Times*, which included feature articles as well as programme schedules for the forthcoming week, had the highest circulations of any general weeklies.

The amount of viewing in Britain was lower than that in the United States throughout the period: in 1984, for example, Americans viewed on average 31

Radio Times cover, 1936.

hours a week, whilst people in Continental European countries viewed less than the British, with the Dutch viewing least of all, 12 hours a week in 1985.

Such comparative figures of national viewing habits, the reasons for which have been inadequately explored, should themselves be compared with comparative studies relating to economic and social differences within particular countries. In Britain, for example, the viewing figures, as they were stated in *Social Trends*, concealed a considerable range of viewing hours per week, with high amounts being associated throughout the period covered with low social class, old (and very young) age, and unemployment. Members of the managerial and professional classes, among the first to acquire television sets, viewed two hours less a day than those in unskilled and semi-skilled occupations. There were also differences between viewing habits at different times of year: *Social Trends* showed that the August viewing figures were always several hours per week less than the winter figures, as people engaged in outdoor activities and went on holiday. The figures quoted above are for February, a prime viewing month.

It is difficult to generalize convincingly about television viewing in different places and at different times, yet some useful comparative studies have been made, particularly by J. P. Robinson, who summarized a range of studies from several countries in 1986. He found that the differences in time spent viewing television between different countries seem to be related less to different amounts of time devoted to necessary household chores and domestic activities than to what he called, with the United States in mind, 'the colonisation of leisure'. For him, 'free time' was becoming a marketable commodity and 'so, in one sense, becoming less free'.

From the evidence of both time-use surveys and from direct observational studies it was apparent that time spent in front of the screen, whether it was continuous or spasmodic viewing, was significant irrespective of the content of what was being shown. Yet the words 'in front of the screen' or 'glued to the screen' obviously became inappropriate as television developed, particularly where 'natural breaks' were devoted to advertising. A study of Germany in 1988 suggested that 'the characteristic look that television produces is the glance'. Likewise, a British time-use diary showed that as early as 1984 'pure' television viewing was relatively rare: people claimed to be watching television and doing other things concurrently, a habit which other studies showed to have been often established in childhood. Conversation was not one of the 'other things'. As Julian Critchley commented in the *Daily Mail* in 1989, 'Silence is golden before the flickering screen . . . The small screen may have reunited the family, but it is generally a silent communion.'

Not surprisingly, the effect of television on the habits—and even the personalities—of children has been the subject of more surveys than any other aspect of the medium. Psychologists, educationalists, moralists, and, of course, parents have taken it for granted that children would be the most vulnerable to the introduction of a television set into the home. Would they stop reading? Would they stop playing? Would they become addicts? Some of them very quickly did.

The conclusions drawn from such surveys have often been contradictory: for example, some surveys suggested that 'quality' children's television programmes gave children more open-minded, better-informed attitudes, while critics complained that children were simply being spoon-fed information which would have been better learned—and retained—the hard traditional way, by reading and classroom teaching. There was argument, too, as to whether children were being stimulated by what they saw on the screen or being made more passive. The most frequently posed question of all—whether television scenes of violence would make children more aggressive or whether they would become indifferent to or even repelled by such scenes—was at different periods answered in different ways in different places.

The first predictions of the effect of television on children were made long before the arrival in 1936 of a scheduled television service in Britain, and long before sociologists began to carry out surveys. In 1928 an advertisement for the *Land and Peoples Encyclopaedia* adopted the 'magic carpet' theme 'Before your children have grown up, television may enable them and you to "see by wireless" any part of the world.' Horizons would be broadened; windows in the world opened. No drawbacks were foreseen.

When television actually came on the scene, however, the assumption was often made, without evidence, that it would do more harm than good. The social psychologist Hilde Himmelweit, interviewed on the BBC in 1972, spoke about the results of her pioneering study of children's viewing behaviour, *Television and the Child* (1958). She commented that in the early years of television a judge might say: 'It is very clear that this boy stole because he was also an addict of television.'

Himmelweit's first research was carried out in 1955 and 1956 at a time early enough in television history for it to be easy to find a control group of children with no sustained access to television. (Indeed, only about one-third of the children in the schools Himmelweit studied had television at home.) Asked where the time children spent viewing television came from, Himmelweit replied, 'What is displaced primarily is non-purposive activity . . . The time previously spent with other children, in clubs and on activities which were always very much enjoyed, by and large remains.' She commented, also, that television is 'the second thing you turn to: it is never the first'.

Some studies disputed this opinion, and also Himmelweit's finding that television had only a temporary adverse effect on children's reading habits. They also emphasized the multiple functions of television. An American social scientist, Bradley Greenberg, who questioned English children to test some of Himmelweit's findings, reported that children gave eight major reasons why they watched television: 'to relieve boredom; in order to forget school, friends, something; to learn about things, how to do things . . . what was going on in the world . . . or about themselves . . . how to cope with life in a more satisfactory manner; for arousal; to relax—they wanted to sit down and not have to think about anything; for companionship when they were lonely; and, finally, for simple enjoyment.'

Whatever the reason, television was often used by parents to keep children quiet so that the cultural critic Alasdair Clayre could conclude in 1972: 'It's been said that children are our guests in the world. It appears that what we do with our guests at the moment is largely to leave them in front of the television set.' At the time that Clayre wrote children were already spending an average of more than three hours daily in front of the set and many critics blamed television for corrupting children's values and deadening their responses.

197

The magic carpet

come abroad...
EVERY EVENING

In October 1922 *The Broadcaster* called its editorial 'Exploring': 'Throughout all the ages of Mankind men have been possessed of "Wanderlust",' it declared, 'but many [now] explore thus:
By the turning of a switch, the adjustment of a tuning coil, or condenser, many "Nations" journey – in the passing of a second of time – to lands afar. Many hear, and fancifully almost see, New York or "The land of the Rising Sun"; or travel to the West where the Amazon rolls in flood to the sea; to the Gateway of the East, Singapore; or to Iceland's one Radio Station.... All by the turning of a switch and the lighting of a Radio Valve.'

A 1928 advertisement for the *Lands and Peoples* Encyclopaedia borrowed the 'magic carpet' theme (*right*). It used the still undeveloped but eagerly anticipated new medium of television as a bait: both books and television would enable readers/viewers to 'see the world'.

Meanwhile they had to be content with radio. In 1935 *World Radio* carried an advertisement for the 'Transatlantic All-Wave Superhet model', 'the set that brings the World to your finger tips' (*above*).

In a *Punch* cartoon of 1936 a butler standing at the wireless asks the Duke, 'Do you wish me to summon Berlin or Rome, your Grace?'

See the World
as by Television

Before your children have grown up, Television may enable them and you to " see by Wireless " any part of the world. This will be unending delight for those who live to enjoy it, but they must wait for wireless vision to be perfected.

You need not wait more than a few hours for a work that gives you in six lavishly illustrated volumes a vision of the interesting lands and peoples of all the world in full colour, and vivid, exciting descriptions of them written in the most engaging manner by eye-witnesses of every scene.

HERE you see the religions, superstitions, witchcraft and magic of tropics and arctic circle. Here the eyes of the great cats haunt the jungle, to stalk the unconscious hunter. There the gorgeous colours of strange birds shift and shine in the sun, volcanoes burst into fire and great waterfalls rush down in foam. Some savage king is heavy with stifling clothes for his naked people to admire, and whole races wear little or nothing. All this and more, in full colour, with thrilling descriptive chapters you will find.

6 VOLUMES SENT TO YOUR HOME FOR 5/-

Here is a FREE Book
that shows you, by samples, the nearest thing yet to television, and tells you what these volumes are like.

Lands & Peoples
SIX SUMPTUOUS VOLUMES

The American sociologist, Urie Bronfenbrenner, speaking in 1972 in a BBC Further Education series on the impact of television on children, warned of the dangers not of the behaviour television produced but of the behaviour it prevented. 'When the TV set is on it freezes everybody: they're all expressionless, focused on the image on the screen, and everything that used to go on between people—the games, the arguments, the emotional scenes, out of which personality and ability develop—is stopped so when you turn on the TV you turn off the process of making human beings human.'

Twelve years later, Cedric Cullingford in an interesting study, *Children and Television*, was less devastating in his judgements. He claimed that children had their own way of dealing with the effects of too much television. The habits they acquired whilst viewing were themselves important. Actually observing children watching television, Cullingford exploded the myth that learning only takes place through conscious attention to programmes. 'The sophistication children learn is that of being able to ignore the stimulation offered . . . the paradox is that of the gap between children's great capacity to appreciate and to be critical and their frequent boredom resulting from overuse of television.'

Children can, of course, learn other things, or rather, be trained into them. Advertising directed at children works on the assumption, as Jules Henry has put it in *Culture against Man* (1965), 'that the claim that gets into the child's brainbox first is most likely to stay there and, that since in contemporary America children manage parents, the former's brainbox is the ante-chamber to the brainbox of the latter.'

Such studies focus largely on individual child viewers, but there has been a sequence of surveys suggesting that viewing is itself a social as well as an individual act, and that the impact of television must always be related to interaction within the family. Jack Lyle, reporting in 1971 to the US Surgeon General's Advisory Committee on Television and Social Behaviour, noted that television viewing in families featured interaction between viewers as well as simple acts of individual viewing as parents and children viewed together. Of course, children also viewed with other children, both siblings and friends, and this aspect of interaction has been less systematically studied.

Interaction concerns adults as well as children and, as in the case of children, friends as well as the family. 'The owner of a television set', wrote one broadcasting critic in 1938, 'should consider it his duty, as a pioneer, to convert friends by inviting them round to enjoy it under domestic conditions . . . take care to choose an evening when there is something good on.' A woman viewer described in 1938 how in her home 'just before nine o'clock chairs are drawn into a circle. Lights are switched off, a screen shuts out any interfering reflections from the fire, and once the tuning signal is radiated silence prevails by common consent.'

Forty years later, across the Atlantic, the agony aunt Abbie van Buren dealt with knotty problems of television manners in the home. Often there were no

opposite Television as 'magic carpet': a 1928 advertisement for the **Land and Peoples Encyclopaedia** borrows the image.

GEC television
advertisement.

solutions. 'Dear Abbie, What can be done about friends who drop in unexpect-
edly while we are watching our favorite TV programs? We hate to be rude, but
we would rather watch our programs than visit with them . . . ' Another letter
to Abbie dealt not with friends but with husbands. 'The minute my husband
comes home from work,' a housewife wrote, 'he turns on the TV and watches
anything that happens to be on . . . He doesn't talk to me or the children. Abbie,
he stays up until 2 o'clock in the morning . . . of course we don't have a sex-life
any more.'

Eight years later, Mary Kenny in a *Sunday Telegraph* column headed 'No telly, please, we're talking' (1986), reported an individual case on the same theme. She described a family who had given up television three years earlier: 'Liz and Neville Compton of Leamington Spa felt that TV was having an insidious effect on their family life. "He'd come in from work in the evening, wanting to tell me about his day", Liz recalled, "and I'd say—shush tell me later—as I hung on for the development in some soap opera." And then there was the effect on their two children. It was nothing dramatic or big and shocking, they both say. It was the gradual clipping away of decent standards, the flip attitudes, the casual acceptance of violence, the trivialisation of love and sex . . . So out the TV went.'

This family had found that the ultimate way of dealing with surfeit and addiction was abstinence, and various studies have examined the effects on families and individuals of watching no television. Some of the earliest of such reports looked at families who from the outset had rejected television altogether, or at those who had renounced it voluntarily after a time, or even, in a few cases, at people who were paid by researchers not to watch for a period. One early Australian survey interviewed householders whose sets had broken down (although the results were misleading, since there was often a second set which could be moved from a bedroom into the living-room). Another Australian survey of 1977 studied 298 non-television-owning families who had responded to an article in a Melbourne newspaper and were interviewed or asked to fill out a questionnaire. The sample was unusual because the participants were 'self-selected, interested and eager to express their points of view' and, one might add, self-satisfied. 'Television steals time, makes people lazier and more passive, and is addictive,' one typical respondent observed. The main reason given by those respondents who blamed television as a waste of time had little to do with programmes and their content but rather with the feeling that time spent on almost any other activity was better used than time watching television: 'there is little to show for those hours'; 'a monster, a lurking presence, exploiting those who watch it'; 'a sedative to keep people in a vaguely somnolent state . . .'.

The results of 'abstinence' surveys have been as contradictory as the results of children's surveys. In both Germany and Britain, where families were paid not to view television for a period, their 'need' for television proved so great that no family was able to continue not viewing despite the payment. In the first difficult week adaptation of various kinds had been achieved, although one of the casualties had been family conversation, a conclusion that set some of the first criticisms of television on its head. A similar American study revealed, however, not surprisingly, that there were varieties of reaction according to a variety of factors, including the age and number of persons in the household and the previous viewing patterns in the home, as well as socio-economic status and the range of other work and leisure activities.

Such reports were illuminating, but most people would reject the idea of total abstinence from viewing, whatever reservations they might feel about the effect of television on themselves and their children. Indeed, a report of 1990 showed

201

that 99 per cent of a British population sample had watched some television during the four weeks before they were questioned. Among this huge group the problem for those families who perceived that there *was* a problem was not whether to view but what to view and there were plenty of would-be family counsellors to advise them.

III

Of course one cannot separate questions relating to viewing behaviour from questions relating to the content of what is seen. The range of television is wide, covering as it does everything from news and current affairs, with a dominating factual content, sometimes violent, to entertainment, presenting various versions of fiction, some of this violent also. News and current affairs programmes have often been concerned with families, not least families in distress in contexts far outside the viewing families' own experience. Entertainment has often incorporated not only fictional families but real families being shown on the screen in quiz and game shows, some of them with glittering prizes, and in other cross-generation contests.

Whether or not all members of the family should have free access to the whole

The family game show: Belgium's version of Fremantle's international hit, **Family Fortunes/ Family Feud**.

television output has always been contentious. The film industry developed a certificating system. Television did not, although in Britain there was for a long period until it was abandoned in 1957 a so-called 'toddlers' truce' between the hours of 6 and 7 o'clock. So-called 'adult' material has often been reserved until later in the evening. For some time 9 o'clock has been treated in Britain as the 'watershed'. In fact, empirical evidence in Britain, at least, suggests that all members of the family watch at 'adult' times (just as adults often view at 'children's' times). The 'watershed' policy has always been criticized for being based on unrealistic assumptions about children's bedtimes and parental control.

Who, if anyone, decides what others should watch or not watch clearly varies from family to family, and many research projects have examined programme selection when there are conflicting views within the family. Sometimes the decision to watch a given programme is the result of democratic discussion, sometimes 'spoiled' children have their way, and sometimes the authoritarian father decides. (Of course the mother, if she is at home, may have had the set to herself during the day.) According to Robert T. Bower, writing in 1973, 'In general, the norms of society prevail when family viewing decisions are made: male dominates female, older children win out over younger children, and father dominates both mother and children.' Despite this, Bower noticed that often parents give way to their children, who thus become arbiters of what the whole family watches. Also, fathers who in fact control the set often perceive their partner or children as the controller(s). Research has also investigated who turned the set on, who changed the channel, and who switched it off. The husband and children were much more likely than the mother to alter the set (only 15 per cent of mothers did so in a 1982 survey of ninety-three British families).

For some families choosing the programme was a matter of indifference and apathy. 'You come home at night and you say you're going to watch a little television and, irrespective of the content, you watch and you turn on the dials to watch the least objectionable programme.' So ran the American Paul Klein's theory of Least Objectionable Programming.

Children's viewing patterns show some differences from adults. Most children of 6–10 years watch a mixture of adult and children's programmes. A typical mixture consists of cartoons, children's serials, and 'magazine' programmes and also sitcoms and soap operas (but little news and current affairs). Very young children mainly watch their own children's programmes and bought or rented children's videos, whilst 10–12-year-olds watch few children's programmes, less television of all kinds than younger children, but what they do watch is intended for adults. Boys watch more sport and 'action' programmes, girls more serials, drama, and comedy.

Would-be family counsellors have been more concerned with what ought to be than with what is, and with what ought to be for adults as well as for children. In Britain, for example, Mary Whitehouse, who became interested in television as a schoolteacher concerned about the effect of 'sex' programmes on her pupils, broadened her range of interests to encompass adults when she founded her Viewers' and Listeners' Association in 1965. Her campaign covered bad language as well as sex and violence and inevitably provoked opposition both from people who thought that she did not understand how twentieth-century families actually lived, and from the BBC, which objected to being offered moral guidance from outside.

The BBC's own study of violence on the television screen, which started in 1969 was specifically based on family reactions. Its Audience Research Department invited fifty families individually to Broadcasting House to watch a programme containing violence. Discussing the project afterwards David Newell, the chief researcher, said that he had often had to push the viewing families quite hard before they would even mention violence. Among the results of an expensive and protracted survey, not published until 1972, it was shown that while there was much violence on television, an average 2.2 incidents per hour, many people did not class programmes showing a few violent incidents as any more violent than those showing just one.

Brian Emmett, Head of BBC Audience Research, was surprised also by the number of people who reacted to violent programmes with 'It's not a bad thing to put the boot in when I think it's needed.'

Other surveys, earlier and later, have attempted to analyse the effect of television violence on viewers in terms of subsequent aggressive conduct and attitudes, but conclusions are indecisive or contradictory. To this day there is, for example, no agreement about the nature of the interaction of mass media violence and aggressive behaviour despite what Simon Carey in *Criminal Justice Matters*, issue of Spring 1993, describes as a surfeit of theories investigating the nature of the link. There is not even the most basic agreement on whether the observation of violence causes the aggression or the aggression causes the observation or whether some other factor such as personality causes both. Nor, given that proofs of causality are not possible, is there even agreement on the *fact* of whether there is a positive or a negative correlation between the viewing of violence and aggression ('arousal' or 'catharsis').

Broadcasters have little control over the flow of events which constitute 'news', but they do have power to decide just what news pictures will be shown on the screen. They have often given warnings, somewhat similar to tobacco health warnings, about items in the news which may not be suitable for whole family viewing.

Most of the studies of violence on viewers carried out since the early days of television have been concerned with fictional violence. Joseph Klapper pointed out as long ago as 1960 that the studies performed for the National Association of Educational Broadcasters 'carefully tally fictional evidence resulting from "act of nature" and "accident" but ignore "because of special problems in definition and methods, violence found in sports, news, weather, public issues and public events programs"'. A study by Leo Bogart in 1956 showed that audiences could stomach, and even enjoy, scenes of violence in a quasi-documentary TV series, provided the shows were prefaced by reassuring announcements.

Whether television violence was fictional or documentary, broadcasters have sometimes, but by no means always, responded sympathetically to the kind of statement made in 1987 by Colin Morris, the BBC's Director of Religious Education, that 'the broadcaster is a guest in the home of the viewer and there are things which guests can be expected not to do whilst enjoying their hosts' hospitality . . . When broadcasters introduce offensive language or images into the family setting, they are guilty of a double offence: they have forced into consciousness issues which may be embarrassing across the generations, and as guests in the home they have breached the laws of hospitality. Hence certain levels of taste and standards in radio and television programmes express the essential courtesies.'

More than three decades after the American sociologist Wilbur Schramm cautiously summed up the findings of a major study, *Television in the Lives of our Children* (by Schramm, Lyle, and Parker, 1961), Simon Carey commented that nothing in subsequent correlational studies suggests any need to modify a single word of it: 'For some children under some conditions,' Schramm had concluded, 'some television is harmful. For other children under the same conditions, or for the same children under other conditions, it may be beneficial. For most children under most conditions, most television is probably neither harmful nor particularly beneficial.' Carey suggests that the failure of massive research efforts to produce clear and useful answers is leading researchers to leave the field of media violence: it has proved, paradoxically, too indecisive and, therefore, too anodyne a subject for systematic study.

This unsatisfactory inconclusiveness has not, of course, prevented many individuals and pressure groups from making judgements. Sex, violence, and bad language on television are subjects on which almost everyone has an opinion.

IV

From inside their own homes viewers saw as a regular item in programmes portrayals of the family itself, fictional or real. They could identify themselves with what they saw, or they could be shocked or envious. Meanwhile, both moralists and sociologists asked, as a leading question, whether what was shown on the screen, fictional or real, reflected or distorted reality. The moralists were also concerned with a second question: did what was seen on the screen affect the real-life behaviour of families?

The family was always at the centre of television thinking and planning: it provided protagonists, situations, and background for sitcoms, soap operas, and contemporary drama. There were as many kinds of families as there were kinds of homes. Yet some homes, whatever happened inside them, came to look reas-

An early—and hugely popular—British television family, **The Larkins**. Pictured from left are daughter Joyce (Ruth Trouncer), son Eddie (Shaun O'Riordan), son-in-law Jeff (Ronan O'Casey), husband Alf (David Kossof), and wife Ada (Peggy Mount).

suringly familiar. As one sociologist put it, 'the narrative space of [these] programmes is dominated by the domestic space of the home'.

Early American television families usually served as comic battlegrounds for farce and slapstick—with henpecked father, domineering mother, and awful children descended directly from seaside-postcard or comic-film stereotypes. By the mid-1950s, however, advertising sponsors grasped that a more realistic—or idealistic—approach could pay, not least in commercials: viewers could be encouraged to aspire to live in the well-designed and well-equipped homes shown in more sophisticated television series. They might even become well-designed nuclear families.

The American *Father Knows Best* (1955) was the earliest mass-audience television sitcom family, neat and nuclear, with Jim Anderson described at the time as 'the first intelligent father on radio or television' and his wife Margaret 'a contented and attractive homemaker', fulfilled by rearing her children and looking after her husband. The *Saturday Evening Post* praised the Andersons for being 'a family that has surprising similarities to real people'. The show was applauded for making 'polite, carefully middle-class, family-type entertainment'. One feminist sociologist has suggested that there was behind-the-scenes pressure to present such wives as role-models since, after World War II, women's skilled jobs were scarce, and most middle-class women were destined whether they liked it or not to remain 'homemakers'. Marginal as such women were as family earners, however, television sponsors correctly targeted them as the major shoppers for household goods.

Contemporary with *Father Knows Best* (1954–63), were sitcoms *Leave it to Beaver* (1957–63), *The Donna Reed Show* (1958–66), *The Dick Van Dyke Show* (1961–6), *Hazel* (1961–6), *Dennis the Menace* (1959–63), and *The Adventures of Ozzie and Harriet* (1952–66). Britain's first television families, *The Grove Family* (1953–6) and *The Larkins* (1958–60) presented a different picture of home and family in a still auster-ity-bound post-war Britain, a life with which lower-middle-class and working-class viewers could identify rather than a source of aspiration, a significant difference from the United States. Since there was as yet no commercial televi-sion there was no sponsors' pressure to show the dream house. Family relation-ships, however, were shown as traditionally—perhaps nostalgically—warm and supportive. It was a world in which homes were run by down-to-earth 'mum'-style housewives rather than American-model youthful homemakers enjoying the leisure made possible by modern household appliances.

As statistics increasingly showed that the nuclear family was in a minority of household groupings, television sitcoms on both sides of the Atlantic showed families of many different kinds, often less than perfect: the British *Till Death Us Do Part* (1966–75) and its American spin-off *All in the Family* (1971–9), with their bigoted husbands, Alf Garnett and Archie Bunker; *Steptoe and Son* in their non-ideal home behind the scrapyard (1962–6 and 1970–4); the grotesque *Addams Family* (1964–6) and *The Munsters* (1964–5), and the all-male, yet innocent, *Odd Couple* (1970–5). There were sitcoms about black families (Cosby), ghetto fami-

A scene from **The Munsters**: America's ideal nuclear family recedes from its television screens.

lies, and all kinds of deviant families, reflecting real life itself. The fictional Lawrences of California were described by a sociologist as 'sitting around waiting for social problems to come knockin' at the door'. By 1980 an American psychologist, Arlene Skolnick, could suggest that the family itself had become 'a media event like politics or athletics, with nightly doses of lump-in-the-throat normalcy and "humorous deviance"'.

Single dramas, too, could, of course, give a picture of home and family life, but the most powerful and still-remembered play was the tragic *Cathy Come Home* (1966, written by Jeremy Sandford and directed by Ken Loach) which brutally laid bare the anguish of families in contemporary Britain who had *no* home.

The soap opera, with its more diffuse structure and longer time-scale, could explore escapist fantasy worlds of improbable plots, extreme passions, and unlikely relationships against backdrops of exotic scenery and high fashion. Adultery, incest, and bigamy thickened many a plot. Yet the family, however extended and deviant, was usually at the heart of the story not only in American and non-British soap opera but in Brazil's *Roda de Fogo* (Wheel of Fire). The hero of *Roda de Fogo*, watched by 50 million people six nights a week, was born into a wealthy family and aspired to become President of Brazil. In France *Symphonie* dealt with an enormously rich watch-making family. In Germany *Das Erbe der Guldenburgs* described a family beer dynasty. In India *Buniyaad* traced the troubles and turmoils of the Gaindamal family over sixty years. *Buniyaad*'s director Kundan Shah believed the show was popular because 'the audience is a voyeur' of the lives of the family.

Such 'voyeurism' could sometimes be the product of loneliness. BBC producer Julia Smith, quoted in *Time* in March 1987, believes 'People watch because they care. There are a lot of lonely people who, owing to the break-up of the family structure, don't live in family groups.' Interviewed in 1992 on the BBC radio programme *Start the Week*, she praised the soap opera for giving people something to talk about when they don't have their own granny and babies. Despite this analysis, however, most British soap operas have focused on groups and locations other than the family: the hospital (*Emergency Ward 10* and *Casualty*); the office (*Compact*); the motel (*Crossroads*); the pub and the neighbourhood (*Coronation Street*, *EastEnders*). The Australian *Neighbours* attracts millions of British fans, some of them, according to a *Daily Telegraph* report of 1990, 'foetuses tuning in to mother's favourite "soap"; hearing the programme's signature tune before they are born, they associate it with the relaxed time she spends while watching it.'

The broadcasting historian Paddy Scannell has pointed out that most soap opera, however outrageous its characters and events may be, exists 'in parallel with real time': between episodes time is assumed to pass as it does in the real world. And, as in life itself, but unlike the case of the classic novel or play, the soap opera deals with several stories running in tandem or overlapping. Characters age as 'real' people do, and the longest running series actually employ archivists

The extremely successful Indian family soap opera **Buniyaad**.

in the production team to avoid discrepancies and anachronisms in the biographies of the characters. Thus, viewers stand in relation to them as they do to people they 'really' know. Like members of their own family who happen to live in a different home they can get to know those characters; and remember past events in their lives.

Comparisons have been made, too, between the 'essentially structureless' nature of domestic work and the disrupted, discontinuous yet never-ending nature of daytime soap opera plots. Home-bound women, it is suggested, therefore feel affinity with soaps.

Research has been carried out on the impact of television's portrayals of family life on children. Are children's notions of what family life is or should be affected by the programmes they watch? Children in one American survey were divided by age and social class and asked questions about whether family members in the programmes they watched 'support, ignore or oppose one another'. The researchers reported that the children derived more positive than negative messages from television, especially children whose parents discussed the programmes with them. In the late 1950s the *Saturday Evening Post* quoted letters from viewers of *Father Knows Best* who praised the programme for being one the *whole family* could enjoy and even learn from. When Susan Sontag noted in *On*

Photography the extraordinary powers of mass-produced images to determine our demands upon reality, she might well have added 'and upon our ideas of relationships'. The feminist Gloria Steinem criticized television commercials for seldom portraying men with any relationship to children, and 'it's still only women who care about our spouses' breakfast food'. Television can fix stereotypes of family relationships.

As with most surveys and opinions on the effect of television on viewers, the verdicts of moralists on family television shows are contradictory. Whilst deviant and selfish television families have been attacked for giving bad examples, as was Alf Garnett's family by Mrs Whitehouse, 'normal' families have been charged with establishing impossible aspirations. 'It's the fantasy, the dream of motherhood that carries them along', said the director of an American study of pregnant addicts, quoted in 1972. 'No matter what realities they've had to face, they continue to imagine themselves in typical television family situations—mother, father, baby, house.' Similarly, a *New Yorker* report of the late 1970s quoted the actor who had years earlier played the Anderson brother in *Father Knows Best*. He regretted having taken part. 'It was all totally false', he said, and 'had caused many Americans to feel inadequate because they thought this was how life was supposed to be and their own lives failed to measure up.'

The strictures of some moralists on the materialism, greed, and lack of traditional family values displayed by the wealthy characters in *Dallas* and *Dynasty* have been counterbalanced by other suggestions that it is salutary to show that riches do not buy happiness or virtue. Cynics, indeed, might believe that such a lesson was the underlying manipulative purpose of these series—to provide a moral opiate for the masses. Such programmes are seen in many countries outside the United States, and in one major cross-cultural sociological study of *Dallas* (by Elihu Katz and Tamar Liebes), episodes were shown to groups from four different ethnic communities in Israel. A group of Russian Jewish immigrants were asked '(learning that in order to be Israelis they had to watch *Dallas*!), "What is the message of the programme?" Together they answered with the other groups, "they're trying to tell us the rich are unhappy . . . But, don't believe it, it's a manipulation; it's what they want us to believe".'

After two decades in which programmes for the family and about the family became staple fare, it was inevitable that eventually television cameras would arrive inside the 'real family'. What the BBC has recently called *verité voyeurism* arrived in Britain in 1969 with Richard Cawston's *Royal Family*, the first television film of the Queen and her family at home. Unique in subject, scope, and television techniques, the film, forty-three hours of footage compressed into barely two, was seen by 350 million viewers around the world.

The making of *Royal Family* showed how the Queen's own attitude to television had evolved: in 1958 she and Prince Philip had decided against allowing the royal children to appear on the Christmas broadcast. 'Some of you have written to say that you would like to see our children on television this afternoon . . . We believe that public life is not a fair burden to place on growing children.' Yet only eleven years later *The Guardian* critic (later to become Editor) Peter Preston, reviewing *Royal Family*, could write, 'The Queen has collaborated; the Queen has permitted a year of camera crews peering over her shoulder; for the first time we see the unvarnished happy family at breakfast, just chatting.' 'Absolutely electrifying, staggering', boasted ITV's publicity—the film was made by a BBC and ITV consortium—whilst *The Times* gave the film a calmer blessing: 'there must be a great many people who have a far clearer picture than they ever had before of what type of person, with what type of family, now reigns in Britain.'

Some doubts about the wisdom of exposing the Royal Family to such intimate scrutiny were expressed at the time—to be repeated often over subsequent years: 'as nothing else, television can trivialize and cheapen', warned the *Sunday Telegraph*. 'Now that we have seen the Queen buying lollipops for Prince Edward . . . will the next solemn procession of the Garter Knights at Windsor, with Her Majesty at the head, seem more dignified, or more ludicrous?' Given subsequent popular press obsession with the most intimate and sometimes scandalous details of the royal family, the remark is dated.

Increasingly sophisticated, 'fly-on-the-wall' television techniques were applied five years later, in 1974, to a very different 'real' family, the Wilkinses of Reading, in Paul Roger's documentary series, *The Family*, which was preceded and inspired by a twelve-part American documentary *An American Family* (1973, for PBS) about the rich Californian Loud family, whose marriage had actually broken up in front of the television cameras. In this context, too, worries of a different kind were expressed. Did the presence in a small terrace house of television crew and cameras—the latter at that time still unwieldy—affect the Wilkinses and cause them either to exaggerate or to downplay their normal conversation and behaviour? It was a question—mirroring a well-known problem in physics—impossible in principle to answer.

Cameraman Philip Bonham-Carter and director Franc Roddam using a council crane to film **The Family**.

Richard Cawston, asked for his views on *The Family*, believed that time could solve this problem. The 'law of increasing returns' would set in, he said, 'a process of familiarisation [an interesting word] when the film crew gradually cease to be strangers. . . . The cameraman, Philip Bonham-Carter, was in the Wilkins' sitting-room for twelve weeks all day with the camera on his shoulder most of the time. They didn't know when it was running and when it wasn't . . . the longer you have a camera team in a closed community', he went on, 'the better are the results for two reasons: one is because people . . . gradually forget the presence of the team . . . and the other is that if you're there long enough, something interesting will happen.' (Mrs Wilkins, for example, divulged on screen that her husband had not been the father of her last child.)

Since *The Family*, in its day described as as 'addictive as any soap opera', the 'soap-umentary' has become a familiar television genre, with the most recent Australian example, *Sylvania Waters* (1992), providing Britain with good prurient fun. As Eric Bailey, the *Daily Telegraph* correspondent pointed out in April 1993,

'Television producers have recognised that programmes which are about "ordinary people" can be both cheap to make and powerful in the ratings—and if these people are willing to make fools of themselves so much the better.'

V

The relationship between television and the family has changed as new technologies of communication have arrived. In the early years of television the gramophone was already a feature in many homes—so, too, was the telephone—but the main comparisons made between the effects of different home communications devices were those between television and the transistor radio, most popular with young listeners for many of whom it became the chief instrument of a youth subculture.

Television commanded special respect in its early years, so that in 1938 a dedicated British television viewer could write sternly that 'you may be a background listener but you can't be a background viewer', adding that 'preparations for watching the television programmes are in our case invested with a certain amount of ceremony'.

Such ideas of ceremony very quickly became obsolete. When hi-fi equipment first entered the home it involved not ceremony but technical expertise. There was room for individual choice—often regarded by the purchaser himself as expertise—in combining different components of varying compatibility to make up the system and later, at home, there were experiments to be made with different permutations of balance and tone.

This self-help element had never been present in the case of television. The television set, technically too complicated to attract the kind of 'hobbyists' who constructed early wireless sets, was a complete object in itself and had by then begun to be taken for granted. It was only after a home acquired more than one television set, however, that the choice of programme to watch on television could become a matter for individual members of a family. By 1985, which was thought of as a turning-point, more than half of British households had more than one television set. By then, too, Barrie Gunter and Michael Svennevig claimed, the television set had in itself become 'almost another member of the family'. But the omnipresent television set and the multi-set household were associated with the decline of family viewing which was itself invested with more than a touch of nostalgia. Laurie Taylor, for example, looked back in 1988 in the *Sunday Telegraph Magazine* to 'the great days of family viewing when, to the delight of everyone round the fireside on a Saturday night, *Dixon of Dock Green* followed hard on the heels of *Dr Who* . . . The second television set and the arrival of more specialist channels', he predicted, would make the box 'as much a solitary companion as that other great focus of family life—the wireless.' This is a recipe for cultural disintegration, say some commentators. 'At the moment television does at least unite us over the goings on in Albert Square [*EastEnders*] or among the neighbours in suburban Sydney.' Taylor concluded, 'In future even that common bond will disappear as television channels divide and multiply and take their specialist audiences with them.'

Television, increasingly international, can now be seen, not in isolation, as only one of a number of information and communication technologies occupying time and space in the home alongside the VCR and the computer and the telephone, the Walkman, the Ansa-phone, the hi-fi, and the radio. Yet, as David Morley and Roger Silverstone have pointed out, 'new media do not simply displace but are also integrated with the old. New forms, such as pop videos, are integrated into traditional modes of communication, such as teenage oral cultures and gossip networks. New technologies may simply displace pre-existing family conflicts into new contexts.'

The biggest changes so far have come with video recording, which gives the viewer the choice of when to see what and, indeed, whether or not to watch the television programmes broadcast on the public channels. Like television sets themselves, videos could be hired and in 1982 the number of shops hiring out video cassettes for the first time exceeded the number of bookshops. 'The image of British families sitting around a television set for an evening's entertainment was no longer true', Britain's Independent Broadcasting Authority stated in January 1986. John Whitney, the Authority's Director-General, who had risen through commercial radio, not television, warned, 'We are no longer the landlords of the screen. The tenants are changing and there will be squatters before long.'

Cable and satellite television added further to the choice. The new cable channels included children's channels and, with more than a touch of euphemism, what came to be known as 'adult' channels. There has been one other use for the television set besides video recording—home computing, including computer games. The Americans used the term 'electronic goodies' to describe what was now on offer to technically sophisticated families. Some of them had been forecast in sketches and cartoons in the early years of wireless before television was invented.

There were new interactions, economic, social, educational, and cultural, as the media became increasingly 'interactive', with buttons, pads, and talk-back. Japan and the United States were pioneers. The Japanese experimented with HI-VIS (highly interactive visual information system) which involved the intrusion into every home of a camera and a microphone linked to the studio by two-way fibre-optic cable. It is not yet clear in this case, as in many others, whether what was being made available was merely gimmickry. One of the most interesting and unforeseen interactions in the United States and Britain was the use of family video and earlier home movies, originally produced within the family setting for family purposes, as broadcast television programmes, not simply to record history, including family history, but to provide mass entertainment.

Having proclaimed electronic plenty, the Americans began to be worried

213

about electronic surfeit. Among the means of coping with it inside the home was a new technical device to make children more selective about what they watched on the television screen. One of the hits at the Consumer Electronic Show in Las Vegas in 1993 was a device called TV Space Allowance. Each child in a family was allocated a weekly ration of viewing. They were then given secret codes to activate the television. Once the allotted time ran out, the set automatically switched off and they would not be able to get it to work until the start of the next week. The system could also block out certain times, such as homework periods, or prevent late-night viewing. By pushing a button the children could see how much time they had left. They could trade time with siblings and carry forward unused time to the following week. The system could also be used to control computer games playing. The engineer who invented it offered to pay his children $50 each time they saved fifty hours. He reported that his children were reading more, doing more things outside the home and learning more skills. 'Abstinence', 1993-style, was back.

Research on television and the family has produced contradictory conclusions, and has been strongly influenced by fashion in prevailing *mores*. London's *Independent* newspaper on 21 April 1993 reported that viewers were demanding a return to family entertainment in a backlash against violence. Programme-makers noted at the Cannes Television Festival a big increase in the sales of documentary and drama series at the expense of programmes of violence. In Britain the regulatory authority has given approval for a new cable and satellite television network that will concentrate on 'family viewing'. It was the *Daily Mirror*, one of the largest mass-circulation papers, which had warned its readers in 1950 that 'if you let a television set through your front door, life can never be the same again'.

9

Taste, Decency, and Standards

Colin Shaw

Like the novel and the theatre in earlier centuries, television and cinema have provided a battleground for rival sets of moral perspectives and disputed assessments of the medium's power to influence its audiences. Debates of that kind about the press have been rarer. In this chapter we are concerned with the issues of 'taste' and 'decency' in a broad sense, including the portrayal of violence and sexual conduct, rather than standards of political impartiality or of technical quality.

Three factors have been important in the distinctive experience of television and, to a lesser extent, radio. The first of them is the power of governments, arising from the system of allocating frequencies for broadcasting by international agreement, to control the means of transmission. In Western Europe the tradition has been for governments to pay considerable attention to what is broadcast by organizations which, in the majority of countries, were, until recently, exclusively operated in the public interest and only rarely for private profit. Not every country imposed such a rigorous form of control. In the United States, for instance, a different approach was adopted. Its governments have traditionally devoted much less attention to what was broadcast, once the broadcaster had received a licence and was, in broad terms, complying with a minimum set of requirements imposed by a government agency as a condition of the licence.

Elsewhere in the world, countries pursued policies between these two extremes. At the more liberal end of the spectrum of attitudes, the Mexican government's approach in the period before 1960 was described by De Noriega and Leach in 1979 as doing no more than react to the broadcasters' more energetic initiatives. At the start of the 1960s, however, there was a sharp change of tack, with new laws which required broadcasters to take much more account of the government's concern to promote certain social goals. In making this change, the Mexicans were falling into line with governments which treated broadcasting and its standards as straightforward instruments of policy, whether in excoriating the state's political or moral enemies or promoting approved forms of private or public conduct.

The second factor has been the arrival of research which goes beyond the simple counting of the audience or assessing the level of an audience's satisfaction. Here again there is a contrast between television and the press, where interest in research has been registered mainly on the marketing side and where the kind of introspective probings initiated among broadcasters themselves, especially in Western Europe, has not been paralleled by the conduct of the managements of newspaper and magazine groups. Yet both broadcasting and print-publishing occupy significant places in modern society.

The third constant factor, held to be stronger in the case of television than in that of the press, is the invasive presence of television in the home (see Chapter 8). While books, magazines, and newspapers are also admitted to the house, they are considered to do so by a more conscious process of selection, the act of purchase involved, than does television. The last, by contrast, enters at the touch of a button, as responsive to the pressure of a child's finger as to that of an adult's. But television trades in images, against which illiteracy provides no real barrier to at least a sketchy kind of understanding. Furthermore, unlike newspapers, television includes much fiction and, like novels and feature films before it, has aroused the traditional suspicions of puritans.

While that lobby was often seeking to protect impressionable minds in general, it found allies among much larger numbers of people concerned that children and young people should be protected from what might be the harmful influences of television. The most commonly cited of those influences were incitement to violence through violent examples and the damage which might result from premature exposure to adult sexual attitudes and behaviour. At a rather later stage, there were fears about the possible effects on children's literacy of a constant diet of images and about children's powers of concentration in the face of a barrage of competing programmes. These later anxieties are harder to match against any system of regulation since they come much closer to the areas of individual behaviour and parental control. They are not, therefore, in the more traditional sense, matters of standards lending themselves to forms of codification.

As a result of the three factors outlined above, there has been, in many countries, an almost continuous discussion of programme standards in television. In the recent past, however, we have seen a proliferation of the means of distribution of television material, making regulation more problematic than before.

Almost simultaneously, we have witnessed the growth of services directed from one country to another by means of satellites. The powers of individual nations to oversee what their subjects watch have become weaker and a corresponding concern has arisen to find some form of international agreement on standards, at least in limited areas, including those which particularly affect minors.

The difficulties of enforcing any such agreement, examples of which exist within the European Community (EC) and within the larger grouping of countries represented in the Council of Europe, are formidable, as can be exemplified by the attempts in 1993 of the British government to suppress a hard-core pornographic channel beamed into the United Kingdom from a base on the mainland of the Continent.

What are Taste, Decency, and Standards?

Since all three words tend to recur frequently in any debate about the moral aspects of television, whirled around indistinguishably like clothes in a washing-machine, it is important to establish their separate identities.

Taste is essentially an ephemeral matter, changing according to changes of fashion. What is good taste one day may turn into bad taste a day later. It can vary at the same time from place to place, from one part of society to another. Decency, however, strikes deeper chords, touching those things which span cultures and generations. It includes respect for the dead, though the rituals of mourning diverge deeply between states and religions. It extends to protection for children and regard for the cherished beliefs of other people.

Standards in broadcasting reflect a blend of the two. Programmes may conflict with prevailing views on taste, causing offence felt more or less deeply among the audience. It is difficult to contemplate a television service of the traditional broad-ranging kind that had any pretensions to quality which did not, from time to time, cause offence of that sort, though usually after signalling, by means of advance information to the audience, the possibility of doing so. The World Council of Churches once declared that a television service without offence was itself offensive. Offences against decency are of a different order, carrying with them, as offences against taste do not, the concept of some actual damage among members of the audience. However, they too may sometimes be justified by the nature of the subject-matter and the quality of its treatment by the programme-makers.

Defining Standards

By whom is it done?

The word 'standards' has different meanings according to the nature of the standard-setter. A broadcasting organization may be expected, in normal circum-

217

stances, to encourage its programme-makers to aim for the best possible level of achievement in a particular genre—the best relay of a ballet, the most amusing comedy, the finest realization of a classic play. In the pursuit of quality, it is helped by the programme-makers' concern to do justice to their own professional skills and their wish for the approval of their peers, which may sometimes be earned in the face of the audience's disapproval. In such circumstances, quality may be regarded less as something to be measured by an objective test than as something felt, in Keats's phrase, on the senses: a code of practice the result rather than the cause of a proper attitude to the medium.

There are three principal ways in which standards may be set from outside a broadcasting organization. The first is through the law, with legislation which prescribes the limits within which broadcasters are free to operate. It would, however, be a very rigid system which required recourse to the courts for every alleged breach of the law in programmes, given the subjective nature of many editorial judgements.

The second way is through the terms of the licence given to the broadcaster, whether directly by the government or by some intermediate agency acting on the government's behalf, such as the Federal Communications Commission in the USA. In such cases, it would be for the agency to police the maintenance of standards and to impose what penalties might be considered appropriate.

The principle of fining offenders exists in some countries: in Britain and France respectively, for example, the Independent Television Commission and the Conseil Supérieur de l'Audiovisuel exercise such powers. While fining may be the appropriate punishment for gross breaches of undertakings, fines for lesser offences can produce difficulties, and risk absurd anomalies, in assessing the degree of culpability for one minor offence against another. Editorial misjudgements are a natural hazard in broadcasting and the wisdom of treating each one as if it were an offence in any real sense is questionable.

The third way lies in judgements retrospectively made by independent agencies. The New Zealand Standards Authority is an example of such a mechanism, invested in that case with strong powers and a degree of legal authority.

It is, of course, possible to combine all three approaches and, indeed, the law is always present to be invoked in extreme instances, even where alternative means of retributive action exist.

The role of the audience

Though standards may be formally defined by the self-regulation of the broadcasters, by the law or by separate institutions, the audience can be a powerful influence on them in at least two ways. A television service, as it becomes established, ceases to be an entirely free agent in its choice of material. It quickly creates expectations in the minds of those who watch it. This can apply equally to the selection of programmes and to the treatment given to their contents. The BBC, many years ago, broadcast an episode of a much-watched police series,

Softly, Softly. In it, a greatly respected (by the audience) Chief Inspector was seen assaulting a suspect in a cell. The public protested vociferously; their weekly expectations of the character's behaviour had been flouted. In a different, more recent and potentially more disturbing example, the BBC broadcast a Hallowe'en programme called *Ghostwatch*. It was, in reality, a fiction, but it was given a documentary flavour by the presence among the cast of some familiar television personalities in whose truthfulness in other programmes the audience was accustomed to trust. The criticisms which followed, once the deception was known, included such words as 'betrayal', as an indication of the audience's shattered expectations of the broadcaster's standard of behaviour.

The audience also exercises an influence on standards through the findings of research. Surveys can not only show the extent to which, as discussed in the previous paragraph, expectations are fulfilled or disappointed. It can also report on the attitudes which the audience brings to programmes. Nobody comes to television without their individual assortment of experiences, beliefs, or information of different kinds, significant or trivial. Research has shown that very young children will attempt, from their own small store of knowledge, to make comprehensible events on the screen of which they can have no real understanding. It is the obvious variety of 'mental baggage' which individual viewers import to their viewing of programmes that makes determining the effects of programmes so elusive. That is not to say there are no effects, but to indicate the difficulty of pinning them down with any precision.

The British Experience

The growth of codes

When the BBC existed as a monopoly, for much of that period only as a radio broadcaster, it occasionally published codes of conduct for its producers, dealing principally with what might now be termed matters of taste and decency, with few references to sexual issues or violence. A 1949 edition, for example, warns against the use of the words 'Wops' and 'Dagos' and of the unnecessary use of 'damn'. Under the heading of 'Horrors and Mortification', it refers only to the possible effects on the audience of such qualities in fiction. The prevailing note of respectful caution in all matters was in acute contrast to the present day, when serious consideration is said to have been given in the United States to the possibility of live coverage of the execution of convicted criminals. The BBC Policy Book on standards issued in 1949 laid down that Members of Parliament should not be allowed to broadcast in a frivolous or derogatory setting. The paragraph concludes dryly: 'This rule has on occasions been enforced against an M.P.'s own wishes.'

As long as the BBC's monopoly existed, the principle safeguard of standards lay in self-regulation. The Governors of the BBC were trusted to keep its programmes within the boundaries acceptable to the British public. With the coming of commercial television to Britain in the mid-1950s, an event which the BBC's first Director-General, John Reith, compared to the advent of the Black Death, a profound change occurred.

The Television Act, 1954, which opened the way to commercial television, contained a clause, repeated in subsequent broadcasting legislation, forbidding, as far as possible, the broadcasting of material calculated to give offence to good taste or likely to incite to violence or other forms of anti-social behaviour. Although not covered by this legislation, the BBC formally undertook to observe the spirit of the clause and has subsequently renewed this undertaking.

The appearance of a direct legislative interest in matters of this sort was to set off a proliferation of codes and guide-lines which has continued to the present day. The initial emphasis was on violence. The BBC produced a Code on Violence in 1960, following it in 1972 with a Note of Guidance produced by an Advisory Group on the Social Effects of Television. The Group's creation was a reaction to an outbreak of public concern about possible links between violent crime and television. A further set of guide-lines was published by the BBC in 1979, each publication a little more detailed than its predecessor.

The Independent Television Authority in the early 1960s was reluctant to draft a Code on Violence, feeling that it could be counter-productive. However, the Authority and its successor, the Independent Broadcasting Authority, were eventually not far behind the BBC in regularly setting out the problems of portraying violence on television for the information of their franchisees. A Code was produced in December 1964, followed by revised versions in 1971 and 1975. The climax to these activities among both sets of broadcasters was the joint publication by the BBC and the IBA in 1980 of the guide-lines which each then had in force. The Authority favoured brevity in its documents, a trend summed up in words used in more than one of them: 'When in doubt, cut.'

In recent years, the momentum of code-making has increased significantly, the reflection both of the specific demands of legislation on the Independent Television Commission and of the belief that, where consensus can no longer be taken for granted, it becomes increasingly necessary for the guide-lines given to producers to be set out for the wider public. There is some support in Britain for the view that a kind of contract exists between the broadcasters and their audiences, with codes outlining the terms on which programmes are transmitted into the homes of their consumers.

The assault on self-regulation

The Pilkington Committee on Broadcasting, reporting in 1962, had been overwhelmingly critical of the service provided by the newly launched Independent Television channel. Its criticisms were, however, principally directed at the alleged triviality of much that was being put out by the new service. But the Independent Television Authority enforced steps to improve the quality of Independent Television programmes and it was upon the BBC that criticism began to fall a few years later.

Much of the critical fire was directed from an Evangelical Christian standpoint. An organization called The Festival of Light, campaigning for the nation's moral renewal, raised the level of controversy and gained a measure of popular support. Its work was complemented by the activities of Mrs Mary Whitehouse, at the time of her first appearances on the national scene in 1963 a schoolmistress in the Midlands. She gained some backing from MPs and was able to bring pressure on the BBC, in particular upon its then Director-General, Hugh Greene (1959–69).

Greene underestimated both Mrs Whitehouse's tenacity and the persistence of the constituency for which she was speaking. As a result, he spurned the 'Clean up TV' campaign, which Mrs Whitehouse and her colleagues launched in 1964. He regarded it as having little weight beside the need to extend the range of BBC programmes, exposing them to new influences, liberal in his mind, terminally permissive in the minds of some of his critics.

Television drama, in particular, was considered by the latter to be an abuse of freedom, although no more than a limited proportion of it represented any departure from the BBC's traditional concern with the classics, detective series like the original Maigret adaptations, and West End revivals. A major controversy, for example, developed over a play, *Up the Junction*, which portrayed the lives of three working-class girls and included an abortion scene and a good deal of bad language. The BBC's opponents made clear that realism had its limits. The play was not repeated.

To drama was added, in 1962, a weekly review, *That Was the Week that Was*, a satirical series in which a generally young and talented team of performers and writers targeted the week's events. It caught a national mood, especially among the young, and drew large audiences. It made enemies among the politicians whom, among others, it attacked with a relish and, often, an acuity not seen before or since in British broadcasting. But its actual life was short and, by the end of 1963, the last edition had been broadcast. The mood which had sustained it had gone and, although other attempts at weekend satire were made by the BBC, none of them evoked the same response and the hands of the critics were strengthened by such incidents as, in 1965, the first use in a television programme of the 'f-word'. Even though it was not used as an expletive, the BBC considered it necessary to issue a formal apology.

In the early 1960s, therefore, Greene created for himself and the BBC two powerful sets of enemies: the group of Christian moralists and a number of politicians. Talk of a Broadcasting Council became common. The cry was heard, 'The BBC must be curbed'. Any similar calls for the curbing of commercial television were muted, partly because the Independent network was thought to give less offence of a political or moral kind, partly because the BBC, as the national instrument of broadcasting, was considered to have particular obligations to uphold national standards, however they might be defined.

The government's eventual response was not a council, but the appointment to the BBC's Board of Governors of a strong chairman. Lord Hill of Luton, who had been a cabinet minister and was currently chairman of the Independent Television Authority, was the choice, the man who, some people hoped, would bring the BBC to heel. Hill's autobiography, however, makes it clear that, if such a purpose existed, it was never declared to him at the time.

Nor, if that was the purpose, did it succeed. The clamour, only a little moderated, continued and, at the start of the 1970s the Conservative government was apparently toying with a proposal for some form of Broadcasting Council. Hill, suspecting something of the kind, side-stepped it by establishing an independent Programmes Complaints Commission, where certain complainants, dissatisfied with the BBC, could seek a second opinion.

The significance of this move, strongly opposed by the now-retired Greene, for the history of taste and decency in British broadcasting is that, for the first time, the BBC's Board of Governors conceded, even if only in the limited field of fairness, a right of appeal from its judgement. The Commission, in whose work the Independent Broadcasting Authority declined to join, lasted until 1981, when it was replaced by a statutory body whose remit extended to Independent Television and Radio.

It was to take another two decades before the principle of independent scrutiny of programmes was invoked for a second time. Once again, something short of a fully comprehensive Broadcasting Council was established. The Broadcasting Standards Council, set up in shadow for its first two-and-a-half years, was given, by the Broadcasting Act, 1990, limited but statutory powers in the areas of violence, sexual conduct, and matters of taste and decency. Its eight members were to be appointed for periods not exceeding five years by the Secretary of State responsible for broadcasting.

The creation of the Council was greeted by many people within and outside the broadcasting industry with much suspicion, some of which it has succeeded in dispelling. It has, however, failed to satisfy those who looked to it to enforce a much more rigid regime on broadcasters, fulfilling, as some would wish it to do, the role of a pressure group for particular sets of values.

When the responsibility for standards is passed to a body whose exclusive concern is with their oversight, then a subtle change occurs and the independent body, monitoring or instigating complaints, is more likely to work through the observance of minimum standards of behaviour. Quality is difficult to articulate and even more difficult to impose from beyond the boundaries of the broadcasting organization itself. An outside body may often be drawn into seeking objective grounds for comment, feeling more secure in that role than in dealing with altogether more subjective issues. As was suggested earlier, the breaking of new ground, essential to the continuing vitality of television, may often compel the suspension of old standards. An authority dealing only with standards needs, therefore, to be wise in the manner of a conservator rather than of a museum-keeper. In the absence of such an approach, standards may be in danger of becoming the enemy of the quality they are intended to protect.

Alerting the audience

Unless standards are laid down, as they may be in highly authoritarian societies, with great precision, their interpretation by both the audience and the programme-makers must be a matter of determining where lines should be drawn. From that, it follows that there must be a shared understanding between them as to where, in particular instances, a line has been drawn. It can be drawn in different places on different channels and at different times of day on the same channel.

The ability to draw the line differently at different times of day is an important protection for the child audience, over whose protection there is generally agreement. It is an audience which dwindles as the evening advances and its gradual departure signals to the broadcasters and their regulators a growing freedom to schedule programmes greater in their demands on the understanding and knowledge of the audience. The problem is more complex than the common perception of it, which is usually concerned with violence and sexual activity. It has to do also with complexity of presentation, the sophistication of discussion, or the choice of subject-matter.

It was an awareness of these realities of the audience's behaviour which led in Britain, as in Australia and other countries, to the concept of the 'watershed' and its companion, the family viewing policy. The concept dates from the 1950s and its implementation set at 9.00 p.m. only slightly later. However, both the BBC and the new Independent Television service were arguing at the end of the 1950s that 7.00 p.m. was the time at which the needs of the grown-up audience should become the dominant factor. It was unreasonable, the BBC declared at that time, that mid-evening programmes should not be able to cater for an audience much larger than that of potential child-viewers. The BBC accepted, however, that nothing unsuitable for children should be broadcast before 9.00 p.m., a subtle difference from the ITA's policy that, up to the watershed, programmes should be suitable for the family audience.

A substantial percentage of British parents (93 per cent in 1992, according to Independent Television Commission research) is aware of the existence of a watershed, with 78 per cent of them, according to the same research, being aware that it occurs at 9.00 p.m. The extent of awareness among parents may be taken as quite striking. In other European countries, the watershed is set at a different time, later in the majority of cases than in Britain. In France, for example, it is set at 10.00 p.m. in the case of 12-rated films and half an hour later in the case of 16-rated films. Comparisons of the effectiveness of the device are, however, not easy since, in Britain, the nature of programmes usually changes gradually, even after

9.00 p.m., on the two majority channels, BBC1 and ITV. Elsewhere in Europe, the passing of the watershed signals a more abrupt change in the kind of programmes which are scheduled.

The 'watershed' gives the audience a broad indication of the kind of programmes which may be expected before and after 9.00 p.m., but in addition, broadcasters use on-air promotion or printed material to tell the audience of the programme choices available. The use of symbols to label different kinds of programmes has been debated but in the end rejected: for the reflection of some-times subtle differences between programmes—compare, for example, the violence which concludes *Hamlet* with that of a James Cagney film—would demand the use of an impractical variety of symbols. Moreover, the huge output of television programmes would make the task of systematic previewing and consistent labelling extremely expensive.

The Main Concerns

While there are many areas of concern for the standards-setter, such as racism, the depiction of people with disabilities, and ageism, the three principal concerns are violence (which takes many forms), the representation of sexual conduct, and bad language.

Violence

Much of the concern expressed about the possible influences of television upon its audiences centres upon violence. But there is an important distinction between the violence reported in news bulletins (or reflected in documentaries and current affairs programmes) and the violence which appears as part of fictional programmes. Violence in news programmes can itself take a variety of forms, for example, the violence of war-reporting, especially now that immedi-ate accounts of battles can be brought to domestic screens thousands of miles away. They may be battles in which the particular domestic audience has a direct interest, as, for example, the American audience had in the Vietnamese war twenty years ago. Some wars, however, may be altogether more remote and scenes of conflict, the motives for which are little known and less understood, can produce a different set of responses in the minds of uninvolved spectators.

Accidents, whether natural or man made, provide further strands of arresting pictures. An air-crash, a pile-up on an autobahn, or an avalanche of mud that swamps a village, all supply violent images. Crime, too, whether at home or abroad, provides many grim scenes, often taken after the action has ended, but not invariably so in days when an amateur's camcorder may provide graphic evidence of an incident as it is occurring.

From the reporting of crimes committed and their consequences, it is a short step for modern technology to go seeking out crime for itself. The past few years have seen an increase in the number of programmes which focus on real-life

Television confronts its audience with the consequences of Nature's violence . . .

. . . as it does with the images of the violence unleashed by man.

crimes. Cameras accompany police patrol-cars, especially in the United States, as they tour the depressed areas of cities in search of criminal activity. Here television can come dangerously close to the border between faithful reporting and the contrivances of fiction, sometimes crossing it without making a conscious attempt to do so.

Another category of programme containing 'real-life' violence is that which sets out to reconstruct crimes, usually with a declared object of giving assistance

225

to the police by encouraging witnesses to come forward as in the case of the BBC's Crimewatch UK, which has solved many crimes after telephone calls from viewers. Sometimes the object is to explore criminal motives by reconstructing crimes committed many years before. It is a form of story-telling of a kind with its own morbid, but strong, appeal. The stories may be told, in times of moral dubiety, with an ambivalence which can lend glamour to criminal activities.

The different treatments of real-life violence which have just been summarized have all given rise to debates about standards. On the one hand, there have been arguments that no television service should seek to conceal the reality of the world from its audiences and that, in democracies at least, the health of society depends on the supply of accurate information about events which may influence its future. On the other hand, there have been claims that a constant flood of violent images distorts the audience's view of the world, giving it a false impression of its own situation as well as of the wider world. The dilemma is well expressed in the Australian Broadcasting Commission's publication, *Editorial and Program Policies*, issued in 1991: 'If (the broadcasters) exclude certain material, are they protecting innocence or perpetuating ignorance, upholding humane values or sheltering prejudices?' In Britain, the view prevails among the principal news broadcasters, the BBC and Independent Television News, that there is an obligation to report the news as truthfully and comprehensively as the story, in the view of the responsible editor, demands. Suppression, whether for good or bad motives, has a way of catching up with those responsible as later events unfold and the lack of a missing piece of evidence becomes clear.

The Rodney King case: television is making increasing use of amateur-shot film and video in order to extend its coverage of events, sometimes resolving controversy, sometimes intensifying it.

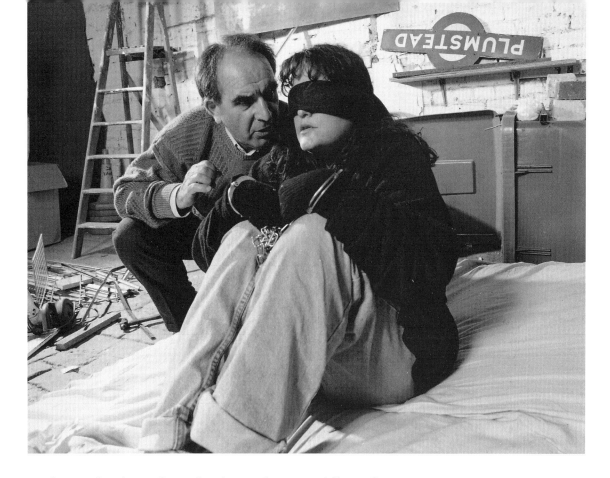

Like actual violence, fictional violence takes many different forms. At one extreme, there is the violence portrayed in cartoons, of which *Tom and Jerry* is the most frequently cited example. There, in the endless struggle between a predatory cat and a wily mouse, countless acts of violence occur, in which neither character sustains lasting damage, even though they may momentarily have been flattened, incinerated, burnt, or bludgeoned in the interests of entertainment. At the other extreme, there is the violence of a Shakespeare play, of which the blinding of Gloucester in *King Lear* may serve as an example. In between comes violence in a variety of guises.

Much of the violence seen on television comes from feature films, made originally for the cinema. In recent years, Hollywood, in particular, has been producing films of an increasingly violent nature, reflecting, as the means of attracting audiences, a reaction to the narrower limits set to violence on television. While some recent feature films have been thought unsuitable for television, experience suggests that the passage of time may eventually make them acceptable. The history of the James Bond films in Britain is illuminating. The earliest of them started out with cinema classifications which made them available only to adult audiences, but they are now acknowledged as suitable family entertainment on Christmas Day. What brings about such a change in standards? Some critics would suggest that the cause is the desensitization of the audience, its familiarity with later excesses making it indifferent to what had once been

Crimewatch UK: The re-enactment of crimes on television may prompt memories to assist the police but, some say, may also increase the public's fear of crime.

Violence on television takes many forms: from the knockabout comedy of well-loved cartoons such as **Tom and Jerry** . . .

regarded as horrific. Others would point to changes in style which diminish the impact of what was once thought frightening.

Apart from changes in attitude which take place with time, some films containing violence are treated as fantasies from the outset. This appears to be true of the American series, *Nightmare on Elm Street*, a sequence of Gothic horrors which, although frightening to some of the audience, were pleasurably so. Yet there is evidence that violence in a familiar setting or among people with whom the audience can readily identify has a disturbing effect. In 1991, for example, BBC Television produced a play, *The Firm*, the story of a gang of football hooligans. It left many of the audience deeply disturbed by its close similarity to aspects of contemporary existence.

The search for a clear link between violence on the screen and violence in real life has been going on for many years. Experiments in the United States have shown apparent increases in aggressive behaviour among subjects exposed to violent images, but their application to other cultures or to people in general has still to be demonstrated. Nor is it altogether clear what should happen if a wide-spread link were discovered. If television is to give a faithful account of the world to its audiences, the presence on the screen of some forms of violence is inescapable. Moreover, there are certain kinds of violence which, in real life, are either applauded or received with ambivalent feelings: for instance, violence used in times of war to defeat an enemy or the violence employed by a father in defence of his family.

. . . to the Gothic fantasy of mainstream horror productions like **Nightmare on Elm Street**.

Many broadcasters would accept that it is wrong to treat violence on television as a matter of slight importance. Thus the Code of Practice issued by the New Zealand Broadcast Standards Authority in 1991 warns against the use of unfamiliar methods of inflicting pain or the combination of violence and sexuality for the purposes of titillation. The Code of Practice published in Britain by the Broadcasting Standards Council in 1989, while acknowledging a legitimate place for violence in fictional programmes, cautions against its inclusion for its own sake as the means of strengthening the impact of otherwise weak material. It concludes, more generally, that an undue proportion of violent material in programme schedules provides an unhealthy element in the viewers' diet.

Sex and sexuality

Neither violence nor the unjustifiable use of swear-words in programmes provokes more public expressions of concern than does the issue of sexual explicitness, though, in comparison with many other countries of Europe, the explicitness permitted in British television has been small. Part of the explanation for the concern created by sexual activity on the screen may be found in the embarrassment which such scenes can cause within the family, where the conventions of different generations may be thrown into conflict. In this, the responses evoked may be different from those evoked by scenes of violence.

The turmoil over sex on television, however, reflects a broad sense of uncertainty in the late twentieth century about sexual conduct. The coming of freely

The problems of realism: the violence of **The Firm** was seen as especially shocking because of the apparent accuracy of its representations.

available means of contraception, the decline of religious restraints on extra-marital activity, and the impact of mass advertising have all played their part in a process of destabilization of attitudes possibly at least as great in perception as in reality. To take a single example, the decriminalization of adult male homosexual acts is not always matched by public tolerance of such acts. It is very difficult to steer broadcasting standards through the confusion.

Both the restraints of the broadcasting authorities and the provisions of the Obscene Publications Act, 1959, which was extended to broadcasting at the start of 1991, ensure that strict limits apply to the depiction of sexual activity. The portrayal of actual sexual intercourse is forbidden and the degree of realism in any simulation is usually judged by the broadcasters in relation to its context. A rare exception to this general rule is a cable station which, under licence from the Independent Television Commission, offers its adult subscribers programmes of soft pornography where the prime interest may be said to lie in the erotic activity rather than in the evolution of the vestigial plots.

After the 9.00 p.m. watershed, however, the audience in Britain shows itself willing to make up its own mind about choosing to view, even those disclaiming any interest in material of a sexual nature recognizing the right of other people to watch if they wish.

The contrast between British attitudes towards sex and those held in many of its European neighbours is striking, the British being regarded in most of Europe as much more inhibited. It is this distinction which has provoked much of the controversy over the hard-core pornographic channel, Red Hot Television, mentioned earlier in this chapter. In contrast, while American films often contain much more violence and bad language than do British films, they contain far less sexual explicitness. In some Scandinavian countries, the view is that it is the British who are too tolerant towards violence on the screen.

As in the case of violence, there is a particular concern for the well-being of children in matters of sexual activity. There are, therefore, in many countries provisions for the protection of children from exposure to sexual scenes. One of the few absolute prohibitions in the European Community Directive on Trans-frontier Broadcasting is concerned with the distribution of material harmful to minors.

Swearing

British broadcasters can usually expect to receive each year at least as many letters of complaint about the use of swear-words in programmes as about any other topic. Like displays of sexual explicitness in programmes, swear-words provoke embarrassment between members of the family circle watching television. In contrast, British radio, where swearing is not unknown, attracts few complaints, the nature of listening being generally different: solitary where viewing tends to be a collective activity.

The legalization of most homosexual behaviour in Britain has not always been matched by a growth in public tolerance. Derek Jarman's **Sebastiane** has, however, found late-night placings which have not provoked strong reactions.

"SEBASTIANE"

A FILM BY DEREK JARMAN

with

RICHARD WARWICK
NEIL KENNEDY
LEONARDO TREVIGLIO

Directed by

DEREK JARMAN and
PAUL HUMFRESS

Music by

BRIAN ENO

RELEASED THROUGH CINEGATE
A MEGALOVISION FILM

The history of the use of bad language on television has been punctuated by a series of scandals. The **Sex Pistols** in 1976 caused one of the loudest outcries.

In considering the problem which swearing presents, those responsible for standards have to make a distinction between the use of the Christian holy names as expletives and the use of other words which some members of the audience would either not employ at all or only within a limited circle of acquaintance: among men at their place of work, for example, or between family members of the same generation.

The Christian holy names present special difficulties since they are not seen by

THE SUN, Thursday, December 2, 1976   **3**

ROCK GROUP START A 4-LETTER TV STORM

By BARRIE MATTEI

VIEWERS jammed a television company's switchboard last night after an interview with a rock group ended in a string of swear words.

And TV personality Bill Grundy was accused of encouraging the language that shocked thousands.

He was talking to "punk rock" group Sex Pistols on Thames Television's Today programme.

One of the group members muttered a four-letter word and Grundy asked him to repeat it.

Then Grundy switched the conversation to one of the group's girl fans— joking about meeting after the show.

One of the musicians made a crack about grundy being a dirty old man.

Flooded

And he retorted by asking the group to be more outrageous.

Grundy was called a dirty old ——, and then came the swearing free-for-all.

Sex Pistol are renowned for their foul language.

But some viewers were lost for words. Others flooded the television company with protests—one even claimed

Viewers in big protest over shock outburst

Sex Pistols ... they shot their mouths off

he had kicked in the screen of his new set.

He was 47-year-old lorry driver James Holmes of Waltham Forest, Herts, who said: "I was so disgusted with this filth that I took a swing with my boot."

Another, Mr Albert Carter, of Orpington, Kent,

said "It was terrible. Many people must have been deeply offended.

"I couldn't switch the television off fast enough. Three of my grandchildren were watching."

Mr Thomas Smith, a sales manager of Walton-on-Thames said: "The whole more than a limited number of people within Britain as particularly offensive. Yet their use can cause very deep offence to some Christians and to some non-Christians who nevertheless feel offended on behalf of believers. It is impractical for the broadcasting authorities to impose a complete ban on a set of words which, whatever significance they may carry for some members of the audience, are part of the normal everyday speech of a more substantial number.

There are further differences between the generations. In general, older people of both sexes object to the use of swear-words to which their juniors raise no objections, although there is a small group of words, mainly sexual in origin, about whose unacceptability, research shows, there is general agreement.

There are differences within Britain over the significance of swear-words from one part of the country to another. Thus, the nouns 'bugger' and 'sod', while remaining terms of serious abuse in some places, can be spoken almost as terms of endearment, certainly as expressions of affectionate admiration. Their use in the imperative as verbs, however, is capable of arousing rather more widespread criticism. The word 'bastard' is also undergoing a transformation, under the influence of changing attitudes towards illegitimacy. While it continues to give much offence to older people, especially those who bore the word as a stigma in their youth, it too is beginning to develop the affectionate resonances just noticed with 'bugger' and 'sod'.

'Fuck' and its derivatives are also undergoing changes. The incidence of these words in American feature films is clearly having an effect on their acceptability to some at least of the British television audience. Although the broadcasters generally observe a ban on their use before the 9.00 p.m. watershed, the words are more likely in the early 1990s to remain uncut after that time. The American film *Platoon*, dealing with soldiers in the Vietnamese war, was transmitted in a late-night slot by the BBC in 1992 without attracting any significant protest from the audience, despite the omnipresence of the word in a variety of forms. The word 'shit' is another that is becoming more commonplace, not as a verb, where the taboo remains strong, but as a noun capable of a number of metaphorical meanings in American mouths.

A significant change which has been noted in British attitudes to the choice of abusive language comes with a growing hostility to the use of words implying disability or racial inferiority. Thus the word 'spastic', which was once commonly used as a synonym for stupidity, was regarded by many respondents to the Broadcasting Standards survey already quoted as unacceptable, as were 'Yid' and 'Wog'.

In attempting to reach conclusions about the use in programmes of words likely to offend, those responsible for standards have to balance carefully the need for clear communication and the need to protect minorities whose vulnerability might otherwise be increased. To insist upon forms of words regarded by their sponsors as politically correct may be to sacrifice the audience's understanding of who is speaking or what is being said. On the other hand, to be unresponsive to gradual changes of popular perception may be to reinforce damaging stereotypes.

The inhibitions which have operated in Britain and other countries are not necessarily shared throughout the world. Global television, with which every country is increasingly having to come to terms, poses problems for those bodies and individuals concerned with issues of taste and decency. The future is likely to see increasing demand for the regulation of standards and, at the same time, increasing difficulty in enforcing whatever standards may be agreed as desirable nationally, or internationally. As long as television is considered to have a particular influence on the minds and intentions of its audiences, politicians and factions of the public are likely to seek means of imposing, openly or covertly, their views of what is desirable to broadcast and what is not desirable. A genuine commitment to excellence in television demands that the professionals and their public both need to be educated in the possibilities of the medium for widening understanding, deepening knowledge, and serving truth.

10

Terrorism

Philip Schlesinger

T he way that television has handled 'terrorism' has been a matter of repeated controversy. The debate has focused almost exclusively on 'insurgent' terrorism, that is on violent action aimed principally against the state by groups acting on the basis of political motives. Furthermore, the media–terrorism relationship has mostly focused on violent left-wing and national separatist politics with little consistent attention paid to the politics of the violent right. Although insurgent political violence is frequently targeted against state officials and the security forces, it may also often involve civilian third parties, and is used to create an atmosphere of fear and unpredictability as well as being an indirect way of putting pressure on the state. Violence from below—with assassinations, hijackings, and bombings as its typical manifestations—has been the main focus of attention in discussions of television and terrorism. By contrast, the repressive actions taken against their own (or others') citizens by states themselves, even when meriting the label of 'state terrorism', have been largely excluded from discussion of the relationship between terrorism and television. Consequently, a historical account that touches upon the received televisual memory of 'terrorism' necessarily tends to reproduce the major biases and limitations of television's own world-view.

It is the often symbolic and spectacular aspects of insurgent terrorism that have made it such a focus of concern rather than the relatively small number of victims that it claims by comparison with those at the sharp end of state repression. Such violence has tended to occur in, or to be targeted against, the capitalist democracies of the West.

In theory, democratic societies operate with a free press, that is, one unconstrained by governmental interference or censorship. In the United States, for instance, constitutional guarantees under the First Amendment aim to preclude government from infringing freedom of expression. However, other democracies—Britain is a case in point—lack entrenched safeguards to secure the freedom to report. And the formal niceties, however well entrenched, are far from invariably observed in the real world of news management by states. The coverage of terrorism—because it deals directly with armed dissent within the political system—persistently raises questions about the freedom to communicate inside democracies, and is of crucial public interest for a democratic citizenry. Whether there is genuine scope for independent reporting of the reasons and motivations for the use of political violence against the established order is always a highly contentious issue. The attitude taken to terrorism by the media in general, and television in particular, cannot remain a matter of indifference to the state. Political violence is invariably judged to be a serious threat by those in power, and the media of communication are seen as crucial instruments to be used in suppressing disorder. Given the key role played by television in the political and cultural lives of most societies today, it is this medium that usually receives most attention and becomes a battleground for access both by those with state power and those fighting against it.

A Matter of Language

'Terrorism' is a term that cannot be innocently applied in categorizing events and actions. It is one of the most value-laden labels in contemporary political discourse. To be called a 'terrorist' is to be accused of perpetrating illegitimate acts of violence, even when such acts may be thought by their perpetrators to have a legitimate political rationale. Nobody wants to be thought of as a 'terrorist', for it is a badge utterly without honour. These points may be highlighted by counterposing the term 'terrorist' to others such as 'guerrilla', 'freedom fighter', or 'member of the resistance'. These, in a contrary sense, invite us to think of particular acts of violence as conducted by honourable people either in the framework of war or that of a struggle for liberation from oppression. When states employ violence outside the context of openly declared wars these tend to be euphemized as 'pacification', 'police actions', 'counter-insurgency', or 'counter-terrorism'. 'State terrorism' is not a label desired by those in authority.

Such semantic considerations make public discourse about political violence a matter of intense struggle. To afix a denigratory label upon your enemies in an armed struggle is to strike a serious blow at them. Hence, how 'terrorism' is defined and characterized, how it is represented through news reporting or fiction, whether or not it is explained, and if it is, how, are no small matter. And in the battle of designate given forms of violent political action as either legitimate or illegitimate—whether by states or those fighting against them—the media of mass communication are the crucial means whereby public interpretations may be substantially shaped.

In this chapter, the term 'terrorism' is therefore seen as inherently contested and always to be understood as within quotation marks, whether used or not.

The Emergence of 'Terrorism'

'Terrorism' first became a major issue for television coverage at the end of the 1960s. The term has come to condition quite profoundly how we think about acts of contemporary political violence. When President John F. Kennedy was assassinated in Dallas in 1963, no one then characterized this as an act of terrorism. However, the attempted assassination of Pope John Paul II in Rome in 1981 was clearly identified as terroristic, even though there was much dispute as to who was really behind it. From the 1970s on, 'terrorism' has been a matter of widespread political concern, spoken of both as an international, or transnational, phenomenon and as a national one. Moreover, until quite recently, both official and popular understandings of terrorism have been profoundly shaped by the Cold War.

Western politicians, the security apparatuses of Western states, and intellectuals and commentators closely allied to officialdom, have been especially prominent in defining the frameworks through which 'terrorism' is understood and the role that the media should play in reporting it. These perspectives often have strongly influenced and constrained the actual performance of television coverage.

One axiom of official thinking has been neatly stated by the Irish writer and sometime government minister, Dr Conor Cruise O'Brien: 'The force used by a democratic state is legitimate while the violence of the terrorist is not legitimate.' Not only is it illegitimate from an official viewpoint but it is also to be refused recognition as having a political character. So characteristically, insurgent terrorism is defined by officialdom as a criminal activity. In the days of the Cold War, before the demise of the Soviet bloc in 1989–90, terrorism in the West was held by many in government and military circles to be orchestrated by Moscow, as part of a plot to destabilize the democracies. At the same time, Western support for repressive regimes in Latin America and elsewhere that employed state terror was justified by asserting that these were only authoritarian states whereas communism was far worse because it was totalitarian. In the orthodoxy popularized by the journalist Claire Sterling, whose writings on terrorism were deeply influenced by her proximity to Western intelligence sources, the supposed 'terror network' that stretched across the continents was orchestrated by the Soviet intelligence service, the KGB. The demise of the Soviet Union, and continued insurgent violence, has left this view rather threadbare.

By 1970, the notion of 'international' or 'transnational' terrorism had entered common currency as a number of quite diverse groups using violence for political ends had begun to engage the attention of the media. Armed action aimed against the liberal-democratic state became apparently so widespread that it lent itself to being seen as a world-wide phenomenon.

In Europe, several major states—mostly democracies—became the locations of violent political action during the 1970s. Espousing variants of neo-Marxist thinking, the Red Army Faction (otherwise known as the Baader-Meinhof group) in the Federal Republic of Germany and the Red Brigades in Italy sought to 'strike at the heart of the state', to provoke repression and to expose the exploitative nature of contemporary capitalism. In the United Kingdom and in Spain (first under the Franco regime and then subsequently in the democratic period) nationalist causes were prosecuted by force of arms, and continue to be so. The Irish Republican Army (IRA) sought Irish unity and the end of British rule in Northern Ireland whereas the separatist Euzkadi Ta Akatasuna (ETA) sought independence for the Basque country.

This was also the moment when the Palestinian national cause entered the global agenda. First, the Popular Front for the Liberation of Palestine hijacked three aircraft belonging to Swissair, TWA, and PanAm with a total of 276 passengers in September 1970, eventually landing all three on a disused airfield in Jordan which was renamed, with the world's media in mind, 'The airport of the revolution'. Ostensibly undertaken to secure the release of prisoners in several Western

Skyjacking for Palestine: planes exploding in Amman in 1970.

countries, as well as Israel, the more fundamental purpose of the hijackings was to draw attention to the existence of the Palestinians. The hostages were eventually released, and the aircraft spectacularly blown up for the television cameras. The event itself unleashed the crushing of the Palestinians in Jordan by King Hussein's forces.

The Palestinians once again commanded world attention by an attack on Israeli athletes at the Munich Olympics on 5 September 1972 carried out by Black September. A day of suspenseful negotiations between the West German authorities and the gunmen was played out live, with commentary, before the world's cameras and a global audience of 800 million. The demand was for the release of 200 prisoners in Israel, which the Israeli government refused. At the end of the day, ten Israeli athletes and their trainer, five gunmen, and one German policeman were dead. This incident, and the previous one, are widely thought to have contributed to the Palestinians' international recognition. Together with armed actions by other contemporary groups such as the Red Army in Japan, the Tupamaros in Uruguay, and the Montoneros in Argentina, such incidents fed the widespread view that a new era of terror had dawned.

Where states felt threatened by political violence, they mobilized to contain and crush their new enemies. Official thinking drew upon counter-insurgency doctrines devised during the post-World War II period. These were most fully elaborated in Britain and France, which had been engaged in long-drawn-out wars of colonial retreat during the 1950s and 1960s, and by the USA, which had taken on the role of world policeman, most notably in Vietnam. American thinking about fighting insurgencies was exported to Latin America and used by the military dictatorships there as part of a 'national security' ideology to justify extreme repressive measures.

Counter-insurgency thinkers concerned themselves, *inter alia*, with 'psychological warfare', or as the Americans termed it, with 'winning hearts and minds'. This meant that the use of media to shape public opinion was regarded as a matter of crucial importance. Television, the dominant medium of the post-war period, which had achieved special importance as a vehicle of political communication, was accorded a major role in the scheme of things. By the time 'terrorism' was perceived as a major problem in the 1970s, television had very much come into its own throughout the advanced capitalist countries, and beyond, as the main vehicle of news coverage.

From an official point of view, terrorists were seen as trying to win the propaganda war by gaining the media's attention and by using them to transmit their views and demands. The task for governments and security forces, then, was to prevent this from happening. For a variety of reasons—their competitiveness in seeking audience-building stories, the desire for sensationalism, supposed sympathy with subversive causes—the media were seen as vulnerable to manipulation by the armed enemies of the state. It is quite commonly believed by governments and the military that if the media would only stop reporting it then

An illustrious victim of the IRA: Lord Mountbatten's funeral in 1979.

terrorism would simply disappear. However, this is to ignore the various social, political, and economic causes that might underlie given violent campaigns. The use of political violence is not solely about communicating dissent.

In official circles it is often argued that the media—television in particular—are instruments to be used by the state in securing its victory. As the British counter-insurgency writer, Major-General Richard Clutterbuck, has aphoristically observed, 'The television camera is like a weapon lying in the street. Either side can pick it up and use it.'

For insurgents too, the media are seen as instruments for fighting a propaganda war. The words of Carlos Marighella, the Brazilian theorist of urban guerrilla warfare, are often cited in evidence. Marighella remarked that 'Modern mass media, simply by announcing what the revolutionaries are doing, are important instruments of propaganda.'

However, this does not tell the whole story. Although such instrumentalism is the mirror image of the official view, 'terrorists' do not always think that all publicity is necessarily good publicity. In nationalist political movements such as Sinn Fein in Ireland, Herri Batasuna in the Basque country in Spain, and the Palestine Liberation Organization, the media are perceived as part and parcel of the capitalist system, as in a conspiratorial relationship with the state, and therefore as inherently hostile. There is often concern about the negative political effects of coverage when there is civilian loss of life. Relevant examples of where violence has been seen as counter-productive by the political rather than the military wings of the nationalist movements just named are: the Enniskillen tragedy in Northern Ireland in November 1987, where eleven were killed by an IRA bomb; the eighteen shoppers killed in a sympathetic working-class area of Barcelona by an ETA bomb in June 1987; the murder on the hijacked cruise ship *Achille Lauro* by the Palestine Liberation Front of Leon Klinghoffer, an elderly and disabled Jewish man in October 1985. The last of these, in particular, achieved global attention because the victim was an American citizen.

From the standpoint of the insurgents, such incidents can mean that the political aims behind political violence become obscured and that only the violence itself achieves attention. An example is the assassination of Queen Elizabeth II's uncle, Earl Mountbatten, by the IRA on 27 August 1979. In the words of their communiqué, the IRA's objective was to 'bring to the attention of the British people the continuing occupation of our country'. However, this goal was effectively ignored by television, radio, and press coverage in Britain, which focused on the victim's heroic stature and aristocratic qualities and the killers' brutality. This was typical, for in the propaganda war fought through television between official and insurgent perspectives, it is generally the views of the state that eventually dominate.

Controlling Coverage

Although 'terrorism' has tended to be seen as a new global problem, in actual fact it has been fundamentally rooted in national circumstances. A common factor is the desire to try and control the media of communication wherever the state perceives a threat to its authority and legitimacy. But the exercise of control by states is not a given, and it needs to be learned in quite specific circumstances. The extent to which conformity may be easily imposed upon the media varies from time to time and place to place. The diversity of the media themselves and the coherence of the state are major factors affecting this.

As overt censorship threatens the legitimacy of the liberal democratic order, more sophisticated official thinkers recognize that they need to try and persuade the media to co-operate in restricting their reporting of insurgent terrorism. However, this does not always work out in practice and sometimes direct censorship is used. Some illustrative national cases show a variety of relations between television, the state, and its armed enemies.

One of the first instances of international note occurred in October 1970, in Montreal, when activists of a cell of the Front de Libération du Quebec (FLQ) kidnapped the British consul in Quebec, James Richard Cross, holding him for fifteen days. As negotiations for his release were proceeding, a different FLQ cell kidnapped the Quebec deputy premier, Pierre Laporte, eventually murdering him. This was an unusual case in which the FLQ initially had extraordinary access to the public through the media before a government clamp-down on communication. When Cross was kidnapped, the FLQ began to send copies of their communiqués listing various demands to the media, thereby outflanking the Quebec government, which had decided on a policy of suppressing information. Most crucial of the demands were the release of FLQ activists from prison and these were accompanied by a death threat (later removed) against the captive consul. When the demands were revealed, a government minister broadcast an official reply on television. Meanwhile, the FLQ ensured that a radio station broadcast its complete manifesto, which was then passed on to the state-run television station and the press. This pattern continued with the direct release of FLQ material to the media being used as a means of circumventing government control. Despite public condemnation of the kidnap itself, there was nevertheless widespread public sympathy in Quebec for the manifesto's nationalist aims, and eventually, after differences of view between the federal and Quebec governments, the official line was to offer certain reforms and safe passage abroad for the kidnappers on Mr Cross's release.

But the situation became more complicated because of the kidnapping of the Quebec deputy premier, Pierre Laporte, by another FLQ cell. Television and radio were completely dominated by this news and went on to an emergency footing. A series of communiqués were released to the media by the second cell, restating the original demands and initially threatening the minister's life. The situation became confused, with each of the two cells stating different conditions for its captive's release. When prominent Quebec figures became involved in the processes of mediation and debate, the federal government in Ottawa became increasingly concerned about the FLQ's access to the media, its evident, if qualified, public support, and the Quebec government's flexible negotiating stand. As the Quebec government continued to negotiate, the federal government, under Prime Minister Pierre Trudeau, prepared to use special powers under the War Measures Act and to engage in security force sweeps to imprison FLQ activists and sympathizers. Trudeau had denounced the media for giving the FLQ the publicity that it was seeking and also refused to call the imprisoned activists whose release was sought 'political prisoners'. 'They're not political prisoners,' he stated, 'they're outlaws. They're criminal prisoners, they're not political prisoners, and they're bandits. That's why they're in jail.'

The eventual introduction of special powers resulted in the outlawing of the FLQ, a wave of police arrests, and the banning of all statements and communications in its favour. The official view henceforth prevailed in the media and redefined the political agenda. It was at this point that the minister was killed, although Mr Cross was released.

Such kidnappings of prominent figures, and hostage-taking more generally, were major focuses of media attention and one of the key ways in which 'terrorism' first came to be represented on television. In Europe, for instance, both the Federal Republic of Germany and Italy were subjected to left-wing armed violence in campaigns that reached their peaks during the 1970s. In the case of

Germany, the origins of violent protest lay in the student movement's campaigns against the USA's conduct of the war in Vietnam. The best-known group to emerge was the Red Army Faction, which espoused a critique of international capitalism and identification with Third World causes.

In one crucial incident, in February–March 1975, a successor group to the RAF, whose leaders were by then all in prison, abducted Peter Lorenz, the Christian Democratic mayoral candidate for Berlin, to bring about the release of six of their gaoled comrades. It was demanded that national television broadcast news of the release, and this was transmitted live and watched by an audience of millions. This was a turning-point for the German government, as may be seen from its subsequent handling of the abduction by members of the RAF of Hanns Martin Schleyer, president of the German industrialists' association on 5 September 1977.

On this occasion, the federal government put into effect an information policy involving a news blackout that lasted for a month. Chancellor Helmut Schmidt set up a crisis committee which included members both of his own Social Democratic Party and the Christian Democratic opposition. The government's information chief, Klaus Bölling, reached a wholesale agreement with the West German television organizations and the rest of the national media to use

Faces of terrorism: the hunt for the Baader-Meinhof group.

243

communications from the kidnappers only after prior consultation. The government continually monitored media output and the crisis committee remained in existence for the entire period of the kidnapping, persuading the media to accept substantial controls. All information deriving from the kidnappers was vetted by the authorities before publication and the crisis committee used its informal contacts with journalists to explain its approach to information policy. The government sought, and obtained, extensive media co-operation in hunting for those responsible for the kidnapping by broadcasting special films on television to mobilize the public and by publishing 'Wanted' posters through the press. Moreover, the authorities succeeded in releasing some disinformation which misled the kidnappers. For instance, the media reported that high-level contacts had been established with Algeria and Libya, implying that the kidnappers' main demand—the liberation of the RAF prisoners in exchange for Schleyer's freedom—would be met.

Although the kidnappers tried hard to have their communiqués published, they largely failed to make any impact on public opinion, or to enter into a bargaining situation with the government. They sought the release of eleven members of the RAF and an aircraft with which to escape from the Federal Republic. On 13 October, an RAF group hijacked one of Lufthansa's Boeings with eighty-six people aboard and repeated the demands. The aircraft had landed at Mogadishu in Somalia and was successfully recaptured by GSG9, the German special forces, on 18 October. That same day, the suicides of three of the RAF prisoners held at Stammheim gaol were discovered. Doubts have been expressed about whether these deaths were genuinely by their own hand or not. Schleyer's body was subsequently discovered on 22 October 1977 in the boot of a car in Mulhouse in France.

In Italy, political violence in the 1970s derived from both left and right. Although the main focus of attention was on the left-wing Red Brigades, there were major outrages, particularly bombings in public places and on trains, perpetrated by the neo-fascist right, with the apparent connivance of elements inside the secret services. Such rightist violence harnessed to the so-called 'strategy of tension' never became a central focus for media attention as did that on the left, a fact not unconnected with the Italian power structure. Well-known instances were the Piazza Fontana bomb in Milan in 1969, the bombing of Bologna railway station in 1980, and the bomb on the train between Naples and Milan in 1984 known as the 'Christmas Massacre'. The bomb explosion at the Uffizi gallery in Florence in May 1993, attributed to the Mafia, was also seen by many as part of a renewed 'strategy of tension'. The causes of leftist violence were widely perceived as rooted in a corrupt political system which worked poorly to represent the full range of demands and interests in society. Whether ostensibly left-wing terrorism was, or was not, sometimes orchestrated by neo-fascist elements inside, or close to, the Italian state, has remained a matter for continued conjecture. The Red Brigades first began to gain serious attention in 1974 when they

A blow to the cultural heart of Italy: bomb damage at the Uffizi gallery in Florence, 1993.

kidnapped an executive from the Fiat motor company. This received major media coverage and was followed by a period in which attention in the media was gained by a variety of means, including the kidnapping and murder of a public prosecutor, the shooting of journalists, and the seizure of broadcasting stations.

The most notorious incident, however, concerned the kidnapping of Aldo Moro, the leading Christian Democrat figure in Italy on 16 March 1978, just as he was departing to parliament to resolve a long-standing governmental crisis. Particularly contentious was the proposed opening towards the Italian Communist Party, at that time intent on effecting the so-called 'historical compromise' with the Christian Democrats. This move was opposed on the political right, but also on the far left. Moro's five bodyguards were killed, a bloodstained image relayed by television and the press that opened a complicated game of communication between the Red Brigades and the media. For fifty-five days Moro was held, during which he was 'tried' and finally murdered. The central focus of political controversy concerned whether or not to negotiate with the Red Brigades. Moro's series of letters to his Christian Democratic colleagues became part of the public debate through the media, and there was much dispute over whether or not they should be taken as genuinely authored by him or as, in effect, dictated by his captors.

The divisions between the politicians over whether to stand on the principle of non-negotiation or to save Moro's life, which were also reflected in the media, meant that there was no overall co-operation between media and state in managing the news. However, the mainstream media were unanimous in taking a stand

245

against the kidnapping and in canonizing Moro. The absence of a clear governmental news management policy, as had occurred in Germany during the Schleyer case, and competition between the media for audiences, allowed the kidnappers to find outlets for their communiqués and the famous photographic image of the captive Moro, pictured in shirtsleeves under the Red Brigades' symbol. Whether the communiqués could be said to have conveyed the intended ideological message to the masses, however, may be doubted, given the obscurity of their language. What the kidnapping succeeded in doing was to grab national attention and to underline the impotence of the state.

When the government finally refused to negotiate Moro's release, his body was dumped in the boot of a car, parked with self-conscious symbolism midway between the Rome headquarters of the Christian Democrats and Communists. This, too, became a celebrated image. The various political divisions were papered over during Moro's state funeral, when the media took a consensual

Aldo Moro, held by the Red Brigades in 1978, is photographed with a newspaper headline suggesting he is dead: an ironic use of the news media by his captors.

stance and reaffirmed the values that Moro was taken to stand for, drawing upon the vocabulary and iconography of the Catholic Church.

Another incident whose images rapidly became part of popular culture and circulated around the world was the siege at the Iranian embassy in London in 1980. The event lasted for six days between 30 April and 5 May 1980 and became celebrated for the dramatic way in which the Special Air Service (SAS) broke the siege. The 'men in black' became an international icon of military efficiency. This was seen as an instance of transnational terrorism, where a political cause located in one part of the world was pursued in another. The Iranian embassy, containing twenty-six hostages, was seized by a group of gunmen claiming to be members of an Arab guerrilla group from Iran who demanded autonomy for their region. Thinking that they would have a chance to present their case through the media, they ran up against a policy of news management which had been worked out over the previous decade by the British government and security forces. Extensive co-operation had already been achieved from the media in general, and broadcasting in particular during such incidents in the past, and these practices once more came into operation. Margaret Thatcher's government set up a special Civil Contingencies Committee to manage the siege as a whole, news coverage included.

The event became best known through the television images of the siege bust, when the SAS broke through the windows at the front of the embassy using 'frame charges', immediately afterwards setting off 'stun grenades' to disorientate the gunmen. The film of the smoke, flames, and figures in black, however, only conveyed the surface action, for it was radio (especially the BBC's news service) that played a role of crucial importance. While one of the express objectives of the hostage-takers was to achieve some publicity for their views, the authorities had an equally express strategy of preventing them from communicating their demands. This was achieved by cutting off all telex and telephone links between the embassy and the outside world, which had been at first used by the media to make contact with the gunmen. The gunmen had radio receivers and consistently monitored them to listen for news of their demands being met, so the process of psychological attrition could be aided by delaying the achievement of their publicity objectives. The security forces knew what these were, because they had the embassy bugged. One of the extraordinary twists in the tale lay in the fact that two BBC television journalists were among the captured hostages. It was they who transmitted the gunmen's initial demands to their newsroom. One of these demands—a request for mediation by the ambassadors of several Arab countries—was apparently suppressed by the BBC at the request of the British government, which was unwilling to yield its control over the bargaining process. In return, the BBC was taken into the confidence of the authorities, it would seem, and its top executives were privy to special security briefings. The BBC became even more deeply involved when one of its senior news executives was brought into the bargaining process and was instrumental

The shadowy figure of an SAS-man in action during the Iranian embassy siege, London, 1980. This image rapidly became an icon of anti-terrorism.

in ensuring that controlled publicity was traded for the release of some of the hostages. The close co-operation of the BBC and of Independent Television News with the security forces meant that when the famous denouement came this was very carefully handled. Both the BBC and ITN offered live coverage only after the action had begun for fear of giving the game away.

Transnational Coverage

The best-known cases involving Americans have tended to have an international dimension. Of course, there were also violent actions in the USA that achieved major television coverage both nationally and internationally. The one that received most attention outside the USA was the attention-grabbing sequestration and conversion into an urban guerrilla of the newspaper heiress Patty Hearst in 1974 by the small and short-lived Symbionese Liberation Army. The bombing of the World Trade Center in New York in early 1993, attributed to an Egyptian

Muslim group, seemed to mark a new departure in the shape of an outside attack on the USA's domestic space.

The USA's dominant presence on the world stage as a superpower has made its citizens, and its aircraft, targets for attack abroad. To a much lesser extent this has also been the case for other Western powers active in international affairs such as Britain and France. In the case of the USA, 'transnational terrorism' has figured predominantly in the shape of hostage-takings, some of which have had major implications for domestic politics. It has already been noted how complicated are the uses of the term 'terrorism'. The taking of hostages at the US embassy in Tehran in November 1979 crystallized the perception in Washington of Iran as a terrorist state. The regime of the USA's close ally in the Gulf, the Shah of Iran, Mohammad Reza Pahlavi, had been overthrown the previous February by followers of the Shi'ite Muslim leader, Ayatollah Ruholla Khomeini. When the Shah was admitted to the USA for medical treatment by the Carter administration in October 1979 this produced outrage in Iran, leading directly to the embassy seizure a fortnight later.

From the start, this officially backed hostage-taking became a leading news story in the United States, as well as elsewhere. The tone was set by ABC News, the first network team into Tehran, which immediately constructed the storyline as 'America held hostage'. The dominant images were of uncontrollable Islamic fanaticism and hatred of the West. Rather than delve into the roots of US involvement in Iran and try to explain the hostility encountered, the bulk of television news coverage became a human interest story focused on the hostages, and showed complete incomprehension of the volatility and complexity of Iranian politics and religion.

The hostage story ran for 444 days, until the captives were released to coincide with the inauguration of Ronald Reagan as President in January 1981, under a cloud of well-founded suspicion that this was part of the pay-off for providing the Iranians with arms.

The continuing coverage of the hostage incident is widely considered to have adversely affected President Carter's re-election prospects. During the first half-year of the story, about one-third of nightly network news coverage was devoted to the fate of the hostages, which some commentators thought very excessive. The celebrated CBS anchorman Walter Cronkite adopted a new way of signing off his evening news programme by counting each day of captivity as it passed. Carter was later to say to him 'that announcement of yours every day didn't help'. In an election year, President Carter made the hostages' release an issue, and his personal standing was increasingly judged by his inability to deliver this.

Consequently, his political fate became tied in with the repeated refusals of the Tehran government to reach an agreement. The Tehran politicians consciously used television, and news reporting more generally, as a means of international communication, especially important in the absence of diplomatic links with Washington. Vice-President Walter Mondale, recognizing the damage that had

Heiress Patty Hearst incarnates terrorist chic in 1974.

been done to the presidential campaign's electoral prospects, later spoke of 'the horror of that evening news guillotine dropping every night'. While the impact of the story must not be exaggerated, it clearly weakened an already enfeebled team opposed by domestic political forces determined to talk tough on 'international terrorism'.

Another celebrated case occurred from 14 to 30 June 1985, when TWA Flight 847 from Cairo to Rome was hijacked by a Lebanese Shi'ite Muslim group at Athens International Airport with 153 passengers on board. Of these, 104 were US citizens. Against the release of the hostages, the hijackers demanded the release of almost 800 Lebanese prisoners, mainly Shi'ite, being held in Israel. The plane was forced to fly from Athens to Beirut to Algiers and then to return to Beirut. At that point forty hostages remained, all Americans. One of the passengers, a serviceman, was killed by the hijackers and his body thrown on to the tarmac. This incident naturally became part of the already dramatic television coverage.

The hijacking was big news for the US networks, ABC, CBS, and NBC, all of which had sent out substantial crews to cover the story in Beirut. In fact, the event received blanket news treatment on all the networks for the whole seventeen days until the hostages were released, with a total of almost 500 reports

'The oxygen of publicity': a controversial image from the TWA hijack in 1985.

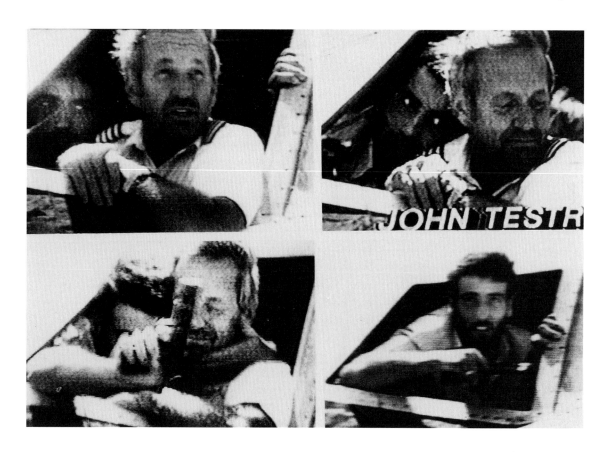

comprising some twelve hours of news time. Some of the most controversial footage occurred when an ABC camera and reporting crew went out on to the runway to interview the aircraft's captain, John L. Trestrake. He was leaning out of the cockpit with a pistol held to his head by a hijacker.

Even more official concern was focused on a televised news conference staged by the hijackers together with five of the hostages. The news conference was used by hostages, at the behest of their captors, to ask President Reagan not to engage in military intervention and also to pressure Israel to release the Shi'ite prisoners. The negotiations with the United States were then fronted by Nabih Berri, head of Amal, the Shi'ite Muslim group, who thereby gained access to network air time. These incidents were to have repercussions back in Britain—as will be seen. The US networks devoted considerable resources to the story, spending some $100,000 per day on it, with substantial crews and top anchor-people flown in specially. Although interviews were carried out with those repre-senting the hijackers, their point of view received about one-tenth of the coverage afforded the views of the US and Israeli governments, which were in turn largely equalled by the attention focused on the hostages themselves. The overall political context that might explain the hijacking was largely absent.

Later, once they had been released, family reunification stories were staged between hostages and their families in Germany—with several re-enactments—*en route* for the USA. Various news media had gone in for 'handholding' the fam-ilies of hostages during their period of captivity with a view to setting up emotional family encounters. Such 'pseudo-events' as the American historian Daniel Boorstin has called them, have become a staple of hostage-releases, now often tied in with the subsequent production of autobiographies and of feature-length movies.

The massive media coverage of the TWA incident had wider ramifications. The focus on the immediate plight of the victims had derailed the longer-term policy goals of the administration of avoiding open negotiation. They spurred on the Iran arms-for-hostages deal, which later came to light.

By contrast with this media overkill, seven US citizens kidnapped before the hijacking, and seen by their families as the 'forgotten hostages', had obtained virtually no news coverage prior to the TWA incident. Its rapid resolution showed what concentrated attention could achieve and brought about a much more organized family lobby with strong media connections, active from 1985 until 1990, when the releases of these US original kidnappees began. These concluded with the freeing of the journalist Terry Anderson, who had been held longest. Analogous to the US case was the lobby for the release of the British journalist John MCarthy, and the repeated efforts by the Church of England to liberate its special envoy, Terry Waite. When the men were finally freed in 1991, their re-emergence into public life was accompanied by considerable media hype and extensive television coverage celebrating their heroism and endurance. Although some of the ex-hostages attempted to explain the political background

251

Terry Waite comes home: the return of Britain's best-known hostage from Lebanon in 1991.

to their captivity, it was the human interest story of how they had survived the ordeal that held the attention.

The Long Television War

From the examples discussed above, it is difficult to judge the long-term impact in a democracy of 'terrorism' on television, and upon television's relationship to the state. However, one case does span the entire period and is a paradigm instance of the toll taken of television's room for manœuvre during a continuing counter-insurgency war.

The latest phase of the 'troubles' in Northern Ireland began in 1969, continuing to the present day. British broadcasting is caught up in a conflict of competing nationalisms. Irish republicanism refuses recognition of Britain's right to rule the province of Northern Ireland and seeks a unified all-Ireland state, whereas Ulster loyalism insists upon the enduring British character of that part of the island and its union with Great Britain. The British state's principal enemy has been the Irish Republican Army, which is officially seen as a terrorist organization. Television has to operate within the boundaries of legality framed by the British state, and, at the same time, in keeping with its historic ethos of public service, must attempt to report with impartiality and independence in the public interest. The historical record, better documented than any other such conflict, shows a long-term process whereby increasing state control has been exercised over television, which correspondingly has largely lost its autonomy to pursue its own agenda in confronting the issues.

The basic rules of the game were first established in 1971 and have tended to become tighter and more nearly all-embracing since then. At that time, the government made it clear that broadcasters could not be impartial between the British state and the 'terrorists' and this was accepted by both the BBC and the Independent Television Authority (ITA), which then regulated the commercial Independent Television (ITV) companies.

From the early 1970s, in response to state pressure for 'responsible' broadcasting, the BBC and the ITA developed detailed internal guide-lines and supervisory practices that amounted to self-censorship. In the 1970s, for instance, despite occasional coverage of these issues by BBC and ITV current affairs programmes, there was a definite tendency to avoid addressing the issue of torture and severe brutality during the interrogation of terrorist suspects. In the 1980s, similarly, allegations that there was a shoot-to-kill policy pursued by the security forces in Northern Ireland were generally treated with kid gloves. It was not just potentially controversial decisions in the fields of news and current affairs that came under scrutiny by senior executives but also the content of television drama and historical documentaries. It took more than a decade from the renewed onset of 'the troubles' for the first major historical series on the roots of the Irish conflict, one produced by the BBC, another by Thames TV, to be broadcast. These were transmitted in 1980–1 and no similar delving into the roots of the crisis has since occurred.

In the early days of the Northern Ireland crisis, there was particular concern inside broadcasting over the airing of interviews with members of banned organizations. During the 1970s, it was the rare screening of such interviews (no more than eight altogether) that caused the most political outrage as these were seen by the government as giving the enemy a direct political voice. The IRA were not interviewed after 1974, when the passage of the Prevention of Terrorism Act in effect made interviews with banned organizations illegal.

It was precisely one such interview—the first in five years—that put BBC TV in the eye of the storm with the newly elected Thatcher government, in July 1979. A spokesman for the Irish National Liberation Army was interviewed on the *Tonight* programme. This republican group had claimed responsibility for the assassination, three months earlier, of Mr Airey Neave, MP, the Conservative party's Northern Ireland spokesman and Mrs Thatcher's close associate. The Attorney-General considered bringing a prosecution against the corporation under the Prevention of Terrorism Act. Although none was brought, this sent a very strong warning signal to all broadcasters.

The incident was rapidly followed by another, in November 1979, when the BBC's *Panorama* programme filmed an IRA roadblock in a Northern Irish village as part of a programme dealing with the military strength of the IRA. This was denounced in Parliament, even though the BBC had not transmitted the film, which was seized by the police, who cited possible infringement of the Prevention of Terrorism Act. Mrs Thatcher opined that it was time for the BBC to 'put its house in order'.

Until 1985, the political establishment had managed to try and control broadcast coverage without using overt censorship. However, in a further major clash in July 1985, the government came close to overt intervention and provoked a major constitutional crisis inside the BBC, as well as raising some basic questions about the corporation's relationship with the government. On this occasion, after some prompting by a Conservative newspaper, the then Home Secretary, Leon Brittan, the minister in charge of broadcasting, asked the BBC's Governors (constitutionally accountable for the corporation) to prevent the screening of a documentary in a series entitled *Real Lives*. The programme portrayed Martin McGuinness, a prominent Sinn Fein figure, widely believed to be the chief of staff of the IRA, and Gregory Campbell of the Democratic Unionists, both uncompromising supporters of the use of violence. The minister made this intervention as part of the 'campaign against terrorism' and said that the programme was contrary to the national interest and would give 'spurious legitimacy' to those who use violence for political ends'. Although ministerial banning powers could have been used, the Governors did the government's work for it. And this despite the fact that the programme had already been carefully vetted internally because of its likelihood of causing controversy. After internal battles in the BBC, involving a serious dispute between the Governors and top management, the programme was eventually screened in October 1985, with additional material intended to underline the IRA's violent nature, and the limited extent of Sinn Fein's electoral support.

In fact, the programme had come at a particularly inauspicious time. Amongst other factors, the American networks were under fire for their coverage of the TWA hijacking, the incident that had provoked Mrs Thatcher's call on journalists, in a speech to the American Bar Association in London, to 'try to find ways to starve the terrorist and the hijacker of the oxygen of publicity on which they depend'.

Another crucial dispute related to 'terrorism' also had its roots in the continuing crisis in Northern Ireland. It concerned the shooting dead in Gibraltar of three IRA members who were planning a bomb attack on British troops stationed there. When killed by the SAS they were unarmed, and the attendant circumstances gave rise to considerable public discussion about whether or not an unstated shoot-to-kill policy existed. This had already been the object of repeated controversy since the early 1970s. So far as the British government was concerned (and this was the view subsequently taken by the inquest into the deaths in Gibraltar) the killings were lawful. For some, however, questions remained, and Thames TV's *This Week* programme investigated the story in March 1988. On the basis of eyewitness evidence, the programme suggested that the three were shot by the SAS without warning, and without making any of the alleged movements towards concealed weapons that were central to the government's version.

This Week's story resulted in a further major row, with hostile interventions by the Prime Minister, the Foreign Secretary, Conservative MPs, and the Conservative press. This time the pressure focused on the Independent Broadcasting Authority (then the commercial television regulatory body) and on the management of Thames TV. In order to establish its journalistic bona fides, Thames Television asked a former Conservative minister, Lord Windlesham, together with a specialist in libel law, Richard Rampton, to investigate its probity, which they subsequently broadly vindicated—although without satisfying the government, which dismissed the findings.

The most overt act of censorship, however, was to occur in October 1988, when the Home Secretary, then Douglas Hurd, used his powers under the BBC's Licence and Agreement and the Broadcasting Act to ban the transmission of the voices of members of proscribed organizations, by, respectively, the BBC and the commercial television and radio companies. Although it did not apply during elections, nor to reported speech, and despite the fact that this ban on direct speech included both republican and loyalist organizations, it was widely recognized that the main purpose was to strike at Sinn Fein, a legal political party. The new directive, which led to such absurdities as the lip-synchronization of actors' voices with the television images of Sinn Fein representatives being interviewed, had a further inhibiting impact on Irish coverage by British television, and a very negative effect on the international standing of British broadcasting, without in any way contributing positively to a resolution of the Northern Ireland conflict.

Silencing Sinn Fein: an actor's voice speaks for Gerry Adams following the government's ban of 1988.

255

The ban was finally lifted on 16 September 1994, some two weeks after the IRA had declared a ceasefire. The Prime Minister, John Major, proclaimed: 'I believe the restrictions are no longer serving the purpose for which they were intended.' The peace process under way since the end of 1993 had made the restriction increasingly anomalous.

Conclusions

The incidents of 'terrorism' that remain in the televisual memory, while certainly having a political content, are also more frequently those that have had a strong human interest and have lent themselves to spectacular and dramatic coverage. The record shows that the interests of those in authority generally prevail and for 'terrorists' to achieve television coverage does not usually mean that they obtain access to put their views across to the public in an unmediated manner. Despite often controlling the range of views and analyses of 'terrorism' available to the public, governments have not seemingly suffered any lasting crises of legitimacy for managing the media and have kept up the pressure for restraint to be exercised. In any case, self-censorship, under the guise of 'responsibility', has tended to mean that overt intervention has not often been needed.

The picture of 'terrorism' offered by television has tended to be seriously distorted, since the repressive actions of states against their citizens have been largely invisible to the camera and, where uncovered, tend not to be labelled 'terrorism' anyway. Television has also tended to be blind in the right eye. In the 1990s, neo-Nazi violence in Europe has not so far been identified as 'terrorism', nor has the brutality perpetrated around the world in the name of ethno-nationalism. So what the public understands as 'terrorism' is largely based upon what is made narrowly visible under that label. The time for rethinking the scope of existing definitions and for enlarging the scope of television's investigative commitment to a more coherent account of political violence in the post-Cold War era is long overdue.

Part Four

Television across the World

11

The American Networks

Les Brown

After some debate in the early 1920s over the possible ways a broadcast system might be financed in the United States, the government chose a course different from that of European countries and consistent with its own *laissez-faire* creed: radio would be built and operated by the private sector—within certain regulatory parameters to safeguard the public interest—and supported by the sale of advertising. Television, when it arrived, was allowed without debate to develop similarly. This made for a system unique in the world, freer than any other, risking all the consequences of mass media shaped by the exigencies of commerce—a system which grew to be so prosperous and powerful that its influence, for better or worse, came to be felt throughout the world.

Though American broadcasting was predicated on localism, with licences awarded to serve every corner of the country, the system quickly became network-centred. National networks attracted lavish-spending national advertisers, and the economies of scale allowed for the presentation of opulent programming with stars of the first rank. Local stations that affiliated with the networks invariably were more prominent in their communities and made more money than those that were forced to programme independently. By the 1960s, each of the three television networks had around 200 affiliated stations giving over some 60 per cent of their air time to national programming.

In such a profits-obsessed system that put the advertisers' interest first, the supreme test for any programme was its popularity, as determined, accurately or not, by the ratings services. Locally and nationally the ratings ruled. Artfulness and worthiness were negative values if they made for limited audience appeal.

259

The American system was much mocked abroad for its devotion to Mammon. It came to represent culture as defined by business, a perverse democracy in which the tastes of the least educated, because they were most prevalent of viewers, prevailed. Yet for all their disparagement of US television, public broadcasters everywhere in the world purchased great quantities of its entertainment programmes—indeed at times fought to get them—because the shows were smartly produced and appealing to their own audiences. Buying American was easily justified because the shows were usually offered cheaply, having recovered their essential costs in the large and thriving home market. Many of the American imports were merely time-fillers in the schedules, but *I Love Lucy*, *Kojak*, *Dallas*, and *Dynasty*, among a score of other US series, were true international hits. American culture, to the extent that it was reflected in TV programmes, thus made itself known and felt, and in some quarters resented, everywhere in the world.

The Industrialist and the Showman

The network system that evolved in America was to a large extent shaped by the friction between two powerful figures—General David Sarnoff, founder of the National Broadcasting Company, and William S. Paley, head of the Columbia Broadcasting System—and by the lively competition between the companies they built and infused with their personal values and mythology.

If anyone can properly be called the father of American broadcasting it would be Sarnoff, who as president of the manufacturing giant, Radio Corporation of America, created the first radio network in 1926 and the first television network in 1940, both through the NBC subsidiary and each with a view to spurring the sale of RCA home receivers. Sarnoff was, moreover, the driving force in bringing television into the consumer market just before World War II. Yet, paradoxically, it was his arch rival Paley who, after trying to hold back television, became the industry's father-figure and reigned as television's spiritual leader almost till the time of his death at the age of 90 in 1990.

Sarnoff, while neither engineer nor consummate showman, was a visionary in his field, and it was his genius for developing and marketing new electronic products that made him one of the great industrialists of the twentieth century. In 1916, when radio was still the wireless, Sarnoff saw its potential as a household utility—'the radio music box', as he characterized it in a prescient memo. As early as 1923 he spoke of television as 'the ultimate and greatest step in mass communication'.

When RCA began manufacturing radios for the home in the 1920s, Sarnoff understood that people were not buying the device for itself but for the information and entertainment it brought to them. The network he created was to be his chief marketing tool—the software, in today's term—and it allowed him to indulge his penchant for extravagance. He brought prestige to the medium early

David Sarnoff opening the RCA pavillion at the 1939 New York World's Fair where television made its public debut. A marketing genius who created the NBC network to help sell radios, Sarnoff could not resist the opportunity the World's Fair afforded even though television technology was not yet perfected. Although television was a star of the Fair, consumers did not rush to buy receivers.

on by hiring no less a resident maestro than the world-renowned Arturo Toscanini to lead the NBC Symphony Orchestra. Some two decades later, to showcase colour television when the receivers were becoming widely affordable, Sarnoff lured away Walt Disney from ABC for a splashy Sunday evening family series whose title, *Walt Disney's Wonderful World of Color*, was implicitly a sales message for RCA.

Paley, while not as visionary or as concerned with technology, was a creative businessman, an indefatigable salesman, and intuitively an impresario for the new broadcast media. For one who was a socialite and lover of the arts, he had a flair for the popular and proved to have remarkable instincts for what would succeed as mass entertainment. Ultimately it was his impresario's knack for befriending and coddling star performers—a talent Sarnoff neglected to cultivate—that allowed CBS television to vault past NBC in overall popularity and stature during the early 1950s, and Paley's remained the premier network for almost a quarter century. During that period CBS boasted of being both the world's largest advertising medium and the 'Tiffany of broadcasting'.

The two industry leaders, both of Russian-Jewish parentage, were a study in contrasts. Sarnoff, who was born in Russia and came penniless to the USA at the age of 9, had one of those legendary rags-to-riches histories—the young wireless operator who through dedication and hard work made his way to the very top of the company and proceeded to build it into a great communications empire. Paley's background was far more privileged. His father owned the prosperous

Congress Cigar Company in Philadelphia, which Paley joined, on completing his schooling, as director of advertising. He became intrigued with radio when he saw how dramatically the sponsorship of a programme boosted the sales of the company's popular brand, La Palina.

Through family connections, Paley came upon an opportunity to enter radio, and leaped at it. For less than $400,000 he bought the controlling interest in United Independent Broadcasters, which operated a faltering young network, the Columbia Phonograph Broadcasting System. In September 1928, at the age of 27, Paley became president of the network renamed CBS. Starting with a paltry twenty-two affiliates and meagre revenues, it presumed to challenge the well-financed and flourishing NBC monopoly, which by then consisted of two networks, the Red and the Blue.

That Paley succeeded against enormous odds in building a communications empire to rival that of Sarnoff's testifies to his entrepreneurial genius and keen eye for executive talent, at least early in his career. (His choice of the brilliant and fastidious Frank Stanton as second in command, on the eve of the television age, gave him a distinct edge on Sarnoff, who was thinking dynastically with his son Robert positioned to succeed him.)

As a neophyte entrepreneur in the late 1920s, Paley assembled a nation-wide line-up of affiliated stations for his fledgling network through the simple device of paying them for the use of their air time, on a scale governed by their market size. NBC was soon forced to do the same or risk losing affiliates to CBS. This practice became standard for all networks. Known as 'station compensation' it carried over into television and binds the local affiliates to their networks to this day.

Paley's first coup, in 1929, was to secure CBS's financial position by selling a 50 per cent stake in it to Paramount Pictures. Paramount's involvement gave CBS credibility with banks, advertisers, and the Hollywood stars sought for some of its programmes. By 1932 CBS had ninety-two affiliates, including five stations it owned. That same year, in a decision the studio regretted for decades after, Paramount allowed CBS to buy back its stock.

But for all its expansion, Paley's upstart operation still had fewer affiliates than Sarnoff's networks and struggled constantly for business since advertisers were drawn to NBC's greater circulation. While NBC had to do little more than let sponsors bring programmes to its networks, CBS set about creating its own programme series for which it aggressively sought advertising sponsorship. This made for a profound and lasting cultural difference between the two networks. In the television era, through the first two decades at least, CBS had an intensely active programme department in whose decisions Paley regularly participated. NBC, in contrast, developed programmes of its own but mainly trusted the MCA (Universal) studios in Hollywood to suggest and provide the big series.

In part because of its circulation handicap in radio days, and its need for programmes of distinction, CBS gave high priority to news broadcasts. With a distinguished news director in Paul White, the network built a staff of stellar correspondents, headed by the journalistic icon, Edward R. Murrow, and including William L. Shirer, H. V. Kaltenborn, Elmer Davis, Raymond Gram Swing, Eric Sevareid, Robert Trout, and Charles Collingwood. The news organization came into its own during World War II and made the daily *CBS World News Roundup* one of radio's most creditable offerings. If CBS continued to trail NBC in circulation and advertising, through news it had become the more respected network.

CBS's steady progress was helped along in 1943 by an action of the third great force in American broadcasting, the Federal Communications Commission. On antitrust grounds, the government agency ordered NBC to divest itself of one of its networks. After contesting the decision and losing the case, NBC sold off for $8 million the less popular Blue Network to Edward J. Noble, manufacturer of Life Savers candy, who renamed it the American Broadcasting Company. The new network fared well enough in radio but, while striving for an identity, was firmly lodged in third place.

Paley and CBS moved to the forefront of broadcasting in 1948. At a strategic moment, taking advantage of Sarnoff's preoccupation with the emergence of television, Paley staged a bold raid on NBC's star talent. In startling succession he spirited away such high-rated performers as Jack Benny, Amos and Andy, Burns and Allen, Red Skelton, Edgar Bergen and Charlie McCarthy, and Frank Sinatra with an innovative business scheme that allowed the artists to save huge amounts of money in taxes. He had them incorporate their shows as companies and sell them to CBS so that they realized a capital gains windfall. Along with helping them become richer, Paley socialized with his new stars. Jack Benny, for one, on making the move, complained that Sarnoff had never taken him to dinner because, as he saw it, the head of RCA deemed such collegiality beneath his station as an industrialist.

The radio audience moved with the stars, and as the CBS ratings boomed new affiliates joined the network and further increased its national circulation. *Variety* dubbed the phenomenon 'Paley's Comet'. Although this occurred in the waning years of the network radio era, the lustre of success carried over into television. And while Paley conducted the raids solely with radio in mind, several of the performers he won over later formed the core of what became CBS's perennially popular, star-laden television schedule.

A Peace Dividend

Well before Paley's raids, Sarnoff had shifted his focus to the development and promotion of television, foreseeing another bonanza for RCA in the sale of home receivers and studio equipment. Paley had shared none of Sarnoff's enthusiasm for the new medium and only dabbled in it during the 1930s to keep pace with his rival. A year after Sarnoff established the first experimental station, CBS went on

263

the air with its own. Six months after NBC began regular broadcasts from the top of the the Empire State Building in 1939, CBS set up its transmitter atop the Chrysler Building and half-heartedly launched its own programme schedule.

The 1939 World's Fair in New York provided RCA with a rich opportunity to introduce television to the consumer market—even though the technology was far from perfected—and Sarnoff made the most of it. The telecast of the glittering opening ceremonies on 30 April, with President Roosevelt's participation, was promoted as marking the official birth of American television since it inaugurated NBC's regular service in New York. RCA's Hall of Television was one of the fair's standout exhibits, displaying NBC's continuous broadcasts on numerous screens in the range of sizes that were being marketed in the stores.

Millions lined up for the demonstrations, and TV cameras were ubiquitous on the fair grounds, but sales of receivers during and after the fair were disappointing. Commentators in the press acknowledged the wonder of television but generally regarded it as a novelty with no practical value in daily life. That view was apparently widely shared. In the midst of the Great Depression, with sets priced from $200 to $600—while movies could be attended for only a few dimes—television was something most consumers could easily do without. A year after the World's Fair, only around 4,000 TV sets were in use in New York.

Though CBS kept its New York station on the air, Paley was as interested in retarding the development of television as Sarnoff was in advancing it. Paley was sworn to radio; it was his essential business, and radio was doing splendidly in the Depression. There seemed no reason to venture beyond, into something as costly and chancy as television, especially since CBS was not involved in the manufacture of the hardware. So when NBC petitioned the FCC for permission to sell advertising on experimental television in the 1930s, CBS opposed it as a danger to radio, and was upheld.

Paley might have moved tentatively into television in the years when it was coming to market but for a fateful development within his company. In 1940 Peter Goldmark, head of CBS Laboratories and the network's resident inventor, came forth with a television system that achieved excellent colour images through the use of a spinning disk. Seeing an opportunity to beat RCA at its own game and to gain lucrative television patents for CBS, Paley applied to the FCC for the acceptance of Goldmark's colour system over the existing monochrome applicants.

The FCC was hesitant because CBS's mechanical system was incompatible with the electronic system already in use and would render all existing TV sets obsolete. Sarnoff urged the FCC to hold off a decision and promised that within six months RCA would present an all-electronic colour system that could be received by both colour and black-and-white sets. The battle over colour was joined, grew fierce with the years, and would not be resolved for more than a decade.

After a bitter struggle involving court appeals and the FCC's approval of the

CBS system followed by a reversal of the decision, RCA finally prevailed. Colour telecasting began in 1953.

At around the time the clash over colour began, an *ad hoc* National Television System Committee was formed at the behest of the FCC to help establish the technical standards for the US industry. After adopting the NTSC recommendations specifying 525 scanning lines and FM sound, the commission in the spring of 1941 finally permitted the thirty-two stations around the country to cease being experimental and to support themselves through the sale of advertising. But just when it appeared that commercial television might be taking off in earnest, the USA entered World War II. Television manufacturing ceased, and the marketing of the new medium was put on indefinite hold. Six stations remained on the air during the war, but most broadcast only a few hours a day and mainly for civil defence purposes.

Sarnoff and Paley both served in non-combatant roles in World War II. Paley took an overseas assignment with the Office of War Information and was given the rank of colonel. Sarnoff became a communications consultant to Eisenhower headquarters in Europe. On his departure in 1944 Sarnoff was promoted to the rank of brigadier-general in the Army Reserve Corps. To him that was tantamount to being knighted, and he so cherished the title *General* that he carried it into business life as his civilian honorific. Within his company he was known ever after as 'The General'.

Their wartime activities seemed to sensitize both Sarnoff and Paley to the importance of news. Both were on a public service high when, on their return, they increased the networks' news programming to more than 20 per cent of their radio schedules. They were also of course reacting to the interest in news that grew during the war, and this inspired a build-up of their journalistic forces beyond the ability of their ragtag competitors to compete. Their news divisions, while loss-leaders, were held sacred; and in television, no less than radio, their networks' primacy in news was Sarnoff's and Paley's greatest source of pride. It was also, of course, politically and socially a unique source of power.

The hiatus for war was in several ways beneficial to television. Developments in radar lent immensely to refinements in video technology. In a most important technical advance, RCA engineers, while working on a military device, invented the image orthicon pickup tube, which made TV cameras easier to use while greatly reducing the light levels the cameras previously required.

But nothing compared in significance to the change in attitude by the American consumer when television re-emerged in the lively post-war economy. No longer minimized as a fair-ground novelty and frill, television was generating enthusiasm and had come to be regarded by the public as a peace dividend. Crowds frequently gathered at store windows to watch the broadcasts from the street, and when prices for TV receivers began to drop as the production of sets accelerated the boom was on.

A mere 0.02 per cent of American households had television in 1946, a year in

A familiar sight in American cities after World War II was crowds watching television through shop windows. Here New Yorkers gather to watch newsreel footage of Queen Elizabeth's Coronation in 1953.

which some 10,000 monochrome sets were sold nationally. But in 1947 sales reached nearly 200,000 and the following year one million. By 1950 household penetration was at 9 per cent, and then the spurt began. Within five years it hit 78 per cent, and television's eclipse of radio was almost complete. Within a mere ten-year span, from 1945 to 1955, television went from a failed idea to one of the necessities of modern life. Five years later it was the biggest and most influential mass medium ever known.

AT&T, the telephone monopoly, had begun laying coaxial cable to interconnect the cities for television as early as 1944. In 1946, with the completion of the link between New York, Philadelphia, and Washington, DC, a three-city telecast of the Joe Louis–Billy Conn heavyweight boxing match gave evidence that television could be networked as easily as radio. By 1948 the major cities in the northern and eastern quadrant of the country were receiving programmes simultaneously. When the east and west coasts were finally linked in 1951, Edward R. Murrow marked that momentous occasion on his CBS programme by showing viewers simultaneous live pictures of the Atlantic and Pacific oceans.

The Brief Golden Age

Four networks were involved in television at the war's end. NBC, CBS, and ABC all had branched into the new medium along with many of their radio affiliates, although CBS had to scramble to buy stations in the major cities because, with its bid for the field sequential colour system, it had withdrawn its applications for monochrome station licences. The fourth contender was the DuMont Network, founded by Allen B. DuMont, an inventor and prosperous manufacturer of television sets and picture tubes.

DuMont Laboratories, in which Paramount Pictures was an investor, had been planning a network from early times. Overshadowed by RCA, it had been the other television exhibitor at the 1939 World's Fair. Its New York flagship was the only television station to continue regular broadcasting during World War II in hopes of getting a jump on the other networks when the war ended. DuMont's handicap was that it had no radio base and thus no ready-made family of affiliates to build upon. But with its two stations in the east tying in with Paramount's two on the west coast, DuMont hoped to string together a national network from the hundreds of new applicants for stations around the country. The FCC was to frustrate that plan. Unprepared as it was for the explosive post-war growth of television, the commission in the autumn of 1948 instituted a freeze on new station licences until it could determine how to allocate the frequencies equitably and in ways to avoid signal clashes. At the time, only 108 stations had been authorized, and eleven cities were left without television service.

The freeze lasted four years. When the FCC finally produced its allocation table, it assigned a maximum of three VHF stations to most metropolitan areas. Though unintended, in practical terms this meant the field would be limited to three networks, since any attempt to compete with an alignment of UHF stations would be unthinkable, given the reception problems with that band.

By 1952, when the freeze ended, NBC and CBS had lined up the new affiliates they needed to assure coverage in the largest and most lucrative population centres. ABC gathered up most of the remainder. DuMont's chances were severely hampered by the FCC's allocation plan and, also, by its own low-budget programme schedule that simply could not compete for prime new affiliates. But the death blow came in 1953 when ABC was significantly strengthened by the completion of its merger with United Paramount Theatres, settling the question of which network would be third.

There was enough advertising at the time to support two networks, scarcely enough for a third, and not at all enough to support four. After nine years of heavy losses DuMont gave up in 1955. The stations it owned were reorganized as Metromedia, which for the next three decades thrived as the largest independent station group. (Interestingly, those stations again became the foundation for a fourth network when Rupert Murdoch purchased the group in 1985. This fourth network, Fox, was far more successful than its early progenitor.)

Because ABC was the newest radio network and a weak third in importance, it moved swiftly into television so as not to get left behind. But ABC was largely owned by one man, and the investment he faced in assembling and operating a network against powerful competition was far more than he could afford. As early as the late 1940s Edward J. Noble began seeking a merger. After rejecting a number of suitors he settled in 1951 on United Paramount Theatres, a theatre chain flush with money after its government-decreed divestiture from Paramount Pictures. But because a transfer of station licences was involved, the transaction required FCC approval, and that turned out to be a two-year process. During the waiting period, with its funds almost depleted, ABC sank even deeper into third place, where it had been scrambling with DuMont for survival.

When the merger was finally effected in 1953, ABC had a new leader in Leonard Goldenson, a lawyer who had been president of the large theatre chain. NBC and CBS already had such dominance of the television audience, such formidable stables of stars, and such tight relationships with the largest advertisers that ABC's existence on the network playing field was bound to be a study in futility. Moreover, Goldenson not only lacked a background in broadcasting, he had none of the hubris or sense of manifest destiny that propelled Sarnoff and Paley. He was a mere life-sized human in the company of godheads.

ABC's was to be a hard climb indeed. Though DuMont's demise gained ABC some affiliates and advertisers, it left ABC the lone victim of network television's poverty cycle, perennially at the short end of what was characterized as a two-

An NBC production of Emlyn Williams' **The Corn is Green** in the late 1950s typified studio activity when most television was live and drama a mainstay of prime time. In what came to be known as American television's Golden Age, the networks, drawing from the talent pool of Broadway theatre, started the careers of noted actors, writers, and directors who later left the new medium for motion pictures.

and-a-half network economy. The big stars shunned ABC for fear of acquiring a loser's taint, so it was helpless against the star power of its rivals. Year after year through the 1950s and 1960s the ABC network lost money, its existence justified in business terms only by its contribution to the profits of the five ABC-owned television stations. Its wretched position in the three-network race forced ABC to compete inventively, and on several occasions its efforts created dramatic changes in the television business.

The ABC merger occurred in a period that is often referred to as American television's golden age—a time when much of the main nightly fare in the new medium was studio drama in the theatre tradition. Television production was centred in New York then, and the networks drew from the talent pool for the Broadway stage, as one live medium feeding off another. In a wave of sponsored anthology series such as Kraft Television Theatre, Philco Playhouse, U.S. Steel Hour, and General Electric Theatre as many as a dozen original plays were presented in prime time each week. The most ambitious series was Playhouse 90 on CBS, which offered a ninety-minute weekly drama.

To talented young people aspiring to the stage, television in the early 1950s afforded an opportunity to be discovered. The network showcases launched the careers of numerous dramatists, including Paddy Chayevsky, Rod Serling, Reginald Rose, Gore Vidal, A. E. Hotchner, and William Gibson; and such directors as Sidney Lumet, Arthur Penn, George Roy Hill, and John Frankenheimer. Among the raft of producers spawned in the golden age were Paul Gregory, John Houseman, Herbert Brodkin, Martin Manulis, and George Schaefer.

But most impressive was the galaxy of young actors who went on to stardom. In their considerable number were Paul Newman, George C. Scott, Lee Remick, Julie Harris, James Dean, Sidney Poitier, Jack Lemmon, Grace Kelly, Peter Falk, Jack Palance, Dina Merrill, Rip Torn, Rod Steiger, Kim Stanley, Jack Warden, and Lee J. Cobb.

Stage adaptations were made of such TV plays as *Marty*, *The Miracle Worker*, *Twelve Angry Men*, *The Bachelor Party*, *Patterns*, *No Time for Sergeants*, and *Visit to a Small Planet*. All were later produced as movies.

The drama anthologies, in their brief hour on the prime-time stage, brought respectability to the new medium and demanded that it be evaluated by critics of substance. Television had not yet come to be scorned by the intelligentsia. But just when it seemed that the networks would be contributing a new and significant body of literature to the national culture, the drama anthologies began to give way to quiz shows and episodic filmed series, mainly Westerns. By the late 1950s television's golden age evaporated, and most of the artists it had nurtured fled to motion pictures and the stage.

At least partly responsible for the networks' abrupt change of direction was television's proliferation in working-class households. In 1953 television was only in 40 per cent of American homes; by 1955 the number had nearly doubled. The first to purchase TV sets were, by and large, the wealthier and better-educated families. Studio drama served such an audience well. But when the masses joined in the viewing, the presentation of serious plays on gloomy themes could not stand up to competition from lighter forms of entertainment.

Other factors contributed to the sudden demise of the drama anthology. One of them was the arrival of videotape in 1956, after which actual live productions were unthinkable. While tape helped eliminate production flaws, it also removed the sense of immediacy that was part of the wonder of a live dramatic performance. The shows, in short, were not as exciting as before.

Most significant, however, was Hollywood's change of heart towards television. The major studios, after years of shunning the new audio-visual medium that was stealing their audience and causing neighbourhood theatres to close around the country, began to see financial salvation in television. One by one they began releasing to the syndication market large packages of old feature films from their vaults. The sudden plethora of movies on the air seemed to satisfy much of the need for drama that the network anthologies had provided.

At around the same time, ABC's new president, Leonard Goldenson, was making his unique contribution to television. Putting to use his Hollywood connections as a former Paramount executive, he succeeded in persuading first Walt Disney and then Warner Bros. to break the Hollywood hold-out and produce weekly film series for the networks. Warner weighed in with a Western, *Cheyenne*, whose hour-long episodes could be shot in five days while incorporating considerable library footage to keep costs low.

When both *Disneyland* and *Cheyenne* became hits for ABC, the other studios began seeking network commissions for weekly series, and few projects were denied. Most were Westerns. By the late 1950s the genre was epidemic, driving out most other forms of programming in prime time. Virtually all that served for balance were some innocuous situation comedies, a scattering of variety shows, and a new genre—opulent and suspensefully orchestrated serialized quiz shows that paid unheard-of awards to the winners. One of the most typical and popular was *The $64,000 Question*. They became a national rage and then a national scandal.

At their very height of popularity, the quiz shows self-destructed. They were banished from the air when they were discovered to have been 'fixed' at the sponsors' behest in ways intended to produce higher ratings. Contestants with demonstrable audience appeal had been fed the answers to ensure their continuance on subsequent shows; those lacking in viewer sympathy or charm were disposed of with questions designed for their elimination. When the hoaxes were found out, the networks were disgraced and the licences of their owned stations placed in jeopardy. They atoned for their sins against the public trust with a commitment to producing social documentaries. This enlivened the news divisions, but only for a few years, until the scandal was forgotten.

The passing of the quiz programmes increased the networks' dependency on Hollywood for entertainment and changed the nature of the prime-time compet-

opposite A couple exults at winning $16,000 in 1955 on CBS's immensely popular **$64,000 Question**, one of the programmes implicated four years later in the quiz show scandal that traumatized the industry. After the Congressional investigation into the deceptive practices of these shows, which involved feeding answers in advance to contestants with high audience appeal, the networks atoned for their sins by peppering their schedules with news documentaries.

As the first major Hollywood studio to produce film series for the networks, Warner Bros. introduced both the 'adult' Western (**Cheyenne** and **Maverick**) and the urban action-adventure hour (**77 Sunset Strip** and **Hawaiian Eye**). Their success prompted the other studios to follow in the late 1950s, and the Western came to dominate prime time for a decade.

ition. Executives who were adept at live television were replaced by those skilled at selecting and scheduling continuing film series. Common practice by the networks was to order thirty-nine episodes of a series and repeat thirteen of them during the summer months. Programmes were created cynically, with intent to destroy the two others in opposition—such was to be the nature of three-network competition for decades after, although for reasons of economy the ratio of first-run to rerun episodes came down to one-to-one.

By 1959 there were thirty-two Western series in prime time. While many of them had relatively complex characters and dealt with social and philosophical issues, all were essentially action shows, and they introduced violence to television on a grand scale. In striving to succeed in the crowded field, the series increasingly resorted to mayhem and often to bizarre forms of torture and murder. This dismal landscape was what Newton Minow, the young FCC chairman in the Kennedy administration, referred to in his famous speech that characterized television as 'a vast wasteland'.

The Ratings War Escalates

In time the filmed shows from Hollywood became too expensive for single sponsors. Advertisers, moreover, began to shrink from the high risk of backing shows for a full year only to have them fare poorly in the ratings and adversely affect product sales. Their desire to retreat from the sponsor system proved opportune for the networks, which had wanted to assume greater control over programming ever since the quiz show scandal when they were held responsible for the nefarious practices of sponsors. Network advertising began to be sold in flights of one-minute spot announcements spread over numerous shows, in the manner of ad pages in magazines, and by the mid-1960s the sponsorship system that had been carried over from radio was gone.

With the networks having full control over prime-time programming (Procter & Gamble continued to hold a grip on certain daytime hours for its soap operas) the ratings war intensified. Ad spots were valued according to the amount of audience reached, so that a programme which placed first in a time period might earn 50 per cent more than one placing third. Every rating point translated into dollars, and a network that finished a season on top by a single average rating point stood to make some $20 million to $30 million more in profits than the network next behind. This had implications for the stock options of network executives, because Wall Street began correlating stock values with the monthly Nielsen rating reports, so the executives' personal fortunes were at stake in the game of numbers.

Caught in a web of venality—one of their own making, to be sure—the networks lost virtually all ability to be boldly venturesome in programming. Scores of pilots for new series were produced each year, and nearly all were mere variations on the proven formulas. Programmes were aligned in the schedules for compatibility, so that one might feed its audience to the next. At the first sign that a series was faltering in its time period, it was either pulled from the schedule or given a second chance in a move to another night. Early cancellation was a form of damage control, even affecting series with several unaired episodes that were already produced and paid for.

The television audience made its unwitting contribution to the programming morass and the lock step of the networks by the sheer predictability of its viewing habits. Audience research found that television viewing levels remained about the same for any hour, week after week, no matter what was being offered on the air. On any Tuesday evening, for example, there would be 75 million people before the set at 8 p.m., 90 million at 9 p.m., and 70 million just after 10 p.m. If NBC offered a programme at 9.00 that viewers did not especially like, they did not switch off but merely tuned to another network. This meant that when a network failed in a time period it compounded the injury by feeding the dissatisfied audience to its rivals, boosting their numbers.

During the 1960s the ratings race was mainly between CBS and NBC, with CBS always finishing first. To a large extent winning was a matter of having star power, and CBS had Lucille Ball, Jack Benny, Danny Kaye, Red Skelton, Jackie Gleason, Ed Sullivan, Dick Van Dyke, Andy Griffith, Carol Burnett, the Smothers Brothers, and Jim Arness. NBC had Bob Hope, Dean Martin, Andy Williams, Rowan and Martin, and other popular performers, but in this sphere CBS proved always to have the edge.

In the dramatic programme forms, NBC excelled in the action-adventure series while CBS was pre-eminent in the sitcom genre. In general, NBC's programming in the 1960s was oriented to the urban viewer while CBS cast a wider net and derived much of its rating strength from the rural areas. Because ABC always ran third, it was somewhat more daring with programming than the others, and occasionally trendy. ABC seemed mainly to succeed with the young. The network raised controversy for the excesses of violence in such shows as *The Untouchables* and *Bus Stop* and for the sexual currents in the *Peyton Place* series— made the worse to ABC's critics by the following among teenagers it had won with shows like *Leave it to Beaver*, *My Three Sons*, *The Adventures of Ozzie and Harriet*, and the animated sitcom *The Flintstones*. Though last in the ratings, ABC was always a factor in the competition and excelled particularly in sports. It even had an occasional entertainment blockbuster with shows like *The Fugitive* and *Batman*. But there were four hours a night of prime time, and in most of those hours ABC did not measure up to its rivals.

Movies that were only a few years out of theatrical release became available to the networks in the mid-1960s, though at great cost, and quickly became a prime-time staple. By 1968 each network had two movie nights and some expanded to three, pitting one against another. The movies were so immensely popular that they were destroying virtually all the TV series in opposition. One reason was that they were racier.

In having to compete for audience with television, producers of theatrical motion pictures exploited whatever was taboo in the family medium and heaped on the flavourings of sex and violence. Even after severe editing, when these movies came to television they usually exceeded the normal standards of acceptance for the medium. Responding to pleas from television producers for the ability to compete, the networks liberalized their standards and opened the new era of permissiveness in TV programming. This was typified by the various Norman Lear series—*All in the Family* and *Maude*, among them—which in dealing with such themes as bigotry, impotency, and abortion altered the character of sitcoms and ended their age of innocence.

Television's voracious appetite for successful movies soon exhausted the supply. MCA, the parent of Universal Pictures and the chief supplier of programming to NBC, offered to produce two-hour features made expressly for television and created a new form—the made-for-TV movie. A crass descendant of the early drama anthologies, it has since become a staple of prime-time schedules.

The Networks' Great Power

Collectively, for having at least half the American population in their thrall on any night, the networks became extemely powerful in the 1960s and a source of concern to many for their influence on the public mind and for visiting change on virtually every institution of society, from politics to professional sports. In mounting the so-called 'Great Debates' between Richard Nixon and John F. Kennedy in the 1960 presidential campaign, the networks established television as the proscenium for national politics, as in time it was to become for local and state politics as well. Ward healers and power brokers selecting candidates in smoke-filled rooms—the essential behind-the-scenes players in old party politics—were rendered obsolete by television.

The televised debates of 1960 not only changed politics but also the course of history, at least to the extent of affecting the order of leadership in the USA. In an earlier time, Nixon would probably have won. As the highly visible vice-president in the popular Eisenhower administration he was a far stronger candidate than the relatively unknown senator from Massachusetts. But the first of the debates, the most crucial of the series of four, proved to be more about image than about where the candidates stood on issues; and on that score the handsome, sun-tanned young senator won handily over the haggard Nixon. Interestingly, most people who had heard the debate on radio thought Nixon the winner. In the aftermath, the event left no doubt about television's ability to create political stars overnight.

Having begun to compete as vigorously with news as with entertainment programming, with prestige as the prize, the networks were at the centre of the turmoil of the 1960s. The civil rights movement gained momentum when the inhumanity of the rabid segregationists towards black demonstrators in cities like Birmingham, Alabama, appeared on the home screens. Images of attack dogs and fire hoses being turned on the blacks seared the consciences of Americans around the country. As public opinion shifted to the civil rights cause, the networks themselves responded. After having portrayed in their programming an essentially lily-white nation up to the late 1960s, the networks lowered the colour bar which had been raised from the belief that series featuring blacks would be rejected by much of the audience. Instead, as it turned out, programmes like *Julia, Sanford and Son,* and *The Jeffersons* became substantial hits, and the mini-series *Roots*, when it aired in 1977, drew the largest audience ever for an entertainment programme.

The great success of sitcoms like **Sanford and Son** in the 1970s gave the lie to the long-held notion at the networks that blacks would not be welcome on screens in many white households. NBC had to cancel a Nat (King) Cole variety series in 1957 because no advertiser would sponsor it, fearing a boycott of its products in the South. With help from the Civil Rights movement, the colour line was effectively broken in 1968 with the hit NBC sitcom, **Julia**, which starred Diahan Carroll.

Along with advancing the civil rights, women's rights, and gay rights movements—none of which could have progressed on the scale experienced without a marked change in public opinion—the television networks were instrumental in ending the US involvement in Vietnam. It was not that they changed attitudes by taking editorial positions against the war—although CBS's revered anchorman, Walter Cronkite, did suggest in a commentary that it was an unwinnable war—but that the networks' daily news coverage revealed as it progressed the horrifying moral decline of the enterprise.

The networks had the power also to bind and comfort the nation through the traumatic wave of assassinations in the 1960s, of President Kennedy, his brother Robert, and Martin Luther King Jr. But the power of the networks, for all the good it actually served, was widely resented and distrusted. Though their programmes were still immensely popular in the Nielsen ratings, the networks themselves were not loved by much of their public. Indeed at times they seemed to have more enemies than friends. Parent groups condemned them for exploiting children as a market and rotting their minds with base Saturday morning

cartoon shows. Educators reviled the networks for providing little of intellectual nourishment, and racial and female activists protested the stereotyping of women and minorities. Social critics deplored television's unrelenting commercialism and the medium's role in supplanting a democracy of citizens with one of consumers.

Moreover, the networks found themselves under fire from the political extremes, assailed from the left as part of the military-industrial complex—wasn't RCA, the parent of NBC News, one of the Pentagon's major contractors?—and from the right as tools of the eastern liberals. Richard Nixon, a champion of the right, was downright paranoid about the media, but particularly the networks, when he became President in 1969. He opened fire on the networks early on, and others in his administration seldom passed up an opportunity to attack them publicly for opposing Nixon from an ideological bias. For years after the Watergate hearings and the Congressional vote to impeach the President, Nixon's right-wing loyalists continued to believe it was the networks that had hounded him out of office.

Revd. Martin Luther King, Jr. pauses for a roadside news conference during a 1965 protest march in the South at the height of the Civil Rights movement. Television became an important instrument in the non-violent campaign to break down colour barriers, searing the American conscience with images of attack dogs and hoses turned on peaceful black demonstrators and of soldiers escorting black students to newly integrated schools.

Public television became a victim of Nixon's war against the media. In 1973 the President vetoed the Congressional appropriation for the system because the money would be going to support a fourth network, PBS, which he believed to be a hotbed of liberalism. The operators of public television stations were made to understand that they would receive the federal funds only if they decentralized the system. PBS was then reduced from an actual network (after only three years in that capacity, as a creation of President Johnson's 'Great Society' programme) to a central body that merely handled the distribution of national programmes. In its decentralized form, with each local station determining what it would air, public television had to content itself with small audiences and never became a factor in the competition among the networks.

If the networks had provoked the public's resentment and the government's anger, they also fuelled a bitterness towards themselves within their own industry for their arrogance and greed. In the 1960s the networks came to dominate nearly every facet of the television business. They made continual demands on stations for more air time, and though the stations objected, they usually complied from fear of reprisal. A network had the ability to drop a recalcitrant broadcaster and switch the affiliation to a neighbouring independent, which indeed happened more than once. The market value of the abandoned stations immediately decreased by at least half.

CBS, NBC, and ABC, moreover, held complete sway over the programme market to the despair of independent producers and programme distributors. The major Hollywood studios were not only frustrated at having nowhere else to go with a project if the networks rejected it, they often were forced to give the networks equity positions in their shows to get them on the air. The networks also presumed to dictate when the reruns of a series could be placed in syndication; invariably it was after the series had run its course in prime time, when its popularity was so thoroughly spent that it posed no serious ratings threat as a competitor. In the syndication field, where the networks also ruled, they tended to favour their own affiliates with the most desirable shows.

Acting on petitions from a number of industry sectors, and after a long series of inquiries, the FCC adopted severe regulations in 1970 that curbed the networks' power and effectively restructured the television market. Under what was called the Prime Time Access Rule, the networks could claim no more than three hours of prime time (the period defined as 7–11 p.m.), except on Sundays where the first hour had to be given over either to programmes for children or to news and public affairs. A companion regulation, the Financial Interest and Syndication Rule (known in industry shorthand as fin-syn), barred the networks from engaging in domestic syndication and the ownership of cable systems, and outlawed their ownership of all or part of the programmes they aired, except for news and public affairs.

The new rules were a boon to the Hollywood studios, which came to realize enormous profits from their network hits, both because they owned the shows

In 1976, in its third year on ABC, the US sitcom **Happy Days** switched its focus from middle-class teenagers to a street-smart supporting character named Fonzie and became the top-rated show for the next eight years. The role made a star of Henry Winkler.

The pioneer shop-at-home channel QVC is leading the way to interactivity. By 1995 it was handling some 20,000 orders a day in the US and grossing $1 billion a year, though four-fifths of households had not yet become customers. It had also begun broadcasting in the UK.

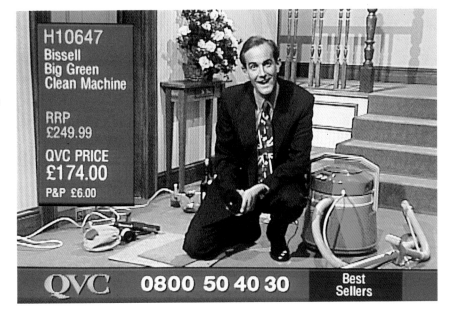

Left: **Hana no Ran**, a popular Sunday serial produced by NHK, depicting the struggle for authority between two Japanese medieval noble women.

Below: a still from **Sword of Conquest**, produced by the Hong Kong-based Chinese Channel for satellite transmission to the Chinese community in Europe.

entirely and because they were able to sell the reruns in syndication while the new episodes on the networks were at their peak of popularity. Twentieth Century Fox, for example, hit the jackpot with *M*A*S*H,* which while running once a week on CBS in its regular slot was also aired five times a week (and in some instances ten) on local independent stations. In the industry's reorganization, the syndication market flourished, allowing small distributors to prosper and independent producers to create shows for the time periods that became available under the Prime Time Access Rule.

In compliance with fin-syn, CBS spun off its syndication and cable divisions into a new independent company, Viacom, which went on to become a force in both the cable and television industries. ABC sold its syndication unit, ABC Films, to a group of its own executives, who named the new company Worldvision. It too continues to live on. NBC chose a different course and sold off its various syndication properties to a scattering of independent distributors.

Despite being reined in by the FCC's action, the networks continued to prosper in the 1970s and, paradoxically, found some of the radical changes in the market working in their favour. ABC was a particular beneficiary, since in being forced to give up seven hours a week of prime-time programming it was able to unburden itself of the weakest shows in its inventory. That served not only to bring ABC closer in line with the other networks in the ratings but also allowed it to shore up its finances and build its evenings around its most dependable programmes.

The tightening of the ratings race, with all three networks in contention, had the effect of firming up the prices of advertising spots. In prior times ABC's frequent offers of bargains produced a more elastic pricing structure at all the networks. Moreover, with their truncated prime-time schedules and 25 per cent fewer spots to sell, the networks found themselves in a most favourable supply-and-demand position. As advertisers wanted more prime-time ad spots than were available to buy, the networks were able to raise their rates 10 per cent or more every year throughout the decade. Such was the demand that every programme made money, even those at the bottom of the ratings charts. The flops were quickly discarded anyway, because the object was to maximize the revenue potential of every time period. Part of the legacy of the FCC's rules, ironically, was to make network television a failure-proof business, at least for the near term.

A Shift in Network Fortunes

The 1970s became ABC's decade. The network not only achieved parity with its rivals at long last, but in 1976 advanced to the front of the field, helped in part by the mysterious passing of the venerable star system. For reasons no one could quite explain, the star system that had hobbled ABC from radio times suddenly stopped functioning. Established stars no longer ensured top ratings; rather, viewers seemed to enjoy the discovery of new performers, and turned them into stars within weeks.

Also favouring ABC was the mania for young demographics that overtook the advertising industry in the late 1960s. Most advertisers, having determined that younger viewers were more likely than the older to try new products or switch brands, were willing to pay twice as much or more for an audience predominantly in the age group of 18 to 34 than for a programme's audience that was more mature. As a network that once was cursed with a teenage following, ABC was better positioned for the change than were either of its rivals.

At CBS, Paley spent most of the 1970s preparing for management succession, the future of CBS without himself. It proved to be his greatest failure. After arranging for his own exemption from the company's mandatory retirement rule at 65, he declined a similar waiver in 1972 for his long-time alter ego and heir apparent, the esteemed Frank Stanton. Instead, he determined that the company should be led by an executive skilled in acquisitions, because he believed CBS should diversify in a way that would make broadcasting a mere facet of a conglomerate rather than a small company's primary business.

The first of his recruited successors-to-be died of a heart attack only months after joining the company, and in rather swift succession Paley hired and fired two others. None of his appointments had had any previous experience with television, or displayed any instinct or talent for programming, and the network began to slide. Paley's final appointment as president of the corporation, Thomas Wyman, brought over from the packaged foods industry, proved to be his undoing. Within two years after his arrival, Wyman manœuvred Paley's semi-retirement as a board decision and assumed the chairmanship.

NBC, meanwhile, had a succession crisis of its own. When General Sarnoff retired from RCA in 1970 (he died the following year) his son Robert succeeded him as chairman and immediately was faced with the onslaught from Japanese manufacturers. During the next five years, RCA's share of the TV receiver market shrivelled, and the company was forced besides to shut down its computer manufacturing operations at a huge loss. With the $10 billion corporation floundering, the RCA board forced Robert Sarnoff's ouster in 1975. After that came two disastrous appointments which left the company in disarray when Thornton F. Bradshaw was named chairman in 1980. Meanwhile, NBC had sunk deeply into third place, the result of a management fiasco of its own.

That had begun in 1978 when, in a blizzard of publicity, RCA wooed away ABC's famed programme chief Fred Silverman by offering him the presidency of the entire National Broadcasting Company, which included the radio, stations, sports, and news divisions. The television network at the time was running last in the ratings race, and the hiring of television's master programmer to turn NBC's fortunes around was viewed as a master stroke. Silverman had made his reputation at CBS in the 1960s as a wunderkind who had an intuitive understanding of the medium that few had ever possessed. Later, as CBS's head of

programming, he divined an imposing string of hits, in a range of genres from *Kojak* to *The Waltons*. ABC, in a stunning coup, hired Silverman away in 1975, and a year later the network soared into first place. Silverman was hailed in the press as the programmer with the golden touch.

He lost that touch completely at NBC, however. Whether because he was distracted by having to oversee the entire company, or because he tried to accomplish too much too soon in doctoring the programme schedule, his frantic three-year stewardship was a humiliating flop. All his programme strategies failed, the ratings continued to decline both in the evening and daytime, several valued NBC affiliates became disenchanted and switched to other networks, and dozens of key NBC executives left, many of them fired by Silverman. By the time he himself was fired in 1981, NBC was a shambles.

The miracle that Silverman had been expected to perform at NBC was instead performed by his successor, Grant Tinker, a noted Hollywood producer and one-time NBC programme executive. In a style that was as calm and civil as Silverman's was hysterical and churlish, Tinker led NBC through one of its most glorious periods. He chose excellent executives and gave them room to do their best. During Tinker's five-year tenure, the network advanced steadily from last place to first, mostly moreover with programmes of exceptional quality, and morale was restored throughout the ranks. NBC had become not only the model network but a model company.

While most US network series sell widely abroad, few have enjoyed the world-wide popularity and durability of **Kojak**, which ended a five-year run on CBS in 1978 but continues to air in foreign markets in the 1990s. The police detective series derived much of its realistic edge from the unglamorous rendition of the hero by Telly Savalas—stocky and totally bald, with an addiction to lollipops. Savalas, a previously obscure actor, became a global star with the series.

The End of the Networks' Prime

It was the last glorious time for any network. Cable had begun to emerge from the background in the late 1970s, and through its convergence with satellite technology brought forth a number of new national television channels that portended the first real competition to the major networks. HBO, the premium channel that offered recent movies uncut and without commercials for a monthly fee, became the engine that drove cable's rapid growth through the 1980s.

The spread of cable across America also fostered a boom in the UHF band, because cable equalized the reception of VHF and UHF signals. As rapidly as cable spread, so did the construction of new UHF stations for both commercial and public television. This extraordinary second growth of terrestrial TV stations allowed Rupert Murdoch to create the first successful fourth network, Fox, using his newly acquired VHF stations that once formed the Metromedia group (and thirty years before, the DuMont Network) as the nucleus. Fox made a substantial claim on the three-network audience in the late 1980s, as did, collectively, some fifty cable networks. (One of them, Ted Turner's twenty-four-hour news channel, CNN, rapidly became television's fourth great news force, and on major running stories, such as the Persian Gulf War in 1991, dominated both the coverage and the viewing.)

In 1986, the year Fox began, all three major networks had changed hands. As if in a single wave the network culture that was born four decades earlier was transformed.

Leonard Goldenson, approaching his 80th birthday, sold ABC to Capital Cities Communications for $3.5 billion, a case of the smaller company consuming the larger. Capital Cities was headed by one of Goldenson's friends in the industry, Thomas Murphy, who was widely recognized in the business world as an exemplary chief executive. Financial analysts later determined that ABC was worth about twice the price, especially since its assets included major equity stakes in three of the most prosperous cable networks: ESPN, Arts & Entertainment, and Lifetime.

At RCA, Thornton Bradshaw, concerned that the company might be prime for a take-over by predators who were running wild on the business landscape in the 1980s, arranged for its purchase for $6.3 billion by the giant General Electric Corporation, a company compatible in electronics manufacturing. The deal included the NBC subsidiary but not Grant Tinker who, previous to the transaction, indicated he would resign and return to Los Angeles. GE seemed appropriate for the acquisition because it had been one of the founding partners of the Radio Corporation of America in 1919. But GE in 1986, under its chairman Jack Welch, had a reputation for toughness in business and brooked no sentimentality. Among GE's first acts was to shut down RCA and to sell off NBC Radio, thereby putting an end also to the world's first broadcasting network.

Meanwhile, a boardroom melodrama unfolded at CBS. Tom Wyman's record as chairman was dismal. The network's ratings were in quicksand, and the news division, disarrayed by internal changes, suffered a decline in stature. The image of the company that Paley and Stanton had so painstakingly burnished over the decades was badly tarnished. That Wyman survived at the helm for six years testified to his skill and energy in dealing with board members. To save his company, the aged Paley mounted a last stand, producing a 'white knight' in Laurence A. Tisch, the billionaire chairman of Loews Corporation, whom Paley did not actually know. Tisch proceeded to purchase close to 25 per cent of the company's stock, more than enough to assume control. When Wyman overplayed his hand with the board in undertaking on his own to find a buyer for the company, he was dismissed, and Tisch immediately took charge.

The new owners of the networks, unlike the founders, were strictly in the business of business. Although the Capital Cities management was the only one of the three that had experience in broadcasting and understood the special nature of it, Thomas Murphy and Daniel Burke prided themselves on running their company in a manner often described as 'lean and mean'. The rule at General Electric was that every division must be profitable, and that included NBC News, which like the news divisions of the other networks had always been a loss leader. Laurence Tisch made his fortune as what Wall Street calls a 'bottom feeder', one who buys sinking companies cheaply and whips them back to profitability by slashing costs, which mainly means reducing staff.

All three new owners immediately proceeded to reduce their payrolls substantially, with the news divisions hit hardest of all because news is the one programme area whose costs the networks can directly control. Also eliminated were the life-style niceties and executive perquisites—the cut flowers, limousines, company planes, hospitality suites at the Plaza, lavish affiliate conventions, *haute cuisine* in the executive dining-rooms, and generous expense accounts— everything that had made working for a network glamorous and exceptional. The new network owners pointed out that television is not the business it once was. That assertion is not only beyond dispute, it almost understates the case.

From the early years through most of the 1970s the networks had commanded at least 90 per cent of the prime-time viewing on any night, but by 1990 the competition from cable and the Fox network had cut their combined share to less than 60 per cent and at times during the summer months even below 50 per cent. Meanwhile, in the latter half of the 1980s video rentals ballooned into a $13 billion a year business that lessened network viewing on weekends and decimated the Saturday night ratings. Most motion pictures made more money from video rentals than from their theatrical runs. Coveting the video rental audience and its burgeoning revenues, and seeing an opportunity to seize them, cable operators in 1993 began to prepare for the greater delivery of pay-per-view attractions and the eventual delivery of video-on-demand. The latter is an electronic form of video rental that allows cable subscribers to order whatever movies or programmes they want, from a catalogue listing hundreds of choices, without leaving their homes. This is the ultimate in *à la carte* television. The regional telephone companies were given permission by the FCC to provide a similar service, called the video dial tone.

In rebuilding their systems to 500-channel capacity, and combining the technologies of fibre optics, digital compression, and packet switching, large cable operators like Telecommunications Inc., Time Warner, and Comcast in effect are paving the start of the electronic superhighway system (or 'national information infrastructure', as it is formally called) whose construction has been one of the ideals of the Clinton Administration.

With television and computer technologies converging, it is clear that the video environment will continue to change for decades to come. But though the commercial television networks are bound to continue losing audience to new forms of television, they will almost surely survive, some of them at any rate, because they provide a unique and widely valued service as the central meeting-place for the nation. They remain, besides, the best and most efficient means by which advertisers can reach a large national audience.

The FCC in 1993 helped immeasurably to secure the networks' future by repealing the Financial Interest and Syndication rule that for twenty years had prevented ABC, CBS, and NBC from fully taking part in the changing marketplace. Allowed once again to produce programmes and secure ownership positions in those produced by others, the networks may find their economic salvation in the expanding world market, which they were scarcely able to exploit while the Hollywood studios reaped the windfall.

As television in America branches into hundreds or even thousands of specialized channels—in technology's democratization of the medium—the old networks, or what remains of them, will by default represent the mainstream. But never again will they be as autocratic as at their height or, paradoxically, as powerful a democratic force.

12

Japan

Hidetoshi Kato

Inventors and Pioneers

Kenjiro Takayanagi, often called the father of television in Japan, was born in 1899 in a small village community 250 kilometres west of Tokyo. As a 10-year-old he was present at a demonstration of Morse code provided by Japanese Imperial Navy officers in his primary school classroom. Later, he learned about David Sarnoff, the wireless engineer who received the signal from the sinking *Titanic*. Impressed and moved by these experiences Takayanagi decided to study electronic signal transmission when he was admitted to Tokyo Polytechnic.

Through scientific journals of Europe and the United States he learned of the establishment in 1920 of the first radio station in Pittsburgh, Pennsylvania, and of its new and popular audience. He envisaged the age of radio in Japan and wondered what would come after radio, pursuing technologies of the further future. One day, inspiration came from a French cartoon magazine he picked up in a bookstore illustrating a fantasy of television. With voice transmission now possible by radio there was no reason why pictures might not be transmitted by similar electronic means.

He already knew that the possibility of television had been explored in Germany and France in the late nineteenth century and that Graham Bell himself, after inventing the telephone in 1876, was fascinated by the idea of visual transmission. Takayanagi was encouraged by this to work on television engineering. As a young assistant professor at Hamamatu Polytechnic in 1924 he proposed to the president of the school, Sokichi Sekiguchi, research on the devel-

Kenjiro Takayanagi (1899–1990) invented the first Japanese television transmission system. He continued his work as the top consultant at JVC until his death.

opment of television. Sekiguchi was puzzled by his proposal but he asked Takayanagi, 'How much money do you need?' Takayanagi told him he needed 3,000 yen a year for ten years. His monthly salary was 40 yen and the sum proposed was extraordinary, but after listening to Takayanagi's idea, the president said he would visit the Ministry of Education and that Takayanagi could start the television project then and there. This was the birth of Japanese television.

Takayanagi studied experiments abroad and discovered that mechanical devices with scanning discs had been used in the United Kingdom by John Baird in the early 1920s. He also followed the state of the art in Austria, Germany, and the USA. The mechanical scanner had technical limitations in terms of speed and density in the transmission of pictures and he considered the possibility of using the Braun tube for television. Developed by Braun in 1897, the tube was used for physical measurement. Takayanagi's idea was to use the cathode rays generated in the tube for visual transmission. In other words he opted for an electronic approach instead of a mechanical one. He was encouraged by a paper by Campbell Swinton in 1911 entitled 'Wireless World'.

His first Braun tube television receiver was made after a year's work in the laboratory and the experiment was successful. He was able to manipulate a small spot on the screen and this simple experiment, conducted in October 1925, made him confident in the promise of the tube in the development of television. The camera, meanwhile, remained mechanical. After a further year, on 25 December 1926, Takayanagi succeeded in sending a written letter *i* electronically. He did not apply for patent rights, partly because there was as yet no final product and partly because he did not have enough money for international patent applications. In fact V. K. Zworykin of RCA in the USA had already patented the idea of television in 1923 with the iconoscope.

At any rate, Takayanagi and his team continued to research and experiment, and in May 1930 the Emperor visited his laboratory to see his invention. By this time his television could transmit more complex letters and even the vague image of a human face. Validated by the imperial visit, Takayanagi's work was officially encouraged and he was given a small independent research institute for the development of television with a dozen staff and ample budget.

In 1934 Takayanagi had an opportunity to visit the USA to meet Zworykin. Both scientists knew each other through respective research papers and they congratulated each other for their parallel research and invention. Regarding the improvement of the Braun tube, Takayanagi's method predated that of Zworykin, whose patent application to Japan was suspended by the Japanese patent office.

1925 was a vintage year for telecommunication science and technology in Japan in the sense that another internationally recognized invention came on to the stage. For the transmission of wireless signals highly sophisticated antennae were indispensable, and Hidetugu Yagi of Tohoku Imperial University succeeded

The first successful television broadcast by Takayanagi in 1926. The letter in the centre is the first letter in the Japanese alphabet.

in developing very high frequency (VHF) and ultra high frequency (UHF) antennae capable of receiving signals with wavelengths of 45 centimetres and frequencies up to 667 MHz. The invention, like many others, was the product of an unexpected event in Yagi's laboratory in 1924, and by 1925 Yagi and his team succeeded in making a directional antenna for microwave.

In 1927 Yagi read his paper at the annual International Conference of Radio Engineering in New York. Audience reaction was extraordinary, and immediately after his presentation, John Delliger, an American government official, called it 'Yagi shock day'. He asked Yagi if the US Aviation Agency could utilize the invention to improve air traffic control. Executives from the American electric and electronic industries approached him about patents, and Yagi generously acceded to these requests. The prototype of the standard television antenna found throughout the world today is Yagi's.

Takayanagi's innovative use of the Braun tube combined with Yagi antenna laid the groundwork for Japanese television engineering, and an experimental television station was established by NHK (Nippon Hoso Kyokai or Japan Public Broadcasting Company), transmitting the first television signals in Tokyo on 13 May 1937. The first commercially inspired television receivers were assembled by both Toshiba and NEC in the same year. This paved the way for the first television drama broadcast on 13 April 1940 by NHK. At that time Japan's government hoped to host the Olympic Games in Tokyo in 1945, and planned to telecast that big event for the first time in history. Takayanagi was appointed as chief engineer of the project.

But this was an unfortunate period in Japanese history. On the one hand

287

economic recession leading to the world-wide depression in 1929 deprived telecommunications technology of both public and private investment, and on the other, Japanese militarists dominated the national government. World War II started and plans for the Olympic Games were cancelled. Takayanagi and Yagi were mobilized by Japan's Imperial Army and Navy to conduct research and development of radar and other military related devices. As a result the development of Japanese television was curtailed until 1945, when Japan surrendered to the Allies.

Ironically, the British and Americans were keener on Yagi's directional antenna, and during World War II a sophisticated radar used by the British Army in Singapore in 1940 surprised the Japanese armed forces. The US Navy used radar called 'YAGI array' to detect and attack Japanese warships in the Pacific. Of course, American sailors did not know the significance of YAGI.

Feverish Beginnings

As the paragraphs above indicate, television engineering in Japan was approaching maturity in the 1930s and the Japanese public was aware of the existence of television. Not surprisingly Japanese broadcasters immediately after the war turned their attention back to the revival of television. From their viewpoint the period from 1940 to 1945 constituted an interruption in the progress of television.

But Japan's social situation in 1945 was miserable. Much of the population was homeless or jobless. Food was scarce. Transportation and infrastructure were devastated. There was rampant inflation and the country and its people were

The glittering opening ceremony of NHK in 1953 marking the start of regular broadcasting in Japan.

pitifully poor. Central government spending was directed to averting starvation. There was no question in the public mind of television before economic reconstruction had been achieved, and it was not until 1953 that Japanese television revived.

The first post-war television broadcast was initiated by the long-established NHK. On 1 February 1953 NHK began television broadcasts, and a commercial station, Nippon Television (NTV), went on the air on 28 August of the same year. The number of television receivers at that time, however, was only 866, and the broadcast area covered by the stations moreover was limited to Tokyo and its environs. The fundamental problem was the financing of television as a business. The price of a television set was far beyond the purchasing power of a Japanese household. A set imported from the USA was 250,000 yen, equal to the entire annual salary of an urban middle-class white-collar worker. As Table 12-1 shows, the ownership pattern of the first sets was limited.

Table 12.1 *Occupational distribution of initial receivers in 1953*

Electric retail shops	303
Business executives	249
Retail shops	76
Government agencies and private firms	61
Retired	33
Hotels and restaurants	28
Students	28
Schools, Museums	11
Agriculture	9
Others	15
Not identified	53
TOTAL	866

As far as NHK was concerned, however, there were good reasons and sufficient money to initiate television broadcasts. As a public broadcaster financed by subscription fees it was feasible and appropriate for NHK to deploy the capital investment necessary to induce interest among the government and the public. But commercial stations required a sufficient audience to secure sponsorship. With fewer than a thousand receivers how could a new station persuade sponsors to part with huge sums of money for advertising? However, Matsutaro Syoriki, a newspaper veteran who was president of the Yomiuri newspaper, had confidence in the new medium and applied to the Ministry of Posts and Telecommunications for a new television station licence. He believed in the promise of the new medium of mass communication and imagined that millions of people would watch TV screens if big sets were placed at major street intersections. As president of NTV, an almost unknown company at that time, he ordered more

In the 1950s, the majority of Japanese could not afford their own television sets, but 'street television'—allowing people to watch but also encouraging them to buy— was very popular.

than a dozen large television receivers from America and had them placed at busy street corners, parks, railway termini, and other places of public gathering. They were nicknamed 'street television' and, as Syoriki predicted, millions of people were attracted to the new mass medium on the street. A newspaper report on 27 October 1953 described an unbelievable scene:

More than 20,000 people gathered in front of a street television to watch a live broadcast of a boxing title fight Sirai vs Allen. The crowd was such that trams were halted. Automobiles were unable to move. Taxi drivers abandoned their cars to watch the match. Spectators who had climbed trees to get a better view fell and were injured. In a neighbourhood residence 20 people fell from a balcony which collapsed under the weight of house guests.

At that time Japan's electronics industry was immature and television sets were for the most part imported from the USA. Panasonic, Toshiba, and others were making televisions but the price of sets was beyond the purchasing power of ordinary people. A locally made fourteen-inch unit in 1953 cost 180,000 yen, compared to an average white-collar worker's salary of 15,000 yen a month. Only the rich could buy the new gadget. But as Table 12.1 shows a number of merchants were canny enough to buy them to attract customers. It started in coffee shops, restaurants, bars, and barbers' shops. When sports shows or other popular programmes were on the owners of such places surcharged customers— and they were willing to pay extra to watch their favourite programmes. Slowly and steadily sales of televisions grew. By March 1954 there were 16,000 TV sets, most of them in commercial establishments.

It was, however, in the late 1950s that the spread of receivers grew dramatically.

Table 12.2. *Number of television stations*

	1953	1954	1955	1956	1957	1958	1959	1960	1961	1962	1963	1964	1965	1966	1967	1968	1969	1970	1971	1972
VHF	2	2	3	5	8	24	40	44	47	48	49	49	49	49	49	49	49	49	49	49
UHF																5	23	33	35	38
TOTAL	2	2	3	5	8	24	40	44	47	48	49	49	49	49	49	54	72	82	84	87

	1973	1974	1975	1976	1977	1978	1979	1980	1981	1982	1983	1984	1985	1986	1987	1988	1989	1990	1991
VHF	50	50	50	50	50	50	50	51	51	51	51	51	51	51	51	51	51	51	51
UHF	39	40	42	42	43	45	47	48	51	52	54	54	55	55	55	55	58	61	67
BS																2	2	2	3
TOTAL	89	90	92	92	93	95	97	99	102	103	105	105	106	106	106	108	111	114	121

The critical factor was introduction of production line methods by television manufacturers. By 1958 the price of a fourteen-inch black-and-white set had dropped by a third to 60,000 yen, by which time average monthly salaries had grown to 25,000 yen. The price was now within the reach of ordinary citizens and Japanese parents were motivated to buy a set rather than let their children view at television-owning neighbours. By now, apart from NHK and NTV, there were six commercial stations and one educational channel and television was recognized as the most popular and attractive home entertainment. By the 1960s television matured into the new mass medium in Japan. Table 12.2 indicates the growth of stations to cover the whole country.

One boost at the end of the 1950s was the televised royal wedding of Prince Akihito and Michiko Shoda. It was a great national event. For one thing it bade goodbye to the wartime era of Emperor Hirohito, who was to a certain degree responsible for the war. For another it was a marriage made by love not by arrangement and as such was a romantic story welcomed by the general public.

The royal wedding was announced in November 1958, almost six months before the actual event on 10 April 1959. Television manufacturers mounted a campaign to persuade the public to watch the wedding parade on television. It was enough to establish television as a key medium of the nation. They anticipated a spectacular programme with thousands of people waving the national flag, royal guards resplendent in uniforms, the horse-drawn imperial carriage, and, above all, the royal couple in ceremonial costume. The stations announced that the whole parade would be broadcast live. And it worked.

In metropolitan Tokyo bits of the parade could be glimpsed by the lucky few but for most people, watching the parade on television was a must. Exhorted by the advertisements of manufacturers, people jammed the retail electrical stores. Within a single year 2 million sets were sold and the great event was the single most important driver of sales. For broadcasters too the grand parade was a chance to demonstrate their technological prowess. Close to 2,000 producers, directors, camera operators, and crew were mobilized with 108 television cameras monitoring the fifty-minute parade along its 9 km route. An estimated 150,000 watched the broadcast.

Electronics manufacturers were not immune to the royal wedding fever. It could even be said that they were the pathogen, because it was they who promised to bring into the living-rooms views of the event which even those on the spot could not see. The fever spread like a new influenza, leaving in its wake a new outlook in Japan. Watching television became an everyday habit, along with eating, brushing teeth, and bathing. The present author published in 1959 a book entitled *The Age of Television* (*Terebi Jidai*), pointing to the changes in Japanese life-style ushered in by the new medium of mass communication. The age of television had arrived. People could not escape it. There was no going back to the past.

If royal wedding fever was type A flu, type B was the Tokyo Olympiad. Just one

The Royal Wedding of 1959 was a great national event and prompted millions of people to buy television sets to watch the live broadcast of the wedding parade.

month after the royal wedding, on 26 May 1959 the International Olympic Committee decided to hold the 1964 Olympics in Tokyo. As mentioned already Japan had expected to host the 1945 Olympics, so the IOC decision created huge excitement. The announcement was treated as a token of recognition of Japan's independence in the eyes of the international community. Unsurprisingly the metropolitan government of Tokyo as well as the central government made special budgetry allocations for the preparations. New construction, building renovations, roads, and highways reflected the new fever. In expectation of hundreds of thousands of foreign visitors, new hotels were built as well as the new express railway, known as the bullet train. It is no exaggeration to say that the Olympic Games constituted one of the major stimuli for post-war economic reconstruction in Japan. Mass media offered Olympics-related news and stories almost every day, and without exception the media preached to the public on the significance of the event for national interest and pride.

Like the royal wedding fever, Olympic fever had a long incubation period. From the IOC's announcement in Munich in 1959 there were five years' lead time to facilitate completion of all construction work before the actual event in the autumn of 1964. And in expectation of another extraordinary spectacular, manufacturers aggressively promoted sales of sets to those who had so far not been infected by the bug. Advertisements promised the best seat to see the games and the public responded. On the one hand people had enough money by that time to buy a television, and on the other, the forthcoming event was enough to justify the purchase.

Moreover, manufacturers had an interest in selling colour televisions along with the traditional black and white. Engineers had confidence in the reliability of their products, and as Fig. 12.1 shows, the mid-1960s was the starting-point of an amazing increase in production of colour televisions. In 1963, when the price of a black-and-white set matched exactly one month's income, three months' salary, if saved, made affordable a colour television (Fig. 12.2). For those who had bought a black-and-white television in the early 1950s, it was a good time to replace it with a colour set. Meanwhile both NHK and commercial stations were gradually switching broadcasts from black and white to colour. As a result, Japan entered the age of colour television in the late 1960s.

Figure 12.1

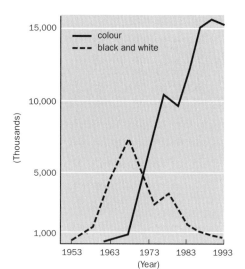

Figure 12.2

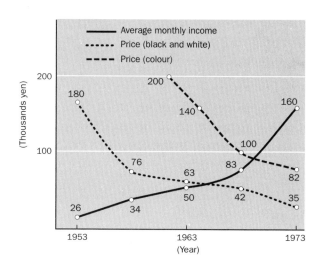

Figure 12.3

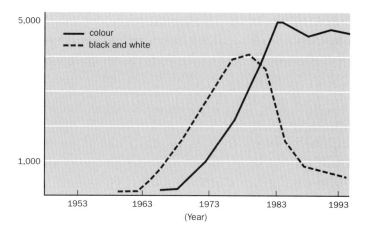

東京オリンピック大会放送
アメリカ、ヨーロッパへ衛星中継(昭39.10.10〜24)

The televising of the 1964 Tokyo Olympics spurred many Japanese to make the change from black and white television sets to colour.

At this stage in the growth of television those who had been reluctant to spend money on what they regarded as childish entertainment finally decided to buy television sets. Purchasing power and enthusiasm for the medium exceeded manufacturers' expectations. Workers at Panasonic, Sony, and other factories assembled sets twenty-four hours a day every day as demand exceeded supply. The mass appeal encouraged manufacturers to set up more sophisticated lines of mass production, which eventually reduced the price of sets. By this time quality control of colour television was satisfactory and retail prices were competitive.

The biggest Olympic Games to date, with 5,586 athletes representing ninety-four countries, was held in Tokyo from 10–24 October 1964. The inauguration ceremony was watched by 65 million people in Japan—84.7 per cent of the population. The event was relayed and broadcast to many countries by satellite. This great event marks the point at which Japanese television reached real maturity. Manufacturers and distributors were confident about the quality of their products and they were ready to export television sets. As Fig. 12.3 indicates black-and-white televisions were first exported in 1962 and exports of colour sets began in 1966. Needless to say, that was the prelude for the expansion of Japan's electronics industry throughout the world.

Changes and Reactions

A remarkable characteristic of purchasing patterns during the period mentioned was the eagerness of rural people for television. Farmers were no longer peasants living in misery, thanks to agrarian reform and price protection for rice.

Moreover, they lacked the entertainments enjoyed by city folk. In the country-side television was an ideal pastime after a hard working day, especially on chilly winter nights. Indeed, in the 1950s a sociologist surveying rural villages was shocked to discover that many farmers' houses had brand new televisions. In other words, television became a bridge spanning the traditional gap between the urban and rural population.

For better or worse the most remarkable resultant phenomenon was the vanishing of local dialects. Although Japan seems to be a small island country, homogeneously populated, each region had its dialect with unique accents and vocabularies. It was said that people from the southernmost islands would have difficulty communicating with people from the northern prefectures. The over-whelming penetration, however, of television brought Tokyo's dialect, spiced by the broadcasters' peculiar accent, often called the NHK dialect, into use as the standard national language, especially among the younger generation. Unlike radio, television brought lip movements and gestures to the audience, and its linguistic homogenizing effect was tremendous.

Another social effect was what critics referred to as the rise of family together-ness, as the whole family became accustomed to congregating in front of the tube to watch their favourite evening programmes. In response broadcasters supplied a new genre of programming known as 'home drama', dealing with situations and problems most Japanese families were now likely to face. Some of these home dramas were serious, others comic.

Home drama had a role in purveying new ideas about life-style to the masses. The furnishing of a new urban middle-class kitchen, for instance, as shown on

Alley Behind the Bus Lane (1958), one of the most popular serial dramas, depicted the lives of typical urban middle-class families.

the screen was often perceived as a model for a new way of living, and such scenes encouraged many families to renovate their own kitchens. The hairdo, dress, speech, and behaviour of the television housewife also influenced viewers, and real households began imitating those portrayed in home dramas. In other words television was psychologically close to the audience, and home drama responded to its desire to regard the characters on screen as quasi-neighbours, so to speak. Unlike movie stars, with whom ordinary people would never dare compare themselves, these heroes and heroines on television were, and had to be, ordinary: people who could be taken for neighbours, dropping in on friends in the living-rooms of private homes.

To stress such psychological proximity, television broadcasters paid close attention to audience-participation programming such as quizzes, singing contests, street debate on public opinion, and so on. Such programming was suggested by American broadcasting back in the days of radio. More than that, audience participation programmes were often the means of recruitment of new talent for Japanese television. A good example is that of NHK's singing contest, which has been aired since the birth of television broadcasting. It is one of the most highly rated Sunday broadcasts, being shown at noon for forty-five minutes. From among hundreds of amateurs and semi-professionals, singers made the transition to professional status.

In this way some audience participation shows took on the status of auditions. This drew television psychologically closer and closer to the audience. As far as Japan is concerned, happy amateurism, rather than the sophisticated profession-alism essential in the tradition of performing arts like theatre and motion pictures, seems to have dominated the world of television. It is a fact that from its inception, such professions as producer and director were not conducted by professionals at all. Some were recruited from motion pictures but many came from newspapers, journalism, and even straight from colleges and universities. Their planning, execution, and broadcasting were fundamentally amateurish and this characteristic remains in today's Japan.

The rise of television ushered in many other effects; *inter alia*, foreign programming, typically from America, was brought through television into Japanese households. *Superman*, broadcast in 1956, was the first imported Amer-ican programme, followed in 1957 by *I Love Lucy*. Though the ratio of imports to domestic programming was below 5 per cent, many people were attracted by this American fare because the shows' scripts were well written and production technique was fresh. At the same time, the Japanese public was eager to absorb the ideal of the American way of life. Naturally, such programmes had to be either dubbed or subtitled. But subtitles offered the opportunity for a certain segment of the population to acquire conversational English.

In that sense, imported programmes, especially those made in the USA, promoted the internationalization, or at least the Americanization, of Japanese popular culture. This experience was revolutionary in the sense that Japanese

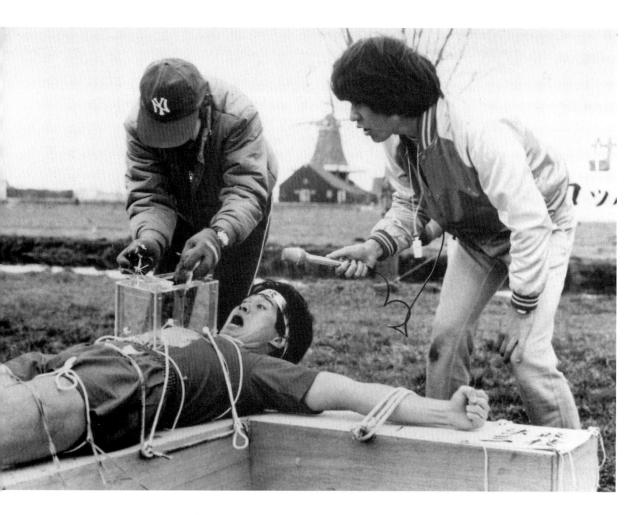

The competition for ratings prompted commercial broadcasters to pioneer programmes such as **Endurance**, designed to test the 'courage' of participants.

homes were now open to visits, as it were, by America, yet without formal introduction. Japanese people welcomed the prospect of foreigners on the TV screen as new neighbours, friends even, almost without hesitation. Not only the audience, but broadcasters themselves were keen to watch American programmes because from them they could acquire knowledge of production techniques.

Television in Japan from its beginning in 1953 was regarded primarily as an entertainment medium, which included sports, drama, quiz shows, and so forth. It was, of course, a new and comprehensive medium for news and, rather like the BBC and other public broadcasters, the 9.00 p.m. NHK news established its authority and reliability. But the essence of television was entertainment. Children in particular fell under its spell, and parents and educators worried about its bad influence on youngsters. It is no coincidence that several Japanese scholars started research on this subject before the end of the 1950s when Hilde Himmerweit in the UK and Wilbur Schramm in the USA conducted similar research in those countries. Critics of television acknowledged the wonder of having a TV set in every home on the grounds that it brought the outside world to every household, but they did express their concern about possible negative effects of television, not only upon children, but upon the public at large.

The most critical comment was made by Soichi Ohya, an influential writer and popular columnist. In a 1958 essay he pointed out the 'peanuts effect' of the television viewing habit: 'once you have a bowl full of peanuts on the table, you automatically and incessantly pick up and put peanuts in your mouth, without even tasting them'. This was endless and without value: 'Like peanut-eating, once you turn on your television, you won't be able to turn it off.' In another essay in which he mocked a quiz programme, he argued cogently that television is nothing more than the new means of 'creating 100 million idiots', thus suggesting that the entire population of Japan would become unintelligent, silly, illiterate, vulgar, and foolish as a result of continuous television viewing. His series of essays about television appeared in major newspapers and magazines, and the phrase '100 million idiots' was popularly quoted by those who attacked television.

As television stations and broadcasting hours increased, not only the number of viewers but also of viewing hours increased rapidly. An interesting research survey, conducted by NHK Research Institute, found that a Japanese in 1960 spent 3 hours and 11 minutes a day on average watching television and 3 hours and 26 minutes a day in 1975. In the case of children aged between 10 and 15 years their average viewing hours reached close to 4 hours a day. This figure dismayed parents and teachers in Japan where, before the advent of television, reading had been strongly encouraged among schoolchildren. Many parents therefore restricted viewing hours to a maximum of one hour or less a day on the grounds that children watching television were sacrificing time for reading and writing, which were essential components of education. Such efforts, however, were for the most part unsuccessful. Parents and educators thought that Ohya's theory of '100 million idiots' might be true, that the next generation could turn out to be illiterate, and that television broadcasters were to blame for their programmes, which were filled with low-quality material, sex, and violence.

In addition, it was proved that, because of relatively heavy viewing habits, Japanese people shortened their sleeping hours. The same survey indicated that average hours of sleep in 1970 were 7 hours 57 minutes, but by 1990 NHK research revealed that people slept on average 7 hours 39 minutes. The research surveys also showed that one-third of Japanese people admitted that they needed more sleep.

In opposition to such negative views, another group of scholars and critics considered that the new medium of television could be educationally useful. They had good reason to stress this potential.

In the first place, the use of radio broadcasting for school education was initiated as early as 1931 by NHK and there were thousands of schoolteachers who already knew the effectiveness of broadcasting in classroom education. They were accustomed to using *School Hours*, broadcast regularly on NHK Radio Channel 2, as a teaching aid. Naturally these teachers were very interested in using television in school, and they knew that television could be even more effective for education than radio. For instance, in teaching physics ordinary elementary or secondary schools did not possess equipment to demonstrate what a vacuum was; but on television delicate experiments on vacuums, air pressure, high voltages, and many other specifics of the natural sciences could be introduced to children. In the instruction of social studies, too, pupils could easily be exposed to such matters as archaeological excavation, the lives of other peoples in the world, and the whole gamut of educational pictures which schools could not provide. These educators welcomed the arrival of television for obvious reasons.

In the second place, more liberal and sometimes radical educators thought traditional textbook-based education would not be sufficient in the years to come, and that new audio-visual literacy must be given to the children so that future generations would be capable of understanding both media and that each would complement the other.

The Ministry of Posts and Telecommunications has also shown its interest in this matter, and from the beginning of television in 1953 the Ministry issued a licence to NHK for a channel dedicated to education. So it was that Japanese public broadcasting opened a channel not just for schools but for adult education. Moreover, the Ministry gave priority to commercial broadcasters who wished to open quasi-educational stations of which the basic condition was that station owners devote at least one-third of air time to educational programmes.

This policy was admirable in intent. But within a few years the quasi-educational broadcasters discovered that commercial sponsors were unwilling to pay for educational programmes. As a result, by 1970 this category of station effectively ceased to exist.

Regardless of station category, it should be added that the most devoted television viewers in Japan have been older people, particular those over 60. According to an NHK Research Institute survey, a man in his sixties has a daily diet of 3 hours 52 minutes of television on average, rising to 4 hours 51 minutes for a man in his seventies. A woman in her sixties spends 4 hours and 27 minutes viewing, rising to 4 hours 49 minutes in her seventies. This is in contrast to the common assumption that young children are the truly heavy viewers. Elderly retired people, who go neither on holiday nor out to theatres, have as their dominant pastime viewing television at home. This fact implies that television today is, in an ageing society like Japan's, serving the cause of social welfare.

Media Complications

The implication of Ohya's '100 million idiots' theory was that people would substitute television for their reading, but the most immediate impact was on the

Figure 12.4

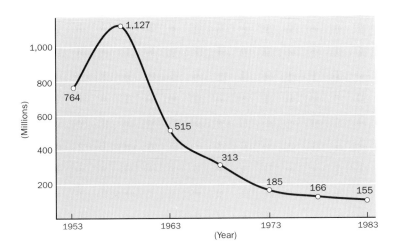

motion picture industry, for obvious reasons. As in other countries, movies used to be one of the most popular entertainment forms, and thousands of film theatres throughout Japan attracted millions of people every year. However, as Fig. 12.4 shows, the number of filmgoers drastically declined from the mid-1960s when Olympic fever affected most Japanese people. Motion picture companies fought a desperate battle against television by producing spectacular films. But films could no longer attract audiences, except for a few works by Akira Kurosawa and other eminent directors.

Indeed, at one point in 1958, Japanese film companies agreed not to offer their properties to television broadcasters, but they discovered that they could not beat television. Finally they surrendered to television, changing themselves into subcontractors to TV stations. Indeed, Toei, Toho, Shochiku, and other major motion picture companies established video production companies as their subsidiaries to respond to the demands from television stations.

Producers who used to make serious films two hours in length once or twice a year were obliged to make forty-five-minute programmes for TV every week under severe budgetary constraints. Many films were sold to television stations but they had to be interrupted by commercials, and were often edited for the interest of time-conscious stations and sponsors. For instance, a film running 2 hours 37 minutes would be cut and edited to meet the requirements of a ninety-minute slot. So, not only movie theatres but motion picture companies of the traditional kind disappeared.

The second victim of television was radio. Before the age of television, radio had been the most attractive medium for most people. Many surveys showed that Japanese people used to listen to radio three hours a day in 1950. But this figure declined to ninety minutes in 1960, dropping to thirty minutes by 1965. The only listeners of radio, a critic pointed out, were drivers, and the observation may have been correct because most taxi drivers in Japan tune in to radio. It was thought that another distinct group of listeners were housewives, who listened to radio while doing household chores. But under the influence of the spread of taped music and, more recently, compact discs, radio is rapidly losing its audience.

As for newspapers, an interesting change occurred. As already mentioned, it was significant that those who were interested in establishing commercial television were newspaper companies, as represented by Mr Syoriki of the *Yomiuri*. People in the newspaper business in fact felt both hope and fear about television. They feared that television might supplant newspaper journalism since the new medium could report on events so much faster than the print medium and with much stronger impact. Their hope was that television stations could become sister organizations so that both media might be made stronger. So, after the *Yomiuri*, the nation's biggest newspaper, took the lead, the *Asahi*, the *Mainichi*, and other major newspapers applied for television licences and eventually these applications were accepted. The result was the emergence after 1960 of what may

The hit NHK drama **Oshin** told the story of a woman born into a peasant's family who eventually rises, despite many hardships and tragedies, to become chief executive of a supermarket chain. The programme was exported to 26 countries, principally in Asia, its phenomenal success described by critics as 'Osyndrome'.

be called information conglomerates. In effect newspaper publishers were eager to subsidize and affiliate with broadcasting stations so that printed pages, radio, and television could coexist harmoniously. A newspaper concerned itself with programmes from the affiliated station and the TV station relied on its mother newspaper for news and commentaries. This was so not only in Tokyo. Local papers mimicked the pattern. The result was a unique information network. In this context it is unsurprising that a newspaper columnist would appear on the late evening TV news as a commentator. Managers were also rotated among the different elements of the conglomerate. It is common in Japan for instance to have a vice-president of a newspaper appointed president of an affiliated TV station, and vice versa.

NHK, a public broadcaster, enjoys a special legal status. Its president is appointed by the Prime Minister. Contrary to popular perception abroad, NHK is not owned by the government. It is wholly financed by fees paid by every Japanese viewer and its mission is to broadcast reliable, unbiased news, entertainment, and educational programmes for the well-being of the public. Its operation is autonomous. Because it is the oldest broadcaster in Japan, having been established in 1925, NHK has a great deal of experience in television as well as in radio. In point of fact, Takayanagi, the inventor back in the 1920s, worked on the technical staff before the war and, as pointed out above, it was NHK which in 1937 opened the first television station.

The technical excellence as well as balanced programming served as the model for subsequent commercial broadcasters. When a new commercial station was established, producers and technical experts were recruited from NHK. Japanese television, therefore, followed the way paved by NHK. This fostered a strange relationship between the public and commercial sectors of television. At one level, commercial stations exercised restraint in deference to NHK's spirit of public service. Conversely, NHK became acutely conscious of the competition with commercial stations offering programmes of greater popular appeal.

As mentioned earlier, both government and public showed intense interest in educational applications of television and one of the outcomes was the establishment in 1981 of the University of the Air, a creation of joint effort by the Ministries of Education and Posts and Telecommunication. The institution is a new type of open university with full use of broadcasting. It has its own TV and FM radio station, and they broadcast university lectures eighteen hours a day throughout the year. As of 1993 some 45,000 people are registered as regular students and it is estimated that about a million citizens listen to or watch programmes offered free by the university. In order to achieve this the university receives technical assistance from NHK.

As of 1968 NHK began experiments in direct satellite broadcasting. The public station has been charged with delivering messages 'to every corner of the globe', and the use of a broadcasting satellite (BS) presented itself as the optimum means

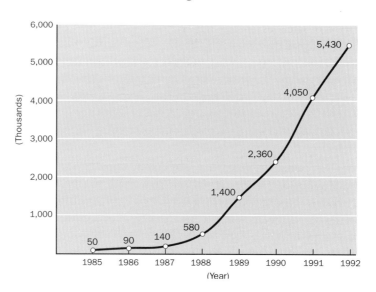

Figure 12.5

of communication in a mountainous island country like Japan. Unlike microwave, BS can send signals directly to homes equipped with a small dish antenna. Audio-visual quality, moreover, of signals sent by BS is superior to conventional microwave broadcasting. It was in the beginning a novelty item, but in the 1980s two NHK-operated channels attracted a new audience numbered in millions. In early 1993 there were 6 million households in Japan with a BS tuner (Fig. 12.5). In addition to NHK a commercial BS station called Japan Satellite Broadcasting Company (JSB) started up in 1991. It is a pay-TV system and subscribers pay 27,000 yen a month to rent a decoder and 3,000 yen as the monthly fee. Since JSB transmits the latest films, both domestic and foreign, without interruption, it appeals to the urban middle class. Early in 1993 1.2 million homes were watching JSB.

New Media Mix

Improvements in telecommunication technologies coupled with rising living standards mean that since the early 1980s television can be received everywhere in Japan. Even in the most remote areas people are able to receive two NHK channels, general and educational, plus a minimum of three commercial channels. If desired they can also receive two NHK BS broadcasts along with JSB. Before the end of the century it is expected that four new BS stations will be operating. This means that Japanese television broadcasting has already passed the saturation point—not only that: some 50,000 cable television stations (CATV) with 7 million subscribers are in existence. Someone with CATV can choose from among thirty channels, including highly specialized ones offering sports, films, shopping, and so on.

Meanwhile, the use of satellites means that the world of television is getting internationalized year by year, day by day. The first experimental use of communication satellite linked to regular broadcasts was between Japan and the USA on 23 November 1963 and Japan was looking forward to the live broadcast from the other side of the Pacific. According to the original plan, President John Kennedy was expected to send his message to the Japanese audience. But this was the day he was assassinated in Texas. The much anticipated greeting was replaced by the shocking news.

Four years after this dramatic experience a world-wide telecast via satellite was conducted in the summer of 1967 with the BBC in London playing the key role. In Japan, NHK participated in this international undertaking when London, New York, Sydney, Tokyo, and many other places around the globe were linked together. The different time zones meant that people in some countries had to wake up at dawn while others had to give up their working hours, but what this experimental link proved was that global television broadcasting was possible. And since the early 1970s Japanese television stations successfully launched their

After 1980 Japanese society became saturated with television sets. Hundreds of stores in central Tokyo sell sets at a considerably discounted price—but customers are still hard to find.

Figure 12.6

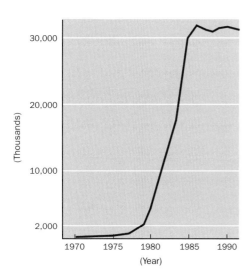
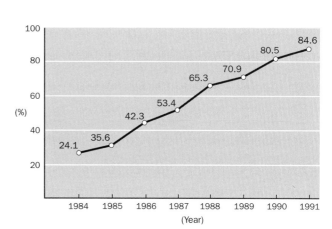

international hook-ups. In sports, not only the Olympic Games but other sporting events such as tennis, golf, and football, taking place anywhere in the world, have been transmitted live to Japan, as well as being pre-recorded to compensate for time differences. Major TV stations have set up offices throughout the world so that any event may be sent live to Tokyo via satellite. In the specific Asian context, under the Asian Broadcasters Union (ABU) initiative, organized in 1964, regular news exchanges called Asiavision were inaugurated in 1986 and news from participating countries of East and South East Asia are relayed and broadcast every evening.

Regardless of reliance on regular television, telecommunication technologies mean that if someone wishes to set up a rotating dish antenna 6 metres in diameter, he can tune to as many as twenty different international channels including Star TV of Hong Kong, BBC International, and CNN. Television in Japan, therefore, is already part of a global network—a development which nobody in the past even dreamed possible. In the spring of 1993 NHK celebrated the fortieth birthday of television in Japan.

A further technical innovation is the development of high-definition television (HDTV), commonly known in Japan as Hi-vision. The essence of this technology is the creation of 1,125 lines of horizontal resolution in contrast to the conventional 525 lines. HDTV at the time of writing is being broadcast five hours a day over BS channels, and the sound and picture quality are impressive. HDTV is, however, still at the experimental stage. Production costs are almost double those of the traditional medium and HDTV receivers are very expensive. Above all, broadcasting time remains limited. It is predicted that a further decade or even two are required before HDTV comes into popular use.

Figure 12.7

Figure 12.8

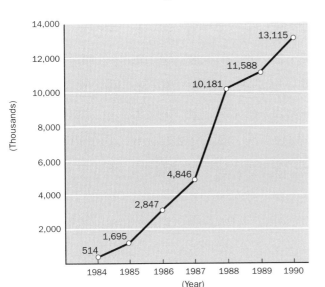

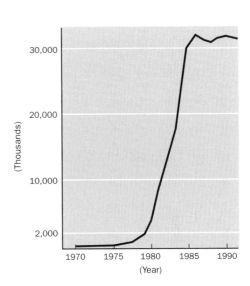

Aside from broadcasting innovations, attention must be paid to the spread of the videotape recorder (VTR) by which users can record programmes on tape. VTR production began in the mid-1960s and, in the beginning, the machine was for the professional use of broadcasters. By 1975, however, electronic manufacturers discovered the home market for VTR. In that year alone they sold 120,000 machines. In the past fifteen years a total of 13 million VTRs were produced and distributed. Fig. 12.6 indicates that over 80 per cent of Japanese households now own a VTR. In contrast to broadcast reception, which forces an audience to wait for a programmed time slot, people can watch their favourite programmes using the VTR at any time.

Fig. 12.7 shows that the number of video rental shops increased at a remarkable rate between 1985 and 1990. Millions of Japanese today rent tape for 400 yen a day, which amounts almost to a nominal price. On average a video rental shop has in stock 2,500 tapes with 4,000 rental customers. In 1991 Japanese rental shops earned 40 billion yen in total from the video rental business. This equates with the budget appropriated to run ninety-five national universities.

A singular effect of this burgeoning development is the disappearance of what was called 'family togetherness' in the old days. Everybody nowadays wants to satisfy their personal viewing habits. It is not strange today for a family to have two or three TV sets placed in separate rooms rather than in the living-room.

The future of television is not predictable. As suggested already, *package* media, encompassing compact disc, audio and video tapes, and laser disc are taking in part the place which has hitherto been monopolized by broadcasting. Communications satellites, which can be used for interactive communication

307

and Integrated Subscriber Digital Networks (ISDN), may be a substitute for television broadcasting depending on the purposes and interests of users. Sophisticated computer systems may be interwoven with broadcasting and package media. The surprising increase in demand for compact video cameras, as shown in Fig. 12.8 may make certain segments of the population at least more *expressive* as distinct from *receptive*.

13

The Third World

Dietrich Berwanger

The term 'Third World' was a proud claim back in the 1950s when it was first coined. The world was divided into two camps, and the superpowers had assumed that the young states of Africa, Asia, and Latin America would have to join one or other of the two. Instead, they decided—first at the Afro-Asian Conference in Bandung in 1955 and then at the Non-aligned Summit in Belgrade in 1961—to take a third path and establish themselves, in a spirit of self-confidence and solidarity, as a 'Third World' between East and West. Now, thirty years further on, one of the superpowers has disappeared, the blocks have disintegrated, and the hope for 'solidarity among the poor' has fallen by the wayside in the harsh world of economic realities.

When the term was first used, television in most regions of the Third World was little more than a technical gimmick. Transmitters covered at best the capital cities, the majority of programmes were imported, and the whole of Africa, Asia, and Latin America accounted for just 3 per cent of the television sets worldwide. Thirty years later, television has become a mass medium in the Third World as elsewhere. Since the early 1960s the viewing public has grown by about 20 per cent per year, and each and every day around half the population of the Third World can be found sitting in front of a television set watching programmes which have mainly been produced locally. International statistics of this kind are not very reliable, but it can be safely assumed that a good 2.5 billion people in the Third World have regular access to television, and this is the majority of the global viewing public.

Translation by Mary Carroll, Language Consultancy, Berlin.

The Early Days

Television started in the various countries and regions of the Third World for many different reasons, but it was seldom if ever as a result of popular demand.

Latin America was the first, because US industry had discovered in the 1950s that a television licence, as the Canadian Lord Thompson was supposed to have said, was a licence to print your own money, and it was eager to introduce this useful invention south of the Rio Grande. The Columbia Broadcasting System went into radio stations in Argentina, Peru, and Venezuela as early as the 1940s, followed by the American Broadcasting Company, which started in 1950 to work with Mexican stations, and later with Venezuelan. Then, in the 1960s, Time Life Inc. tried to gain access to the Latin American market by investing in Mexico, Argentina, Venezuela, and Brazil.

These ventures were anything but lucrative for the North American companies. Their junior partners in Latin America soon became competitors who were quick to make use of the political advantage they had on their home turf. A typical example is the role played by Time Life Inc. in establishing what is now the Brazilian television company Rede Globo, now one of the biggest broadcasters in the world. Time Life initially only wanted to sell the new TV station consultancy services and programmes, but very soon, in order to stay in business, had to take a 50 per cent share in it. Then, in 1968, after its money and expertise had helped TV Globo get started, Time Life found itself being squeezed out. North American television analysts reached the conclusion by the mid-1970s that 'the networks took a beating in their Latin American investment'.

South of the Sahara, from the very outset foreign television companies saw few opportunities for fast profits. The best-known example of this was an English-Canadian-US consortium which introduced television to Kenya in 1963 and was soon taken over by a local agency. Normally the only area where European and US firms made money was when they set up and equipped new television stations. A good example of this was Thomson Television International being commissioned to set up a TV station in Ethiopia in time for the coronation jubilee of Haile Selassie on 2 November 1964.

In most cases the development of television in Africa had been initiated by the colonial powers and was established just in time for the new countries to celebrate their independence and gratify their founding fathers. By 1965 national television stations had been set up in many former colonies including Nigeria, Zambia, Kenya, Burkina Faso, Ivory Coast, Gabon, Congo, Sudan, Uganda, Ghana, and Mauritius. Rhodesia (today Zimbabwe) had also acquired television, partly in the unfounded hope that well-made propaganda could convince the black majority of the advantages of white minority rule.

In the 1970s Zaïre, Niger, Togo, the Central African Republic, Angola, Mozambique, and Djibouti joined the league. In the early 1970s the small island republic of Zanzibar, which together with Tanganyika makes up the federal state of

Facing: the Latin American telenovela—pioneered in particular by TV Globo in Brazil and Televisa in Mexico—has also been successful when exported abroad. TV Globo has sold programmes to more than 100 countries: shown here is a poster advertising the German transmission of **Vale Tudo**.

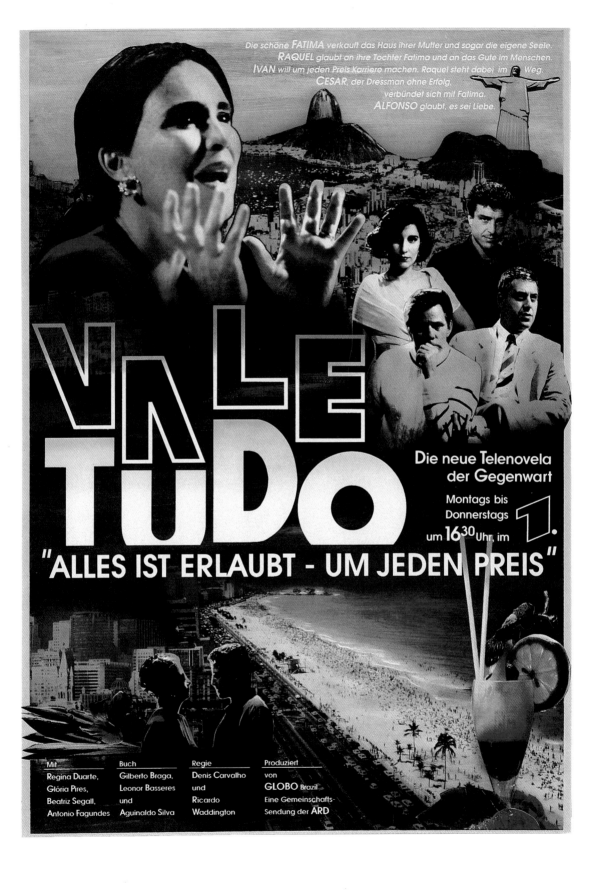

Right: the Mursi tribe of Ethiopia. The difficult task for African television is to maintain, in the face of a flood of programming from America and Europe, a sensitivity to the diverse cultural roots of African societies and simultaneously to work toward the development and sustenance of African culture itself.

Below: a television studio in Oman. Oman was one of a number of Middle Eastern states which set up national television stations from the mid-1960s onwards, a development preceded and accompanied by a lively debate about the religious and cultural implications of the new medium.

Tanzania, used a boom in the price of cloves, its main export commodity, to establish a TV station even against the wishes of the central government. Since then the studios and stations have slowly disintegrated because the price of cloves soon collapsed and European manufacturers were unwilling to barter spare parts for spices.

In the Islamic world of the Middle East and North Africa the introduction of television was preceded by a lively debate about the religious and cultural implications of this new medium. It was related partly to the ban on idolatry and partly to doubts in conservative circles about lady athletes in shorts and other kinds of Western immorality. More secular states like Iraq, Lebanon, Egypt, Algeria, and Syria had fewer problems and introduced TV around 1960. Egypt not only built a huge broadcasting centre but also a factory to produce television sets, both with the help of a soft loan from the USA. Such was the logic of the Cold War: the Soviet Union had been commissioned to build the Aswan Dam.

Countries such as Saudi Arabia, the United Arab Emirates, Qatar, Oman, and North Yemen followed suit and set up national TV stations from the mid-1960s onwards—usually under the strict supervision of pious censors and with their programmes containing a heavy dose of Koran readings. And then, as always in the Middle East, there was the special question of Israel. Because Arabic programmes from Syria could be received in Israel, the latter—after another lively debate about the religious and cultural implications—began in 1968 to broadcast TV programmes in Hebrew and Arabic. Jordan promptly responded with TV programmes for Israeli viewers.

An additional reason why the Gulf states were eager to introduce their own TV services was that, while the camps of the American oil companies were otherwise cordoned off, their TV broadcasts spilt over into virtually every living-room.

In Asia, too, especially in the Philippines and South Korea, the problem of spill-over—this time from army and naval bases—was one of the reasons why national television was introduced. The other reason was that, as in Latin America, and equally in vain, US companies were hoping for long-term profit.

As far as the other states of Asia are concerned, it is hard to discern a consistent pattern regarding the introduction of television. For regional superpowers such as China (TV introduced in 1958), India (1959), and Indonesia (1962), TV and the local production of communications technology was part of their general industrial policy. In other countries such as Taiwan (1962), Malaysia (1963), Singapore (1963), and Hong Kong (1967) television was an integral part of their strategies for social and economic renewal. Bangladesh and Pakistan (both 1964) felt it necessary to respond to the penetration of their territory by Indian broadcasts, which was partly unavoidable and partly deliberate, by setting up their own transmitter chains, especially along their borders with India. And the oil-rich state of Brunei was able to afford television in 1975 just as it could afford anything its rulers deemed desirable.

TV Taipei, Taiwan.

By the mid-1970s virtually every country of the Third World with a population over 10 million had introduced television. One of the few stragglers was South Africa (1976), which, fearing—justifiably—that broadcast signals would transcend the constraints of apartheid, spent years trying to develop separate programmes for the different audiences. But Colour Television in Black and White was no more successful than the other attempts to achieve 'separate development'. By the early 1980s, apart from a few minor states, only Tanganyika did not yet have television, and it has been trying ever since to make up the ground it lost in the era of colonial parting gifts and soft loans. In the meantime its inhabitants are directing their aerials towards Kenya, Uganda, Zambia, Zanzibar, or international satellites.

Technical Development

In these days when any tourist can use a hand-held camcorder to make broadcast-quality pictures, it is useful to remember just how cumbersome, complicated, and expensive early TV technology was. It was a strange mixture of precision engineering, electronics, and photochemistry.

The television originally introduced in the Third World was black and white, but hardly had it been installed and hardly had stations established their production routines than the Commonwealth Broadcasting Conference of 1972 came out with the recommendation that 'new television services should be planned on the basis of acquiring colour transmission and production facilities right at the outset in order to avoid early obsolescence, re-wiring, and costly replacement of monochrome gear'. Thus the existing stations were already obsolete, and conversion to colour broadcasting often turned out to be more expensive than the basic equipping for black and white.

Up to the late 1950s, television throughout the world only transmitted films and live studio broadcasts. It was not until the early 1960s that videotape recorders—at first inordinately expensive—became widespread. Their two-inch tapes could be cut and stuck together again, but this could not be called editing.

Newscasts, documentaries, and TV games were produced on film which then had to be developed and printed in laboratories. These not only required extremely complex equipment and highly qualified staff, but also a regular supply of chemicals and other expendables—which is not a problem unless the supplier is separated from the lab by 3,000 miles, two customs offices, and the currency controls of at least one central bank.

It was not until the mid-1970s that people started to use video cameras with 'portable' recorders—which at first were so heavy that they were transported on a sort of wheelbarrow and so complicated that they required an extra technician to operate them. Not until the mid-1980s did professional camcorders with post-production facilities become available, thus liberating television from photo-chemistry once and for all.

You do not require an understanding of microelectronics to be able to grasp the full impact it had both technically and economically on the mass media. Anyone who is old enough to remember wristwatches with springs, radios with valves, and electric typewriters knows just how much better quartz watches, transistor radios, and personal computers are in terms of reliability, energy consumption, performance, and price. The same goes for television. For complex systems such as a TV station, it is particularly important that equipment based on the same technology can be used for a variety of tasks. It means that there is no longer a need to train and deploy specialized staff on a large number of different technologies.

Because of the many local factors which have to be included, it is difficult to calculate valid figures for the amount of investment required for the new production equipment as compared to the old. But industry estimates put it at between 10 and 30 per cent. Staff costs can be reduced by between 30 and 50 per cent and video reduces the cost of the copying necessary for distribution, exchange, and selling of programmes to less than a tenth of that for film.

In the early years, TV in the industrialized countries could use the services of the film industry and benefit from a highly developed industrial infrastructure and the work of the research and development departments of the manufacturers. In the Third World TV had to wait for the arrival of a fully developed new technology before it could grow to its full potential.

313

The Price to the National Economy

We have to talk about money here first because poor countries have to economize and secondly because well-meaning friends of the Third World love to complain about the Third World squandering its money. Even with new technology, television does not come cheap, but it can only be called expensive if you do not see it for what it can be, and still is in many cases—a public service.

It suffices here to indicate the general magnitude of the costs involved. In most Western European countries public broadcasters supply at least two TV channels and several radio programmes for a fee which is less than the price of a subscription to a good daily newspaper. Similar costs are involved for viewers in the Third World, and it is irrelevant whether these take the form of a TV licence or a surcharge on the products which are advertised on TV. (Only in countries where licence-fee-financed and commercial broadcasters compete do viewers have to pay double.)

For the national economy it is relevant, however, that the technical hardware usually has to be imported. This applies not just to developing countries but to most industrialized countries as well, only the largest of which manufacture at least some of their equipment themselves—and even these often import many of the components. The basic investment for a medium-sized TV station is between 5 and 10 million US dollars. A roughly similar sum is required for a network of transmitters to cover at least the most densely populated areas of a smaller country. These are sums which perhaps could or should be used for other purposes by many developing countries, but they are relatively small compared with other burdens on the balance of trade. For the cost of one of the biggest national TV satellite systems in the Third World, that of Indonesia, the comparison has been made that the price of the toll roads with their fly-overs and other bridges built in Jakarta alone was the same as the costs of the initial PALAPA satellites with forty earth stations.

In addition to the investment costs for studios and transmitters met by the state or by private investors, i.e. the viewers in their role as taxpayers or consumers, the national economy has to bear the additional cost for the private television sets of viewers. The acquisition of television sets by private individuals always constitutes the bulk of the total national investment. And this usually involves highly personal decisions, as there are no known cases of a government ordering its citizens to acquire TV sets even though there have been plenty of cases where a government has tried to prevent or restrict such 'luxury consumption' only to find that, despite import restrictions, special taxes and administrative hurdles, the number of television sets in the country has exceeded all expectations and official statistics. Television sets lend themselves well to being smuggled or brought back from trips abroad.

Nevertheless the question as to whether there is any point in introducing television into countries where the annual cash income of many a farmer or worker

Television and hi-fi
equipment advertisements
in Shanghai.

is not enough for him to be able to afford a television set remains a valid one. But
one should not ignore the fact that several hundred million farmers and workers
in China, Nigeria, and Brazil have regarded a television set as something they
could sensibly afford. The decision becomes more comprehensible if you do not
compare the purchase price with an individual's income but with the family's
income. In Beijing and Canton the author found in the mid-1980s that an average
family, in statistical terms, had to spend between 5 and 8 per cent of its annual net
income to buy a black-and-white television set. This is approximately the same
percentage as an average family in Western Europe has to spend on a colour television set. The same applies to the Arab countries, all newly industrializing countries, and most urban areas in Africa.

All in all, neither the governments nor the potential viewers seem to regard
the investment costs for television as being an unacceptable burden on their
budgets. Television is expensive, but not prohibitively so. For private households
it probably often represents the most expensive single purchase, but it is not
excessively costly compared with other purchases such as gas cookers, bicycles,
or refrigerators.

What cannot be denied, however, is the fact that for the foreseeable future the
Third World will be dependent for its TV technology on supplies from the industrialized countries. But the intense competition among manufacturers in the
latter provides the developing countries with considerable space to manœuvre.
And this will grow as competition between the old industrialized countries and
the newly industrializing ones continues to increase.

Many writers in the Third World see electronics as a means of leapfrogging
some of the stages of development which Europe went through. Vijay Menon,
for example, has written about Asia: 'Having missed out on the first Industrial

315

Revolution, Asian countries are keen that they should not be bypassed by the second.' His words apply to the rest of the Third World as well.

Cultural Imperialism and Public Taste

One term inextricably associated with the introduction and spread of television in the Third World is that of 'cultural imperialism'. It became popular in the context of the debate about the New International Information Order which started in Unesco in the early 1960s, became the dominant theme in the mid-1970s, and then disappeared off the agenda with the end of the Cold War in the 1980s. Committed communication scientists saw cultural imperialism through communication as the spearhead of US imperialism. Television apparently had no other task than to secure and maintain economic domination and political hegemony. Titles such as 'Mass Communications and American Empire' (Herbert Schiller, 1969), 'Picture Tube Imperialism' (A. Wells, 1972), and 'Communication and Cultural Domination' (Luis Beltran, 1978) are indicative of the conclusions reached by a number of investigations. According to one the sole aim of US television programmes was to get people to say 'Coca-Cola' when they felt thirsty.

Viewers in the Third World were less susceptible to manipulation than some had hoped and others had feared. Since the appearance of the first TV aerials on the thatched rooftops, it has been maintained, but rarely proved, that television exerts a malign influence on the Third World, specifically that it has a devastating effect on local culture. No one can deny that Western civilization has influenced all, changed most, and destroyed much traditional culture in the Third World, but it would be hard to argue that television has made any major contribution to this process, compared with the effects of Western religion, economy, and weaponry. Some experts have even maintained that television has given a new lease of life to some forms of traditional culture.

The most succinct statement on the present state of knowledge on the popularity and impact of Western television culture on the Third World remains that made by Michael Tracey:

In most countries 'Dallas' is not as popular as home-produced soaps, and it is completely ignored in countries as diverse as Brazil and Japan, which nevertheless have well-established and highly popular domestic dramas as part of their main TV offerings . . . In fact it is simply untrue to say that imported television programmes, from the US or other metropolitan countries, always have a dominant presence within an indigenous television culture. Certainly they do not always attract larger audiences than home-made programmes, nor do they always threaten national production . . . As far as we can tell, audiences discriminate and tend to prefer home-produced television, rather than slavishly pursuing imported programmes.

In 1974 and 1986 Unesco presented the results of statistical surveys of the international flow of television programmes, which included figures which were not entirely uncontroversial, but nevertheless prove that in the television stations of the Third World the proportion of foreign programmes broadcast declined on average by over 15 per cent between 1973 and 1983. In 1985 Everett Rogers and Livia Antola published an investigation according to which the proportion of imported programmes in the six largest countries of Latin America fell by 29 per cent between 1972 and 1982. In 1986 Third World stations on average filled between 20 and 40 per cent of their total programme time with imported material, with the proportion dropping the bigger and more densely populated the country was.

A comparison of figures for industrialized and developing countries shows that countries of the south are hardly different from those of the north in this respect. Only large states such as the USA, Japan, China, India, and the Soviet Union filled less than 10 per cent of their programme time with imported materials. Indonesia, South Korea, the Philippines, Pakistan, Cuba, Czechoslovakia, Ethiopia, and Vietnam, and also France, Great Britain, Italy, Germany, Australia, Norway, and the Netherlands had between 11 and 30 per cent. Those with over 50 per cent included Senegal, Algeria, Singapore, Tunisia, Mauritius, Zimbabwe, Ecuador, and Zaïre, but also Ireland, Cyprus, Iceland, and New Zealand. If the tables give an accurate reflection of trends over recent years, then it can be assumed that in the future only the largest industrialized and developing countries will be able to manage with less than 10 per cent imported material in the long term, with only the very small and/or poor countries meeting less than half of their programme requirements with domestic productions. All the others, i.e. the vast majority of countries, may settle on a figure of about 30 per cent. Anyone familiar with the largely domestic productions of the USA or the former Soviet Union is unlikely to object to the fact that only a few large states can afford the luxury of restricting their programmes to homespun productions, and will more likely welcome a certain proportion of foreign programmes.

The fact that the proportion of foreign programmes broadcast by many small stations in small and/or poor countries is relatively high and likely to remain so is the result of a peculiarity of the exchange value of TV programmes. Manuel Alvarado gives a graphic description of the situation: 'A motor car will always have a certain basic price below which it can never fall. A programme that is made for £1 million could be sold for £100,000 to the USA but to Burkina Faso for £100. In fact, in both cases the eventual price of the programme is more likely to be determined by the cost of selling it than by the production cost.'

But Third World producers can make more money more easily in the Third World than their American or Western European competitors because they are more popular for cultural and language reasons. This has led in recent years to a distinct shift in the composition of imports. While the proportion from the region or from other developing countries has significantly increased, imports from Western industrialized countries have suffered a sharp decline.

317

A still from the Chinese Channel's **Thief of Time**. The Chinese Channel broadcasts news and programmes (principally from Hong Kong) by satellite from Asia to the Chinese diaspora in Europe.

Television in Latin America broadcasts Latin American productions—particularly ones from Brazil, which has become a world exporter of programmes, but also from Mexico, Argentina, and Venezuela. Arab TV stations supplement their own programmes with ones from other Arabic stations, especially Egypt, but also, to some extent, from Jordan and Syria, and, in the future, perhaps also from Lebanon again. In Asia, programmes from India, China, or Hong Kong are shown in areas with a high Indian or Chinese population. In sub-Saharan Africa the traditional suppliers in Western Europe and the USA are facing growing competition from other continents. It would also seem that an increasing number of programmes are on offer from Africa itself now that the non-profit-making Programme Exchange Centre of the African Broadcasting Union (URTNA) has slowly become fully operational.

In many Third World countries imports from the industrialized nations only play a minor role compared with domestic productions and imports from the immediate region. This applies particularly to the large, heavily populated countries which are home to the majority of the people living in the Third World. If TV programmes from the industrialized North were ever the spearhead of cultural imperialism they were supposed to be, then the spearhead has long since been blunted.

Traditional Culture and New Media

Supporters, and also connoisseurs, of the traditional cultures of the Third World occasionally argue that the direct influence of US and Western European programmes may have declined, but the indirect influence is all the stronger, as local productions have taken over the style and content of foreign programmes. This may apply in many cases, but most of the time the opposite seems to be true.

This is not the place to look at subtle theories of cultural change from confrontation via acculturation to assimilation. It will have to suffice to recall that culture is not static. It is a process.

The process of cultural change may start with plagiarizing a foreign cultural technique, be it cuneiform script or film, but it does not stop there. Mary Bitterman describes the process using the example of Indian film:

Cinema, as an art form and medium of entertainment, is a Western import, but from the creation of their first full-length Indian movie in 1913 to the present day, the Indian cinema has assumed an identity of its own. Indian films reveal their descent from the classical Indian theatre and folk theatre; they deal very often with mystical and historical themes; and they place emphasis on song, mime, dance, spectacle, and episodic presentation . . . A Westerner watching a popular Indian movie must be struck by its inescapable 'Indianess'.

The example often used for television is the Brazilian TV series known as the telenovela. Telenovelas are basically soap operas Brazilian style. The difference between an archetypal soap and a Brazilian telenovela is easy to see and hard to describe. (For a good summary of academic and other writing on telenovelas see Richard Paterson's account in Chapter 4.)

The outward characteristics are the easiest to describe: individual episodes are shown every day except Sundays and public holidays. They last between thirty and forty-five minutes and are only produced a few days before transmission. The television stations can therefore take into account the audience's reactions to the latest episodes when developing characters and the plot. Nearly all Brazilian television stations show a number of telenovelas every evening between 7 and 9 p.m., pausing only for the news and for adverts.

All one can say in general about the dramatic structure of telenovelas is that they consist of a finite number of episodes and have a closed plot with a curve of dramatic tension that extends throughout the entire work, rather than being a basically endless series of closed episodes as in most US series.

As to the content, Maria Klagsbrunn suggests their 'basic thematic elements are the striving after love, social prestige, riches and power'. They use a lively, everyday language and in terms of aesthetics and content correspond to the 'attitudes, lifestyle and expectations of the Brazilian middle classes . . . the milieu in which the stories take place, the types depicted, the language spoken, the

319

themes—all are topical in a double sense: they are of our times and reflect them, they refer to the Brazilian milieu. The viewers recognize on television something of contemporary Brazil . . . they (the viewers) either live in similar circumstances themselves or—as is the case mostly—the life of the middle classes which is depicted is what they and their families aspire to.' Telenovelas are always on the side of ordinary people and the fact that the viewers actually expect critical realism is demonstrated by the way they flock to the more critical competition as soon as a telenovela depicts life in Brazil in too conformist a manner.

Popular success for socially critical series is not confined to Brazil. It is reported from India that one of the greatest public successes was a series which portrayed a one-woman crusade against the evils of corruption. It depicted the day-to-day problems of the viewers with crooked petroleum dealers and taxi-drivers, sellers of quack medicines, the arrogant town officialdom, and the corruption which is prevalent in many aspects of Indian life.

In a study of viewer behaviour in Egypt, Samir Allam discovered that 'identification with the people in a series . . . is more likely to occur when they are portrayed in a realistic manner'. He is referring mainly to the portrayal of corruption, which because of state censorship may only be depicted on television as being the result of individual immorality, while the viewers all know that it actually has material causes, e.g. the excessively low wages of state employees.

It is reported from Nigeria that the most popular figure produced by local television is 'Mr Andrew', who returns to Nigeria after a long stay in the USA. He finds his home country hot and dirty, with an incompetent administration and corrupt politicians. His critique is witty, aggressive, and self-confident. The viewers can vicariously relive all the irritations and problems of everyday life, and at the same time can laugh at the well-known figure of the bragging returner. 'Mr Andrew' is popular because he thinks and says what the viewers think and say—only he does it better and more wittily.

Many traditional forms of art would be less popular today, or would even have disappeared altogether if television had not given them a new lease of life. 'The televising of bag puppetry has brought it to a new period of visibility and popularity,' Mary Bitterman reports from Taiwan. And from India: 'To radio and now television can be attributed much of the recent widespread stimulus to folk music of different regions. A new sense of identity and even pride had come to rural and tribal singers, who are now beginning to refine their modes of presentation.'

The way that traditional and modern culture have merged and mutually support each other on Third World television is not something that people in the industrialized countries are particularly aware of. There are probably many possible explanations for this, but the simplest is also the most likely: Western experts do not understand the language it all takes place in.

New Life in the Living-room

Whatever the reputation of television, it is usually regarded as being neither conducive to family life nor an instrument of social enlightenment. Leaving aside the question of whether this is true in industrialized countries, the situation in the Third World would certainly seem to be a different one.

In recent years a series of surveys from the Third World have been published which all agree that the television set in the living-room—whatever the programme being watched—has brought about changes in patterns of social behaviour which could not have been predicted on the basis of experience in the industrialized countries. At the start of his study, Leoncio Barrios is referring to investigations in Western societies when he states that it is a classic criticism of TV watching that it undermines family communication. His field study shows, on the contrary, that in Venezuela 'TV viewing can enhance communication in the family . . . TV watching was a time for sitting together, talking to each other (about several themes, even different from TV issues), touching, and caring for each other . . . At times TV viewing seems to be more enjoyable than the TV show itself.'

The situation would appear to be no different in the case of the urban middle classes in India, as J. S. Yadava and Usha V. Reddi observed: 'Watching television in Indian homes is more a social activity than a private act . . . Preparation and eating of the evening meals are timed with television programs. In many families in Delhi the time for eating supper coincides with the Hindi or English newscasts.'

Neena Behl studied the effects of television in an Indian village and presented

her results under the significant title of 'Equalizing Status: Television and Tradition in an Indian Village'. What she is referring to is mainly the status of the woman in the household. The television set is usually located in the women's living quarters which, though always accessible to the whole family, were hitherto seldom frequented by the men. 'Television viewing means now that men frequent the women's quarters for a much greater length of time. Men and women share much more time together. This unification also applies to age—younger and older people now spend much more time together with the TV in the house.'

With the arrival of television, Sunday now punctuates the week by taking the form of a holiday, a new concept for the farmer. For the evening meal on Sunday, women prepare those items of food that can easily and quickly be cooked. They do not make chappatis for the evening meal, as it takes a long time to bake . . . and the supreme new symbol of food consumption shown on TV—the dining room table—has been adopted.

Among the major changes that television has brought to the household Behl lists the fact that 'the orientation to the TV set as a cultural object frees the women from the control of men' and also 'an increased democratization of human relations with respect to the statuses of gender and age especially'.

Finally, James Lull and Se-Wen Sun looked at the effects of Chinese television on families in Beijing, Guangzhou, and Xian. The most important aspects of their results do not differ from the ones already mentioned. The authors sum up the social effects of television as follows: 'The introduction of television into the homes of Chinese families may be the most important cultural development in the People's Republic since the effective end of the Cultural Revolution in the mid-1970s.' Television 'has brought with it revolutionary cultural changes, including a fundamental restructuring of daily life in homes and neighbourhoods, a new means for obtaining entertainment and information, and a gradual redefining of the most basic and the most subtle aspects of the relationship between the government and the people.'

As regards the political role of television, Lull and Sun observe that the government still regards television as a primary instrument of national development and social control, but the viewers see it in a completely different light: 'Some viewers told us, for instance, that when they watch the international news, they pay more attention to street scenes from foreign cities than to the political reporting that accompanies the pictures.' One viewer summed up the result as follows: 'The government . . . can't just tell us "China is the best country on Earth". We know better.'

Public Opinion and Social Behaviour

There were many hopes and many fears attached to the introduction of television in the Third World. In the more narrow, political sense some hoped and

opposite The meeting of traditional narratives and modern technology: India's **Mahabharat**.

others feared that state monopoly broadcasters would control and manipulate public opinion. All in all this did not turn out to be the case, and one might even say that television benefited those in government least of all—as the viewing public received an overdose of their faces and their opinions on the small screen. A politically and economically unsuccessful regime that tries to influence the public through television propaganda soon finds itself in a dilemma—the more it talks about itself the more it reveals itself.

Until he had to leave Iran, Mohammed Reza Pahlevi enjoyed unlimited control of huge oil revenues, an army, a secret police, and one of the most modern television systems in the Third World. Prior to the introduction of television, writes Mowlana, occasional appearances in public had done nothing to damage the image which his subjects were supposed to—and in many cases did—have of the 'King of Kings, Shadow of God and Light of the Aryans'. It was only when he started appearing regularly on television screens that the nation discovered what hitherto had only been known to court circles—namely that the language and tone of voice of Mohammed Reza Pahlevi revealed him to be a parvenu who was not equal to the demands made by his office. Television did not bring about the fall of the Shah, but neither did it help him. It showed him as he was, and thus made him vulnerable.

The Nigerian communication researcher Luke Uka Uche comes out against overestimating the mass media in his country: 'Research finds the audiences of the Nigerian mass media in crisis situations to be extraordinarily independently opinioned, suspicious of the media contents, active rather than passive audiences of the media, and intelligently questioning the legitimacy of any new leadership and the contents of the media . . . The audience knows when it is being manipulated through mass media.'

If television can do little for those in power, what can it do for the viewers? To prove any changes in attitude brought about by television it is necessary to carry out long-term studies, which cost a lot of money and therefore are few and far between (also because the social sciences seem strangely uninterested in the effects of the biggest mass medium of our times). The best known long-term study is that of Chu, Alfian, and Schramm on the social impact of television in rural Indonesia. In an initial survey (1976) they looked at the social behavioural patterns and attitudes of men and women in selected villages in Indonesia prior to the introduction of television. Six years later they carried out a second survey of the same groups. By then television had been introduced to half of the villages, and because otherwise little had changed in this secluded region, any changes could reasonably plausibly be attributed to the influence of television.

What was particularly striking was the change which had occurred in the economic behaviour of the farmers and the attitudes of the women towards family planning. Television had recommended to the farmers direct marketing of their products and warned them against private money-lenders. The result was that twice as many viewers as non-viewers pocketed the middleman's profits and twice as many had an account with the local savings bank and had taken out loans from the rural credit institutes on better terms than those offered by the money-lenders.

Among the women, the viewers were better informed about family planning and were eight times more likely to use IUDs and four times more likely to use the contraceptive pill than non-viewers. Prior to the introduction of television over 40 per cent of women had relied on 'wise women' rather than trained midwives when they gave birth; afterwards the figures for viewers were 23 per cent but still 45 per cent for non-viewers. Prior to television about 20 per cent of all women were members of Family Planning Associations, afterwards 44 per cent of viewers and 20 per cent of non-viewers. Television also contributed to the spread of Bahasa Indonesian as the lingua franca throughout the entire country. Among those without a school education the percentage who could at least understand Bahasa rose among viewers from 69 to 91 per cent, whereas the figure remained at 69 per cent among non-viewers.

These were desirable results from the point of view of the government's development policy, but there were undesirable ones too. Among viewers, consumption of goods advertised on television—most of which were imported—such as shampoo, hair cream, toothpaste, soft drinks, cigarettes, and detergents increased so sharply that in April 1981 the Indonesian government banned all television advertising. And viewers were less likely to remain loyal to the 'Mengaji' than non-viewers.

'Mengaji' refers to the custom among village dwellers of coming together in the evening and reciting the Koran 'in a sing-song voice' in Arabic—a language which they hardly understand and cannot pronounce correctly. Half of the viewers gave up this age-old custom and watched television instead—including religious broadcasts, which are a common and popular part of programming. The decline of the 'Mengajis' was welcomed by educated Muslims because the somewhat superstitious village practices had always been regarded as suspect. Thanks to television the farmer could now for the first time hear the Koran in the correctly pronounced language of the prophet, and for the first time also the addresses given by the best Islamic teachers were able to reach all believers in the land.

In a study of 'Broadcasting and Cultural Change', Sid-Ahmed Nugdalla, a communication researcher from Sudan, states that it is difficult to measure 'the impact of the media on what may be considered "core values and attitudes"', but he goes on to say:

The question of women represents a striking example of the role of broadcasting in our cultural renewal. Irrespective of the form and content of programmes, the mere appearance of women in radio and television is a serious crack in the crust of tradition; for women to sing and act on radio and television is an unforgivable sin in the eyes of the religious fanatics and the rigid traditionalists. Not long ago, even male singers were spoken of as 'vagabonds' . . . Broadcasting has made them popular and given them a touch of respectability in a relatively stagnant and traditional society where art, like labour, is regarded as the vocation of the poor masses at the base of the social pyramid.

What we are talking about is change in traditional cultures—not their complete disappearance—even if this change involves the disappearance of certain privileges, for example the claim which the men of Sanaa in Yemen have to absolute obedience from their wives. In the past, women among the arch-conservative urban population of Sanaa saw very little of life outside their living quarters and met virtually no one who did not belong to their immediate family circle—until television arrived. Society in Sanaa is still conservative, and the women are still devout Muslims who wear a veil reaching to their feet when they go out in the street. But a lot has changed. Gabriele von Bruck suggests that 'The influence of the Egyptian and Syrian family serials broadcast daily on Yemeni television on women's attitude towards marriage is very strong. The discrepancy between the world portrayed in films and their own circumstances makes women think about their own situation. They follow with great interest the ways women who are neglected by their husbands tackle the problem . . . Women say that these scenes cause them to have more reservations about entering into a polygamous marriage or one with a man who is significantly older than them.'

Family serials are not intended to be counselling sessions on day-to-day living, and the women in Sanaa do not misinterpret them as such, but television—from family serials to news programmes—shows them in their seclusion, that one can be a good Muslim from a respectable family and nevertheless behave in a different way from what has been the norm hitherto in Sanaa. It is no doubt difficult to assess the impact on Yemeni women of the sight of the wife of the Egyptian

The Egyptian family serial,
Layali Al-Helmia.

President in Western clothes or a Syrian woman professor disagreeing with a male government minister in a television debate—but it is true that Yemeni men complain that television gives women ideas above their station.

Television and Language

For Western observers television in the Third World has many unexpected consequences. Who would have thought that television would be used—in the words of a Korean expert, Choe Chungho—'for liberating Korean culture from Chinese culture, which has dominated the former for one thousand years'? (1986)

According to Chungho, Korean culture is a culture of the written word—written in Chinese characters. To write Korean one had to study classical Chinese first, so access to Korean literature was denied to all except a small circle of court officials and Confucian scholars. Below the level of courtly culture there was nothing but 'a swamp of absolute poverty in the cultural field', with comedians, magicians, and singing beggars as typical representatives of the spoken word and the language of the common people. Written texts were so artificial that they were even incomprehensible when read aloud in Korean to those who could not read the script. An alphabetic script called Han'gul, which had developed since the fifteenth century, offered a straightforward phonetic way of writing the Korean language, but it was considered base and used mainly by women and in novels written for them.

It was only when a need arose for radio and television scripts which had to be comprehensible when read aloud that Han'gul's hour had arrived. 'The nation-wide popularization of the electronic media developed a new culture of spoken words, reversed the position of written words and spoken words, culminated in the exclusive use of Han'gul in our daily language,' and led, according to Chungho, for the first time, to a 'democratization of culture' in Korea.

If television has enabled Korea to liberate itself linguistically and culturally from its over-powerful neighbour, China, then the latter has been able to use TV to achieve one of its most important cultural goals: the lasting introduction of Putonghua. Putonghua, or Modern Standard Chinese, is often referred to abroad as 'Mandarin'. Ignoring certain finer linguistic points it is, by and large, the language which is spoken in modern Beijing, and is officially the language of administration and education in China. About 70 per cent of the population can speak it more or less correctly, but the remaining 30 per cent still amount to several hundred million people, living mainly in the south of the country. Despite all official attempts, Putonghua failed to spread in the south, partly because it and the local dialects are mutually virtually incomprehensible. On television Putonghua cannot only be heard day in, day out, but also—thanks to the regularly used subtitles in the Chinese characters common to all Chinese dialects—it can be understood. Putonghua has been the official language of China since the thirteenth century, but only since the introduction of television has it had a chance of becoming its national language proper.

It is one of the ironies of modern communications that television, of all things, has furthered a national language and with it also a national literature. The example of Bahasa in Indonesia has already been mentioned. Studies in the Arabic-speaking world have shown that Egyptian films and TV series have resulted in Egyptian Arabic increasingly becoming the pan-Arabic language of everyday life. And it is reported from Brazil that television has gradually led to a standardization of the spoken language there too.

In other regions of the Third World, too, television is playing a similar role of popularizing the official national language or helping create a regional lingua franca—or will do so in the near future. One example is Swahili, which is the official language in Kenya, Tanzania, and Uganda (with a total of over 60 million inhabitants between them), but is not yet spoken with any accuracy except along the coastal strip between Mombasa and Dar es Salaam.

Satellite and Third World Television

When the Soviet Union launched the first artificial satellite, *Sputnik*, in 1957, and the USA put the first communications satellite, *Early Bird*, into operation in 1965, these events made headlines all over the world. In 1992 the fact that China put five satellites into orbit was only briefly reported in trade journals. Since the days of *Sputnik* and *Early Bird* the number, service life, and performance of communications satellites have increased to such an extent that a world-wide over-capacity exists today, and transmitting costs have fallen by over 90 per cent since the late 1960s. Virtually all countries of the Third World now have ground stations which can send and receive signals, and simple reception aerials can be purchased for a few hundred US dollars.

This means, for example, that with a satellite receiver, which you can buy virtually anywhere in Malaysia, you can receive twenty-nine television programmes—including four from the USA and Thailand respectively, three from England, two from Australia, Indonesia, and Hong Kong, and one each from France, New Zealand, Russia, China, the Philippines, Iran, and Pakistan. This is officially forbidden—with the exception of foreign embassies and the royal family, no one in Malaysia is allowed to receive satellite broadcasts direct—but it is possible. In China direct reception has also been forbidden since 1989, but this did not prevent the Ministry of Engineering from producing 30,000 satellite dishes—referred to popularly as 'white ears'—in 1992 and advertising them publicly. At 3,000 Yuan (about $US500) they are not cheap by Chinese standards, but it would appear to be worth investing in them, for in China, as in other parts of the Third World, cable networks are shooting out of the ground like mushrooms. According to the official Chinese News Agency, at the start of 1993 there were about 1,200 local TV cable networks, usually for the internal use of firms, and 10,000 private ones. The unofficial figure for further illegal ones is 100,000.

The formula for these so-called 'cable networks' is the same everywhere: a small satellite dish, some ordinary aerial cabling, and a few couplings—and already you have a distribution system for a neighbourhood. The lucky owner can then start demanding a modest contribution for programmes which he receives for nothing and merely has to pass on at his own expense.

This practice, which has been common in the Caribbean for the past few decades, has been turned into the official business policy of Star TV, a healthy Hong Kong company. It broadcasts five programmes via a satellite which can be received throughout the length and breadth of Asia. These programmes are sometimes rebroadcast by big TV stations and sometimes they are received direct by private individuals, who often then distribute them by cable. This is not only free of charge for the private receivers, but they are also even able to make money out of it, as Star TV positively encourages them to build up their own little cable business and even sells them aerials suitable for the purpose. The larger the private network is—whether legal, semi-legal, or illegal—the more money Star TV makes; the bigger the number of viewers the more they make from advertising.

In early 1993, Star TV had five programmes: an English-language channel with music videos, a US twenty-four-hour sports channel, a Chinese movie channel, an entertainment channel called Star Plus, and the BBC World Television Service. At that point, only two years after it had first started, Star TV claimed it was making a profit. Not only did it have a significant share of the Taiwan, Hong Kong, and Israeli cable markets, it had also reached at least two million households in China and India respectively. And, it claimed, a further 200,000 households were joining the ranks every week. By the end of 1993 Rupert Murdoch had acquired a controlling interest in Star TV. Star TV and the large number of cable channels available in Malaysia are the exception rather than the rule at present, but they indicate the direction things are taking. For their international PR work the Western industrialized nations are setting up their own programmes, made up partly of material from their own domestic channels and partly from material produced at their own expense. Large commercial broadcasters are internationalizing their programmes at little extra cost, and benefiting from the extra revenue from international marketing. And countries which cannot afford this sort of money are broadcasting their programmes via their own or foreign satellites like a sort of electronic mailshot.

The attractions of satellite in the 1990s are widening. In the first few weeks of 1993 alone the trade journals reported that the Turkic republics of the former Soviet Union (with about 40 million inhabitants) had just started receiving the international service of Turkish state television, that the South African programme M-Net was now being received in Lesotho, Swaziland, Kenya, Ghana, and Zimbabwe, that in tiny Namibia 12,000 households were now

Television's global footprint: children in Samoa watching an advertisement for Levi jeans.

subscribing to M-Net, and that international satellite programmes were now being distributed in Bombay via at least 8,000 illegal cable networks which anybody can lease for about a dollar a month.

The people in charge of television stations in the Third World have no illusions. A representative of Malaysian Television said in November 1992: 'The decade of the nineties ushers in the era of satellite broadcasting in Asia. The year 2000 and beyond will see the proliferation of satellite networks, whose footprints will cover the continent of Asia as well as the island nations of the Pacific. At the same time more national satellite broadcasts will come into play as more countries in Asia are acquiring their own domestic satellites.' But they are not discouraged—they even glimpse some opportunities in this development, for if viewers start to compare local programmes to those of supranational broadcasters, the local broadcasters will be reminded 'that good local programming always beats foreign programming'.

One could maintain that the biggest hurdle television in the Third World has faced hitherto has been the lack of interest local governments have shown in the technical and journalistic quality of national television. So long as television was politically tame and could be used as a kind of governmental public address system, those holding the reins were quite content. It is the hope of many journalists, producers, and engineers in the television stations of the Third World, that international competition will at last force their governments to give them the freedom they need.

14

Australia

Elizabeth Jacka and Lesley Johnson

The Tyranny of Distance

T he themes of distance, region, and nation are continuing ones in Australia's communications history. Indeed one way of understanding Australian television history is as a continuing tension between centralizing and regionalizing pressures, a struggle between large commercial television proprietors who wish to extend their reach over the entire nation (and increasingly beyond) and those interests that seek to preserve the local and regional character of television, a struggle which has always been biased towards the former.

The big proprietors have not been interested in trying to reach the truly remote areas of Australia, those vast tracts of sparsely populated land in the Northern Territory, Western Australia, North Queensland, and the north of South Australia. As late as 1978 10 per cent of Australians, a total of 1.4 million people, had an impaired television reception or no service at all. The advent of a national satellite in the early 1980s was a crucial factor in the further development of the system. Its space-compressing capacities created the potential to reach outback parts of Australia, including remote Aboriginal communities but cost (of transponders) was still to prove an impediment to the extension of television to all parts of Australia. The history of television in Australia has been a slow but inexorable pull towards what James Carey calls a 'high communications policy', that is, one 'aimed at spreading messages further in space and reducing the cost of transmission'.

At the same time this history has been strangely retarded. Television was not

331

introduced until 1956, considerably later than comparable countries; national networking in the commercial system was not achieved until the late 1980s; and Australia is the last industrialized nation without some system of pay television, at a time when such systems are increasingly appearing in other regions of the world such as Latin America and Asia. The small size of the population (16.8 million) could be the reason for this last feature of the Australian television service, but other comparable countries like Canada and the much smaller New Zealand (3 million) have pay TV. The reason is more likely to be found in the extraordinary lobbying power that the commercial television industry has always been able to exert over Australian governments of either political persuasion to ensure that their secure position is not disturbed. Another reason may be that, for its size, Australia, with its three commercial networks and its two national broadcasters, has had a large amount of television choice.

Television historian and analyst Tom O'Regan has suggested a set of terms by which the history of Australian television might be grasped. He sees television being structured first of all by an interaction, usually of an antagonistic kind, between international, national, regional, and local forces and, secondly, by the needs of different kinds of audiences, which he terms minoritarian, ethnic, indigenous, and 'established'. The different kinds of audiences are of course not always discrete; sometimes they overlap, so that for example, audiences can be both 'minoritarian' (for example, women) and 'ethnic' at the same time.

Some of these terms have appeared on the television policy stage only recently; Aboriginal Australians and those born outside Australia whose first language is not English have been catered for only since the 1980s in the broadcasting mix. Until the late 1970s the audience was very much conceived of as Anglo-Celtic and the only diversity built into the system was that between the supposedly more cultivated taste catered to by the Australian Broadcasting Commission (ABC), renamed Australian Broadcasting Corporation in 1983, and the more popular one addressed by the commercial system. However, from the very beginning of television, international, national, regional, and local forces have been at play in the system. These four terms will structure the administrative and industrial history of the Australian television system in the next section of our essay.

Australian Television: The 'Dual System'

The natural models for Australia's broadcasting institutions were, unsurprisingly, Britain and the USA. However, Australia has always had it both ways by having a dual system, first of all in radio and later in television. This was not achieved smoothly. The Chifley Labor government of the 1940s wanted to have only a national, that is, a public service system, which would be run by the ABC; it passed legislation in 1948 prohibiting the granting of commercial TV licences.

The Liberal-Country party coalition, led by Robert Menzies, favoured a commercial system. As early as 1944 commercial interests had been agitating for the introduction of commercial television but the government preferred to bide its time and review experiences in other countries before it ventured into such a big investment in the fragile post-war economy. There was a great deal of disquiet amongst various sections of the community about whether Australia needed television at all, with fear expressed about the negative model presented by American television and about the corruption of morals and the erosion of family life that television might bring.

In 1949 the Menzies government came to power without a definite policy for television but by 1953, when the new government established a Royal Commission to examine the details of the introduction of television, it was clear that there would be a dual system. Its report recommended that there should be two commercial licences in each of Sydney and Melbourne and that the ABC should run the national system which would have one station in each capital city. It saw the Australian Broadcasting Control Board (ABCB), which had been established by the Chifley government in 1948, as the appropriate body to regulate the commercial sector, though, as it would turn out, its status as advisory rather than an independent statutory authority meant that it often proved rather toothless; and it recommended leaving the ABC to regulate itself.

The ABCB immediately began hearings to determine the first licences and to no one's surprise they went to consortia dominated by the big newspaper proprietors. They remained in the same hands until the late 1980s. In Sydney the Channel 9 licence was awarded to the group associated with Sir Frank Packer's Consolidated Press, publishers of the *Daily Telegraph* and *Sunday Telegraph* in Sydney and of top-selling magazines, including the *Australian Women's Weekly*. The Channel 7 licence was awarded to a group led by Fairfax Newspapers and the powerful Macquarie radio network. Fairfax was the publisher of the prestige newspaper the *Sydney Morning Herald*. In Melbourne the successful bidders were the Herald and Weekly Times Group for the Channel 7 station and the publishers of the *Age* newspaper won the other licence.

The domination of Australian television by big newspaper interests was to be a feature of the scene until 1987. It was, and remains, an intensely controversial issue in Australia. The press itself is quite concentrated and has become more so in recent years. To have this concentration increased by giving it dominance of the electronic media as well seemed to some sections of the community extremely undemocratic, tending to make politicians beholden to the media proprietors who might control their political prospects. Australian television history is full of examples where the politicians of both conservative and progressive bent have looked after what are in Australia called the 'media mates'.

All but one of the six stations (four commercial and two ABC) were on air in time for the Melbourne Olympics in November 1956 and all were broadcasting by January 1957. That year both ABC and commercial services were extended to the 'BAPH' cities—Brisbane, Adelaide, Perth, and Hobart. There had been controversy about whether these smaller markets could sustain two services, but there was pressure from the operators in Sydney and Melbourne who favoured parity with the two biggest cities. The Sydney–Melbourne owners quickly developed informal networking arrangements and in 1961 the Packer interests succeeded in acquiring GTV9 in Melbourne. Concentration rules limited owners to two stations in total and meant that they could not have full national networking as they would have liked, but having two stations in each major market enabled the Sydney–Melbourne axis to set up programme-sharing arrangements which helped to defray their costs and which eventually led to their domination of the whole Australian system. Against the advice of the ABCB the government allowed two licences in each of Adelaide and Brisbane and one each in Perth and Adelaide.

By 1961 television had been extended to thirty-three country areas. Again the big proprietors favoured extension of networking arrangements to allow them to broadcast nationally, but it was firm government policy to have regional stations owned by regional interests. This policy was undoubtedly heavily influenced by the Country Party pressure within the Menzies coalition government. Until the major media changes of the late 1980s the regional stations were controlled by local interests; Bonney reports that in 1984 there were thirty independent owners amongst the owners of a total of forty-one television stations. The viability of regional television between 1961 and 1989 was helped by the fact that regional stations had a monopoly in their markets and unlike the 'BAPH' stations were able to avoid total domination by the Sydney–Melbourne axis.

In 1963 the government announced that there would be a third commercial licence in each of Sydney, Melbourne, Adelaide, and Brisbane and a second for Perth in spite of widespread criticism that these markets were not big enough to sustain a third commercial channel (after all a country as large as the USA only had three). The ABCB recommended against a third licence in Adelaide and Brisbane but were again overruled, confirming critics' sense that they were ineffective as a regulatory body. Their predictions were confirmed when within six months of the award of the new licences a bidding war for overseas programmes broke out, their price doubled, and transmission hours were reduced. Australia had had relatively extensive transmission hours quite quickly: by the end of 1959 there were eighty hours a week compared with less than seventy in the UK as late as 1974.

With the addition of the regional stations from 1961 and the third commercial licences in 1963 the system became set in a pattern that would last until 1980 when the Special Broadcasting Service Television Service (SBS-TV) was added to the national system. There were no major changes in the commercial system until the mid-1980s when the Hawke Labor government introduced its policy of equalization (see below).

Consolidation of an Institution

Only 5,000 television sets had been sold by the time the Olympic Games began in November 1956. But many Melbourne people watched the events on sets displayed in the windows of electrical and department stores in city and surburban streets. International tensions, particularly around the invasion of Hungary by the USSR, as well as more general Cold War animosities and the Middle East crisis provoked considerable anxiety among the organizers in the last few weeks leading up to the Games, yet, by the time they had finished, politics was considered to have intruded only occasionally among participants or spectators during the competitions and surrounding events. Live telecasts enhanced the sense of excitement around the Games and were seen to contribute to the amicable atmosphere by creating a sense of public support and enthusiasm for what was represented as a major step in the development of Australia as a young nation.

For the members of the fledgling television service it was the beginning of a key role for sport on Australian television. After the Games, sports news and telecasts quickly became an important feature of all television stations programming particularly on Saturdays. At first live telecasts could only be received in the city of origin, but many sports programmes were considered only of local significance. Different regional traditions of football in Sydney and Melbourne, for instance, remained sacrosanct until the 1980s.

It was not until the installation of a coaxial cable between Sydney and Melbourne in 1960 and the introduction of videotape facilities in 1962 that live programmes could be exchanged with relative ease between the different capital cities of Australia. Before this time, a programme televised live in one city was recorded by pointing a camera at a television screen and the film then flown to other cities. But such difficulties did not prevent the ABC from placing an increasing emphasis on sport, with a much higher proportion of time given to these programmes on television than radio and twice as much sport provided as on commercial stations. From 1962 onwards it became possible to send programmes down the cable between major cities and from 1966 onwards microwave links existed between Sydney and Melbourne on the one hand, and regional stations on the other. It was a mark of the importance accorded to sports coverage, and its ascendance over the commercial channels in this respect, that as late as 1966 the national relay system was being used by the ABC for little else than broadcasting cricket and tennis. Though commercial stations were keen to develop this aspect of their services, it was to take them some time, as Inglis points out, before they were to work out how to sell sports programmes to advertisers.

Though personnel connected with sports programmes had begun experimenting during the Olympic Games with ways of exploiting effectively the particularity of television as a medium, many associated with its early development in Australia understood it primarily as simply 'radio with pictures'. Indeed, a number of quiz and variety shows that had become very successful on

Six O'Clock Rock
appeared on the ABC from
1959 and was compèred by
Australia's own rock star,
Johnny O'Keefe.

commercial radio were simply 'simulcast' on both radio and television in the
1950s. The ABC's initial stance towards television was that this service would
merely be about furnishing visuals for the same kind of programmes they had
been providing on radio for the last twenty years. This was reflected in the fact
that the ABC, unlike the BBC, did not have a separate television organization.
The drama department, for example, or the news department, would prepare
programmes for both radio and television.

In other ways, however, the ABC was very much modelled on the BBC. The
first ABC operatives and announcers were sent to the BBC for training and on
return trained their colleagues in methods learnt from the 'mother' system and
from the beginning the ABC had an exclusive arrangement with the ABC of first
refusal on all BBC programmes. Commercial channels initially, however,

obtained all of their imported programmes from Hollywood. To avoid driving prices up by competing with each other, in 1963 the operators of the three commercial networks set up a buying pool. In 1967–8 there was a stand-off with the Motion Picture Exporters' Association of America, who wanted to increase the price for Australia. The pool resisted and no programmes at all were acquired that year.

In the first years of television, currency restrictions and thus limits on imports meant that, whether they wanted to or not, the stations had to produce local programmes. The absence of an Australian film industry meant that at first these consisted mostly of the relatively low-cost variety shows. Some had a quiz format; others like the very successful *In Melbourne Tonight*, which began in 1957, hosted by Graham Kennedy, relied on a light entertainment format. Teenage shows also were of a similar genre and the first two programmes beginning in 1958 looked remarkably like those devised for adult audiences. Brian Henderson's *Bandstand* on Sydney's TCN 9 and Brian Naylor's *Swallow's Junior* in Melbourne looked sedate and sober alongside the ABC's more distinctively 'teenage show', *Six O'Clock Rock*, compered by the Australian rock'n'roll star, Johnny O'Keefe, which opened in Sydney in 1959. Apart from these types of shows, local content was chiefly made up of sports and the as yet undeveloped news, current affairs, and documentary programmes.

Though the locally produced variety shows were popular with Australian audiences, imported domestic and situation comedy programmes from the USA on the commercial stations quickly became the top-rating programmes. Up until 1962 less than 50 per cent of Australian television was locally produced. Shows from the USA like *I Love Lucy*, *Father Knows Best*, *77 Sunset Strip*, and *The Untouchables* vied with *Sunday Night Movies* and *Alfred Hitchcock Presents*. US programmes were seen as making similar local shows look amateurish and stilted. But their cultural impact was more profound. Contemporary cultural critic, Meaghan Morris, describes the effect in her family as the raucous, relentless voice of Lucille Ball drove her father to distraction, yet delighted her mother and herself. Such shows were viewed with alarm by many as evidence of an increasing Americanization of Australian society and a destruction of Australia's connection with and the proper authority of things British. But Lucy's voice, according to Morris, also had a potentially galvanizing and emancipating effect for Australian women. As screaming hysteric, a woman 'out-of-control' in language and body, she was 'one of the first signs of a growing sense that women making a lot of noise did not need to be confined to the harem-like rituals of morning and afternoon tea, or the washing up'. Recent television commentators have suggested too that Australian television has been shaped by the way in which it has sought to juggle British and US models, and how this, in turn, has reflected and enhanced a distinctive pluralism in Australian cultural history.

While the ABC relied less heavily on imports than commercial stations, it too showed US programmes as well as those from the BBC, including documentaries and programmes on natural history and the arts as well as light entertainment, drama, and comedy. More significant by the early 1960s, however, was the introduction of locally produced programmes based on BBC innovations particularly in the field of news and current affairs. The first such major programme was *4 Corners*, modelled on the BBC's *Panorama*, which first went to air in Sydney in August 1961. By early 1962, this programme was being recorded on videotape, making it possible to distribute it quickly to each state. As Inglis notes, Australia now had a weekly national television news and current affairs programme at a time when there was as yet no national newspaper and only one national news weekly, the *Bulletin*.

Commercial stations began to follow suit experimenting with various current affairs programmes. Channel 10 in Sydney for a brief time ran an early evening news magazine *Telescope*, which went to air in 1965 four nights a week, modelled on the BBC's *Tonight*; and regional ABC stations in Hobart and Adelaide experimented with similar style programmes. In April 1967, the ABC launched *This Day Tonight* (*TDT*) with Bill Peach, who had worked on *Telescope* as anchorman. Though drawing on the BBC's *Tonight* programme format and style of a daily, racy current affairs show, the ABC programmers set out to make *TDT* what they saw as distinctively Australian. Bill Peach was central to their strategy. Inglis

4 Corners: Australia's foremost investigative current affairs programme has been running continuously since 1961 on the ABC.

The low-budget variety show **In Melbourne Tonight**, compèred by Graham Kennedy, presented an affectionate parody of Australian larrikinism.

describes his accent as 'unusually Australian' by ABC standards; he 'sounded knowledgeable, but not at all pedantic'. Interviews with public figures were conducted with a lack of deference, sometimes with cheek, and Peach maintained a low-key, cheerful, and energetic style for the programme.

TDT was televised nationally from Sydney in the first year, then in 1968 local programmes were fully established with segments of the Sydney version flown to each state to be used by producers the next day if they so desired. It was a hard-hitting programme which became enormously influential in the development of television news and current affairs in Australia and stayed on air until 1979. It was the training ground for a whole generation of television journalists, including Peter Luck, Mike Carlton, Peter Manning, Mike Willesee, and Caroline Jones. The ABC's news and current affairs programmes became amongst its most popular and controversial. The news was and is by far the highest consistently rating programme on the ABC and the first compère of *4 Corners*, Michael Charlton, was named most popular personality by the readers of the Murdoch-owned *TV Week* in 1962. *4 Corners*, still on air after thirty-two years, continues to be Australian television's most important investigative programme. Its exposé of police corruption in Bjielke Petersen's Queensland was the first step in the demise of that government.

In the first fifteen years of television in Australia, some of the most innovative programming was in the field of variety and entertainment, beginning with Graham Kennedy's *In Melbourne Tonight*, which went to air in 1957. Drawing on traditions of vaudeville theatre, these programmes exploited a stereotypical

The Mavis Bramston Show: this hugely popular satirical sketch comedy show led to several sitcom spin-offs in the mid-1960s.

Australian larrikinism, overturning conventions, parodying each other and themselves, and inserting an element of anarchy into evening entertainment. Kennedy had been the protégé of two radio personalities, Nicky and Nancy Lee, who had developed techniques of ad libbing and practical jokes that had revolutionized commercial radio programming style in the 1930s. Kennedy expanded and exploited this style successfully on television, developing his own form of burlesque humour, in a programme that went to air five nights a week.

In 1965 *The Mavis Bramston Show* began on ATN-7. A stagy, revue-style programme, it developed a reputation for the clever acting of a number of its stars, including Gordon Chater, and for its witty political barbs. Also important in this period was the ABC's surprise success *The Aunty Jack Show* (1972), with its humour very much in the tradition of the BBC's *The Goon Show*. Norman Gunston, played by Garry McDonald, had been one of the figures from the second series of this show in 1973, billed as the 'most boring man in Wollongong'. In his own show, *The Norman Gunston Show*, launched in 1975 on the ABC,

McDonald carried out a brilliant parody of television and newspaper conventions of interviewing, as well as the Australian cultural cringe itself. He interviewed international stars visiting Australia, many of whom were unaware of the nature of his programme. Some were outraged, some highly amused, as they encountered his inane, insistent questions and his peculiar attire. In a rather different style, yet also challenging the conventions of television and variety shows, Paul Hogan made a name for himself initially on a talent quest show, *New Faces*, in 1974. Slow-talking, relaxed, he charmed his way into stardom as a parody of the archetypal 'Aussie' male and was given his own programme, *The Paul Hogan Show*, which soon began to appear in the list of top ten programmes.

Paul Hogan perfected his Australian 'ocker' persona in his own television show of the 1970s.

341

Australian Content and the Development of an Australian Production Industry

Of all the debates about television which have convulsed Australian society in the last thirty-five years none has been so passionate or had so much ink spilled over it as the issue of Australian content. The issue had been of concern since at least the 1920s when there were campaigns for more support for an indigenous film industry. When the introduction of television was being discussed in the 1950s the concern continued but the Royal Commission Report made no specific recommendations about Australian programmes, although Section 114 of the Broadcasting and Television Act said that as far as possible the stations should use the services of Australians in the production and presentation of programmes. As we have seen, in the first three years of television, currency restrictions forced the stations to produce Australian material, mainly variety and game shows (as well of course as sport and news), but there was little drama done by the commercial industry until *Homicide* (1964).

There were no specific Australian content rules until 1960 when the ABCB introduced the extremely modest requirement that overall content was to be 40 per cent with four hours a day in peak time. The first drama quota did not appear until 1966 as a result of pressure created by the 1963 report of a Senate Select Committee (known as the Vincent Committee after its Chair) which recommended vigorous measures to support the film and television industry. The first drama quota required two hours a month in peak time. Perhaps the biggest fillip to the developing production industry was the 1960 requirement that all advertisements broadcast on television should be produced in Australia. This assured the existence of a reasonable infrastructure to support production and nurtured the skills of Australian creative and technical personnel. Moran has persuasively argued that the increasing Australian drama quotas that were progressively introduced between 1966 and 1976 (104 hours a year) were never set at levels above what the industry was already achieving. Thus they did not actually stimulate production but rather acted as a safety net, ensuring that once certain levels had been achieved the industry as a whole could not fall below them. Over the years, two of the three networks have regularly exceeded the drama quota, but for the third, the Nine Network, whose forte is news, current affairs, and sport, the quota has operated as a coercive measure which they have often barely complied with.

Facing: the Warlpiri Media Association has 'invented' Aboriginal television 300 kilometres west of Alice Springs. The children's programme **Manyu Wana** helps in cultural and linguistic maintenance among the Warlpiri at Yuendumu and provides an alternative to programmes imported from white Australia and the US.

By the mid-1960s a local television drama production industry was beginning to emerge. In 1964 the Melbourne-based Crawford Productions began making the very successful *Homicide*. Set in Melbourne's inner suburbs, this detective series strove for a distinctively Australian feel in its attention to local detail and Australian accents and idiom. Other police series followed, for example *Division 4* and *Matlock Police*. The ABC established a separate TV drama department in 1965, and in 1967 launched *Bellbird*, Australia's first 'stripped' serial, that ran four

Above: television abolishes the 'tyranny of distance': outdoor television in remote central Australia.

Right: Graham Kennedy exploited Sydney-Melbourne rivalries in his sketch comedy and variety programme, **In Melbourne Tonight**, in which he pioneered the style of quick-witted, irreverent, and vulgar humour that has made him an Australian icon.

Above: Silvio Berlusconi became Prime Minister of Italy with the help of his three wholly owned national television networks. As Prime Minister he also controlled the three public channels of RAI. Public opposition to his media dominance helped bring about his fall from power, after only six months, in 1995.

Left: the unstoppable 'media machine' with the rapacious appetite. In the 1980s many thought that in SKY Rupert Murdoch would overreach himself and his empire implode. Within a decade however SKY was producing a profit of several million dollars a week.

The 1990s has been the decade of satellite television. The new channels fed a worldwide hunger for entertainment, but also for reliable news in the post-Communist and developing worlds.

nights a week for ten years. A precursor in many ways to other very successful soap operas that began to appear in the 1970s, *Bellbird* drew on British examples like *Coronation Street* and *Crossroads* but also on the highly popular and long-running ABC radio serial *Blue Hills*. While the detective series depicted Australian cities and their backstreets, this soap took an Australian country town as its 'typically Australian' setting.

The first stripped serial to appear on prime-time Australian television was the phenomenally successful *Number 96* (1972), produced for the Ten Network by Cash–Harmon. Before *Number 96* there was talk of the government removing its licence on the grounds that Australia could not support three commercial networks but the success of the programme changed all that. Set in a Sydney, inner-city apartment block, it was sexually frank for the time and also very progressive in its politics: one of the leading characters was a homosexual, certainly a breakthrough for Australian television.

However, it was the Grundy organization that was to become synonymous with soap opera in Australia. The Grundy organization already completely dominated the Australian quiz and game show scene with versions of *Wheel of Fortune*, *Sale of the Century*, *The Great Temptation*, and many others, when it also began to dominate the supply of stripped serials in the early evening time slot with titles like *Class of 74* (1974), *The Young Doctors* (1976) (still playing on British television), *The Restless Years*, *Sons and Daughters*, and of course its best-known exports, *Prisoner* and *Neighbours*.

Like *Number 96*, *Prisoner* was an innovation in soap opera form and content. As Curthoys and Docker note, it won twenty-one awards in Australia and maintained high ratings throughout the eight years of its production. Set in 'Wentworth', a female prison, it provided strong character roles for Australian actresses and has fascinated Australian television critics and academics. A number of scholarly analyses have been written examining its popularity with children and young people, as well as the way it parodied the soap opera form at the same time as using it successfully to challenge social norms about deviance, normality, womanhood, and sexual difference.

At the same time as the commercial television drama industry was attaining a certain scale and maturity, in the early to mid-1970s the ABC too increased significantly the scale and scope of its drama production. The victory of a Labor government led by Gough Whitlam in 1972 after twenty-three years of Liberal rule was the culmination of a flowering of Australian cultural nationalism that had begun in the 1960s. The Whitlam government increased the ABC budget by 30 per cent in two successive years and the level of Australian content leapt to over 60 per cent. In 1973–4 the ABC broadcast 130 hours of Australian drama—much of it being soap opera, including the path-breaking *Certain Women*—more than at any time before or since. However, the good times did not last; as Australia went into recession and the Labor government began to falter, funding to the ABC began to fall. In 1975 the Labor government was defeated and the new

343

Liberal-National Party coalition began to cut funding to the ABC even more. While the commercial sector began to expand its drama production with local soap operas and mini-series, often drawing on and seeking to emulate successful ABC programmes, for instance, with *The Sullivans* (1976) and *A Town like Alice* (1981), the ABC turned inwards as it entered a long process of review and reform.

Probably the biggest stimulus to the development of an Australian production industry were the measures introduced by successive governments to assist the film industry. From 1970 on various government bodies, for example the Australian Film Commission established in 1975, provided script development money and made investments in and loans to Australian film and television drama. The policy was successful and soon films like *Picnic at Hanging Rock*, *Sunday Too Far Away*, *My Brilliant Career*, *Breaker Morant*, and *Gallipoli* were attracting large Australian audiences and receiving favourable attention in the international market. In 1980 the government introduced a generous system of tax concessions, known as '10BA' after the section of the Taxation Act that embodied them. These concessions produced a huge upsurge in production levels and budgets, and films like *The Man from Snowy River*, *Crocodile Dundee*, *Bliss*, *Mad Max II*, *Malcolm*, and *Young Einstein* were assisted by them.

Their significance for the television industry was immense. Independent producers with access to the 10BA concessions began producing high-budget, high-quality mini-series and telemovies. This gave television stations access to this prestige product for about a third of its actual production cost and the networks seized the chance with alacrity. The early 1980s was the heyday of the Australian mini-series. Perhaps the most innovative production house was Kennedy–Miller, who had made the Mad Max films. They produced *The Dismissal* (1983), a ten-hour mini-series which outlined the fall of the Whitlam government in 1975, and which scored ratings in the high 30s over four nights. They were also responsible for *The Cowra Breakout* (1984), *Bodyline* (1984), *Dirt-water Dynasty* (1987), and the finest of all, the ten-hour *Vietnam* (1986), tracing the history of a single family through Australia's involvement in the war from 1966 to 1972.

The obsession with historical subjects which had earlier been the province of the Australian cinema was taken over by the mini-series. Between 1984 and 1987 twenty-seven with a historical theme were made out of a total of thirty-four. Titles included *The Anzacs* (1984), *Captain James Cook* (1986), *The Dunera Boys* (1985), *Melba* (1986), and *The Petrov Affair* (1986). Australian mini-series rated consistently far higher than most imported ones and many of them sold well overseas, for example Crawford's *All the Rivers Run* (1983) and *Return to Eden* (1983) produced by the McElroy Brothers. The boom in production consolidated the industry and increased its sophistication and level of skill.

Scheduling practices began to change in the late 1970s and early 1980s. As well as seeking to build up loyal audiences primarily through 'stripping', Australian television began to follow developments which had emerged in the USA with the

opposite **Homicide**: the first Australian-made drama to present national accents, idioms, and settings.

The Cowra Breakout: The innovative production house Kennedy–Miller made the only mini-series on commercial television with subtitles—the story of the escape of Japanese prisoners-of-war from an Australian prison-camp.

televising of the 1976 Olympics. 'Specials' taking up large amounts of prime time over several nights began to be used for sports programmes, drama, movies, and variety. Mini-series worked this way, although they tended to be shown over a longer period of time than other 'specials'.

Along with the changes in programming format went a shift to national programming from lower-budget local programming. Kerry Packer's involvement in televised cricket was one of the early moves in this direction. He had sought exclusive television rights to Test Cricket for the Nine Network in 1976, but had been rebuffed by the Australian Cricket Board (ACB). He proceeded to set up his own opposition to established cricket by signing up leading international cricketers and organizing 'World Series Cricket' (WSC). Australian cricket fans were stunned and many of them initially antagonistic to the showy entertainment-style matches that abandoned many of the conventions of cricket, which in the past had been considered untouchable. Although WSC only existed for a short time—a *rapprochement* was negotiated between Packer and the ACB in 1979—it profoundly altered, as Quick points out, 'the way cricket was presented, packaged and even perceived by a sporting public'. Though Packer was seeking to establish a nation-wide audience for his televised cricket, there were consumers in search of entertainment rather than a loyal citizenry wanting to barrack respectfully for their local team.

By 1986 the ABC would emerge from the long trauma into which the Dix Inquiry would plunge it (see below) and under new management revamped its moribund drama policy. By making alliances with independent producers for the first time, and thus accessing the 10BA concessions, the ABC increased its drama levels from thirty-eight hours in 1987 to over 100 in 1988. Like its commercial counterparts it began to engage in international co-production, most commonly with UK broadcasters, and, using 10BA and co-ventures with overseas partners, produced a large amount of high-quality drama after 1987, including *Edens Lost* (1988), *Act of Betrayal* (1988), and *Bodysurfer* (1989). It also tried out a couple of long-running series before coming up with a winner in *GP*, produced by Roadshow Coote and Carroll and on air since 1989, and more recently, the great local and export success, *Police Rescue* series (1991).

The 10BA concessions were scrapped in 1988 in favour of a new government film investment body, the Film Finance Corporation. This led to a slight contraction in production levels, greatly exacerbated in the television industry by the collapse that was to occur after 1987. With two of the networks in receivership and the third carrying unacceptable levels of debt, from 1990 on there was a period of severe stringency in the industry from which it only began to emerge in 1992. During this period only the ABC made any high-budget drama with the commercial channels relying more than usually on the volume of soap opera—*Neighbours*, *E Street*, *Home and Away*, *Chances*, *A Country Practice*—to fulfil their quota requirements.

Oddly enough, in this atmosphere of crisis, there was a flurry of experimentation and innovation, especially in comedy. A number of brilliant new sketch comedy programmes made their appearance in the late 1980s—*Fast Forward*, *The Comedy Company*, *The Big Gig*, and all of the programmes made by the ABC's new comedy star, Andrew Denton. Situation comedy too became a more prominent part of Australian schedules; the ABC had had the hit, *Mother and Son*, since the mid-1980s and Seven responded with the long-running *Hey Dad!* Both of these have sold overseas.

Australian content regulation continued as a highly contentious issue throughout the 1980s. The Australian Broadcasting Tribunal (ABT) commenced an inquiry into the issue in 1983 which was only completed in 1989 after a number of court battles caused protracted delays. During this inquiry, as expected, the networks argued against regulation and the various interest and community groups, most notably the entertainment unions, argued for the importance of continued quotas. In 1990 the ABT introduced a new regulation which did not alter the level of Australian content requirements but made them more flexible and strengthened the definition of 'Australian' because of a perceived threat from the increased prevalence of international co-production. As the regulation stood in 1993, a drama programme could only qualify for full Australian quota if it was written, directed, and produced by Australians and if the script had an Australian theme or 'perspective'.

Policy Debates

Two significant government inquiries into broadcasting and television were set up in the late 1970s: the Green Inquiry into the broadcasting system which began in 1976 and the lengthy and exhaustive Dix Inquiry into the ABC, which began in 1979 and lasted for two years. The most important recommendation of the former report was to abolish the ABCB and to replace it with a body with strengthened powers, the Australian Broadcasting Tribunal. The ABCB, which was only an advisory board, had received much criticism over the years for being too weak and too close to the industry it was regulating. The ABT would be an independent statutory authority and would have the power to grant, renew, and revoke licences, set standards, authorize changes in ownership and control, and, most important of all, it would hold its inquiries in public. The Green report also recognized that technological change was about to transform broadcasting and accordingly recommended that a task force be set up to inquire into cable television and radio and satellite broadcasting systems. Australia was to move with infinite reluctance to embrace the possibilities of new technologies and even now has no cable or DBS services.

The Dix Report into the ABC strongly reaffirmed the importance of the ABC to the Australian community; it undertook research that indicated that 80 per cent of people wanted the ABC to serve the whole community and 93 per cent said they tuned in at least once a week. However, it criticized ABC management for the poor morale it found among staff, outdated management and budgeting practices, and inflexible organizational structures. In the wake of the Dix Report the ABC began an agonizing and protracted period of reform in 1981 which was hardly completed by 1986 when present Managing Director, David Hill, took over. The process chewed up at least one Managing Director (Geoffrey White-head), whose proposals for change were greeted with suspicion by staff, management, and the public alike. After five years of erosion and demoralization under Fraser any change at all looked like an attack on the now sacred ideals of public service broadcasting and the ABC's independence.

The new ABT immediately attracted criticism from broadcasting campaigners when the government appointed its first chairman, Bruce Gyngell, and as a member Jim Oswin, former General Manager of the Seven Network. Having been associated with first the Nine and then the Seven Networks in Australia and with Lew Grade's ATV in Britain, Gyngell was regarded as being far too identified with the commercial industry, and, hardly a discreet or circumspect man, he had often made clear his scepticism about regulation. However, the new tribunal's first major task, an Inquiry into Self-Regulation, gave the campaigners some heart. It reaffirmed the importance of direct regulation in the crucial areas of Australian content and children's television, the two areas which of course bite deepest financially, although Chairman Gyngell put in a dissenting report on the question of quotas for Australian content.

In 1980 the ABT thwarted Rupert Murdoch's attempts to develop a network on a par with that owned by the Packer and Fairfax *Herald* and *Weekly Times* interests by refusing to approve his acquisition of Channel 10 in Melbourne. The Tribunal had previously approved his take-over of the Channel 10 in Sydney even though his Australian residential status was dubious. Murdoch took the matter to appeal and there was every sign that he would lose but the Fraser government obligingly stepped in, and with the notorious 'Murdoch amendments' of 1981 changed the Broadcasting and Television Act to facilitate his plans. These changes weakened the public interest considerations that the ABT was permitted to take into account when considering transfers of ownership. This meant that by the early 1980s the four big media barons were firmly in control of Australian television. Packer's (by now it was Kerry not Sir Frank) Consolidated Press owned TCN-9 Sydney and GTV-9 in Melbourne. Fairfax owned Channel 7 in Sydney while the Seven station in Melbourne was owned by the *Herald* and *Weekly Times* and Rupert Murdoch owned the two Channel 10 stations in Sydney and Melbourne.

In 1978 a government task force had concluded that Australia needed to develop a domestic satellite which would be government-owned and which would bring broadcasting services to remote parts of Australia. The Packer interests made a detailed submission to the inquiry arguing again for the establishment of national networking of television services. As result of this the government made a commitment to a domestic satellite and in 1981 AUSSAT was formed to own and operate the system. The ABC used the satellite to begin broadcasting to remote areas through its Homestead and Community Broadcasting Satellite Services (HACBSS) scheme.

During the early 1980s the Tribunal conducted inquiries into satellite, cable, and RSTV services, basically recommending that such services should be introduced with certain safeguards. However, the new Labor government proved extremely cautious about the idea of introducing more services into the television mix, inviting the inference that they were responding to pressure from established television interests who feared competition. After a flurry of activity around various options for pay television in the early 1980s, the government introduced a moratorium on its introduction which was to last until 1990; they preferred to concentrate on their plans to extend television choice to regional Australia—the so-called equalization policy (see below).

However, in the second half of the 1980s the government did authorize the establishment of a new class of licence, the Remote Commercial Television Licence (RCTS), which would use the satellite to broadcast to three remote areas of the continent, Central (the Northern Territory and the north of South Australia), North Queensland, and Western Australia. In each of these vast areas

349

there are only a few tens of thousands of inhabitants and thus they do not form viable advertising markets. The services require and receive varying amounts of subsidy from their respective state governments. Because of the large numbers of Aborigines in their reception area they are obliged to programme Aboriginal content.

The licence in the Central region, Imparja, is operated by an Aboriginal-controlled group, CAAMA (the Central Australian Aboriginal Media Association). While the bulk of the programming on Imparja is of a general commercial nature there is also a high level of Aboriginal content, with programmes in a variety of Aboriginal languages. Although these remote services are very marginal and fragile, they have provided a focus and a stimulus for Aboriginal people to make programmes and to be trained as operators.

Redefining the Television Audience

Perhaps the most significant development in both reflecting and shaping changes in the way the television audience has been conceptualized in Australia was the establishment of SBS-TV in October 1980. An ethnic television service had been an election promise by Malcolm Fraser, the then Prime Minister, during the Federal election campaign of 1977. According to Andrew Jakubowicz, Fraser believed that 'a liberal conservative society could best be maintained by an acceptance of cultural diversity, where this did not threaten the basic economic relations of the society'. The issue of 'ethnic' or multicultural broadcasting, and of multiculturalism more generally, became a subject of sometimes bitter debate throughout the 1980s. For the ethnic communities it represented formal recognition of their political importance and cultural legitimacy. Others saw multiculturalism and SBS as socially divisive and opposed any cultural and social initiatives which were not assimilationist. Left-wing and some ethnic critics of SBS saw it catering too much to middle-class tastes for European movies and specialist arts programmes.

What is clear is that SBS-TV has transformed the nature of public service television in Australia. Its programming policy is deliberately minoritarian, seeking to build different audiences for different programmes, rather than attempting to please 'a general audience'. Language groups constitute a significant proportion of its target audiences, as well as socially disadvantaged groups like women, Aboriginal Australians, religious groups, the hearing impaired, and gays and lesbians. It also caters for minority arts-cultural constituencies. In focusing on language groupings as a definition of ethnicity rather than nationality, it has managed to avoid—although not totally—some of the more strident nationalist or separatist politics that periodically divides ethnic communities. Particular programmes, as well as the mix of programmes it provides, also create new audiences across these groupings, thereby ensuring that SBS does not simply reflect but is actively involved in shaping current forms of social identification.

In a typical week a viewer can see arts documentaries from Europe, the USA and Canada, feature films from Greece, Iran, Egypt, Poland, Turkey, Russia, China, etc., soap operas from Holland, Brazil, and Japan, and soccer from Italy. Russian viewers can see a daily news in Russian but all other programmes are subtitled in English, which is of course the common language across different groups and reinforces the idea that multicultural television is also for viewers of Anglo-Celtic origin. There is a good daily news service emphasizing overseas news from Asia, the Middle East, and Latin America as the more traditional sources, news in Greek and Italian, the most widely spoken community languages, and a weekly community participation show, *Vox Populi*.

Sydney writer and critic, Anna Maria Dell'oso, pays tribute to the way in which SBS offered new forms of social identification. Born of rural immigrant Italian parents, growing up in Melbourne in the 1960s, she recalls the importance of television in her search to find out how to behave in Australian society. But 'the average family' she saw on 'The Box' was nothing like hers: it was English-speaking and American, living in a world of gingham curtains, country sofas, fathers' 'dens', and angora sweaters. Father worked in an office, mother stayed home all day, keeping the house neat, and the daughters all had boyfriends, wore make-up, and had heart-to-heart chats with their parents. Dell'oso had left home by the time SBS-TV went to air. Her first viewing of this new form of Australian television had a dramatic impact:

When I first saw SBS television, in my 20s, I cried. . . . I was living in a share-house of young artists and journalists in inner-city Sydney, we all tuned in to the first broadcast. I hoped that none of my flatmates saw how it was affecting me. I didn't expect to get so emotional . . . Maybe I cried because I felt some part [*sic*] my story, the drama of my life, had finally been officially placed into the jigsaw puzzle that is society, Australian life. Maybe I cried because someone was speaking not only to me but to people all around the country in my accent, in the language of my parents. Maybe it was simply the sight of another wog reading the evening news—a news service that connected Australia with the rest of the world and not just a few murders in Sydney and Melbourne before turning over to sport—that impressed me.

Dell'oso points here to the way SBS-TV challenged all previous notions of what Australian television was. As well as being a space where different languages could be heard, SBS asserted the place of the accented voice in notions of Australian English.

ABC television had been formed within a notion of public service broadcasting as shaping a modern citizenry of loyal and educated individuals who all shared a set of common values and interests. It had interpreted this mission in 'high-brow' terms as requiring the cultivation of taste in the general public and for a long time looked to the BBC as a central cultural authority in defining if not providing 'taste'. As early as 1962 there were calls for a second ABC channel so as to accommodate both more popular and more specialist needs and these were to continue throughout the 1970s but the ABC was never to persuade the government of the need. The advent of the SBS in 1980 more or less put paid to the ABC's hopes though throughout the 1980s they continued to press to take over operation of the SBS network.

Though SBS-TV achieves a smaller audience share than the ABC, with about 3 per cent in prime time as against the ABC's 15 per cent, and is also driven in part by the desire to seek a larger proportion of the television audience, it has successfully introduced a quite different notion of public service into the world of Australian television. Through its news programmes, its emphasis on a wide range of sporting interests, through its importing policies, and through its own programmes, SBS-TV has become a public television service that not only speaks of the diversity but actively shapes this feature of the Australian population. It has defined public service television as concerned with reflecting and contributing to a new definition of citizenship in which diversity is recognized and valued.

Yet another form of public service television was introduced in Australia in

Aboriginal communities are using 1990s' technology to reinforce their 40,000 year-old culture by satellite broadcasting programmes in Aboriginal language.

1987 with the establishment of the Broadcasting for Remote Aboriginal Communities Scheme (BRACS). Set up as the result of the Federal Government Task Force, chaired by Eric Wilmot, on existing and potential Aboriginal media needs, the basic philosophy behind this scheme, according to Helen Molnar, was 'to give Aborigines in remote areas the means of making radio and television programs as a mechanism for the promotion and preservation of local languages, culture and lifestyles'. Basic equipment and some training in its use is provided, but communities have to provide an air conditioned building themselves and pay for electricity, videos, and cassettes. Though a significant number of communities have been equipped with BRACS units (eighty are in place in 1993), these requirements are prohibitive for many communities. The units can receive both ABC and commercial radio and television, as well as enabling local communities to make and transmit their own programmes, embedding this material into the mainstream programming by turning off the main signal and transmitting their own programmes locally. Commercial broadcasters were initially reluctant for their programmes to be interrupted and used selectively in this way, but new legislation introduced in 1993 for community television licences which enables each BRACS unit to become a licensed broadcaster has circumvented this problem.

Controversy has surrounded this scheme from the time of its inception. Eric Michaels, a researcher for the Australian Institute of Aboriginal Studies, criticized the Wilmot Task Force for failing to consult sufficiently with the Aboriginal communities themselves. His report *The Aboriginal Invention of Television* and subsequent publications pointed to the complexity of issues involved that went far beyond the initial paternalistic philosophy of cultural preservation of the BRACS scheme. He documented the way at least some remote communities had already begun their own television services, using pirated equipment and VCRs to transmit their own locally produced content, primarily in their own language. These initiatives, he argued, need to be understood in the context of a considerable interest and yet also concern among Aborigines in the early 1980s about television becoming available to remote communities. In particular, the issue of Aboriginal languages was a major issue:

The problem of language signals a more general problem of social diversity that introduced media pose for indigenous peoples everywhere: how to respond to the insistent pressure towards standardisation, the homogenising tendencies of contemporary world culture?

Policies of multiculturalism, Michaels argued, threaten to reduce Aboriginal people to 'Aborigines', a life-style or 'cultural heritage' collectivity rather than a diverse group of peoples. His research provided evidence of how particular Aboriginal communities had already found, before the introduction of BRACS, ways to use television technology that conformed to the basic premises of their traditions and enabled them to find ways of strengthening, revitalizing their

353

cultures, rather than protecting them as museum pieces. Although there is little documentation available about how the BRACS units are being used, there is some evidence, however, that they too are now functioning in this way in many instances.

Media Upheavals in the 1980s and 1990s

The establishment of the national satellite system in the early 1980s had set the groundwork for national networking. In November 1986 the Communications Minister announced a new policy for television: there would be 'equalization' of services between the city and the country (country Australia would now get three commercial stations instead of one); bigger and thus more viable service areas in the country would be created by a process of 'aggregation' of smaller ones; competition in media would be created by introducing for the first time cross-media ownership limits. In the then Treasurer, Paul Keating's colourful words, media owners would have to decide whether to be 'princes of print or queens of the screen'. In spite of the fact that the Labor government which came to office in 1983 has often seemed to look after the interests of the big media owners quite as much as the conservative Liberal-National Party ever did, this move to lessen concentration seems to have been based on a genuine desire to increase media diversity in Australia. It may have stemmed from a conviction that the Fairfaxes, the Packers, and Rupert Murdoch had never been particularly pro-Labor, though this changed from time to time.

This seemingly large blow to the big media proprietors was softened by the fact that the infamous 'two-station' rule (no one could own more than two stations) was to be removed. It was replaced, after bitter debate on both sides of politics, by a 'media-reach' rule which limited individual owners to stations which were capable of reaching no more than 60 per cent of the population. This, together with the equalization policy, opened the way to national networking across Australia. The 60 per cent rule meant that a single proprietor could own stations in the four biggest markets of Sydney, Melbourne, Adelaide, and Brisbane and stay just within 60 per cent of the Australian population.

The possibilities offered by this new arrangement made television licences even more attractive than they had been before. When all of the big proprietors, Kerry Packer, the Fairfax organization (which had bought HSV7 from the *Herald and Weekly Times* in 1987) and Rupert Murdoch (who had taken over the *Herald and Weekly Times* in the same year amid determined community opposition) opted to be 'princes of print', there were new players available only too eager to buy into this medium with apparently boundless possibilities. West Australian beer and property baron Alan Bond bought the Nine Network for $1 billion, an unprecedentedly high sum, the Seven Network went to Christopher Skase, and the Ten Network to a supermarket development company, Westfield Holdings. A stockbroking firm estimated the value of the Nine and Ten network before the changes to have been $800,000. They were sold for $1.8 billion in highly geared deals.

Sadly, the disaster that ensued probably did more to put Australian media on the international map than anything else. Alan Bond was the first in trouble, with an ABT inquiry into whether he was a 'fit and proper person' to own a television licence resulting from his attempt to bribe the Queensland Premier, Sir Joh Bjielke Petersen. However, it was the rise in interest rates, and collapse of stock prices, after the stock market crash of 1987, combined with ruinous extravagance in management styles and bidding wars for overseas programmes that finally brought all the new media owners down. By 1990 the Seven and Ten networks were in receivership and Kerry Packer had bought back the Nine network for $200 million.

In the mid-1980s the government initiated a debate about the shape of the Australian broadcasting landscape and the need to amend the Broadcasting Act to introduce more competition and to recognize the changes that were occurring because of new technology. A series of departmental reports and parliamentary inquiries were held, culminating at the end of 1991 in the release, not of a policy paper for a new broadcasting regime, but a draft bill. This proposed a quite new framework for Australian broadcasting, one that was supposedly technology-neutral, that envisaged a combination of 'light-touch' regulation, self-regulation in the area of content, and considerable deregulation, especially in the area of radio where it abolished cross-media and foreign ownership rules. In television it proposed the introduction of satellite pay television and further competition in television after 1997. It also introduced price-based auctions for licences and virtually automatic licence renewal. The requirement for public inquiries was also removed. The ABT was to be replaced by the Australian Broadcasting Authority.

The rationale for these changes was that new technologies had replaced 'spectrum scarcity' with 'spectrum plenitude' and thus the task of responding to consumer preferences could be left to market mechanisms to a greater extent than before. The only areas of content in which it was envisaged that the regulator would have a role were Australian content and childrens' programming. During 1992 a slightly modified version of this bill became law. However, at time of writing the area of pay television is in total confusion. Because of a number of bungles and unforeseen circumstances it is unlikely that Australia will have pay television delivered by satellite before 1995.

Australian Programmes to the World

In spite of the financial problems in the Australian television industry in the late 1980s and in spite of the bungled nature of the broadcasting changes of the early 1990s, the Australian television scene is surprisingly robust. Due largely to the consistency and comparative stringency of Australian content requirements

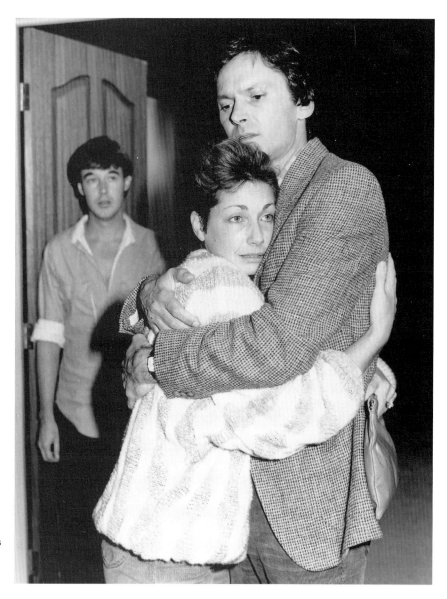

Sons and Daughters: one of a number of Grundy serials now being reformatted for various European television markets.

since 1976 and to the strong support given to film and television production, Australia has developed an industry that is making an impact in the world television market out of proportion to the size of the population. It is helped in this by the fact that it makes programmes in English; this increasingly is a 'language of advantage' in the world television scene. Australian television has been protected from competition from services on alternative delivery mechanisms and from cross-border flows longer than any comparable country. This has assured it of reasonably stable advertising revenues in real terms and enabled it to continue to provide a high level of quality Australian programming.

Since 1988 Australia has been looking increasingly overseas for financing and markets. A number of companies now exist which are successful packagers of programmes for export. By far the most spectacular success belongs to the Grundy organization, which has branches in about ten countries and which has become one of the largest packagers of game shows in the world. In 1991 it produced fifty hours of television a week world-wide. It is currently enjoying considerable success in format-selling; at present it is making Dutch and German versions of its 1977 soap, *The Restless Years* and similar versions of *Prisoner* are planned. Other producers with good overseas records include Crawfords, Roadshow Coote and Carroll, Village Roadshow, Southern Star, Film Australia, Beyond International, the Australian Children's Television Foundation, and the ABC. The ABC established an advertiser-supported satellite service to South East Asia in 1993 and other television entrepreneurs, for example Kerry Packer, will follow.

The broadcasting changes of the early 1990s were concerned mainly with the commercial system but during this period changes were occurring in the national broadcasters too. In 1992 the SBS was placed under its own Act of Parliament and it was authorized to accept advertisements as a source of finance. Advertising is limited to the spaces between programmes and so far appears to have done little to influence the programming philosophy of the network, although it is probably too early to judge fully.

The ABC has been becoming progressively more entrepreneurial while still retaining its public service mission. In addition to its quasi-commercial satellite service in Asia, it will also be a player in pay TV. Though some commentators have found these moves controversial, it continues to offer independent news and current affairs programmes and high-quality drama with some modest forays into innovation and the development of new talent (for example *Seven Deadly Sins*). It continues to cater to minority interests in sport; it produces lifestyle programmes and a new current affairs programme, *Attitudes*, especially for young people; it produces an Aboriginal magazine and arts programme, and programmes for rural Australia; and it is attempting to address issues of multiculturalism in its hiring practices and programming. The debate about public service broadcasting that has preoccupied other societies, for example the UK, as the deregulatory reforms of the 1980s take effect seems to be muted in Australia. Perhaps this is only a temporary effect of the preoccupation with the commercial sector. Australia is still on the edge of changes that occurred elsewhere ten years earlier. How a 'multi-channel environment' affects and interacts with the cultural fabric of Australian society, how it modifies the sense of a 'public sphere', how it creates or closes down spaces for a diversity of voices is not yet in view. The next ten years will probably see more changes in Australia's television landscape than occurred in the first thirty-five.

15

Africa

Charles Okigbo

Television and National Independence

Africa—that sprawling continent that will never cease to amaze both natives and foreigners alike—is not one unit. Historically, geographically, and politically, it is the epitome of diversity. Above all else, it is characterized by contrapuntal attributes. For instance, though it is the oldest continent, the study of its history 'came of age' only in the 1960s, coinciding with the emergence of many newly independent modern African states. One can only attempt therefore a somewhat cursory and arbitrary excursion into the history, role, and future of television in certain African countries.

There is evidence that Africa is the birthplace not only of the human species, but also of many technological innovations of the ancient world of human prehistory. The reality today is that Africa is not leading in any area of modern technology, least of all television, which, among the modern mass media, is a late-comer to the continent. Other parts of the developing world beat Africa in the race for introducing television.

Mexico had its first television in 1950, and two years later Venezuela and the Dominican Republic got theirs, followed by the Philippines in 1953, Columbia in 1954, with Guatemala, Nicaragua, and Uruguay achieving that status in 1956. In 1958 Chile, Peru, and Iran established their first television stations.

Some African countries did not lag far behind. In many cases, television seemed to be the handmaiden of political independence. In 1954 Morocco established its television station, followed two years later by Algeria. Nigeria, the giant of Africa, established hers in 1959, on the eve of her independence in 1960.

Between 1962 and 1965 television was introduced to Kenya, Uganda, the Congo (Brazzaville), the Sudan, Zambia, Upper Volta, Gabon, Côte d'Ivoire, Senegal, and Ghana. Making the link between the new television stations and the political developments of the period, Dietrich Berwanger rightly argues that 'it was the time when most of the colonies in Africa were becoming independent, and quite often a television station found its way into the colonial powers' farewell gifts'. That might well be the case for some countries, but in a great many others local initiative and the desire to use television as a political weapon played vital roles.

Considering the relatively low technological developments in most of the African countries at the time, it is amazing that so many of them were able to afford the initial high costs involved in introducing television. In this respect, African countries were not far behind more prosperous and modernizing countries, among which Korea and Taiwan established their television stations in 1961 and 1962 respectively, only after Morocco, Algeria, and Nigeria. Singapore and Malaysia joined the club in 1963, the same year as Ghana. Kenya beat them to it by one year, establishing its first television station in 1962, a year before independence, as with Nigeria. But unlike Nigeria, where a regional government in

Independence celebrations in Kenya, 1963. African countries did not lag behind more prosperous and modernizing countries like Korea and Taiwan, which established their first stations in 1961 and 1962 after Morocco, Algeria, and Nigeria.

359

opposition had taken the lead, in Kenya it was the central government that did this, primarily for the settler community of Europeans and Indians.

In Zambia, television came in 1961 at the instance of a private firm, London Rhodesia Company (Lonrho), which established its television operations at Kitwe. Realizing the political impact of the medium, which can be used for mass mobilization of even illiterate viewers, the government bought the facility in 1964 and subsequently opened another station at the capital city of Lusaka. From the most humble beginning, television broadcasting in Zambia developed fast to the point that by 1986, as Francis Kasoma explains, most of rural Zambia could, technically, watch television, although many of the people could not afford the sets and, in some cases, electrical power was not available. Microwave links had brought the television signal to the provincial centres of Chipata, Kasama, Solwezi, Mongu, and Livingstone.

The introduction of television in many African countries takes a coloration that in some respects reflects the geopolitical culture and/or commercial character of the states. For instance, in Nigeria, with its wide variety of ethnic groups and highly developed social organizations, many of which compete with the federal government for power and influence, television first came at the instance of a regional government. Following the removal of broadcasting from the exclusive (central government) list as a result of the 1953 constitutional conference, the 1954 Constitution provided that regional governments could establish broadcasting stations.

Thus it was that the Western Nigerian government, in association with a British firm, Overseas Re-Diffusion Limited, established the Western Nigeria Broadcasting Service-Western Nigerian Television (WNBS-WNTV) to operate a radio station and also a television station, the latter becoming operational just a year before national independence on 1 October 1960. WNTV's slogan was: 'First in Africa' (notwithstanding that Algeria and Morocco already had operational television stations). The stage was set in Nigeria for interregional rivalry in television operations.

Thus, one year after the establishment of WNTV, the Eastern Nigerian government established its own television station, appropriately called the Eastern Nigerian Television Service (ENTV), with the slogan 'Second to None'. This was later to make a historic contribution in the prosecution of the Nigeria–Biafra war that raged between 1967 and 1970. Many objective Nigerians agree with Biafrans and international observers that Biafra won the propaganda war, which was orchestrated by Radio Biafra, the wartime name of the Eastern Nigerian Broadcasting Service, an amalgamation of the radio and television operations.

The other political region in Nigeria—the North—accepted it was lagging behind in the race for television operations, but was determined to improve its position. In March 1962 it established its television station, Radio Television Kaduna, as an arm of the Broadcasting Company of Northern Nigeria (BCNN), and with that, the war of the regions temporarily cooled down. In April 1962 the

opposite Watching football on television in Lusaka, Zambia. Zambian television was inaugurated in 1961 by a private firm, the London Rhodesian Company (Lonrho).

federal government balanced the equation by establishing the federal television station, the Nigerian Television Service (NTS) on Victoria Island, Lagos.

The strong hand of foreign partners was everywhere evident in the early attempts to establish television stations. In the case of the Nigerian Television Service (NTS) the foreign partner was the American giant RCA, which outbid Siemens and Marconi in the tenders for the establishment of national television services. The contract with RCA was signed on 23 February 1961, though actual telecasting started in April 1962 on Channel 10, Lagos.

The history of television in Nigeria is intimately linked to the political history of the country, not only in the sense that the regions pre-empted the federal government and thereby set the agenda for managing television, but also in respect of the control and use of the medium as a political weapon. New structures of state administration invariably led to new structures of television establishment, control, and use. With the abolition of the regional governments and the subsequent creation of states in 1969, the new states that did not inherit television stations felt the first need was to establish one. A further balkanization exercise in 1975 left the country with a nineteen-state structure, instead of the original twelve-state arrangement. The new states again felt they had to have their own television (and radio) stations, and they now have.

The federal government, always trailing behind, in April 1976 promulgated Decree No. 24 to establish the Nigerian Television Authority (NTA), the umbrella organization for managing all federal government-owned television stations in the federal and state capitals. Today the federal government in Nigeria controls television and radio stations located in the old and new federal capitals of Lagos and Abuja, as well as those located in the individual capital cities of the thirty states in the country. Additionally, nearly all the thirty states have their own state-controlled radio and television stations—as these are now accepted as the first order of business for any newly created state.

Another African country that has an interesting history of television is the People's Republic of the Congo, a largely French-speaking Central African country located on the Atlantic Coast and with a modest population of about 2 million people. Congo is reputed to be the first French-speaking African country to establish a television station, and the third country in tropical Africa to do so, after Nigeria and Kenya. Congo started transmission on 28 November 1962, twenty-seven years after it had established its first radio station in 1935.

The reasons for establishing a television station in the Congo were neither to pre-empt the federal government, as was the case in Nigeria, nor to satisfy the needs of foreigners, as was the case in Kenya. It was not a marriage of the private and public sectors as was the case in Zambia, where Lonrho initiated and government took over. Rather it was uniquely French in conception. It was France's intention to deck out the Congo as a show-case of its post-colonial policy in Africa. But even when that policy changed a short while later, the television service remained. The Congolese Radio and Television Service (Office de Radiodiffusion et Télévision Congolaise—ORTC) was originally run by French staff until indigenous personnel who had gone to France for training returned a few months later. Within one year, all but three staff members were Congolese nationals.

Television use is very popular in the Congo, where there is now, in the 1990s, about one television set per fifty inhabitants, with more than 10 per cent of all sets being colour receivers. Part of the rapid development of television in the Congo is attributable to the rivalry occasioned by the clarity of transmissions from Kinshasa (Zaïre), which provides the viewing public in Brazzaville with a second channel using the same languages in addition to Kiswahili and Tchilouba.

Though television was already firmly established in some African countries in the early 1960s, there was still a pocket of countries where the novel medium was not established even in the 1980s. Today, mainland Tanzania still lacks a television station, though it receives signals from neighbouring Zanzibar. Among those countries that have been classified as the laggards are Niger, which launched her television station in 1980, Lesotho and Cameroon (1985), and Chad (only in 1987).

The promise of television has not been realized yet as the medium is still the least active medium, with many stations running somewhat haphazard operations that are remarkable only in their failure to inspire any strong following. The difficulty is compounded by the paucity of television sets, now aggravated by the poor economic conditions. Taking the continent as a whole, 1965 showed there were 1.9 television sets per 1,000 inhabitants. In 1975, this increased to 6.2, and in 1986 it went up to 25, but even at this, it was a far cry from what obtained in other parts of the world. There was also a wide disparity between individual countries, with Egypt posting the highest figure at 83 receivers per 1,000, followed by pre-war Sudan with 52. Congo and Gabon (both French-speaking) recorded 20, while Ghana was 10, Uganda 6.2, Kenya 5.4, Nigeria 5.6, and Niger 2.4.

Themes on African Television

The themes on African television are as varied as the motives and philosophical principles that undergird the stations. In some cases, these change as often as the managements of the individual stations change; and often station management changes with the government. It is a standing joke among the staff of the Organization of African Unity (OAU) that no Minister of Information in any of the member states has managed to attend three successive meetings of the OAU Council of Ministers. This is because of incessant cabinet changes, and, in some cases, changes of government.

Politics

Regardless of what type of government an African state might have, a permanent theme on African television is politics. It is safe to assume that the apolitical television station in Africa does not exist, for it is in the nature of the general mass media in Africa to be seen and used as political tools, if not on the offensive, at least for warding off the inevitable personal attacks that are part of African politics.

In the typical case of Nigeria, the seed was sown when the Premier of the Western Region, the late Chief Obafemi Awolowo, was denied permission 'to air his views through the national radio services' in reply to allegedly false accusations levelled against his party by the Governor, Sir John Stuart MacPherson. According to Mike Egbon:

Chief Awolowo was disappointed by this denial of access. He considered [that] the only way out of such a dilemma in the future would be to have his own regionally controlled mass medium. The idea was nursed and it grew until the Western Region of Nigeria decided to set up its own broadcasting services . . . October 31, 1959.

Politics has continued to be a major variable informing many decisions, about establishing television stations as well as about choosing events and news makers to cover. Many Africans accept this without apology, as the rightful role for television. According to Chen Chimutengwende, Zimbabwean Minister of Infor-

Presidents Arap Moi, Barre, Mugabe, Chissano, Kaunda, Mwinyi. Television and radio stations have more armoured vehicles and ammunition than some military or border posts.

mation and Broadcasting, 'the purpose of broadcasting in underdeveloped [*sic*] societies is not merely to educate, inform and entertain as is the case in the West. Mass Communication has a direct political mission . . . the "agitational" or "propaganda" element has to be there if mass mobilisation is to take place.'

The political import has now taken a new dimension with the critical role broadcasting stations play during military *coups d'état*. The vicinity of radio and television stations in Africa is usually full of tanks and artillery always in readiness to ward off coup makers who know that their success or failure probably depends on how soon they take control of the broadcasting stations.

It may not be purely accidental that the era of the first military coups in Africa coincides with the introduction of television in the 1960s. The first Nigerian coup of January 1966, as well as the second one of July 1966, made good use of the broadcasting stations, and in both cases the young officers were emboldened by the success stories of their colleagues in other developing countries where military regimes had replaced elected governments. Among these are Zaïre (Congo Brazzaville), where Mobutu successfully led the military revolt of 25 November 1965; Upper Volta (now Burkina Faso), where Lamizana overthrew the civilian government on 3 January 1966; Algeria, where Boumedienne came to power on 19 June 1965, and Benin Republic, where Christopher Soglo led the revolt of 22 December 1965; while in the Central African Republic Jean Bedel Bokassa took over power on 1 January 1966.

It may be argued that radio plays a more critical role in attempts to take power by force, but it is also true that television stations play decisive roles in supporting or refusing to go along with the radio messages. In Nigeria, for instance, supportive television stations fly the national flag on the screen, play military music, and intermittently broadcast the message of the mutineers. Whenever coups occur, government agencies, ministries, departments, and parastatals are always found to be in great disarray as a leadership vacuum is created, and the broadcasting stations become the *de facto* government.

Though the military is becoming more unpopular as a political actor in Africa, its love affair with television is not about to cool, as military dictators now use the medium more than ever before in their new-found strategy of resigning their military positions only to run for the Presidency and declare themselves winners. All across the continent, the picture of the incumbent President is the most permanent icon in television news. So the theme of politics will probably remain an evergreen in African television programming.

Education

Next in importance to the political is the educational role of television. Education is always a vote catcher and all governments are also genuinely altruistic towards education to some extent. Thus the politicians present the education argument to the people in order to secure their massive approval and support for the introduction or expansion of television. In recognition of the educational role of television, Chief Obafemi Awolowo, the first politician to canvass for the establishment of a television station in tropical Africa, argued that 'television [would] serve as teacher and entertainer, and as a stimulus to us all to transform Nigeria into a modern and prosperous nation'.

Early television in Africa was a strong instructional medium which was used for both formal training in academic subjects and general information on civics, health, agriculture, and even morals. In addition to instructional academic programmes imported from the United States and Europe, some African television stations now have locally produced lessons in mathematics and the natural sciences. Other instructional packages come in the form of quizzes or school competitions for college students. Television is being used extensively for public service and civic behaviour campaigns.

Referring to the situation in Nigeria, Sylvanus Ekwelie has argued that it is no longer in doubt, if ever it was, that the mass media can and do supplement existing educational facilities, nor that the media (including television) can at times supplant these facilities. Wilbur Schramm once reported, at the time when many African countries were launching their television stations, that television could be as good (sometimes better) a teacher as conventional classroom instructors. According to his report of 1964 'out of 393 experimental comparisons of classes taught chiefly by television with classes taught by conventional classroom methods, there was no difference (in what the pupils could do in the final examination) in the case of 65 per cent of all the comparisons; in 21 per cent of the cases, the television class wrote significantly better examinations than the conventional class, and only in 14 per cent was the conventional class superior'.

On the whole, the promise that television is supposed to hold for educational purposes in Africa has gone largely unrealized because of the inherent limitations of the medium (limited reach) and also the motive behind television use (fun, game, and play). Tapio Varis in his 1985 study of the structure of television programmes in six African countries (Côte d'Ivoire, Kenya, Nigeria, Senegal, Uganda, and Zimbabwe) found that 'on the whole, educational and cultural or generally developmental broadcasts do not appear to have gained significant attention'. He noted further that 'the improvement of production standards is constrained by lack of trained personnel and other necessary resources'.

Joseph Mbindyo's study of Kenyan television viewers did not show any habitual viewing of educational programmes. Rather it showed that, whereas 22 per cent 'had no particular favourite programme', 18 per cent mentioned news as their favourite, 15 per cent chose sport, and 8 per cent chose movies. Zambia had an ambitious programme when in October 1964 it established the Educational Broadcasting Service (EBS), which produced its first programmes for schools in February 1965. According to Francis Kasoma, 'EBS was set up to help improve the quality of teaching and learning for teachers and students and in schools and colleges . . . Thousands of radio and television sets were distributed to schools throughout the country.' Teachers were recruited to present the lessons on radio and television. But in spite of all these, by 1986 'both the television equipment in Kitwe and the sound recording studios in Lusaka were not operational', and thus the educational television project died naturally (though the radio wing survived).

In the Congo, though the two vernacular languages of Lingala and Munuku-tumba are used for the evening news, nutrition, education, and health programmes, the Congolese audience was found to have a decided preference for American action series and some local productions. In many parts of Africa today, educational television is not the instant university that the early advocates of instructional electronic media hoped it would be.

Entertainment

African television is primarily an entertainment medium, much in the character of such traditional forums as the village square, the community market, and the age-grade gathering, which are all communication situations that facilitate the common exchange of information and sharing of values. The entertainment motive was not lost on the early advocates of television in Africa. Not surprisingly, traditional dances and other forms of entertainment were some of the most common contents. Central to the entertainment functions of television is this taxonomy provided by Denis McQuail for all media: 'escaping, or being diverted from problems, relaxing, getting intrinsic cultural or aesthetic enjoyment, filling time, emotional release and sexual arousal.'

From its inception, the entertainment function of television and other electronic media in Nigeria as in other African countries was not in doubt. According to Ekwelie, 'the bulk of media entertainment comes from radio, television and the cinema. As is well known, entertainment is the selling point of all three.' In his earlier (1968) study of broadcasting in Nigeria he found that Eastern Nigerian Television devoted 62.49 per cent of its broadcast time to entertainment, as against 73 and 60.75 per cent on Western Nigerian Television and Radio Nigeria.

Television in the Congo is remarkable in its celebration of entertainment, which comes in many guises, especially, in the words of a 1990 UNESCO report by Peter Larsen, 'variety shows, video-taped performances of traditional dancing and singing, concerts by well-known dance bands, coverage of public events to be considered of national importance such as the arrival and departure of visiting presidents and reporting of civic, social and economic affairs'. In addition to these local programmes, Congolese television screens some popular foreign entertainment programmes such as *Dallas* (which was a huge success before it was discontinued due to financial reasons), *Starsky and Hutch*, *Derrick*, and *Der Alte*.

A certain number of entertainment programmes, especially variety shows, are exchanged with those of other African countries. Such exchanges are now promoted by regional bodies like AIDEC, which is based in Ouagadougou (Burkina Faso). In the film areas, though the three French-speaking countries of Mali,

Senegal, and Burkina Faso have achieved enviable heights in international film culture, their popularity is more noticed beyond Africa, and least of all in African television. This is mostly because many African television stations find it cheaper to receive foreign films, which usually have more than paid their way, unlike African films, which may not have had a wide enough distribution to ensure they break even and turn in a profit.

Television is well patronized by youth, with young women seeming to prefer entertainment to news or public affairs. An empirical and qualitative study of television use by young Nigerians found that 63.9 per cent reported watching television daily while 23.3 per cent said they watched only occasionally. But by far the most dominant factor determining their preference among TV programmes was 'entertainment', followed by 'national affairs'. Whereas the boys preferred national affairs, the girls voted overwhelmingly for entertainment. Though popular TV programmes were watched for their entertainment value, television news still got the highest rate of approval.

All across the continent there is a wide variety of entertainment programmes available for the local television audience. In Nigeria, Kenya, Ghana, and the French-speaking countries of Congo, Côte d'Ivoire, and Senegal, local audiences are thrilled by drama series, situation comedies, and live performance by indigenous or popular music groups, with most of these being in the national languages of the individual countries.

The foreign often appears to the African to be more exotic than the indigenous, and so, even with official policies that require up to 70 per cent of local programming in many African stations, there is still considerable play given to American soap operas (*Another Life*, *General Hospital*, and *As the World Turns*) and British comedies, especially those using many Black artists. On Nigerian television, late night movies, which are usually reruns of old American films, are popular on state-owned television stations and the NTA2 Channel 5, Lagos.

In Kenya, the establishment in 1991 of a private-enterprise television station

New Village Headmaster *left* and **Things Fall Apart** *right* (both NTA, Nigeria). African television programmes reflect the geopolitical culture and commercial character of the individual countries. Nigeria leads the way in the variety and quantity of nationally produced programmes following a government directive limiting foreign shows to 30 per cent of total broadcasting.

(KTN) has seen the unrestrained presentation of entertainment programmes, nearly all of which are imported from the United States and Europe. Though the local audience is not complaining, such unbalanced programming is usually the focus for charges of new media imperialism from nationals concerned at the uncontrolled importation of foreign entertainment programmes.

Languages and cultural differences as well as infrastructural poverty make it difficult to engage in inter-country exchange of television programmes of the magnitude one would expect, considering that there are long-standing regional blocs that should have facilitated this. A report on the possibilities for such exchange of programmes in Africa showed that 'programme exchange . . . has a long way to go' for these reasons:

1. lack of adequate personnel to produce or put together programmes for exchange;
2. stations are too preoccupied with day-to-day problems of broadcasting to pay attention to the needs of programme exchange;
3. lack of adequate resources to cope with programme exchange;
4. the reasons for programme exchange are vague and remote as far as practising broadcasters are concerned;
5. many broadcasters do not feel that what they produce for their stations is good enough or relevant for the needs of other stations.

Though the Union des Radiodiffusions et Télévision Nationale d'Afrique (URTNA) is working vigorously to promote inter-country exchange of programmes, there is a great need for more action by national governments and national broadcasting unions to augment its efforts in this direction. There is a regional monthly exchange between Gambia, Sierra Leone, Ghana, and Nigeria (English-speaking West African states with a common colonial background). The Nigerian Television Authority also uses a lot of footage in its news and screens some entertaining programmes from Afrovision. But the extent of exchange is still less than desirable. Though the URTNA Programme Exchange Centre in Nairobi has studied the exchange situation and problems, it is still hampered in its operations by poor financial resources and ageing equipment for dubbing and translating entertainment programmes. So, even when the will is there the might to make exchange possible is often lacking.

In recent years, many African television stations have started treating their viewers to international live programmes, many of which are pure entertainment. In this respect, sport and musical shows dominate, with occasional state visits involving the Pope or some other international personality sometimes qualifying for telecasting. This is made possible by the ground satellite-receiving facilities in nearly all the television stations in Africa. These can allow for the exchange of programmes, though despite the availability of these facilities, not many programmes are exchanged through the satellite systems in Africa because the tariff in using satellite is prohibitive. It is only in the case of a few international sports events that URTNA, the Commonwealth Broadcasting Association

(CBA), and/or the European Broadcasting Union (EBU) facilitate the sharing of costs to bring the coverage—either live or recorded—to African viewers.

Cultural Identity and Unity

Of all the modern media of communication, none has a more serious implication for cultural development than television, which has the unique advantage of sight and sound, and whose range of creative manipulation is limited only by the aptitude of its users. Referring to culture as an anchor for society, Ogbu Kalu has argued that Africa has witnessed 'a shell-burst from foreign cultures [and] much of her history is . . . imprisoned within European histories'; some historians like Hugh Trevor-Roper even suggest that Africa has no history. Culture covers all aspects of life, from the technological and economic to language and religion, and can provide the anchor to prevent a changing society from drifting: television must be central to it.

The era of the earliest television in Africa was also the period of the nationalist struggles that culminated in political independence in many countries. The nature of the European occupation of each African country and the character of the independence struggle that led to political autonomy have tended to colour the cultural use and impact of television, even up to the present. In Kenya, for instance, known as the East African Protectorate until 1920, the British viewed the territory as a colony for white settlement. This was because the area offered a favourable climate and fertile soils and was served by the newly completed Uganda Railway. It took the ferocity of the Mau-Mau freedom struggle to establish the principle of African majority rule for Kenya in 1960. Independence eventually came in December 1963. But that early British policy of permanent settlement coupled with a large presence of Indians whose ancestors came for the railway projects has left an indelible mark on the culture of Kenyans and on the main contents of Kenyan television.

Early Kenyan television catered more for the tastes of the foreigners who controlled the economy than for the indigenous population, who suffered deliberate marginalization. Apart from the use of Kiswahili in some programmes, there is not much of Kenyan traditional culture evident on television. The greatest shock for a first-time West African visitor to Nairobi is the realization that the English suit and tie (the blouse and skirt) appear to be the national dress for this independent African country.

Nigeria took a different route to independence, and also to the establishment of her television stations. The hot and humid climate, abundant mosquitoes that threatened every European with fatal malaria, and the rancour of an indeterminate number of local ethnic groups which were locked in perpetual battles with each other, all combined to impress on the British colonial administration that it had a limited tenure in that West African territory, which before 1 January 1900 was administered by the Royal Niger Company, a British enterprise. Not only were the British ready to relinquish power easily without imposing British culture on the people, but the indigenous people were notoriously proud of their African cultural heritage. Not surprisingly, this found expression in the earliest television programmes, and has continued to the present, in spite of the increasing influence of foreign cultural values arising from the globalization and Americanization of communication generally, and the electronic visual media in particular.

Masai tribe and satellite dish. African television is primarily an entertainment medium, whose promise for education has gone largely unrealized because of the limitations of the medium and its commercial and political motivation.

371

At independence, the task for television was simple. It was to portray a true picture of the people's culture and accurately render an account of the political climate, which showed Nigeria to be vastly diversified, and blessed with enormous wealth, natural resources, and manpower. She was perceived as the greatest, the most promising, and the best hope for the black man and as having the fewest tensions. This dual mandate of promoting the cultural heritage while depicting the political promise was ably handled by the early managers of Nigerian television. However, in a vast country of about 80 million people, 256 ethnic groups, and 400 different languages, it is impossible to achieve the promotion of cultural unity through only three regional television stations, and so by 1966 the television stations were part of the political machinery for aggravating the civil strife that ensued.

In the French colonies, the situation was closer to what obtained in Kenya. By deliberate policy the French originally sought to 'assimilate' their colonial subjects into being cultural Frenchmen, regardless of their skin colour. They were to have the full legal and political rights of French citizenship, including the right to send representatives to the French parliament in Paris. This proved impractical because of large-scale colonization and thus was later abandoned except for some Senegalese towns and a select few highly educated, French-speaking Africans, though 'potential assimilation' was held as an ideal which all French-speaking Africans should strive for. This colonial policy has affected the cultural role of television in the former French colonies, where much of indigenous African culture has been subjugated and suppressed by the desire of the native people to be more French than their colonizers. This is more evident in a bilingual country like Cameroon, where the French-speaking *indigènes* are more foreign in outlook and orientation than their English-speaking counterparts, who appear more African (though these perceptual differences are definitely subjective, there being no truly empirical measures of Africanness, apart from such arbitrary characteristics as clothes, food, and language use).

The expectation that television in Africa would help bind the various ethnic groups together has largely gone unrealized from one country to another, regardless of whether the people suffered from the British maltreatment of Indirect Rule or the French policy of Assimilation or the Portuguese version (*assimilado*) or the Belgian *évolué*. Television must be seen as a mirror that reflects what is happening in society. This passivist perspective needs to be balanced, however, with an activist one which posits that television can be used as an agent for cultural development.

In this regard, each society must decide for itself how it sees its culture and how television can play a positive role in the management and promotion of that culture, including national cultural unity, if this is one of the goals it has set for television. The experience of the Western world does not support the view that television can easily bring about cultural unity, even among nationals of a country. This is not to discount the role of the media (including television) in the propagation of culture. In Nigeria the early newspapers, and television also later on, created and sustained Nigerian culture. If television in Africa has not lived up to its expectations in the promotion of African culture, it is because the programmers have not applied themselves seriously to that task, nor has the audience demanded it. What is not in doubt is that the medium can rise to this challenge. If it can be used as a major source of local national and international news, as is usually the case, it can also be a source of cultural values and education.

News Content

The news function of television is one of its most critical roles, and, because this usually has political implications, it attracts considerable attention from both television operators and the owners, mostly governments in the case of African countries. News on African television is as predictable and routinized as what we have in any other part of the world. Commenting on this feature of television news generally, Denis McQuail once noted that 'what is striking is the extent to which a presumably unpredictable universe of events seems open to incorporation, day after day, into much the same temporal or spatial frame'. Though there might be deviations from this routine (e.g. during crises), 'the news form is posited on the notion of normality and routine and might be thought to reinforce the notion of normality through its regularity', McQuail concluded.

Allied to the routinized presentation is the indication of significance suggested by the arrangements of news items on television. All across the continent, television news starts with the President or some activity at Government House, continues with focus on the most important cabinet ministers, before it is spiced with some remote events, including international news. This is not a unique African feature, as it obtains in most television news operations world-wide. The Glasgow Media Group referred to this in 1980 as 'Viewers' Maxims', by which is meant the principle that first-appearing items are more important than those that come later. Much of the news on African television can be classified as protocol news since it arises mostly from the comings and goings at Government House. This kind of coverage has also been noticed in the presentation and news-selection styles of Third World news agencies.

Whereas Western journalists strive for objectivity and neutrality, many African television journalists have a view of the world which is essentially ideological—reflecting the positions of the governments of the day. It is amazing how this world-view changes immediately a new regime comes to power, especially when this results from a *coup d'état*. There is a very thin line dividing news and propaganda, and credibility is not one of the strongest attributes of African television news. Some aspects of television news on the continent are absurd and ludicrous, bordering on pure entertainment or pedantic nonsense. This is more often the case during election campaigns, when the airwaves are put to greatest use by the incumbent heads of government, most of whom cannot distinguish between 'state' and 'party'. The result is erosion of the medium's credibility.

The coverage of the world on African television varies from country to country, though one can easily identify a pattern of old colonial ties still influencing the nature of foreign news reporting in each African country. Erwin Atwood found from his study of how the international press covers Africa that British and French media coverage of sub-Saharan African countries is strongly associated with the country's membership in the British Commonwealth and the French Community. Similarly, the content of African television stations is directly related to the historical ties of individual countries. There is more about Nigeria on Kenyan television than about other African nations, and vice versa. There is also more about Côte d'Ivoire on Senegalese television, and vice versa. On the other hand, there is not much about former British colonies in the television of former French colonies, and vice versa.

The proportion of foreign news in African television has been found to be higher than obtains in some other regions of the world. This can be explained by the historical and commercial linkages many African countries share with the West and East. But even in this there are regional variations, with former French colonies and East African countries giving more play to foreign news. On Kenyan television, Western countries account for about 32 per cent of foreign news, followed by African countries, which account for 21.9 per cent.

In the case of Nigerian television, it has been found that (as with the Nigerian press generally) foreign news is not given much attention. It has been reported that as much as 82.9 per cent of Nigerian television news is local while only 17.1 per cent is foreign. The Third World accounts for a disproportionately high percentage of the news stories (94.3 per cent), with the Western world providing only 4.1 per cent. Eastern Europe and other parts of the world provide only 1.6 per cent of the television news whole. The dominant contents all across the continent are usually politics, business, and human interest. Because of the commonality of training programmes, the presentation of the news is usually similar right across the continent, and in fact is the same as in Europe and America, except that there is less 'sweet talk' among news presenters on African television. Lately, some African stations have started experimenting with weather reports on television, but these weather men / women are not as effective as characters as their counterparts on American television.

African Television Culture

In spite of the wide variety of television stations in Africa, and also the different colorations of television use, there is general agreement that the medium should be deployed in the forefront of the war for accelerated development. This expectation that television should be given a serious and purposive role in the social engineering process in Africa runs in the face of both empirical and episodic evidence of how people (Africans and all others) react to television. There is hardly any African television station that does not incorporate educational and mass mobilization elements in its programme structure, even though entertainment is the dominant ware and the main attraction.

It is very difficult to come up with one notion of African television culture,

Kenyan **Radio and TV Times**. Many African countries now publish popular magazines of this type, listing programmes and generating interest in shows and television personalities.

because there is no one African people unified in a common approach to television, nor is there one single methodology of television in Africa. It is not only possible, but also instructive, to consider the proposition that, right across the continent, television content is predominantly skewed towards foreign or local plays, drama, soap opera, story-telling, and sport. There is also an increasing incidence of religious and political programmes which tend to be so similar that it is sometimes difficult to distinguish between them. Both preachers and politicians harangue their audiences at religious and political rallies in much the same manner and style.

A review of the programme schedule of many African television stations shows that, among local programmes, fictional content, in the form of drama in local languages, soap opera in English or French, and story narration by or for children, is some of the commonest fare. In Kenya, weekend viewers are treated to long hours of entertainment that start at noon with such programmes or films as *Wild Rose*, *The Littlest Hobo Year*, *Joy Bringers*, and *Rambo* (on Saturdays).

On Sunday, the menu includes *Disneyland*, *Children Variety*, and *Classical Music*. Weekend programming is incomplete without sport, for which there are usually three programmes on Saturday (*Football Coaching*, *KBC Sport Hour*, and *Premier League*). On Sundays, sports fans are treated to *Sports Machine* and *Gillette World Sports Special*. The programmes on the independent and private-enterprise television station (KTN) are almost entirely foreign, with the following being some of the most popular: cartoons, *Desmond's*, *Beauty and the Beast*, *Neighbours*, *Knotts Landing*, *Oprah Winfrey*, and *Showbiz Today*.

Among the local entertainment drama are: *Shulko Mawaidha*, *Kinimacho Baloonology*, and *Hukuma*. There is usually a thrilling feature film late every night, before the prayers that precede closedown at 11.33 p.m. African television culture is evidently entertainment-oriented.

The final picture that emerges shows that television is regarded as the modern equivalent of many traditional media forms which are used mostly for entertainment and the transmission of the cultural heritage. Many Africans make a clear distinction between serious use of the traditional/modern mass media as instructional channels and their use for enjoyment. Television use is more for the latter. This has informed not only how African viewers react to or use the medium, but, equally importantly, how African programmers package the daily television menu. The popularization of satellite networks is more on the basis of pure entertainment than for education. This has serious implications for the future of television in Africa, though the use of the medium for instructional and mobilizational purposes should not be completely discounted.

The Future of Television in Africa

All over Africa, even within those countries that established their television stations as long ago as the 1950s and 1960s, television is still a novelty. In the beginning, all the television sets were black and white, but now they are mostly full colour. The recent developments are in the sizes of the sets, some of which now approximate cinema screens. Of great significance also is the popularization of satellite channels. Though a regional satellite system (the Regional African Satellite Communication System—RASCOM) was launched in early 1987 to develop an efficient, reliable, and economic means of telecommunications, including sound and television broadcasting, inter-country exchange of television news and programmes is yet to develop beyond the trial stage.

By far the greatest impact of satellite broadcasting is coming from direct transmissions from European and American stations. All across the continent, a wide variety of foreign stations are received either directly or through diffusion arrangements with local stations. For instance, in April 1989 the French television network Canal France International started a daily four-hour direct satellite transmission to television stations in twenty four French- and Portuguese-speaking African countries, among which are Benin, Côte d'Ivoire, Niger, and Senegal. Kenya's private television channel (KTN) relays regular satellite programmes from the American Cable News Network (CNN) on an hourly basis, creating the impression that its local programmes are fillers. In Nigeria, satellite antennae that make it possible to receive CNN, BBC, UK Gold, Sky, MTV, C-Span, and at least six other channels are now so cheap that nearly every household in the big cities has one. They have also become so popular that there is now a microversion that is specially designed for folding and fitting in a travelling bag for weekend trips to the villages.

The result of the introduction of satellite television among African states has been an increase in the one-sided flow of information, from the developed countries to Africa. The satellite news and programmes that are now becoming the common content of African television do not reflect African realities, and, if anything, they paint a negative picture of Africa as a continent that is at war, hunger-stricken, or drought-ravaged. The uncontrolled flow of satellite television programmes from European and American stations is a serious threat to the future development of television in Africa. Many urban dwellers in Africa prefer the foreign programmes to their local competitors', which suffer from the usual sicknesses of modern African mass media: lack of money, poverty of creativity, inadequate equipment, political pressure, and bureaucracy, among others. African governments need to invest more in regional satellite systems that will promote inter-country exchange of resources and television programmes; otherwise they will remain for ever at the receiving end of the global satellite networks, leading to a perpetuation of the media dependency syndrome.

Unfortunately, the poor economic health of many African countries means that not much can be achieved in the immediate future, no matter how well intentioned the governments might be about television development. The gloomy outlook has forced the World Bank to the view that the sub-Saharan region is more underdeveloped even than South Asia. Some of the predicaments for tomorrow's Africa are rapid population growth and scarce water resources, two problems that can slow down the rate of development.

According to United Nations projections, the population of Africa is expected to quadruple before stabilizing at the end of the twenty-first century. The perennial drought in parts of the continent is another major handicap to development. Much of the African continent lies in a zone which for part of the year is arid and where recurrent drought severely disturbs agriculture, leading to a chain of adverse reactions that ultimately result in underdevelopment.

In these circumstances, growth and expansion in communications, including television, are likely to be frustrated. Even the expansion in population is not yet of much advantage to television development since there is usually no equivalent expansion in advertising revenue. The challenge to policy-makers in Africa is to turn the growing population of the continent to advantage.

One observer has pointed out that the populations of the less developed world have made no vow of permanent poverty while their economic policies are oriented toward maximum feasible material growth. Television in Africa has to be placed within a new vision of expanded development and growth. Television stations have yet to realize the potentials of the medium as a strong advertising revenue earner. In 1985 Tapio Varis found that, on many stations, advertisements account for as little as 1.6 per cent of the overall total broadcasts and 3.3 per cent during prime time. About a third of all television advertisements were found to be foreign. The low volume of advertisements leads to reduced revenue in many countries. On Ethiopian television, for example, advertisements account for only 3.8 per cent of total revenue. In Algeria advertisements on radio and television

Zimbabwe: family watching television at home. In many urban centres today television is easily the most common form of family entertainment.

combined account for only 5 per cent of total revenue but the figures for Ghana and Benin are 11 per cent and 26 per cent respectively.

Mauritius and Zimbabwe point to the possibility that African stations cannot only be self-sustaining in future, but might also be significant profit centres. Unesco figures for Zimbabwean television reveal that advertisements yield 52 per cent of total revenue while the figure for radio and television stations in Mauritius is 47.3 per cent. If the potential is to be realized, the managers of African television stations need to be more business-like in their advertising sales operations. Many still behave like civil servants and expect advertisers to beg for their time.

The distinctive feature of American broadcasting is the marketing abilities of even the smallest stations. American radio and television stations are primarily marketing tools, and, not surprisingly, there is a deliberate effort to position each station according to the consumer outlook for the area. Because of the paucity of radio and television stations in Africa, the marketing approach to programming, station positioning, and promotion has not yet been adopted. African television stations now need to target their programmes for defined market segments. This was not the habit of government-owned television but the new privately-owned stations will usher in an era of aggressive marketing and bring about a revolution in television management. In recent times, there has been a serious call for countries of the south to co-operate more among themselves. One of the pressure groups for this is the South Commission, formally established in 1987, after years of informal discussion among intellectual and political élites of the south. In its manifesto, *Challenge to the South*, the Commission analysed the problems of southern development and proffered far-reaching solutions, many of which have serious implications for the media, especially television.

According to the Commission, 'it is important that the public should have access to information on the activities of the government. In this respect, the role of the media becomes vital.' It goes further, recommending that 'the existing co-operation among the media of developing countries should be greatly intensified and diversified, and the necessary infrastructural links improved . . . The South has to act collectively so as to minimize its dependence on Northern sources.' Information is a key resource that needs to be managed for the protection and promotion of southern interests. In this regard, television, especially its satellite operations, must be employed in the strategic task of ensuring public access to vital government information, the promotion of south–south development, and the enhancement of the cultural dimension of development.

In its expansive view of culture the Commission includes 'values, attitudes, beliefs, and customs of a society' as well as 'activities . . . which express and enrich, while at the same time transforming those values, attitudes, beliefs, and customs'. Television must be sensitive to the cultural roots of African societies and at the same time must include as a goal the development and sustenance of African culture itself—not an easy task.

The future of television cannot be divorced from the future of African societies. In the daily struggle of the medium to be a relevant actor in the socio-political and technological development of Africa it has to find a solution to the one-sided flow of satellite programmes and thus to reduce dependence on the north. It has to capitalize on the growing size of African populations, and it has to orient itself to the task of marketing while at the same time fulfilling its mission as agency of sustainable development.

African television is so varied in its nature and characteristics that one cannot describe it in simple terms. At one end there are developed systems like the Nigerian Television Authority with a network of thirty federal and state stations linked to the central station for network news and special programmes. At the other end, there is Tanzania, just about to establish her first mainland station, and there is Lesotho, where television was established in 1986, but transmits its programmes for only one hour a day from 6.00 to 7.00 p.m. with the evening news taking the last fifteen minutes of broadcasting. With three South African channels (TV.1, CCV, and MNET) available, one cannot see much future for the expansive growth of Lesotho Television in this country of 1.6 million people. Television in Africa is largely a political weapon, not a tool of marketing as in the West. It is this that makes the ownership and control of the medium so important to African governments. Like Western education and religion, it arrived at the instance of colonial powers who left their mark.

In an era of political armies, radio and television stations as well as the people who work there have acquired added significance because of their roles during *coups d'état*. Not surprisingly, some radio and television stations now have more tanks than government houses and barracks. In the future of politics in Africa, the role of television cannot be disguised. The mismanagement of the medium is the beginning of failure for any regime.

Africa's dwindling economic fortunes will have severe results in the development of the medium, which every African likes, but only few can now afford. Unesco figures show that television has become nearly invisible in some African countries, especially Angola, with 5.3 sets per 1,000 people; in Tanzania with 0.6; in Burundi with 0.2; and in Mali with 0.1. Many countries are establishing community viewing centres as a way of overcoming the diminishing presence of television.

In spite of its promise in Africa, television has not lived up to people's expectations, and after more than thirty years on the continent it is still largely foreign in orientation. An Africanization revolution is inevitable if the medium is ever to realize its potential as an instrument of culture; without this it will continue to be only a filler of time.

Epilogue
The Future

Richard Paterson and Anthony Smith

The ever-increasing role of television as support for a range of new services makes certain that the future is uncertain. This is the case both for those in the different parts of the television business, whether programme-makers, broadcasters, or cable operators, and for those who seek to explore the novelties of the television screen in the telecommunications and multi-media companies. But it must inevitably be the tastes of the audience which will in large part determine who will succeed and who will lose, while leisure diversions compete for the consumer dollar, ECU, or yen.

During the twentieth century moving-image entertainment has undergone a remarkable transformation from an activity interposed at the edges of the working day to a range of industries which attempt to provide for all the leisure time available. The possibilities of mass home entertainment (as well, in the politically troubled 1920s and 1930s, as mass propaganda or education) were first developed in radio. Entertainment and information, particularly through the medium of television, have since gradually taken over and transformed the organization of the home. With further technological advances a proliferation in home technology seems inevitable.

Television's audience was initially addressed as a family unit, but, over time, influenced by advertising needs and changing social mores, this has changed so that increasingly groups and specialized interests are targeted: more programmes (and channels) have emerged designed for sections of the audience. Film production, recently dominated by genres designed to appeal to an under-

Television as global medium. For the Third World, television was a symbol of modernization, one which found its way rapidly in some countries into a place in local culture.

30 market (because this group had become the main cinema audience), has now begun to change with a new demand pattern. The arrival of the video recorder and cable and pay TV, and the importance of film viewing in their use, has been central to this process.

Audiences (as citizens and as consumers) want the most pleasurable and effective media available in the most convenient place. Film in cinema was overwhelmed in the 1950s by television in the home. The radio experience, essentially domestic until the transistor, duly became more mobile. We are now confronted with further possible changes: first, in the quality of the aesthetic experience of watching television with wide-screen and high-definition television (although it is not certain whether these will have the significance of black-and-white TV's replacement by colour); secondly, in the convergence between the computer, telecommunications, and entertainment industries and the development of new modes of distribution with video-on-demand and other 'premium' services. Giving audiences greater choice and also ease of access to the programmes of choice, but also the chance to interact with the screen, may prove to be the next convergence and the next leap forward. Indeed, many of the largest media conglomerates are beginning to plan their business strategies around the notion of the 'information society', which after many false starts now seems to be becoming a reality.

Interactivity and multi-media developments may be the key to a wholly new phase. Consumer multi-media programmes can be delivered via traditional networks (whether terrestrial, satellite, cable, or phone) or as packaged commodities such as optical discs. The most concrete, and successful, example of entertainment multi-media so far is the video game, which has provided an increasingly vivid interactive experience. In parallel there is a small but developing market for mostly reference-type material on CD-ROM discs which can contain a mixture of text, audio, graphics, stills, and motion video. The next stage in the development of the multi-media market will see the introduction of more sophisticated hardware and software with greatly improved image quality using compact discs as the storage and playback medium.

Key to this next stage will be the development of 'smart TV'—basically the

Cinema overwhelmed. By the boom of the mid-1950s, the USA had acquired over 500 television stations—including two dozen struggling educational stations—and 85 per cent of US homes were watching an average of five hours of television per day.

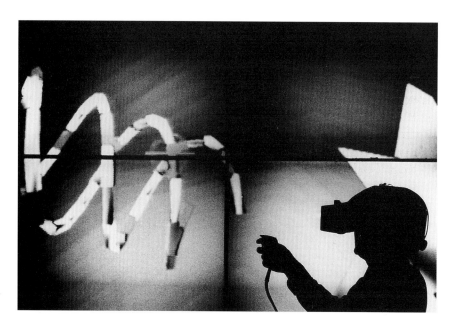

Virtual reality: a vision of the further future?

increasing integration of the television set with computer intelligence. Networked multi-media will evolve from ancillary services such as teletext when both digital transmission capacity and digital storage capacity become cheaply available. Poor-quality teletext graphics will be superseded by full-quality still pictures and audio—making the screen more like a magazine delivered to those subscribers who have paid to receive it.

At the same time the digital compression of the television signal, using fast computer techniques, will make it possible to compress the hundreds of megabits of raw digital data generated when a TV signal is digitized down into a much lower data stream below 20 megabits per second. This will allow a greatly increased number of programmes to be transmitted terrestrially, by satellite or by cable. Indeed some cable systems, based on optical fibre architectures, will offer 500 or more channels. Equally there are many other applications possible for this potentially low-cost extra capacity, including stereo picture transmission to 'virtual reality' type helmets using either real or computer-generated scenery.

For television executives adaptability to the fast-changing world of technology will become a key to future success across all parts of industry. New options for serving audiences are manifold. But amidst all of the concern about technological change and the customer's willingness to buy there is an enduring and underlying continuity: the programmes—the software of the moving image. And one central question now is whether the programming will change. It seems certain that television's routinized genres of soap opera, game shows, and news will continue. But in coming decades a new generation will find a place for entertainment that assists escape from the home into places less fraught with social and financial stress. A new tendency towards the big, outdoor electronics-

above Educational television: Britain's Open University has exploited the opportunities offered for distance learning by television.

left 'Real life' dramas such as the US **Emergency Call** are increasingly prominent on prime-time schedules.

The communal 'event': In the Telethon, viewers and studio audience are linked in day-long fundraising events, which bring in millions for local and international charities.

assisted spectacle is under way. In the blockbuster films of Steven Spielberg, in theme parks like the Disneylands and Universal Studios, and in the emerging medium of virtual reality there are pointers towards the start of a new outdoor range of gratifications. The moving image may spread outwards again, beyond the home.

At the same time the possibilities (in the developed world) for electronic democracy continue to advance. Television has been an important adjunct of the democratic (and when misused authoritarian) polities for the last forty years. The democratic uses of the interactive screen are still at a very early stage of development—but if electronic home shopping is a success, surely some involvement of electorates through the medium of television will be attempted. As private selection and individuation become inscribed into the culture at all levels, we might then expect changes in our mode of governance as well as in our entertainment.

In the past new technologies have been add-ons—the audio-visual market seems to offer a fertile adaptative environment. Soap opera on radio becomes soap opera on TV, film studios produce television series. Hybrid programmes emerge, different media adopt and adapt the same programming. Technological advances may alter our perceptions of our world but much of the technology will remain unsuccessful if unable to persuade audiences of opportunities for new pleasures as well as augmented old ones. Some innovations will succeed but it is worth bearing in mind the fickle nature of consumer behaviour. Many a new product failed to reach the 'must-have' status. Betamax, D-MAC, disc cameras are all examples of failed dreams of the 1980s, like quadraphonic sound in the 1970s.

There is a growing belief that interactivity will be a strong selling point and with this belief the desire for *control*. Even an either/or choice in the ending to a story on television might prove attractive. But will interactive entertainment ever replace the enjoyment of a realized, complex narrative? It seems doubtful.

What seems more likely is a drift in two directions in the business of providing this fare: on the one hand towards ever larger, more powerful conglomerates producing high-cost entertainment (until new anti-monopoly rules are introduced) and on the other hand towards lower-cost, national and community-based production.

There have been many 'synergistic' take-overs which seem to confirm the inevitability of convergence between telecommunications and the media. The Sony and Matsushita strategies of buying Hollywood studios was based on a belief that they needed to control the software for use on their hardware. It is new media in the shape of telecommunications and computer-linked companies which in the 1990s are searching for software. These business strategies seem to be based on further exploitation of software—new and old. Libraries of films and programmes have taken on a new value.

The linking of telecommunications and the entertainment industries has long been predicted. In the 1990s this seems to be happening and the much vaunted electronic superhighways are being translated into reality. But convergence goes much further. The interfacing of the computer with telecoms and the domestic

The rise of community programming: the BBC's **Video Diaries** gives viewers and citizens the chance to tell their own stories and present their own images.

screen remains an unexploited resource, but one which is clearly seen as potentially hugely profitable.

So there are parallel trends, of different kinds, which may come to characterize the next era in entertainment. The big spectacular communal experience will return, with stylish venues and media-aided technology. The prevailing aesthetic will demand the most completely convincing representations, whether of history, contemporary event, or fantasy. At the same time the popular acceptance of interactivity might lead to a medium of 'dial-up' virtual fictions which give access to an intangible but more wholly enthralling experience. The marketing will be enhanced to try to ensure a rate of return on the huge initial investment.

But there is a third trend too. People will be induced to spend money when equipment brings them a more intense and enthralling image, but they will spend when they are offered empowerment too. And this empowerment will be extended to self-production of images. If you have your own camcorder and digital edit suite you can make your own images and, if community stations grow in number, it will be increasingly possible to show them to a wider audience.

The software business led by the Hollywood majors stands to be the most likely victor. Consumers are subject to an unquenchable appetite for entertainment. It is almost certain that with the changing profile of the industry much energy will be focused on programming. The ever longer income streams for major films act as an incentive to Hollywood's vertically integrated majors to invest in large-scale productions. The concentration in this market is likely to grow and barriers to entry might become greater. No matter how sophisticated the search facilities of interactive CDs and the new one-to-one communication facilities available on cable, established by banks and shops, it is high-profile entertainment which will offer the greatest rewards to distributors who can use the whole of the new range of electronic 'delivery' methods.

In the future of television 'events' will then probably take on a much more important role alongside the usual schedule of quiz shows, soap operas, and chat shows. And these events will be global rather than national in their address. In sport the Olympics and the World Cup show the way. The success of a film like *Jurassic Park* may be dwarfed in size of return by a similar event on pay television. We may see the premières of high-cost programmes via 'pay-per-view' to millions of viewers across the globe: an alternative to the current system in which the print and advertising expenditure for cinema release is the foundation for success (and income) further down the exhibition chain—video, pay-TV, and terrestrial TV. In effect, the order in which things are shown may change, with pay television taking the first and largest slice of revenues.

A new version of cultural domination seems likely. American dominance of the world's cinema screens was partly transferred to the TV screen but national control of the channels and their output also determined that much domestic production came about. Hollywood has regained much ground in the video

opposite The rise of 'pay-TV': Sky—majority owner Rupert Murdoch—is one of the successful operators of multi-channel satellite television but it had to struggle in the late 1980s, securing audiences with major sports events and first-run films. It has had a difficult and competitive relationship with terrestrial channels. Murdoch has adopted a similar strategy in Asia, establishing Star TV.

The way we were? Prime-time entertainment programming was constructed around the needs of the bread-winner and followed the early-evening news. Few alarming documentaries disturbed the viewer's sense of the psychological fortress offered by the medium.

boom and with the emergence of satellite channels is able to evade national regulation for the screening of predominantly American-originated material. With the growth of electronic superhighways that dominance looks irreversible across the globe. Hence the caution of the European Community in its audio-visual trade regulation, and the eagerness of major enterprises (Murdoch's News Corporation, the BBC) to extend the markets (for both news and entertainment) to the Asian land mass. The regulatory environment of China, Malaysia, and India may come to exert a powerful impact on the contents of world culture. It is always the growing market rather than the fully established one which concentrates the energies of the supplier.

But it is an unpredictable future. What seems likely is that ever larger global corporations will offer high-premium events; with more numerous local stations offering lower-cost fare to region, neighbourhood, and nation. Linguistic factors do seem to matter and will provide some protection. Radio has long been the potential fully global medium but it has never breached national boundaries sufficiently to pose a threat to cultural autonomy. National television systems started at a time when Hollywood dominated cinema world-wide and thus our ways of seeing. One more generation from now and, despite massive changes in technology as well as the businesses involved, we could feel that nothing has really changed.

Further Reading

CHAPTER 1

Albert Abramson, 'Pioneers of Television: Vladimir Kosma Zworykin', *Jour SMPTE* 90 (July 1981), 579–90.

—— 'Pioneers of Television: Charles Francis Jenkins', *Jour SMPTE* 95 (Feb. 1986), 224–38.

—— *The History of Television: 1880–1941* (Jefferson, NC: McFarland, 1987).

—— 'Pioneers of Television: Philo Taylor Farnsworth', *Jour SMPTE* 101 (Nov. 1992), 770–84.

Gleason L. Archer, *History of Radio to 1926* (New York: American Historical Journal, 1938).

Erik Barnouw, *A Tower in Babel* (New York: Oxford University Press, 1966).

Kenneth Bilby, *The General: David Sarnoff and the Rise of the Communications Industry* (New York: Harper & Row, 1986), 132–4.

Asa Briggs, *The Golden Age of Wireless* (London: Oxford University Press, 1965).

—— *Sound & Vision* (Oxford: Oxford University Press, 1979).

Robert W. Burns, *British Television: The Formative Years* (London: Peter Peregrinus Ltd., 1986).

George Everson, *The Story of Television: The Life of Philo T. Farnsworth'* (New York: W. W. Norton, 1949).

Peter C. Goldmark, *Maverick Inventor: My Turbulent Years at CBS* (New York: Saturday Review Press/E. P. Dutton & Co., Inc., 1973).

Robert Grimshaw, 'The Telegraphic Eye', *Scientific American*, 104 (1 Apr. 1911).

Sydney Mosely, *John Baird: The Romance and Tragedy of the Pioneer of Television* (London: Odhams Press, 1952).

John J. Perry and W. E. Ayrton, 'Seeing by Electricity', *Nature*, 21 (22 Apr. 1880).

A. A. Campbell Swinton, 'Distant Electric Vision', *Nature*, 78 (18 June 1908).

Ronald F. Tiltman, *Baird of Television: The Life Story of John Logie Baird* (London: Seeley Service & Co., 1933).

CHAPTER 2

William Boddy, *Fifties Television: The Industry and its Critics* (Urbana, Ill.: University of Illinois Press, 1990).

Leo Bogart, *The Age of Television: A Study of Viewing Habits and the Impact of Television on American Life* (New York: Ungar, 1956).

Douglas Gomery, 'Failed Opportunities: The Integration of the U.S. Motion Picture and Television Industries', *Quarterly Review of Film Studies*, 9 (Summer 1984), 219–28.

——'Theater Television: The Missing Link of Technological Change in the U.S. Motion Picture Industry', *Velvet Light Trap*, 21 (Summer 1985), 44–54.

——*Shared Pleasures: A History of Movie Presentation in the United States* (Madison, Wis.: University of Wisconsin Press, 1992).

Michelle Hilmes, *Hollywood and Broadcasting: From Radio to Cable* (Urbana, Ill.: University of Illinois Press, 1990).

J. Fred MacDonald, *One Nation under Television: The Rise and Decline of Network TV* (New York: Pantheon, 1990).

Dallas Smythe, 'A National Policy on Television?', *Public Opinion Quarterly*, 14/3 (Autumn 1950).

——'Reality as Presented on Television', *Public Opinion Quarterly*, 18/2 (Summer 1954), 148–50.

Lynn Spigel, *Make Room for TV: Television and the Family Ideal in Postwar America* (Chicago: University of Chicago Press, 1992).

CHAPTER 3

Asa Briggs, *The BBC: The First Fifty Years* (Oxford: Oxford University Press, 1985).

Donald R. Browne, *Comparing Broadcast Systems: The Experiences of Six Industrialized Nations* (Ames, Ia.: Iowa State University Press, 1989).

Richard Burke, *Comparative Broadcasting Systems*, Modules in Mass Communication Series (Chicago: Science Research Associates, 1984).

Barry Cole and Mal Oettinger, *Reluctant Regulators: The FCC and the Broadcast Audience* (Reading, Mass.: Addison-Wesley, 1978).

Walter Emery, *National and International Systems of Broadcasting* (East Lansing, Mich.: Michigan State University Press, 1969).

Bernard Guillou and Jean-Gustave Padioleau, *La Régulation de la télévision* (Paris: La Documentation Française, 1988).

Sydney Head, *World Broadcasting Systems* (Belmont: Wadsworth, 1985).

Raymond Kuhn (ed.), *The Politics of Broadcasting* (New York: St Martin's Press, 1985).

Anthony Smith (ed.), *Politics and Political Life* (London: Macmillan, 1979).

CHAPTER 4

Manuel Alvarado and John Stewart, *Made for Television: Euston Films Ltd.* (London: BFI/Thames Methuen, 1985).

Ien Ang, *Watching Dallas* (London: Methuen, 1985).

George Brandt (ed.), *British Television Drama in the 1980s* (Cambridge: Cambridge University Press, 1993).

David Buxton, *From 'The Avengers' to 'Miami Vice'* (Manchester: Manchester University Press, 1990).

John Corner (ed.), *Popular Television in Britain* (London: BFI, 1991).

Richard Dyer *et al.*, *Coronation Street* (London: BFI, 1981).

Jane Feuer, Paul Kerr, and Tise Vahimagi (eds.), *MTM: 'Quality Television'* (London: BFI, 1984).

Christine Geraghty, *Women and Soap Opera* (Cambridge: Polity Press, 1991).

Todd Gitlin, *Inside Prime Time* (New York: Pantheon, 1985).

Gerd Hallenberger and Joachim Kaps, *Hatten Sie's Gewusst? Die Quizsendungen und Game Shows des deutschen Fernsehens* (Marburg: Jones Verlag, 1991).

Cristina Lasagni and Giuseppe Richeri, *L'altro mondo quotidiano: Telenovelas TV brasiliana e dintorni* (Rome: Edizioni RAI, 1986).

Michele and Armand Mattelart, *The Carnival of the Images: Brazilian Television Fiction* (New York: Bergin & Garvey, 1990).

Albert Moran, *Images and Industry: Television Drama Production in Australia* (Sydney: Currency Press, 1985).

Steve Neale and Frank Krutnik, *Popular Film and Television Comedy* (London: Routledge, 1990).

Martha Nochimson, *No End to Her: Soap Opera and the Female Subject* (Berkeley, Calif.: University of California Press, 1992).

Helena Sheehan, *Irish Television Drama: A Society and its Stories* (Dublin: RTE, 1987).

Irene Shubik, *Play for Today: The Evolution of Television Drama* (London: Davis-Poynter, 1975).

Alessandro Silj, *East of Dallas: The European Challenge to American Television* (London: BFI, 1988).

Michael Skovmand and Kim Christian Schroder (eds.), *Media Cultures: Reappraising Transnational Media* (London: Routledge, 1992).

Richard Sparks, *Television and the Drama of Crime* (Buckingham: Open University Press, 1992).

John Tulloch, *Television Drama: Agency, Audience and Myth* (London: Routledge, 1990).

CHAPTER 5

John Corner (ed.), *Documentary and the Mass Media* (London: Edward Arnold, 1986).

——(ed.), *Popular Television in Britain: Studies in Cultural History* (London: BFI, 1991).

Wilson P. Dizard, *Television: A World View* (New York: Syracuse University Press, 1966).

Robert M. Entman, *Democracy without Citizens: Media and the Decay of American Politics* (New York: Oxford University Press, 1989).

Edward Jay Epstein, *News from Nowhere: Television and the News* (New York: Vintage Books, 1974).

Alexander Kendrick, *Prime Time: The Life of Edward R. Murrow* (London: Dent, 1970).

Robert MacNeil, *The People Machine: The Influence of Television on American Politics* (London: Eyre & Spottiswoode, 1970).

Lloyd Morrisett, 'A New Main Street: President's Essay', John and Mary R. Markle Foundation, Annual Report, 1990.

Burton Paulu, *Radio and Television Broadcasting on the European Continent* (Minneapolis: University of Minnesota Press, 1967).

Don R. Pember, *Mass Media in America* (6th edn. New York: Macmillan, 1992).

Irving Settel, *A Pictorial History of Television* (New York: Ungar Pub. Co., 1983).

Colin Seymour Ure, *The Political Impact of the Mass Media* (London: Constable, 1974).

Anthony Smith, *The Shadow in the Cave: A Study of the Relationship between the Broadcaster, his Audience and the State* (London: Allen & Unwin, 1973).

Michael Tracey, *The Production of Political Television* (London: Routledge & Kegan Paul, 1977).

John Whale, *The Half-Shut Eye: Television and Politics in Britain and America* (London: Macmillan, 1969).

Francis Wheen, *Television: A History* (New York: Century Publications, 1985).

Michael Winship, *Television* (New York: Random House, 1988).

John Wyver, *The Moving Image: An International History of Film, Television and Video* (London: Basil Blackwell, 1989).

CHAPTER 6

Steven Barnett, *Games and Sets: The Changing Face of Sport on Television* (London: British Film Institute, 1990).

Bill Bonney, *Packer and Televised Cricket*, Faculty of Humanities and Social Sciences media paper no. 2 (Sydney: New South Wales Institute of Technology, 1980).

Asa Briggs, *History of Broadcasting in the United Kingdom*, iv (London: Oxford University Press, 1979).

Edward Buscombe (ed.), *Football on Television*, BFI Television Monograph (London: British Film Institute, 1975).

Joan M. Chandler, *Television and National Sport: The United States and Britain* (Chicago: University of Illinois Press, 1988).

Peter Dimmock (ed.), *Sports in View* (London: Faber & Faber, 1964).

David Docherty, *Running the Show: 21 Years of London Weekend Television* (London: Boxtree, 1992).

John Goldlust, *Playing for Keeps: Sport, the Media and Society* (Melbourne: Longman Cheshire, 1987).

Allen Guttmann, *Sports Spectators* (New York: Columbia University Press, 1986).

Denis Howell *et al.*, *Committee of Enquiry into Sports Sponsorship* ('The Howell Report') (London: Central Council of Physical Recreation, 1983).

David A. Klatell and Norman Marcus, *Sports for Sale: Television, Money and the Fans* (New York: Oxford University Press, 1988).

Jeremy Potter, *Independent Television in Britain*, iii: *Politics and Control, 1968–80* (London: Macmillan, 1988).

Benjamin G. Rader, *In its Own Image: How Television has Transformed Sports* (New York: Free Press (Macmillan), 1984).

Bernard Sendall, *Independent Television in Britain*, i: *Origin and Foundation, 1946–62* (London: Macmillan, 1982).

——*Independent Television in Britain*, ii: *Expansion and Change 1958–68* (London: Macmillan, 1983).

Garry Whannel, *Fields in Vision: Television Sport and Cultural Transformation* (London: Routledge, 1992).

CHAPTER 7

Jeffery Alexander, 'Culture and Political Crisis', in Jeffery Alexander (ed.), *Durkheimian Sociology* (New York: Cambridge University Press, 1988).

Timothy G. Ash, *The Magic Lantern: The Revolution of '89 Witnessed in Warsaw, Budapest, Berlin, and Prague* (New York: Random House, 1990).

Walter Benjamin, 'Theses on the Philosophy of History', and 'The Work of Art in the Age of Mechanical Reproduction', in Hannah Arendt (ed.), *Illuminations* (New York: Harcourt & Brace, 1968).

Daniel Boorstin, *The Image: A Guide to Pseudo Events in America* (New York: Harper & Row, 1964).

Peter Brown, *The Cult of the Saints* (Chicago: University of Chicago Press, 1981).

Clifford Geertz, 'Center, Kings and Charisma', in J. Ben-David and T. Clark (eds.), *Culture and its Creators* (Chicago: University of Chicago Press, 1980).

Eric Hobsbawm and Terry Ranger (eds.), *The Invention of Tradition* (New York: Cambridge University Press, 1983).

S. Kraus (ed.), *The Great Debates: Background, Perspective, Effects* (Bloomington, Ind.: Indiana University Press, 1962).

Kurt Lang and Gladys Lang, *The Battle for Public Opinion* (New York: Columbia University Press, 1983).

Pierre Nora, 'L'Événement monstre', *Communications*, 18 (Paris: Le Seuil, 1972).

——*Les Lieux de mémoire*, i (Paris: Gallimard, 1984).

Edward Shils, *Center and Periphery: Essays in Macrosociology* (Chicago: University of Chicago Press, 1975).

Victor Turner and Edith Turner, *Image and Pilgrimage in Christian Culture: Anthropological Perspectives* (New York: Columbia University Press, 1978).

William Uricchio, 'Rituals of Reception, Patterns of Neglect: Nazi Television and its Postwar Representation', *Wide Angle: A Film Quarterly*, 11 (1988), 48–66.

Lucette Valensi, *Fables de la mémoire: La Glorieuse Bataille des trois rois* (Paris: Seuil, 1992).

Robin Erica Wagner-Pacifici, *The Moro Morality Play* (Chicago: University of Chicago Press, 1986).

Max Weber, *From Max Weber: Essays in Sociology* (New York: Oxford University Press, 1946).

H. Y. Yerushalmi, *Zakhor: Jewish History and Jewish Memory* (Seattle: University of Washington Press, 1982).

Barbie Zelizer, *Covering the Body: The Kennedy Assassination, the Media and the Shaping of Collective Memory* (Chicago: University of Chicago Press, 1992).

CHAPTER 8

Robert T. Bower, *Television and the Public* (London: Holt, Rinehart & Winston, 1973).

Susan Briggs, *Those Radio Times* (London: Weidenfeld & Nicolson, 1985).

Cedric Cullingford, *Children and Television* (Aldershot: Gower, 1984).

Jules Henry, *Culture against Man* (New York: McGraw, 1965).

Hilde Himmelweit, A. N. Oppenheim, and P. Vince, *Television and the Child* (Oxford: Oxford University Press, 1958).

Derek Horton, *Television's Story and Challenge* (London: Harrap, 1951).

Elihu Katz and Tamar Liebes, *The Export of Meaning: Cross-Cultural Readings of Dallas* (Oxford: Oxford University Press, 1990).

Joseph T. Klapper, *The Effects of Mass Communication* (New York: Free Press, 1960).

Jack Lyle and Heidi R. Hoffman, 'Television in the Daily Lives of our Children', paper presented at the symposium 'The Early Window: The Role of Television in Childhood', at the annual meeting of the American Psychological Association, Washington DC, 4 Sept. 1971.

Jack Lyle and Heidi R. Hoffman, 'Children's Use of Television and Other Media', in Eli A. Rubinstein *et al.* (eds.), *Television and Social Behaviour: Reports and Papers*, iv: *Television in Day-to-Day Life: Patterns of Use* (Washington, DC: US Government Printing Office, 1972), 129–256.

David Morley, *Family Television: Cultural Power and Domestic Leisure* (London: Comedia, 1986).

John P. Robinson, 'Toward Defining the Functions of Television', in Eli A. Rubinstein *et al.* (eds.), *Television and Social Behaviour: Reports and Papers*, iv: *Television in Day-to-Day Life: Patterns of Use* (Washington, DC: US Government Printing Office, 1972).

——and Jerald G. Backman, 'Television Viewing Habits and Aggression', in George A. Comstock *et al.* (eds.), *Television and Social Behaviour: Reports and Papers*, iii: *Television and Adolescent Aggressiveness* (Washington, DC: US Government Printing Office, 1972), 327–82.

CHAPTER 9

Broadcasting Standards Council, *A Matter of Manners?* (London, 1991).

Guy Cumberbatch and Dennis Howitt, *A Measure of Uncertainty: The Effects of the Mass Media* (London: BSC/Libbey, 1991).

Luis Antonio De Noriega and Frances Leach, *Broadcasting in Mexico* (London: Routledge & Kegan Paul, 1979).

Charles Hill, *Behind the Screen* (London: Sidgwick & Jackson, 1974).

Ian McIntyre, *The Expense of Glory* (Life of John Reith) (London: Harper Collins, 1993).

Colin Morris, *Drawing the Line* (London: BBC Books, 1987).

T. Newburn, *Permission and Regulation: Law & Morals in Post-war Britain* (London: Routledge, 1991).

Report of the Committee on Broadcasting (Pilkington Committee), Cmnd. 1753 (London: HMSO, 1962), esp. ch. III.

Paddy Scannell and David Cardiff, *A Social History of British Broadcasting*, i (Oxford: Blackwell, 1991).

Bernard Sendall, *Independent Television in Britain*, ii (London: Macmillan, 1983).

Michael Tracey, *A Variety of Lives* (Life of Hugh Greene) (London: Bodley Head, 1983).

CHAPTER 10

E. S. Herman and N. Chomsky, *Manufacturing Consent: The Political Economy of the Mass Media* (New York: Pantheon Books, 1988).

D. L. Paletz and A. P. Schmid (eds.), *Terrorism and the Media* (London: Sage, 1992).

M. Rodrigo, *Los medios de comunicación ante el terrorismo* (Barcelona: Icaria Editorial, 1991).

E. Said, *Covering Islam: How the Media and the Experts Determine How we See the Rest of the World* (London: Routledge & Kegan Paul, 1981).

P. Schlesinger, *Media, State and Nation: Political Violence and Collective Identities* (London: Sage, 1991).

——G. Murdock, and P. Elliott, *Televising 'Terrorism': Political Violence in Popular Culture* (London: Comedia, 1983).

A. P. Schmid, and J. de Graaf, *Violence as Communication: Insurgent Terrorism and the Western News Media* (London: Sage, 1982).

R. E. Wagner-Pacifici, *The Moro Morality Play: Terrorism as Social Drama* (Chicago: University of Chicago Press, 1986).

M. Wieviorka and D. Wolton, *Terrorisme à la une: média, terrorisme et démocratie* (Paris: Éditions Gallimard, 1987).

CHAPTER 11

Ken Auletta, *Three Blind Mice* (New York: Random House, 1991).

Erik Barnouw, *Tube of Plenty: The Evolution of American Television* (Oxford: Oxford University Press, 1990).

Kenneth Bilby, *The General: David Sarnoff and the Rise of the Communications Industry* (New York: Harper & Row, 1986).

Les Brown, *Television: The Business behind the Box* (New York: Harcourt Brace Jovanovich, 1971).

——*Les Brown's Encyclopedia of Television* (3rd edn., New York: Gale Research, 1992).

Robert L. Hilliard and Michael C. Keith, *The Broadcast Century* (London: Focal Press, 1992).

Sally Bedell Smith, *In All his Glory: The Life of William S. Paley* (New York: Simon & Schuster, 1990).

Christopher H. Sterling and John M. Kittross, *Stay Tuned: A Concise History of American Broadcasting* (Belmont, Calif.: Wadsworth, 1978).

CHAPTER 12

Alex S. Edelstein, John E. Bowes, and Sheldon M. Harsel, *Information Societies: Comparing the Japanese and American Experiences* (Seattle: International Communication Centre, 1978).

Masami Ito, *Broadcasting in Japan* (London: Routledge and Kegan Paul, 1978).

Yasusada Kitahara, *Information Network System: Telecommunications in the 21st Century* (London: Hutchison, 1983).

NHK, *The History of Broadcasting in Japan* (Tokyo: Nippon Hoso Kyokai, 1967).

——*Fifty Years of Japanese Broadcasting* (Tokyo: Nippon Hoso Kyokai, 1977).

——*Studies of Broadcasting* (annual publication) (Tokyo: NHK, Radio & TV Culture Research Institute).

CHAPTER 13

Mohammed Salleh Pateh Akhir, 'Challenge by Transnational Satellite Channels', unpublished Discussion Paper, ABU, 25th Standing Programme Committee Meeting, Kuala Lumpur, 1992.

Samir Allam, *Fernsehserien, Wertvorstellungen und Zensur in Ägypten* ('Television Series, Values and Censorship in Egypt') (Munich: Edition Orient, 1983).

Manuel Alvarado, 'The International Markets for TV Fiction', paper presented at the NOS Consultation on the International Dissemination of TV Drama, Hilversum, 1988.

Leoncio Barrios, 'Television, Telenovelas and Family Life in Venezuela', in James Lull (ed.), *World Families Watch Television* (Beverly Hills, Calif.: Sage, 1988).

Neena Behl, 'Equalizing Status: Television and Tradition in an Indian Village', in James Lull (ed.), *World Families Watch Television* (Beverly Hills, Calif.: Sage, 1988).

Luis R. Beltran, 'Communication and Cultural Domination: USA–Latin American Case', *Media Asia* (1978).

Dietrich Berwanger, *Television in the Third World: New Technologies and Social Change* (Bonn: Friedrich Ebert Foundation, 1987).

Belkis Bhegani, 'Television for a Continent', *TV World* (May 1986).

Mary G. F. Bitterman, 'Mass Communication and Social Change', *Media Asia*, 1 (1985).

Gabriele von Bruck, 'Identität und Wandel: Frauen in Sanaa' ('Identity and Change: Women in Sanaa'), in Werner Daum (ed.), *Jemen* (Innsbruck, 1987).

Godwin C. Chu, Alfian, and Wilbur Schramm, *Social Impact of Satellite Television in Rural Indonesia* (Singapore: Asian Mass Communication Research and Information Centre, 1991).

Choe Chungho, 'Korea's Communication Culture: An Inquiry into Spoken and Written Words', *Korea Journal*, 8 (1980).

——'Traditional Culture and Television in Korea', *Third Channel*, 1 (1986).

Marta Maria Klagsbrunn, *Brasiliens Fernsehserien: Telenovela* (Brazil's Television Series: Telenovela') (Mettlingen: Institüt für Brasilienkunde, 1987).

James Lull (ed.) *World Families Watch Television* (Beverly Hills, Calif.: Sage, 1988).

——and Se-Wen Sun, 'Agent of Modernization: Television and Urban Chinese Families', in James Lull (ed.), *World Families Watch Television* (Beverly Hills, Calif.: Sage, 1988).

Vijay Menon, 'Introduction' in *AMIC: Satellite Technology* (Singapore: Asian Mass Communication Research and Information Centre, 1985).

Hamid Mowlana, 'Trends in Middle Eastern Societies', in George Gerbner, *Mass Media Policies* (New York: Wilney-Interscene Publication, 1977).

Sid-Ahmed Nugdalla, 'Broadcasting and Cultural Change', in George Wedell (ed.), *Making Broadcasting Useful: The African Experience* (Manchester: Manchester University Press, 1986).

Segun Olusola, 'Television for Mobilisation', *Inter Media*, 4–5 (1985).

Everett M. Rogers and Livia Antola, 'Telenovelas: A Latin American Success Story', *Journal of Communication* (Autumn 1985).

Gopal Saksena, 'Growing the Serial Crop', *TV World* (May 1986).

Herbert I. Schiller, *Mass Communication and American Empire* (New York, 1969).

Luke Uka Uche, 'Political Socialization, Functional and Dysfunctional Information: Aspects of Broadcasting in Nigeria during National Crises', *Third Channel*, 1 (1985).

Niko Vink, *The Telenovela and Emancipation: A Study on TV and Social Change in Brazil* (Amsterdam: Royal Tropical Institute, 1988).

A. Wells, *Picture-Tube Imperialism? The Impact of U.S. Television on Latin America* (New York, 1972).

Brian Winston, 'Survival of National Networks in an Age of Abundance', *Inter Media*, 6 (1986).

J. S. Yadava and Usha V. Reddi, 'Television in Urban Indian Homes', in James Lull (ed.), *World Families Watch Television* (Beverly Hills, Calif.: Sage, 1988).

CHAPTER 14

Peter Beilby (ed.), *Australian TV: The First Twenty Five Years* (Melbourne: Nelson in association with Cinema Papers, 1981).

James Carey, *Communications as Culture: Essays on Media and Society*, (London: Routledge, 1992).

Ann Curthoys and John Docker, 'In Praise of *Prisoner*', in John Tulloch and Graeme Turner (eds.), *Australian Television: Programs, Pleasures and Politics* (Sydney: Allen and Unwin, 1989).

——and John Merritt (eds.), *Better Dead than Red: Australia's First Cold War: 1949–1959* (Sydney: Allen & Unwin, 1986).

Susan Dermody and Elizabeth Jacka, *The Screening of Australia*, i: *Anatomy of a Film Industry* (Sydney: Currency Press, 1987).

————*The Imaginary Industry: Australian Film in the Late Eighties* (North Ryde: Australian Film Television and Radio School, 1987).

Sandra Hall, *Supertoy: 20 Years of Australian Television* (Melbourne: Sun Books, 1976).

——*Turning on, Turning off: Australian Television in the Eighties* (Sydney: Cassell Australia, 1981).

K. S. Inglis, *This is the ABC: The Australian Broadcasting Commission 1932–1983* (Melbourne: Melbourne University Press, 1983).

Elizabeth Jacka, *The ABC of Drama: 1975–80* (Sydney: Australian Film Television and Radio School, 1990).

Andrew Jakubowicz, 'Days of our Lives: Multiculturalism, Mainstreaming and "Special" Broadcasting', *Media Information Australia*, 45 (Aug. 1987).

Julie James Bailey, 'Australian Television: Why it is the Way it is', *Cinema Papers* (Melbourne), 23 (Sept.–Oct. 1979), 513–85.

Lesley Johnson, *The Unseen Voice: A Cultural Study of Early Australian Radio* (London: Routledge, 1988).

Mungo MacCallum (ed.), *Ten Years of Television* (Melbourne: Sun Books, 1968).

Eric Michaels, *The Aboriginal Invention of Television in Central Australia* (Canberra: Australian Institute of Aboriginal Studies, 1986).

Heler Molnar, 'The Broadcasting for Remote Aborigines Scheme: Small versus Big Media', *Media Information Australia*, 58 (1990).

Albert Moran, *Images and Industry: Television Drama Production in Australia* (Sydney: Currency Press, 1985).

Meaghan Morris, 'Banality in Cultural Studies', *Discourse*, 10/2 (1988).

Tom O'Regan, *Australian Television Culture* (Sydney: Allen & Unwin, 1988).

Bill Peach, *This Day Tonight: How Australian Current Affairs TV Came of Age* (Sydney: ABC, 1992).

John Tulloch, and Graeme Turner (eds.), *Australian Television: Programs, Pleasures and Politics* (Sydney: Allen & Unwin, 1989).

David Watson and Denise Corrigan (eds.), *TV Times: 35 Years of Watching Television in Australia* (Sydney: Museum of Contemporary Art, 1991).

Helen Wilson (ed.), *Australian Communications and the Public Sphere* (Melbourne: Macmillan, Australia, 1989).

CHAPTER 15

L. Erwin Atwood, 'Who Covers Africa', in Charles Okigbo (ed.), *New Perspectives in International News Flow* (Lagos: CRP, 1992).

Dietrich Berwanger, *Television in the Third World* (Bonn: FES, 1987).

Chen Chimutengwende, 'Manpower Development for Broadcasting Organisations', in

George Wedell (ed.), *Making Broadcasting Useful: The Development of Radio and Television in Africa in the 1980s* (Manchester: Manchester University Press, 1986).

Mike Egbon, 'Western Nigeria Television Service: Oldest in Tropical Africa', *Journalism Quarterly* 60/2 (Summer 1983).

Sylvanus A. Ekwelie, 'The Content of Broadcasting in Nigeria' (unpublished MA Thesis, University of Wisconsin, 1968).

——'Mass Media and National Development', in Ogbu Kalu (ed.), *African Cultural Development: Readings in African Humanities* (Enugu: Fourth Dimension, 1978).

William Hachten, 'Broadcasting and Political Crisis', in Sydney Head (ed.), *Broadcasting in Africa: A Continental Survey of Radio and Television* (Philadelphia: Temple University Press, 1974).

Sydney Head (ed.), *Broadcasting in Africa* (Philadelphia: Temple University Press, 1974).

Ogbu U. Kalu, *Readings in African Humanities: African Cultural Development* (Enugu: Fourth Dimension, 1978).

Francis P. Kasoma, *Communication Policies in Zambia* (Tampere: University of Tampere, 1990).

Peter Larsen (ed.), *Import/Export: International Flow of Television Fiction* (Paris: Unesco, 1990).

Joseph Mbindyo, 'The Structure and Flow of Foreign News and Programmes in Kenyan Mass Media', in Will Teichert (ed.), *Images* (Bonn: FES, 1986).

H. Nwosu and O. U. Kalu, 'The Study of African Culture', in Ogbu Kalu (ed.), *Readings in African Humanities* (Enugu: Fourth Dimension, 1978).

Charles Okigbo, 'Television in the Lives of Nigerian Youths', *Third Channel*, 5 (July 1987).

——'Military Intervention in Nigerian Politics: A Philosophical Appraisal' (unpublished thesis, University of Nigeria, Nsukka, 1992).

R. Chude Okonkwor, 'The Press and Cultural Development: A Historical Perspective', in Ogbu Kalu (ed.), *Readings in African Humanities* (Enugu: Fourth Dimension, 1978).

Kevin Shillington, *History of Africa* (London: Macmillan, 1989).

Robert Stevenson, 'New News for the New World Information Order', in Charles Okigbo (ed.), *New Perspectives in International News Flow* (Lagos: CRP, 1992).

Luke Uka Uche, 'Radio Biafra and the Nigeria Civil War: Study of War Propaganda on a Target Audience', *Third Channel*, 5 (July 1987).

Charles Ume, 'The Advent and Growth of Television Broadcasting in Nigeria: Its Political and Educational Overtones', ACCE Conference Paper (Jos, 1988).

Tapio Varis, *International Flow of Television Programmes*, Reports and Papers on Mass Communication 100 (Paris: Unesco, 1985).

Television Museums and Archives

There now exist a number of museums dedicated to the history of television, often in the context of the history of film. There are also several archives around the world with occasional or regular public access and often with facilities for members of the public to look through various television programmes. What follows is a list of some of the best known of these.

AMERICAN MUSEUM OF THE MOVING IMAGE
36-01 35TH AVENUE
ASTORIA
NEW YORK 11106
USA
TEL (718) 784 4520

Television technical and production history.
Television production retrospectives, television programmes reference library.

AMERICAN CINEMATHÈQUE
1717 HIGHLAND AVENUE
SUITE 814
HOLLYWOOD 90028
USA
TEL (213) 461 9622

Television projections and retrospectives.

BRITISH KINEMATOGRAPH, SOUND AND TELEVISION SOCIETY
547/549 VICTORIA HOUSE
VERNON PLACE
LONDON WC1B 4DJ
GREAT BRITAIN
TEL 0171 242 8400

Learned society concerned with technical aspects of television. Demonstration on technical aspects and production techniques.

CENTRE GEORGES POMPIDOU
75191 PARIS CEDEX 04

FRANCE

TEL 142 77 12 33

Changing television exhibition and television programme projections.

CINÉROTHÈQUE/CINESCOPE

NFB

1564 ST DENIS STREET

MONTREAL

QUEBEC H2X 3K2

TEL (514) 496 6304

FAX (514) 283 0225

Most advanced videothèque in the world. The entire NFB film and television production stored, accessible on 4,680 double-sided video discs.

CITÉ DES SCIENCES ET DE L'INDUSTRIE

30 AVENUE CORENTIN

CARIOU

75930

PARIS

CEDEX 9

TEL (1) 4005 7010

Technological history and demonstrations. Video programmes.

GRANADA TELEVISION TOURS

MANCHESTER

GREAT BRITAIN

TEL 0161 832 9090

Coronation St. British television soap exhibition with programme reference.

INSTITUT NATIONAL DE L'AUDIOVISUEL

4 AVENUE DE L'EUROPE

94366 BRY-SUR-MARNE CEDEX

FRANCE

TEL (1) 49 83 20 00

Radio and television archive of France. Giant reference library opened to professionals.

MUSEUM OF BROADCAST COMMUNICATIONS

800 SOUTH WELLS STREET

CHICAGO

ILLINOIS 60607 4536

USA

TEL (312) 987 1515

Reference library of USA and world television programmes.

MUSEUM OF BROADCASTING

NEW YORK

USA

Video library of USA and world television.

MUSEUM OF THE MOVING IMAGE
SOUTH BANK ARTS CENTRE
WATERLOO
LONDON
SE1 8XT
TEL 0171 928 3535

History of television technology and production. Television programmes and retrospectives. Baird television collection.

MUSEUM FÜR DEUTSCHE FERNSEHGESCHICHTE RFM EV
HINDEMITHSTRASSE 1–5
D-6500 MAINZ 31
GERMANY
TEL (061) 317 789

Television technology and production history (museum in preparation).

MUSÉE POUR RIRE
2111 BOUL. SAINT-LAURENT
MONTREAL
QUEBEC
CANADA
H2X 2TS
TEL (514) 845 1200

Projections and library world television comedians.

NATIONAL MUSEUM OF PHOTOGRAPHY
FILM AND TELEVISION
PRINCE'S VIEW
BRADFORD
WEST YORKSHIRE
BD5 OTR
TEL 0274 727488

Technical history of television. Television projections. Videothèque of key television programmes.

POWERHOUSE MUSEUM
PO BOX K 346
HAYMARKET
NSW 200
500 HARRIS ST
ULTIMO
SYDNEY
TEL (02) 217 0111

Television technology and programmes within a social history, decorative arts, and science museum.

403

SCIENCE MUSEUM

EXHIBITION ROAD

LONDON

SW7 2DD

TEL 0171 938 8000

Technical history including John Logie Baird equipment.

VIDEOTHÈQUE DE PARIS

PORTE SAINT-EUSTACHE

75001 PARIS

FRANCE

TEL (1) 4026 3060

Video history of all film and television production (world-wide) on the subject of Paris.

Picture Sources

The editor and publishers wish to thank the following who have kindly supplied, and given permission to reproduce, illustrations on the pages indicated. (Copyright holders listed in parentheses.)

AP/Wide World Photos 44, 51, 96, 129, 159, 250, 261, 271
AP/Wide World Photos (Dick Cavett Productions) 166
ABC Document Archives, Sydney 336
BBC 134, 211, 230, 255
BBC, photograph Michael Taylor 227
BFI 13, 21, 106, 125, 155, 195, 320, 390
BFI (ABC TV, Australia) 338
BFI (BBC) 82, 101, 143, 381, 387
BFI (B.R.Films, Bombay and Rethell International, London) 309, 322
BFI (CBS Inc.) 99
BFI (Channel Four Television) 88
BFI (Columbia Tri-Star Television) 276
BFI (Eurosport) 148, 162
BFI (Fremantle International) 112 top and bottom
BFI (Granada Television) 171
BFI (Grundy Television) 356
BFI (ITC Entertainment Ltd) 206
BFI (Kennedy-Miller Productions) 346
BFI (Megalovision; photograph Gerald Incandela) 215, 231
BFI (NBC) 46
BFI (New Line Cinema Corporation) 229
BFI (New Star Entertainment) 285, 298
BFI (Nine Network Australia Ltd) 339
BFI (Pragati Chitra International) 209
BFI (Rimfire Films) 341
BFI (c. 1940 Turner Entertainment Co. All Rights Reserved) 228
BFI (Copyright © by Universal City Studios, Inc. Courtesy of MCA Publishing Rights, a Division of MCA Inc.) 191, 207, 259, 281
BFI (Warner Brothers International Television) 102, 272
Bodleian Library, Oxford 187
Susan Briggs 83
CANAL+ 115

(Chrysalis Sport) 168
CNN International 145
CyBC, Cyprus 105
ETRU, Turkey 326
(Mrs Pem Farnsworth) 24
Fremantle International 202
(Genesis Entertainment Inc. a New World Entertainment company) 144 left and right, 385 bottom
Hulton Deutsch Collection 53, 81, 121, 152, 172, 175, 240, 359, 371
Hulton Deutsch Collection (Thames Television) 386
Hutchison Library/Michael MacIntyre 330
Hutchison Library/Mischa Slaver 315
Hutchison Library/Iba Taylor 378
Hidetoshi Kato 305
The Independent/Nicholas Turpin 384
Independent Television Commission Library (The Sun Newspaper) 232
(P. K.Gorokhov, Boris L'Vovich Rosing, Moscow Hayka 1964) 18 (Charles Jenkins, Radio Movies, Radiovision, Television, Jenkins Laboratories 1929) 22
Nick Lockett 352
Bruno Barbey/Magnum Photos 382
National Film and Sound Archive, Canberra (Seven Network Ltd) 340
National Film and Sound Archive, Canberra (Crawfords Australia) 331, 344
Network/Gideon Mendel 361
Newslink Africa, London 358, 364, 375
NHK, Japan 288, 296, 302
Nigerian High Commission/NTA 368 left and right
Novosti, London 62, 74, 75, 169, 181
The Open University 385 top
Phase Three Productions, Jamaica 107
Popperfoto 225 bottom, 235, 246

405

(Punch's Almanac for 1879) 15
Range/Bettmann 35, 36, 39, 42, 184 top, 266, 383
Range/Bettmann (Broadway Video
    Entertainment) 59
Range/Bettmann (NBC) 268
Range/Bettmann/UPI 1, 3, 6, 118, 124, 126, 127,
    138, 176, 177, 184 bottom, 238, 248, 249, 277
Range/Bettmann/UPI (NBC) 132
(Albert Robida, Le Vingtieme Siecle: La Vie
    Electrique, Paris G.Decaux 1883) 14
Roger-Viollet 67, 68
Russian State Television 75
(David Sarnoff Research Center) 27
BSkyB 388
Suddeutscher Verlag 64, 77, 79, 149
Sygma 70, 243
D. Hudson/Sygma 186

Allan Tannenbaum/Sygma 225 top
KTLA/Sygma 226
Albert Pizzoli/Sygma 245
Mathieu Polak/Sygma 252
Trip/Helene Rogers 312
TRT, Turkey 110
TVB Ltd/Chinese Channel Ltd 318
WDR/K. H.Vogelmann 95, 109
Wisconsin Center for Film and Theatre Research
    (NBC) 98

In a few instances we have been unable to trace the
copyright holder prior to publication. If notified
the publishers will be pleased to amend the
acknowledgements in any future edition.

Index